MW00723298

ISRAEL UNDER SIEGE

ISRAEL UNDER SIEGE

The Politics of Insecurity and the Rise of

the Israeli Neo-Revisionist Right

RAFFAELLA A. DEL SARTO

Georgetown University Press | *Washington DC*

© 2017 Georgetown University Press. All rights reserved. No part of this book may be reproduced or utilized in any form or by any means, electronic or mechanical, including photocopying and recording, or by any information storage and retrieval system, without permission in writing from the publisher.

The publisher is not responsible for third-party websites or their content. URL links were active at time of publication.

Library of Congress Cataloging-in-Publication Data

Names: Del Sarto, Raffaella A., author.
Title: Israel under Siege : The Politics of Insecurity and the Rise of the Israeli
    Neo-Revisionist Right / Raffaella A. Del Sarto.
Description: Washington, DC : Georgetown University Press, 2017. | Includes bibli-
    ographical references and index.
Identifiers: LCCN 2016024176 (print) | LCCN 2016040475 (ebook) | ISBN
    9781626164062 (hc : alk. paper) | ISBN 9781626164079 (pb : alk. paper) | ISBN
    9781626164086 (eb)
Subjects: LCSH: Israel—Foreign relations—21st century. | Israel—Politics and
    government—1993– | Right and left (Political science)—Israel. | National security—
    Israel.
Classification: LCC DS119.6 .D45 2017 (print) | LCC DS119.6 (ebook) | DDC 327.5694—
    dc23
LC record available at https://lccn.loc.gov/2016024176

♾ This book is printed on acid-free paper meeting the requirements of the American National Standard for Permanence in Paper for Printed Library Materials.

18 17   9 8 7 6 5 4 3 2
First printing

Printed in the United States of America

Cover design by Martyn Schmoll.
Israel–Egypt barrier, Wikimedia Commons image (ISR-EGY border 6521a.jpg)
This file is licensed under the Creative Commons Attribution-Share Alike 3.0 Unported,
2.5 Generic, 2.0 Generic and 1.0 Generic license.

To N.

CONTENTS

PREFACE

The idea for this book first emerged while I was a Pears-Rich Fellow in Israel and Mediterranean Studies at the Middle East Centre of St. Antony's College at Oxford University between 2007 and 2011. In that period, the first Gaza war between Israel and Hamas took place, termed Operation Cast Lead by Israel and lasting from December 2008 to January 2009. In September 2009 the so-called Goldstone Report of the UN Fact Finding Mission on the Gaza Conflict was published, accusing both the Israeli army and Palestinian militants of war crimes and possible crimes against humanity during that war. In May 2010 the Israeli navy stormed the Turkish-owned flagship of a flotilla of vessels, the *Mavi Marmara*, which was crewed by pro-Palestinian activists trying to break the Israeli–Egyptian blockade of the Gaza Strip; nine Turkish citizens were killed in the incident. The heated discussions about these and other Middle East events with students, colleagues, and friends in these years convinced me that specific notions and policies, together with the question of who is to blame, had become "common sense" and were thus widely uncontested in Israeli politics and society. However, from an outside perspective, Israeli policies were becoming increasingly incomprehensible. Fierce and polemic disputes between supporters and critics of Israeli policies, with their respective justifications, characterized that period and the following years. The growing international criticism of Israeli policies would, however, only reinforce the domestic consensus in Israel, together with the sense of besiegement that had taken hold of Israeli society in those years. Toward the end of the 2000s, the Israeli body politic had thus considerably changed from the Israel I had come to know earlier, while living, studying, and working there (and in the Palestinian territories) for almost eight years. That period comprised the years of the Oslo peace process, in which cooperation with the Palestinians, however difficult, was a reality. It was also a time in which contestation and heated debates in Israeli politics on anything related to relations with the Palestinians and the wider region, the future borders of the state, and Israel's place in the region were the norm. All of this would change following the outbreak of the Second Intifada, with its dramatic increase in suicide bombings, and the subsequent end of the Oslo process. While Israeli politics shifted to the right, it was possible to detect the emergence of a dominant political discourse on threats and regional order, together with a strong domestic consensus on Israeli policy preferences, however questionable and counterproductive some of these seemed. Israeli politics and the prevailing political discourse had thus also come under siege by the fear-based consensus on security threats and the politics of insecurity promoted by consecutive right wing and neo-revisionist Israeli governments.

This process would not see any reversal in the following years. An attempt to understand and explain this development and the growing lack of domestic dissent on crucial political issues seemed to be of utmost importance. Initially intended as a research paper, this work, I soon realized, required a proper analysis and consideration of a whole web of interlocking factors and developments. A further motivation for writing this book is the absence of any comparable study covering Israeli politics and society after the end of the Oslo process.

Many colleagues and friends have contributed to this book in different ways, by taking the time to discuss with me its main ideas, by providing valuable input and critique, and by their encouragement. As I have worked on the book for a number of years, as a sort of a side project to my main research and teaching activities, it has involved discussions with many individuals, and I cannot possibly list them all. However, I would like to mention Emanuel Adler, Ellen Dahrendorf, Dirk Moses, Sabaï Ramedhan-Levi, Avi Shlaim, David Unger, and Susan Vahabzadeh, to whom I am very grateful for discussing the ideas of the book at its various stages and/or for reading parts of the manuscript. I am also indebted to a number of officials, or former officials, of Israel's Ministry of Foreign Affairs who took the time to talk to me off the record. I would also like to thank members of Israel's Council for Peace and Security for their time and valuable insights, and Avner Azoulay for facilitating these contacts. Of course, the content of the book is entirely my own responsibility. Special thanks to Lee Levy and Julie Northey for research assistance and language editing. At Georgetown University Press, I would like to thank Donald Jacobs, Glenn Saltzman, Sarah Cough, and Patti Bower as well as two anonymous referees contacted by GUP, who provided much appreciated feedback.

I am grateful to the Robert Schuman Centre at the European University Institute, where I directed the BORDERLANDS research project between 2011 and 2016, funded by the European Research Council, for providing a wonderfully peaceful working environment. A sincere word of thanks also goes to my colleagues and students at SAIS Europe, Johns Hopkins University, for providing an extremely stimulating academic setting.

And as always, my final word of thanks goes to my better half, for putting up with me while writing this book in between many other commitments and deadlines, and for providing the logistical backup—and even making me laugh in stressful times.

A NOTE ON TRANSLITERATION

Names and terms in Hebrew and Arabic have been spelled according to the conventional rules of transliteration but without the diacritical marks. An exception is the sign ' (indicating the letter 'ayn / 'ayin in Hebrew and Arabic) and, in a very few Arabic names, the sign ' (indicating the Arabic *hamza*). In many cases, however, the spelling of Hebrew and Arabic names and terms follow the commonly accepted English version, such as "intifada" instead of "intifadah"; "Netanya" instead of "Netanyiah"; "Tzahal" instead of "Tsahal"; "Tzipi Livni" instead of "Tsipi Livni"; and "Yasser Arafat" instead of "Yasir 'Arafat."

ABBREVIATIONS

EU	European Union
IAEA	International Atomic Energy Agency
IDF	Israel Defense Forces
IMF	International Monetary Fund
MK	member of Knesset
NGO	nongovernmental organization
NPT	Non-Proliferation Treaty
OECD	Organisation for Economic Co-operation and Development
PA	Palestinian Authority
PFLP	Popular Front for the Liberation of Palestine
PLC	Palestinian Legislative Council
PLO	Palestine Liberation Organization
R2P	responsibility to protect
SLA	South Lebanese Army
UNRWA	United Nations Relief and Works Agency for Palestine Refugees in the Near East
UNSCR	United Nations Security Council Resolution

Introduction

Israel's New Foreign Policy Consensus after
the Oslo Peace Process, 2000–2010

Heated debates about the priorities, means, and ends of Israel's relations with its neighbors have characterized Israeli politics ever since the state was created in 1948. In the early 1970s Michael Brecher noted of Israeli foreign policy that "the Israeli electorate was deluged with competitive opinions and panaceas during the first twenty years."[1] Divisions over the state's foreign relations typically also occurred within Israeli governments; the conflicting approaches of David Ben-Gurion and Moshe Sharett toward relations with the Arabs in the mid-1950s are a particularly good example here.[2] The future of the territories Israel conquered in the June 1967 war (the Six-Day War) has been a major bone of contention in Israeli politics since, indeed, 1967. Fifteen years later, in 1982, the Israeli army's invasion of Lebanon prompted the largest public protest against the government that Israel had seen thus far. Contestation and dissent also characterized the years of the Madrid and Oslo peace processes in the 1990s. In fact, in this period Israel's domestic disputes over the modalities of peacemaking and the desirability of territorial compromise reached an unprecedented level.[3] The assassination of Prime Minister Yitzhak Rabin by an Israeli Jewish religious extremist was probably the most dramatic expression of this state of affairs.

However, in the decade following the collapse of the Oslo peace process, from 2000 to 2010, Israeli politics presented a very different picture, and to a large extent still do. Preceding the so-called Arab Spring, which was to alter several parameters of the regional order, the first post-Oslo decade was marked by the disintegration of the Israeli Zionist Left and a general shift to the right, as consecutive elections in that period evidenced. Even more surprising was the emergence of a conspicuously strong consensus, spanning Israel's political and security establishments, on the type of threats Israel was facing, the nature of the regional order in the Middle East, and the prospects for peace with the Palestinians within this equation. What is this consensus about, and why is its emergence intriguing?

Consensus in a Traditionally Fragmented Polity

Shared by a vast majority of the Israeli public, the new foreign policy consensus emerging after the demise of the Oslo process consists of three main building blocks. To begin with, and perhaps unsurprisingly, in the first years of the raging second Palestinian intifada, with its numerous suicide attacks, the fight against terrorism was identified as one of the most pressing issues. Second, following the collapse of the Israeli–Palestinian summit at Camp David in July 2000, consecutive Israeli governments stressed that there was "no partner for peace" (*ein partner le-shalom*) on the Palestinian side, and that "there is no one to talk to" (*ein 'im mi ledaber*). Prime Minister Ehud Barak deserves the credit for coining these phrases, which were to remain a major feature of Israel's political discourse for the years to come. Third, a few years later, the growing influence of Iran became the main concern in Israeli politics. Tehran's nuclear ambitions only reinforced Israeli anxiety.[4] Undoubtedly, the rise of Iran was a major unintended—but not entirely unpredictable—consequence of the US-led invasion of Iraq in 2003. The decision of the George W. Bush administration to remove Saddam Hussein from power had left Iran without its most important enemy and regional counterweight. Concurrently, the notion of a rising "Shi'a Crescent," as Jordan's King Abdallah II termed it, gained currency in Israeli politics (and beyond). Believed to include Iran and its proxies and to stretch from Beirut (via Damascus, Baghdad, and Tehran) to Gaza and the Arabian Peninsula, Israeli politicians were united in ascribing great danger to this new regional order that seemed to be dominated by Shi'a Islam.[5]

Taken together, the three elements of the consensus converge toward one main point: Israel feels under siege and sees its very survival as at risk. In this situation, questions of identity become crucial. As ethnoreligious conceptions of "us" and "them" began to prevail, so the conflicts with the Palestinians and the wider "Arab world" (or "Muslim world") began to be reinterpreted. These conflicts were now increasingly perceived as an ethnic or ethnoreligious conflict and no longer as a dispute over land and borders.[6] Significantly, the new Israeli consensus on threats and regional order echoes the worldview of neo-revisionist Zionism, a more radical version of classical revisionist Zionism: it combines the perception of an inherently hostile environment—hence the need for forceful policies and deterrence—with ethnoreligious conceptions of politics and the principle of territorial maximalism. The latter may stem from nationalism, messianic beliefs, or security considerations. With some notable exceptions, such as the renewal of peace talks between the Israeli government under Ehud Olmert and Palestinian president Mahmoud Abbas (Abu Mazen) in 2007–8, Israeli policies toward the region followed the worldview and prescriptions of the new consensus.

Of course, the consensus had, and still has, a consistent and very real material basis. Political developments in that period seemingly confirmed the bleak regional outlook that took hold of Israeli politics and society. Thus, in the first years of the second Palestinian intifada, terrorist attacks against Israeli civilians occurred on an almost daily basis, with the Palestinian chairman, Yasser Arafat, unable or unwilling to stop the violence. Hamas, which was responsible for the lion's share of these attacks, won the Palestinian elections in January 2006. While ousting its rival, Fatah, it took control over the Gaza Strip in July 2007. Well before the Israeli government decided to withdraw from Gaza in the summer of 2005, the organization had started launching rockets on population centers in southern Israel, and it would continue to do so in the following years. For the Israeli government, stopping the rocket attacks was the major justification for the launching of a war on the Hamas-ruled Gaza Strip in the winter of 2008–9, and again in 2012 and 2014. The divide between Fatah and Hamas during much of the rest of the decade, together with the (alleged) weakness of Palestinian Authority chairman Mahmoud Abbas to deliver a peace deal, seemed to further corroborate the Israeli assessment that there was no Palestinian partner for peace.

In addition, the growing power and militancy of Hamas, which Tehran supported, only seemed to confirm the notion of a hegemonic Iran that was seeking to control the region through various proxies. Iran's other major ally, the Lebanese Hizballah (which, like Hamas, is defined as a terrorist organization by the United States, the European Union, Israel, and others), also became increasingly defiant. In the summer of 2006 Hizballah fighters crossed into northern Israel and kidnapped 2 Israeli soldiers, killed 3 others, and wounded 2. In the ensuing war between Israel and Hizballah, the Lebanese organization launched a barrage of rockets on northern Israel, paralyzing the country for several weeks and killing 43 Israeli civilians and 119 soldiers. According to the Lebanese authorities, Israeli air strikes and the subsequent ground invasion killed over 1,100 Lebanese, injured over 4,400 people, partly destroyed the infrastructure in the south of the country, and prompted the displacement of over 900,000 people—almost one-quarter of the Lebanese population.[7] It is disputed how many of the Lebanese fatalities were Hizballah fighters, with Lebanese sources putting their number at 200, and Israeli sources at around 700. However, notwithstanding the obvious asymmetry in power and damage, a sense of besiegement prevailed in Israel during the war. Hostile statements of Iranian president Mahmoud Ahmadinejad, such as his call for Israel to be "wiped off the map," reinforced the Israeli perception of being encircled by particularly evil forces.[8] Tehran's efforts to develop a nuclear program certainly did not soothe these fears. According to a report of the International Atomic Energy Agency (IAEA) of November 2011, it seemed indeed "credible" that Iran was trying to develop a nuclear device.[9]

Significantly, the Israeli public—particularly its Jewish majority— overwhelmingly accepted what became the hegemonic political discourse in Israel, as numerous public opinion polls demonstrated. Thus, in that decade, the vast majority of Jewish Israelis were predominantly concerned with terrorism and the Iranian threat. Surveys also consistently showed that most Jewish Israelis no longer believed—if they ever did—that there was a partner for peace on the Palestinian side. Various opinion polls over the years evidenced a widespread conviction that the Palestinians were not interested in peace and that the conflict would therefore not be resolved anytime soon. Post-Oslo, the Jewish Israeli public was decidedly disillusioned and fearful, and increasingly tired and disinterested. But it was also surprisingly united in its assessment of the regional environment and the resulting policy prescriptions. On the other hand, a majority of Israel's Palestinian citizens, who constitute about 20 percent of the population, opposed the prevailing hegemonic vision. Thus, in the first decade post-Oslo, the gap between Jewish Israelis and the Palestinian Israeli public widened considerably.[10]

There is generally no point in arguing with entrenched beliefs of individuals, let alone with those of entire collectives. And neither is this the scope of this book. Without doubt, the assessment of threats and regional order prevailing in Israel post-Oslo is based on a number of material facts and developments. Indeed, terrorist organizations and hostile regimes are real, and so are bombs and rockets. However, a crucial caveat is in order. A broad agreement over the fact that the sun rises every day is generally not a matter of surprise. But the post-Oslo consensus in Israel does not involve this kind of facts, or not solely. Rather, it is based on a combination of observations and—confirmed or unconfirmed—assumptions about the nature of events, their sequencing and causality, and the intention of actors. These "social facts" may be subject to very different interpretations. Moreover, even in the event of agreement on the meaning of these facts, different lines of policy may still be called for.

To give an example, it is uncontested that Iran adopted an increasingly defiant posture on the international stage after 2003. A growing weapons arsenal or the development of nuclear weapons, for that matter, counts as material evidence that is hard to challenge. However, a state may still arm itself for different reasons: it may want to attack another state, or it may feel threatened, or it may want to be recognized as a regional power according to the rules of international politics. But even if we agree that the regime in Tehran sought to acquire nuclear weapons because it has been maintaining an expansionist and aggressive foreign policy since the 1979 revolution (and there is evidence to support such a claim[11]), there may still be different prescriptions as to how to counter these aspirations. A strike on Iran's nuclear facilities is but one among a range of options.

By the same token, Iran's alliance with Hizballah and Hamas during much of the recent decades is well documented. However, it may be argued that regional developments after the collapse of the Oslo process were not as clear-cut as Israel's prevailing notion of regional order would have it. The 2002 Saudi peace initiative, which was endorsed by the twenty-two member states of the Arab League and which offered Israel peace in exchange for an Israeli withdrawal to the pre-1967 war borders, is the best example here. Likewise, leaked secret cables from US embassies to the US State Department confirmed that several Arab governments shared the Israeli concern with Tehran's aspirations for regional hegemony: behind closed doors, a number of Arab states were pressuring Washington to strike Iran's nuclear facilities.[12] These developments point to partially convergent interests in the region in the 2000s against the backdrop of altered strategic conditions in the Middle East following the US invasion of Iraq. Seen in this light, Israel's acceptance of the Saudi peace initiative could be, or could have been, a valid alternative by which to counter the Iranian threat. Of course, this course of action may not have been feasible or desirable for a variety of reasons. However, one would at least expect there to have been a significant domestic debate in Israel on this option.

Precisely because we are dealing with social facts, disagreement over their nature, interpretation, and the policy prescriptions that flow from them are almost inevitable in any fairly open and democratic political system. To be sure, alternative understandings of the regional order and different prescriptions as to how to enhance Israel's security are still present in Israeli politics and society. However, these voices do not have any comparable weight. Hence, considering the traditionally fragmented nature of Israeli politics, the emergence of a hegemonic vision of threats and regional order is a phenomenon that begs for an explanation.

It can be argued that the violence of the Second Intifada, in conjunction with external threats, explains the lack of domestic dissent in that decade, as situations of insecurity and acute crisis always tend to mute domestic contestation. Thus, the terror attacks of the Second Intifada, and the rockets launched by Hizballah and Hamas across the northern and southern borders, respectively, combined with Ahmadinejad's threatening statements, had a profound psychological effect on Israelis. But is this sufficient to explain the sudden lack of dissent in Israeli politics? How can we account for Israel's prevailing sense of being under siege, especially if we consider the country's status as a regional power and its alliance with Washington? How can we explain this discrepancy? How did the sudden lack of dissent in Israeli politics come about, and why did one particular notion of threats and regional order become predominant, together with a set of widely accepted lines of policy? Why was there almost no opposition to the hegemonic discourse in post-Oslo Israel? Why did the influence of opposing voices remain so limited? And what are the domestic and international implications of this state of affairs? These are the questions this book will answer.

Explanations on Offer, and Why It Matters

How can we think about hegemonic beliefs dominating a society? What explains their emergence, and what is their impact? Hegemony in the Gramscian sense is defined as the dominance of specific commonsense ideas and beliefs that affect a society with the purpose of maintaining the status quo. In essence, the construction of hegemony demands that specific collective beliefs emerge, become common sense, and are taken for granted, thus inhibiting the articulation of alternative opinions. Hegemonic ideas and convictions also act as prisms through which incoming information on specific events is filtered, thereby reinforcing those previously held beliefs. Hegemony is also maintained through the continuous reproduction of dominant notions and beliefs, while dissenting voices are sidelined and become increasingly illegitimate.

Perhaps unsurprisingly, the processes by which hegemony emerges and consolidates itself are extremely complex. They involve material conditions and developments, actors and multiple feedback dynamics.[13] Agency plays a crucial role in these processes, including, inter alia, the political elites, public intellectuals, the state bureaucracy, the media, and the education system. Usually, various actors working at different levels contribute to the construction and maintenance of hegemony, either consciously or unconsciously. It is important to consider that political elites have a conspicuous interest in controlling the commonsensical understanding of events and developments as well as of social reality more generally, in order to justify specific courses of action. This is what politics is essentially about.[14] In other words, defining what constitutes reality is a mode of legitimizing the existing order and the dominant role of those same elites within it.

The power of political elites to define the taken-for-granted understanding of reality is not absolute, however. It depends on their authority and legitimacy but also on preexisting beliefs and convictions. Thus, in addition to examining material facts and the role of agents, an investigation into Israel's hegemonic perspective on the region post-Oslo must consider preexisting cognitive structures. Israel's intellectual history, together with the historical narratives that have defined the Israeli experience since the founding of the state, is a good starting point here.[15] As discussed in more detail below, the dominance of Labor Zionism in the first decades of statehood not only defined the way in which Israelis came to perceive of themselves and of the world but also laid the foundations of Israeli foreign policy. The decline of Labor Zionism and the constant rise of neo-revisionism since the 1970s are equally important. As neo-revisionism allied itself with religious Zionism and grew constantly stronger, specific ideas on the nature of threats and Israel's place in the region became increasingly relevant.[16] Thus, while it is possible to posit that revisionism's "Iron Wall" doctrine has constantly been on the rise since the late 1970s, this book shows that, for a combination of reasons, neo-revisionist thought became hegemonic in post-Oslo Israel, serving as the ideological matrix of the new consensus on threats and regional order.[17]

The interplay of specific political and socioeconomic developments may also explain the emergence and consolidation of particular notions in a society. Without doubt, one of the reasons for the strengthening of neo-revisionist thought was the devastating psychological impact of the terror of the Second Intifada in a post-9/11 international climate together with the general sense of desolation that took hold of the Israeli polity in the 2000s. These developments discredited the optimists who believed that peace with the Palestinians was possible.

As for the actors, this study considers the role played by politicians and the security establishment, together with other "trusted" public figures, in the construction of Israel's post-Oslo consensus. The contribution of the media is also taken into account.

At this point, it must be asked whether the consensus on threat and regional order in Israel post-Oslo is relevant. Indeed, why would it matter? The book maintains that Israel's foreign policy consensus in the 2000s, and the neo-revisionist hegemony sustaining it, is highly significant for a number of reasons. First, the strong consensus on terrorism, Iran, and the absence of a Palestinian partner for peace legitimizes specific foreign policy choices. At the same time, it delegitimizes other options. As specific perceptions of the regional order turn into a taken-for-granted truth, the space for challenging those conceptions and for discussing alternatives narrows. For instance, according to prevailing conceptions in Israel, there does not seem to be much difference between Iran, Hamas, Hizballah, and possibly also al-Qaeda and the self-declared Islamic State. As a result, endogenous reasons for the strengthening of Hamas in the Palestinian territories are no longer considered. Similarly, the question of why Sunni Hamas turned to Shi'a Iran for support—in contradiction to the idea of a rising Shi'a Crescent—was seldom asked. The Iranian threat also overshadowed the question of how to resolve the Israeli–Palestinian conflict, with no noteworthy opposition questioning this hegemonic set of priorities.

Second, the Israeli consensus on what defined the regional reality and the resulting lines of action increasingly contrasted with government positions and public opinion in other countries. Regarding Arab and Muslim majority countries, where publics are generally quick to portray Israel as the main villain, Israel's hegemonic discourse is likely to contribute to the perpetuation of the Arab–Israeli conflict. This is highly probable, as protracted conflicts always entail a self-sustaining clash of narratives.[18] In fact, an analysis of the hegemonic conception of the conflict that prevails among Arab publics would complement this book. Although the lack of dissent in Arab states and societies can largely be attributed to the history and politics of authoritarianism, a critical analysis of the dominant explanations of the conflict in those societies is long overdue. Support for Israeli positions and policies, however, has been dramatically declining in other parts of the world as well—for instance, in Europe. According to a 2007 Pew survey, a large percentage of European respondents said they did not sympathize with either side in the Israeli–Palestinian conflict, with greater numbers in France, Great Britain, Sweden, and Spain sympathizing more strongly with the Palestinians than with Israel.[19] The support for Israeli policies and positions has also been declining in the US, albeit to a lesser extent. Altogether, while the perceptions of threats and regional order prevailing in Israel may be internally logical and coherent, the country's policies—together with the broad public support they enjoy—are increasingly difficult to comprehend for "outsiders." Conversely, Israelis fail to grasp why others do not share their understanding of the region and the world, thus dismissing any type of criticism right away. In this widening gap in the perception of reality, Israel tends to close in and to close ranks, thereby perceiving the criticism as an assault on its legitimacy, as an attack on its very existence. Israel's hegemonic notion of threats and regional order thus also affects the country's foreign relations far beyond the Middle East.

Third, the Israeli consensus on Middle Eastern reality, together with the resulting policy choices, is relevant since it may have contributed to the cementing of precisely that regional order. In this vein, it is conceivable that Israeli policies have, *nolens volens*, played a part in the strengthening of Hizballah and Hamas, contributed to the alienation of former allies, and caused the growing delegitimization of those Arab parties that were most interested in finding an accommodation with Israel. Needless to say, this possibility deserves a thorough investigation.

Fourth, Israel's transformation within a relatively short period of time from an open society where fervent political debates were the norm to a country characterized by a set of extremely powerful hegemonic narratives and explanations is a puzzling development. An understanding of this transformation may generate important insights into the specific conditions and circumstances prompting significant political and societal change in general. More importantly, however, Israel's new foreign policy consensus and the hegemony of neo-revisionist thought in which it is anchored may have significant domestic implications. As the new domestic consensus considerably reduces the space for dissent, it may undermine Israel's democratic structures. Moreover, in light of the existence of a significant non-Jewish population in Israel, the reproduction of an essentially ethnoreligious understanding of threats and regional order, together with the politics of insecurity and fear adopted by consecutive Israeli right-wing governments since the collapse of Oslo, potentially challenges any liberal conception of citizenship in a state.[20]

Finally, an investigation of the emergence and salience of a specific hegemonic notion of threats and regional order helps to shed light on the powerful social and interpretative dimension of international relations. It shows that, similar to the idea of humanitarian intervention or the taboo on nuclear weapons, specific notions of threats and regional order are, while "real," at least to a large extent a product of social construction.[21] Without denying that Israel faces a number of formidable threats and security challenges, and that security and survival are the main interests of any state, this study specifically investigates the role domestic politics play in framing foreign policies. It also highlights the importance of collective beliefs in this process. From the same vantage point, the book demonstrates that alternative understandings of threat and regional order are possible, with these alternative readings potentially legitimizing different lines of policy. These alternatives may not necessarily be more convincing or adequate. However, an acknowledgment of the existence of different choices is necessary if Israel wishes to escape the sense of siege and perceived lack of options after Oslo, together with its growing international isolation.

The investigation into Israel's consensus on regional policies post-Oslo rests on a number of conceptual and theoretical considerations that may not be self-evident. Therefore, the next section briefly reflects on the concepts underwriting this study. Readers who are not passionate about social science theory may easily skip these paragraphs.

Some Concepts and Some Theory

In a basically anarchical international order, states and nations are first and foremost concerned with their security and survival, and next with the maximization of wealth and power. Israel is certainly no exception here. The existence of a domestic consensus on the most adequate strategies to meet these objectives may not necessarily warrant any further reflection. The case under discussion is a bit more intricate, raising a different set of questions. For one, this case involves the emergence and consolidation of an exceptionally strong and largely unchallenged consensus on threats and regional order. However, these conceptions are not self-evident. Rather, a number of developments suggest that alternative Israeli policies and strategies could have been sensible, and perhaps even more effective. In fact, the remarkably strong foreign policy consensus under discussion is partially ideological in nature and, arguably, potentially counterproductive both for Israel's security and for its international standing. Hence, the question of how this type of hegemonic notion underpinning foreign policy emerges and is maintained becomes central. This necessitates a reflection on how to conceptualize the nature and implications of a strong domestic consensus on threats and regional order together with hegemonic narratives on specific "facts."

To be clear, not every consensus on a given issue in a particular society would lend itself to further investigation. A strong agreement on a scientifically proven fact of the material world, such as "the world is round," is not particularly surprising.[22] The Israeli consensus post-Oslo, however, does not exclusively concern material facts, such as "the world is round." The "fact" that, for example, Arafat did not do everything in his power to resolve the conflict with Israel is a different kind of "fact": it is a social fact. Of course, social facts, including threats and dangers, may be very real— as social reality is always subjectively "real." It is also important to stress that social reality is always based on hard material facts. However, those facts may be interpreted in quite different ways. For instance, an enemy piling up weapons (a material fact) may constitute a threat. However, an ally increasing its weapons arsenal would hardly be perceived as a threat, with "ally" or "enemy" already being social categories in world politics. As Alexander Wendt markedly put it, "500 British nuclear weapons are less threatening to the United States than 5 North Korean nuclear weapons, because the British are friends of the United States and the North Koreans are not."[23] Hence, social facts are not given or uncontestable. But how can we think about the creation of social facts? Which features and dynamics are involved in these processes?

While this study is committed to scientific realism as its ontological reference point and to pragmatism as its epistemological basis, processes of creating social reality are, of course, of a very complex nature.[24] They involve agency as well as preexisting norms and values that are shared by a collective. Without going into detail, social reality becomes "real" through complex feedback processes that involve collective interpretations as well as social institutionalization. Put differently, social conventions, collective beliefs, norms, practices, customs, and everything else the social world is made of emerge as an agreement among a group of individuals and become a shared understanding among the members of that group. Subsequently, these understandings become institutionalized and codified through different rules, practices, and institutions. Social conventions and norms in turn influence actors by providing guidelines for ethical, just, and appropriate behavior. But they also act as lenses or "cognitive maps" through which reality is seen and understood.[25]

Shared understandings that make up social reality exist at different levels of community. For instance, marriage is a social convention at the level of society; it exists because of a previous collective agreement on what "marriage" means and on which practices it involves. Shared beliefs also define the community of states and international relations. As John Searle has put it, "part of being a war is being thought to be a war."[26] In other words, a war depends on a previous collective agreement on its meanings and its rules. Likewise, the concept of state sovereignty and the principle of noninterference in domestic affairs are examples of socially constructed norms that regulate international relations. To give another example, it is a convention in international relations that a state's power is defined by the strength of its army and the degree of sophistication of its weapons, as opposed to, say, the production of culture. In this vein, states "have a say" on the international stage if they possess atomic weapons, as reflected in the composition and powers of the UN Security Council.

The question of why specific concepts become predominant, as opposed to others, is a particularly difficult one, and there is no clear answer in the literature. Possible explanations draw on the legitimacy and intrinsic qualities of norms, the timing, and the power of those actors promoting them, among others.[27] It is important to note here that collective understandings tend to be contested from within and without the community. Their relevance or meaning may also change over time. The rather recent principle of the responsibility to protect (R2P) is a case in point. Stipulating that if governments fail to protect their citizens from genocide, war crimes, ethnic cleansing, and crimes against humanity, the international community shall have the responsibility to take collective action to ensure that protection, the R2P principle poses a challenge to the long-established norm of noninterference in international politics.[28] At the societal level, an example of a contested principle is the growing but still disputed legitimacy of same-sex marriage. In fact, competition between different norms and shared understandings is the rule. It is a general lack of contestation of social facts that is surprising. This raises the question of how this lack of dissent in a given society—and, with it, the existence of hegemonic conceptions of the social world—can be conceptualized and explained.

As noted earlier, hegemony in the Gramscian sense occurs when specific concepts and norms are shared by an overwhelming majority and turn into an axiomatic truth that goes unquestioned. In other words, they become common sense. Highlighting the importance of agency, Gramsci also pointed out that the construction of hegemony serves the legitimization of a specific social and political order. While lending additional powers to dominant groups to present their particular interest as universally valid, hegemony also forges consensus among those groups that are dominated.[29] Hence, elites have a crucial interest in defining and naming specific facts and events, and in exerting power over the political lexicon more in general. The struggle over defining these commonsense notions or the background knowledge is thus a fundamentally political endeavor.[30] Likewise, hegemonic notions of reality may serve as powerful frames. Frames are defined as interpretative structures within a political discourse that impact on how people think about an issue or event.[31] In general, the successful framing or "packaging" of a message or policy will define the extent of its support in society. Hence, in situations of hegemony—and thus in the absence of meaningful dissent on what social reality is about—a skillful framing process will succeed in convincing a vast majority of the population of the legitimacy of specific policies. It will also sustain the authority of the government, the state institutions, and the political elites. Likewise, in the event of failure of those policies, it will be relatively easy to assign blame to something or someone else. Situations of insecurity—or the prevailing perception thereof—will only reinforce the self-sustaining nature of hegemony. The main reason is that situations of threat and danger tend to mute domestic criticism while strengthening support for policies that may otherwise be highly questionable.[32]

The social science approach that there is no purely objective reality when it comes to the social world may hit a raw nerve for those facing terrorism or being part of protracted conflicts. While this proposition does not postulate that wars or terrorism are imaginary, or that people do not really get killed, the approach opens the door to thinking about ways of reframing messages, modifying prevailing norms, and restructuring discourse so as to overcome conflict and violence.[33] In fact, a plethora of studies on different aspects of the socially constructed world and its implications for global politics have marked international relations scholarship in the last decades.[34] The insight that belief systems and the normative environment influence foreign policy decisions has an even longer history, and so has the finding that decision makers act upon their perception of reality.[35]

Positing that both elites and the normative environment contribute to the construction of hegemony, how can we think about the relationship between agency and structure? What comes first? It has indeed remained difficult to disentangle the role of the normative environment, which may constrain decision makers, from the contribution of those decision makers in shaping that same environment. Indeed, given that mutually constitutive feedback processes are in place, the choice to focus either on agency or on structure is a largely arbitrary one, with both options being equally valid.[36] This book seeks to refrain from the theoretical chicken-or-egg debate. Instead, it postulates that specific explanations in foreign policy "work" because they reflect or reinforce preexisting collective beliefs on these matters. These shared beliefs often evoke deeply entrenched historical narratives and identity themes, thus enabling actors to successfully advance a specific understanding of social reality. Regarding agency, it is important to note who the promoters of specific notions and explanations are. Various studies suggest that authoritative sources and personalities, termed "epistemic authorities," are able to influence public opinion in a determinative way. Epistemic authority is defined as the source of information that an individual relies on while he or she seeks to acquire and internalize knowledge about a specific issue. Expertise, empathy, and reliability of the information source act as incentive on the individual to absorb the message.[37]

Moreover, major events or political developments that deeply affect society, such as conflicts, a natural disaster, or even the advent of peace, are crucial as they open the door for a collective reinterpretation of reality. In such situations, authoritative sources may seek to promote narratives that provide crucial information on these events, thus possibly altering public attitudes and beliefs. It goes without saying that the information may be incomplete or incorrect even though it may be provided in good faith—or perhaps not. Likewise, it is important to note that successful processes of collective reinterpretation of reality usually go hand in hand with the delegitimization of a previously dominant collective belief.[38] This observation seems to be particularly relevant regarding the complete disintegration of the Israeli political Left, the discrediting of the logic of the Oslo process, and the hitherto relevant belief among many Israelis that peace was possible.

A final consideration concerns the issue of impact and causality. This study suggests that the hegemonic notion of threats and regional order in post-Oslo Israel informs specific policies in the sense that it makes them intelligible and legitimate while delegitimizing alternative courses of action. In other words, a societal agreement on the type of threats Israel is facing, or on the intentions of the neighbors, offers a range of possible alternatives in terms of policies but excludes others.[39] This is not to say that collective understandings directly cause policies. First, foreign policy-making processes are extremely complex and messy as they involve bureaucracies, procedures, personalities, intelligence, instrumentalization, and politicking. This is to say that political leaders may adopt policies that depart from a preexisting domestic consensus and, if successful, even change those dominant conceptions. Second, from a theory of science perspective, it is important to point out that the social sciences operate with a different concept of causality than the natural sciences. This is because investigations into the social world involve open systems, the difficulty in comparing across time and place, and—most importantly—individual agency. Thus, social sciences should aim to explain the meaning of human action in a specific social, cultural, and historical context.[40]

The objective of this book, then, is to explain how a majority of Israelis view their regional environment post-Oslo, what policymakers think they are doing, what a given policy means in a specific context, what the implications are, and why hegemonic notions on these issues can be challenged. This study relies on a large amount of data and inference, which is particularly relevant considering the clash of logics, visions, and justifications in the Middle East and beyond.

To sum up, with its study of the nature of the Israeli foreign policy consensus post-Oslo, this book aims to explain how and why specific notions of threats and regional order emerged and became hegemonic in Israel, together with the far-reaching international, regional, and domestic implications of this development. The book thus sheds light on a complex phenomenon with significant political implications not only for Israel but also for the wider region and beyond. In conceptual and theoretical terms, the book makes three main contributions to the literature. First, it provides a comprehensive study of the emergence and maintenance of hegemony and the growing lack of dissent on foreign policy issues in a previously fairly open and politically diverse society. It does so by integrating various endogenous and exogenous explanatory factors at different levels, including the material basis of specific perceptions, historical developments, preexisting cognitive structures, practices of foreign and security policies, the question of agency, and the impact of more recent domestic and regional developments. Second, the study highlights the power of hegemony in sustaining the narrow interests of specific domestic groups and elites while persistently undermining the relevance of dissenting voices and alternative preferences. Third, by focusing on the dynamics that legitimize specific foreign and security policies and delegitimize others, this book puts the spotlight on a particularly significant aspect of the nexus between domestic politics, on the one hand, and foreign and security policies and the prospects of conflict resolution, on the other.

Organization of the Book

Focusing on the decade following the collapse of the Oslo negotiations and the outbreak of the second Palestinian intifada (2000–2010), the book investigates Israel's hegemonic notions of threats and regional order. It critically examines the Israeli sense of besiegement that this perspective embodies and explores the factors explaining the lack of any relevant dissent on these matters. In particular, the theme of terrorism that is described as being endemic to the Palestinians and the Middle East *tout court*, the absence of a Palestinian "partner for peace," and the Iran-dominated regional order are identified as the main building blocks of the Israeli consensus post-Oslo. Taken together, these elements constitute a consistent belief system that is deeply anchored in neo-revisionist thought and that seemingly prescribes a set of rather coherent policies. Chapter 1 begins by looking in more detail at the nature of Israel's hegemonic vision of regional reality after the collapse of the Oslo process, together with the material basis of these notions. It thus discusses the main political developments and the regional environment in the first post-Oslo decade. The chapter also considers possible alternative interpretations of Middle Eastern reality and the regional order, thus already touching upon the political implications of Israel's foreign policy consensus post-Oslo.

Chapter 2 investigates the impact of the foreign policy consensus on Israeli policies vis-à-vis the Palestinians, Hizballah, and Iran in the first post-Oslo decade. The discussion specifically focuses on the legitimization of policies. The chapter subsequently engages in the question of whether these policies have achieved the desired effect or whether, *nolens volens*, they have been counterproductive by possibly perpetuating the conflict and strengthening the emerging regional order. We then move to assess the impact of the consensus on Israel's international relations. Finally, the chapter considers its domestic repercussions, particularly in terms of relations between the Jewish majority and the Arab minority within Israel.

Chapter 3 looks at possible explanations for the surprising lack of dissent in Israeli politics after Oslo. A combination of factors is taken into account here: first, I discuss the particular construction of Israel's collective identity and the dominant historical narratives that define the Israeli experience. It is assumed that the way Israelis think about themselves is far more conducive to one specific understanding of regional developments than others—particularly if terrorist attacks and saber-rattling neighbors characterize these developments. Second, the chapter engages in an excursion into the structure and doctrinal foundations of Israeli foreign policy. The striking similarities between the key doctrine of Israeli foreign policy and the collective understanding of threats and regional order post-Oslo may explain, at least partly, the salience of Israel's hegemonic vision. Third, key political developments in Israel over recent decades are considered. In particular, the study discusses the rise of neo-revisionism and its alliance with religious Zionism. This alliance forged a particular ethnoreligious definition of national identity and political preferences while also witnessing a notable political and societal consolidation of Israel's settlement project in Palestinian territories. The discussion suggests that neo-revisionist thought has become hegemonic in Israel, acting as the ideological matrix of the foreign policy consensus post-Oslo. Fourth, the psychological impact of the end of the peace process and the terrorism of the second Palestinian intifada on Israeli politics and society is evaluated. The last part of the investigation focuses on the role of agents in promoting what became the new consensus. It relies specifically on significant studies highlighting the role of "authoritative" politicians such as Ehud Barak and the Israel Defense Forces, together with the part played by the Israeli media.

The so-called Arab Spring of 2011, which was triggered by the desperate act of self-immolation of the Tunisian vegetable-seller Mohamed Bouazizi in December 2010, in a way marks the end of the post-Oslo decade. As some have claimed with a grain of irony, the contestation of political power in Arab states in that period seemed to have reached Israel, which witnessed a wave of protests against the high costs of living in the summer of 2011 and again in 2012.[41] Although the protest movement did not focus on Israel's relations with its neighbors, it did seem to point to the return of dissent to the Israeli polity. Further confirming this trend, former key figures of the Israeli security establishment publicly criticized Prime Minister Binyamin Netanyahu's preferred option of dealing with Iran—namely, a military attack on Iran's nuclear facilities—causing a heated public debate on national security issues.[42] Thus, a discussion of the possible return of political contestation in Israel in the 2010s along with a consideration of public opinion during the third Israel–Gaza war of the summer of 2014 is the subject of the last chapter.

In the conclusion, I synthesize the insights gained in the course of the study on how and under which conditions hegemonic worldviews are constructed and maintained, and why this matters. It is worth noting here that for most Israelis and for staunch supporters of Israeli policies post-Oslo, the foreign policy consensus that this book problematizes is utterly self-evident and beyond questioning, thus squarely proving the main point of the book.

Notes

1. Brecher, *Foreign Policy System of Israel*, 163.

2. Shlaim, "Conflicting Approaches to Israel's Relations with the Arabs."

3. See, for example, Hermann and Yuchtmann-Yaar, *Israeli Society and the Challenge of Transition*; Del Sarto, *Contested State Identities*, chap. 4; and Weissbrod, "Israeli Identity in Transition."

4. See, for example, Toby Greene, "Fearing Iran," *Guardian*, January 26, 2007.

5. Michael Broening, "The Myth of the Shia Crescent," *Haaretz*, June 12, 2008.

6. Klein, *The Shift*.

7. United Nations General Assembly, *Report of the Commission of Inquiry on Lebanon*; and United Nations, *Report of the Secretary-General on the United Nations Interim Force in Lebanon*.

8. Nazila Fath, "Wipe Israel 'Off the Map' Iranian Says," *New York Times*, October 27, 2005.

9. IAEA, *Implementation of the NPT Safeguards Agreement*.

10. For more on this issue, see chapter 3.

11. Hunter, *Iran and the World*, 36–41; and Parsi, *Treacherous Alliance*, chap. 8.

12. See, for example, "US Embassy Cables: Saudi King Urges US Strike on Iran," *Guardian*, November 28, 2010.

13. Gramsci, *Quaderni dal carcere*. For the concept of hegemony in international relations, see Cox, "Gramsci, Hegemony and International Relations."

14. Ish-Shalom, "Defining by Naming."

15. See, for example, Zerubavel, *Recovered Roots*.

16. Kimmerling, *Invention and Decline of Israeliness*, chap. 3; Seliktar, *New Zionism and the Foreign Policy System*; and Peleg, *Begin's Foreign Policy*.

17. For the impact of the Iron Wall doctrine on Israel's foreign policy toward Arab states, see Shlaim, *The Iron Wall*.

18. See, for example, Kacowicz, "Rashomon in the Middle East"; and Caplan, *Israel–Palestine Conflict*.

19. Pew Research Center, *Global Unease with Major World Powers: 47-Nation Pew Global Attitudes Survey*, Global Attitudes Project, June 27, 2007, http://pewglobal.org/files/pdf/256.pdf. For more on this issue, see chapter 3.

20. See, for example, Rouhana and Sultany, "Redrawing the Boundaries of Citizenship."

21. See, for example, Katzenstein, *Culture of National Security*; and Wendt, *Social Theory of International Politics*.

22. Certainly, even this statement must be taken *cum grano salis*. Scientific inquiry in the natural sciences may lead to new observations and paradigmatic shifts, Galileo's discovery that the earth moves around the sun being a case in point.

23. Wendt, "Constructing International Politics," 73.

24. See Bhaskar, *A Realist Theory of Science*; and Goodman, *Pragmatism*.

25. Berger and Luckmann, *Social Construction of Reality*.

26. Searle, *Construction of Social Reality*, esp. 31–32.

27. See, for example, Finnemore and Sikkink, "International Norm Dynamics."

28. The "responsibility to protect" principle was launched in 2005 at the UN World Summit. Resolution 1973 of March 17, 2011, which legitimized the intervention by France, the UK, the US, and other NATO allies to enforce a no-fly zone in Libya and to take steps to support rebel forces in their civil war against Muammar Gaddafi was a significant operationalization of the R2P principle. However, contradicting the principle of noninterference, the legitimacy of this intervention was also contested.

29. Gramsci, *Quaderni Dal Carcere*.

30. Ish-Shalom, "Defining by Naming."

31. Chong and Druckman, "Framing Theory"; and Polletta and Ho, "Frames and Their Consequences."

32. See, for example, Buzan, Wæver, and de Wilde, *Security*.

33. Barnett, "Culture, Strategy and Foreign Policy Change"; and Adler, "Damned If You Do."

34. The literature is far too extensive to mention, but see, for instance, Wendt, *Social Theory of International Politics*; Onuf, *World of Our Making*; Katzenstein, *Culture of National Security*; and Adler and Pouliot, *International Practices*.

35. See, for example, Boulding, *Image*; Jervis, *Perception and Misperception*; Vertzberger, *World in Their Minds*; and Holsti, *Change in the International System*.

36. On the agent-structure problem in international relations, see Dessler, "What's at Stake in the Agent-Structure Debate"; and Doty, "Aporia."

37. Kruglanski, *Lay Epistemics and Human Knowledge*; and Hovland, Janis, and Kelley, *Communication and Persuasion*.

38. On the processes of delegitimization and political alienation, see, for example, Eldridge, *Images of Conflict*.

39. For a good discussion of the relationship between belief systems and foreign policy decisions, see Seliktar, *New Zionism and the Foreign Policy System.*

40. Weber, *Gesammelte Aufsätze,* 503.

41. Al-Jazeera, "Has the Arab Spring Arrived in Israel?" Inside Story, *Al-Jazeera,* July 31, 2011.

42. Barnea, "Lahats Atomi" [Atomic pressure], *Yedioth Aharonot,* October 28, 2011.

1

Feeling under Siege

Conflicts, Threats, and Regional Order

Israel is undoubtedly facing a number of significant external security threats, together with an enduring regional hostility. Among the populations of many of Israel's neighbors, animosity and hatred toward Israel are often a blind reflex. But while disagreements over the desirable policy toward "the Arabs" have been a constant feature of Israeli politics, after the end of the Oslo peace process a remarkable shift took place: the country's politicians now increasingly concurred on one specific vision of regional politics. In fact, it was the Zionist Left that converged toward the positions of Israel's political center and right-of-center, with the vast majority of the Israeli public sharing its assessments.

Three major themes came to define the regional foreign policy agenda and public discourse in Israel after the collapse of the Oslo process. The first is the issue of terrorism, a topic that was particularly predominant during the first years of the Second Intifada. Terrorist attacks—mainly in the form of suicide bombings in Israeli buses and shopping malls—deeply affected the Israeli collective psyche and impacted how Israeli governments henceforth portrayed the nature of the Israeli–Palestinian conflict. Second, there was a growing conviction that there "is no partner for peace" on the Palestinian side. This notion would remain predominant during the 2000s and beyond. Third, Israel's political establishment and the public came to view the regional environment through the lens of the rising power of Iran, a country that also supported hostile nonstate actors in the immediate neighborhood.

The three core elements of the new foreign policy consensus are interlinked, forming a rather coherent understanding of Israel's regional environment and strategic position. They also convey a strong sense of besiegement. This chapter looks closely at the new consensus by focusing in particular on the first decade after the demise of the Oslo process, from 2000 to 2010. What is the material basis of the domestic consensus? Which features characterized Israel's security situation and its regional environment in that period? What exactly do the main elements of the consensus mean and imply? Which lines of policy did these themes inform, and what are the political implications of these choices? And who were the main actors contributing to the emergence of Israel's hegemonic vision on threats and regional order? While hegemonic notions are, by definition, axiomatic for those who maintain them, the discussion here assumes that at least some aspects of Israel's hegemonic vision post-Oslo can be challenged.

Terrorism, on All Fronts

Against the background of the numerous Israeli victims created by the terrorist attacks of the second Palestinian intifada, the preoccupation with terrorism took center stage in Israeli politics in the first post-Oslo decade (and beyond). Together with the involvement in the violence of Fatah security forces—which Israel had helped arming—and other gruesome events, such as the lynching of two Israeli soldiers in Ramallah in early October 2000, the suicide attacks left Israelis in shock, fear, and anger. Repeated rocket attacks from Hamas and Hizballah across the southern and northern border, respectively, also forged a broad agreement across Israel's political elite and the public on the need to fight the phenomenon of terrorism forcefully.

However, before proceeding, a note on the notion of terrorism is necessary. Perhaps unsurprisingly, there is no universally accepted definition of who is a terrorist. In legal terms, virtually all forms of terrorism are prohibited by one of twelve international counterterrorism conventions, international customary law, the Geneva Conventions, or the Rome Statutes of the International Criminal Court. Yet, in spite of this scattered list of conventions and little-known provisions in specific treaties, a compelling normative framework surrounding the question of terrorism is lacking. A particularly contested issue is the legitimacy of means adopted by liberation movements and by people living under occupation; the expression "one's terrorist is another's freedom fighter" clearly conveys this state of affairs.[1] The question of whether states may be considered as engaging in terrorism is disputed as well.

However, a number of primary factors have been identified as bearing on terrorism. These include the systematic and intentional use of violence with the aim of creating fear, not just among the direct victims but also among a wider audience, with the objective of achieving political goals. In this vein, the UN Secretary-General High Level Panel on Threats, Challenges and Change suggested in 2004 that terrorism should be defined as any action "that is intended to cause death or serious bodily harm to civilians or non-combatants, when the purpose of such act, by its nature or context, is to intimidate a population, or to compel a Government or an international organization to do or to abstain from doing any act."[2]

The argument that acts of terrorism solely involve the intentional killing of civilians and noncombatants (as opposed to combatant security personnel) is disputed as well. The 1983 barracks bombing in Beirut that targeted US and French soldiers, who were not engaged in any fighting, was widely defined as an act of terrorism. Those disputing this definition would point to their role as a foreign "occupation force," thus designating them as a legitimate target of "resistance." What is undisputed is that the deliberate killing of civilians violates international humanitarian law and counts as a war crime. According to these criteria, this book adopts the position that suicide bombings targeting civilians, as well as the deliberate firing of rockets on town and cities, violate international law and can be considered as acts of terrorism. When perpetrated in a systematic way and with the clear objective of creating fear as a means to achieve political goals, attacks carried out by Israeli settlers on the Palestinian population in the territories can also be considered as acts of terrorism. Provided that the same conditions are met, actions of the Israeli army against unarmed Palestinian civilians may fall into the same category.

It should also be mentioned that Israeli governments officially espouse a rather broad definition of terrorism: attacks on Israeli security personnel are considered as terrorist acts. Israel also defines Hamas and Hizballah as terrorist organizations—a position it shares with the United States, the European Union, and the governments of many other states. It goes without saying that these positions are contested by others, with Israel being sometimes accused of engaging in "state terrorism."

Background: Terrorist Attacks Before and During the Second Intifada

Terrorism was not a new phenomenon that emerged with the Second Intifada. In fact, terrorist incidents have accompanied the entire history of the Israeli–Palestinian conflict. Significantly, attacks against Israeli civilians and security personnel carried out by different Palestinian factions— particularly Hamas and Islamic Jihad—also marked the period in which Israel negotiated the Oslo agreements with the Palestine Liberation

Organization (PLO) in the 1990s. The novelty of the attacks starting in 1993 was that they targeted civilian population centers and were directed at central locations in major cities.[3] From the signing of the Declaration of Principles on September 13, 1993, to the outbreak of the Second Intifada in late September 2000, Palestinian organizations that opposed the Oslo Accords carried out fourteen suicide bombings against Israeli civilians. Together with shooting, axing, and stabbing attacks, more than 180 Israeli civilians and over 80 soldiers were killed in that period.[4]

Under the interim premiership of Shimon Peres from 1995 to 1996, which followed Yitzhak Rabin's assassination in November 1995, Hamas unleashed a series of suicide attacks within the pre-1967 Green Line, that is, within the internationally recognized borders of the State of Israel.[5] Against the advice of some of his security advisers, Peres had ordered the assassination of Yehia Ayyash, the popular chief bomb maker of Hamas. Also known as "the engineer," Ayyash had built several suicide bombs that had caused the deaths of about ninety Israelis. Hamas's retaliation, the bloody series of attacks during Israel's electoral campaign in the spring of 1996, had a major impact on the voting results, with Binyamin Netanyahu winning over Peres (albeit narrowly). This was exactly what Hamas had wanted: a Likud victory that would slow down or derail the peace process it detested.

During the Oslo process the question of how to handle Palestinian terrorism was a highly divisive issue in Israeli politics. The Rabin government declared that it would fight terror as if there was no peace process and that it would pursue the peace process as if there was no terror. Repeated many times by the Rabin government, this principle paraphrases David Ben-Gurion's famous dictum at the outbreak of World War II, stipulating that the Jewish community in Palestine should fight the British government's 1939 White Paper (which limited Jewish immigration to Mandatory Palestine) as if there was no war against the Nazis, and that it should fight the Nazis on the side of Great Britain as if there was no White Paper. Peres, on the other hand, coined the phrase that Israelis killed in Palestinian suicide attacks were the "victims of peace," a notion that the Israeli public was reluctant to accept. While continuing to negotiate with the PLO, the governments of Rabin and Peres imposed closures on the Palestinian territories and restricted the movement of people and goods in response to repeated attacks.[6] The subsequent government under Netanyahu (1996–99) had a very different approach to Palestinian terror. Netanyahu decided to suspend the implementation of the Oslo Accords and to renew it subject only to the complete cessation of Palestinian violence.

If this was the situation during the Oslo process, the worst was still to come. In the decade following the eruption of the Second Intifada, the number of Israeli fatalities from Palestinian terrorist attacks almost tripled. Between the end of September 2000 and the end of October 2010, different Palestinian factions carried out over eighty suicide bombings against Israeli civilians. Together with shootings, stabbings, or intentional killing by other means, these attacks claimed the life of more than 700 Israeli civilians in that period. In addition, over 330 members of the Israeli security forces were killed in Palestinian attacks, bringing the total number of Israeli fatalities to over 1,000.[7] In January 2002 Israel captured a ship, the *Karine A*, with fifty tons of concealed weapons—including Katyusha rockets, antitank missiles, assault rifles, and explosives—that were most probably destined for Arafat's Palestinian Authority. From 2001 different Palestinian factions in Gaza also started firing rockets into southern Israel as well as on Israeli settlements in the Gaza Strip.

Ariel Sharon, who became prime minister after the 2001 Israeli elections and had repeatedly declared that the Oslo Accords were null and void, reverted to the Likud approach to Palestinian terrorism, stressing that no negotiations would be held "under fire."[8] Sharon's prime concern of seeking to crush terrorism witnessed the adoption of particularly repressive policies toward the Palestinians, marked by vast military operations in the West Bank and the Gaza Strip and, from 2002 on, the reoccupation of territories from which the Israeli army had withdrawn under the Oslo Accords. Thus, following a suicide bombing during Passover in Netanya in 2002 that killed twenty-eight Israeli civilians, the Israeli army undertook the largest military operation in the West Bank since the 1967 war. During the so-called Operation Defensive Shield of March and April 2002, the Israeli army reoccupied most West Bank cities and considerably damaged the Jenin refugee camp. Closures, curfews, administrative detentions, house demolitions, and extrajudicial killings were part and parcel of Israel's counterterrorism policies in the territories.

Sharon's policies took a heavy toll on the Palestinians. During his premiership between early 2001 and January 2006, over 2,900 Palestinians were killed by Israeli security forces in the occupied territories. According to the Israeli human rights organization B'Tselem, more than 1,400 of these Palestinian fatalities (that is, almost half) were not taking part in hostilities at the time they were killed. This number does not include Palestinians who were the object of targeted killings, amounting to 182 people between 2001 and the end of 2005.[9] The Palestinian leadership across the political spectrum was not spared: Israel assassinated Sheikh Yassin and Abdel Aziz

al-Rantisi of Hamas; the leading Fatah activist and commander of the al-
Aqsa Brigade in Tulkarem, Ra'ed al-Karmi; and Abu Ali Mustafa of the
Popular Front for the Liberation of Palestine. It imprisoned the popular
Fatah leader Marwan Barghouti, convicted by an Israeli court of orchestrating numerous attacks and suicide bombings against Israeli civilians.
The subsequent Popular Front secretary-general, Ahmed Sadat, was also
incarcerated. In early 2002 the Israeli army placed Yasser Arafat under siege
in his Muqata headquarters in Ramallah, where he remained confined until
close to the time of his death. Altogether, Israel's essentially military and
unilateral response to Palestinian terrorism was a clear departure from the
policies that had characterized much of the previous decade.[10]

Sharon and Terrorism: Consensus and Reinterpretation

The numerous terrorist attacks of the Second Intifada—defined as acts
of resistance by their perpetrators—are an incontestable fact. However,
it is interesting to observe how Sharon's specific prescription to fight terrorism not only forged a broad consensus in Israel but also entailed a
reinterpretation of the conflict with the Palestinians itself. Thus, with the
ongoing carnage caused by Palestinian terrorist attacks, which peaked in
2002–3, and against the backdrop of the "war on terror" that US president George W. Bush had declared after the attacks of 9/11, "terror" and
"terrorism" became the most important words in Israel's political lexicon.
Examples are too numerous to mention. To provide but one striking illustration, in October 2002 Sharon addressed Bush at a joint conference as
follows: "I would like to express our deep appreciation to your leadership
facing the world of terror. We regard terror as the most dangerous thing,
and seeing the terror spread now, seeing that under your leadership the
world will be able to face the terror and contain terror and stop terror.
We have been facing terror for over 120 years, and we still face terror."[11]

Israeli journalist Doron Rosenblum sarcastically remarked on the
highly inflationary use of the term "terrorism" in those years that "every
form of combat and military operation [in Israel] has been upgraded to
a 'war against terrorism,'" noting that the "chief of staff and his cabinet
ministers make sure to stick the word 'terrorism' into every sentence three
times." Stressing that "if everything is terrorism, anything goes," Rosenblum also pointed to the use of the notion of terrorism as a means of
legitimizing otherwise questionable actions.[12]

Identifying terrorism as the main problem facing the Middle East, Israel under Sharon defined the cessation of the latter as *conditio sine qua*

non for the resumption of peace talks with the Palestinians. Equally, the government in Jerusalem repeatedly pointed to the failure of the Palestinian Authority (PA) under Yasser Arafat to fight terrorism, as it had committed itself in the Oslo Accords as well as in the so-called Roadmap for Middle East Peace of 2003.[13]

Crucially, from the outset Sharon's "war against terror" implied that Israel's conflict with the Palestinians was reinterpreted as an exclusive problem of terrorism. Therefore, the conflict was not, or was no longer, a clash between two national movements, a fight over the same piece of land, or a question of rights. Devoid of any historical dimension, Palestinian terrorism was singled out as the main issue preventing a peaceful solution to the conflict. Concurrently, terrorism was identified as a much broader phenomenon at the regional and global level. No doubt, Israel's unconditional positioning in the war on terror on the side of the "free world" also served the government's strategic aim of strengthening relations with the US administration under George W. Bush, as noted elsewhere.[14] In fact, the pattern of concentrating on wider regional and global threats "while relegating to a secondary priority the need to create and exploit opportunities for an Arab-Israeli peace" is a recurrent pattern in the relationship between Israeli center-right governments and Republican administrations in Washington.[15]

The government's policies in the face of the terrorism of the Second Intifada, together with the altered understanding of the conflict with the Palestinians it promoted, relied on an extremely broad Israeli consensus. The 2003 elections confirming Sharon's leadership—the Likud party under his guidance won a resounding victory in these elections—proves this point. It is also relevant that Sharon led a grand coalition with the Labor Party from 2001 to 2003 and again from 2005 until he suffered an incapacitating stroke in January 2006.[16] Sharon's popularity in that period is particularly striking considering the contempt that large parts of Israel's political establishment had previously had for him because of his role in the 1982 Lebanon War. Then acting as minister of defense, Sharon had lied to Prime Minister Menachem Begin regarding the war aims as the Israeli army marched without government authorization into Beirut (the declared war aim was to push 40 km into southern Lebanon). Israel's Kahan Commission of Inquiry also found that Sharon bore personal responsibility for the massacres in the Palestinian refugee camps Sabra and Shatila in Beirut in 1982. Perpetrated by Lebanese Maronite militias after the assassination of Lebanese president Bashir Gemayel, the Israeli army was guarding the camps and allowed the militias to enter them, ignoring the danger of bloodshed and revenge and without doing anything to prevent it. Yet numerous public opinion polls conducted during the first years of the Second Intifada point to a strong consensus around Sharon's positions and policies. For instance, according to a poll of 2001, a vast majority of Jewish Israelis (89 percent) was in favor of eliminating (that is, assassinating without any legal proceedings) those accused of terrorism; 71 percent supported the use of tanks and fighter aircraft against the Palestinians, 68 percent favored the use of closures and economic sanctions, and 57 percent of respondents supported an Israeli invasion of area A, the territories under Palestinian control as stipulated by the Oslo Accords.[17] In 2003 the support among the Jewish Israeli public remained very high for targeted killings of terrorists (92 percent), for destroying the homes of the families of terrorists (88 percent), for using closures and economic sanctions (72 percent), for using tanks and aircraft against the Palestinians (79 percent), and for invading Area A (76 percent).[18] Two years later 77 percent of respondents of a poll believed that the intifada could be controlled by military action, and 65 percent of those polled were in favor of postponing negotiations with the Palestinians until Arafat was replaced.[19]

Israelis also indicated that they had become more militant since the intifada started, with 41 percent of respondents saying in 2002 that they were prepared to make fewer concessions to the Palestinians since the beginning of the uprising. Most significantly, in 2002 a staggering 57 percent of Jewish Israelis thought that government policies toward the Second Intifada were "too soft." A year later, 58 percent of those polled thought that the measures employed by the government to ensure quiet in the territories were adequate, while 29 percent still believed that they were "too soft."[20] The slogan (and car sticker) of that period, "tnu le-Tsahal lenatseah" (let the IDF win), bluntly expressed this position.

The Israeli media played a significant part in the consensus-building process. In covering the unfolding events in the territories, the media usually identified with the positions of the political and military establishment. Stressing the need to fight and prevent Palestinian terrorism, the media rarely questioned the adequacy, purpose, or proportionality of Israeli policies. A study by Daniel Dor of the coverage of Operation Defensive Shield during March and April 2002 demonstrates this matter. Focusing on Israel's most important print media—*Maariv, Yediot Aharonot,* and *Haaretz*—and the news coverage on Israel's two major television stations, Channel 1 and Channel 2, the study shows that the media was united in denouncing the international community's growing condemnation of Israeli policies in the territories. With some differences in stance, the media unanimously depicted the criticism of Israel's human rights violations as proof of an inherent hostility toward the country. At the same time, the Israeli media tended to suppress reports that could be perceived as incriminating. Thus, with almost no exception, reports from generally respected military sources that were critical of the purely defensive nature of "Operation Defensive Shield" or its proportionality tended to be placed far away from the main news pages or editorials in the print media. Similarly, they were only mentioned en passant, if at all, in the TV news. These reports suggested, for instance, that the primary objective of Israel's military operation was to destroy the PA and avoid a return to the Oslo peace process. According to Dor, the media prevented any critical discussion of Israeli policies, let alone of the question of responsibility and blame. Instead, the media contributed to a particular construction of Israeli identity as a nation under siege, while forging a strong sense of community.[21]

A more comprehensive study by the same author of how the Israeli print media reported the outbreak of the Second Intifada reaches similar conclusions.[22] Likewise, an analysis of Israeli media reports on the policy of extrajudicial killings—the targeted assassinations of Palestinian terrorists or suspected terrorists—points to a complete lack of critical inquiry regarding the effectiveness, legality, or morality of these measures. Instead, the media largely accepted the official justification of this practice, together with the version of events as presented by the Israeli army and government. It also adopted without any further reflection the euphemistic Hebrew term "*hisul memukad*," that is, "targeted liquidation," which of course sounds much better than "extrajudicial killing" or "assassination."[23] It is worth noting here that even within Israel's security establishment, the policy of targeted killings is controversial because of its high collateral damage—the killing or wounding of innocent civilians. Its contribution to the spiraling of violence has also been criticized, as Palestinian suicide attacks also occurred in revenge for Israel's assassination of Hamas and Islamic Jihad leaders or other political figures, or the killing of civilians in the course of action.

In the first years of the Second Intifada, Palestinian terrorism developed into a major disrupting factor in Israeli life, affecting the economy, the morale of Israeli citizens, and the general public agenda. The repeated attacks, the casualties, and the almost daily gruesome footage of these events on television screens created a climate of fear and anger. Significantly, Palestinian terrorism also informed a number of key policy decisions on the Israeli side, implicitly or explicitly. For instance, terrorism was the main reason for building the West Bank barrier. According to Israel's Foreign Ministry, "had there been no terrorism, Israel would not have been compelled to build a fence to protect its citizens."[24] Palestinian terrorism, particularly Hamas's attacks on the Gush Katif block in the Gaza Strip during the Second Intifada, was also the main—albeit tacit—reason behind Israel's withdrawal from the Gaza Strip in August 2005.[25] According to its architect, Ariel Sharon, the purpose of the disengagement was "to reduce terror as much as possible and grant Israeli citizens the maximum level of security," as he publicly stated in December 2003.[26]

Rocket Attacks by Hamas and Hizballah

The Israeli experience with terrorism was not confined to bombing and other attacks within the Green Line or in the occupied territories. Israeli citizens were also subjected to rockets launched across the northern and southern borders of the country. As for the situation in the south, Israel's unilateral withdrawal from the Gaza Strip in 2005—although widely supported at that time[27]—did not exactly have the desired effect on Israel's security. On the contrary, the number of rockets hitting civilian targets in southern Israel, fired in particular by Hamas, increased exponentially after Israel withdrew its soldiers and settlers from the strip. If the total number of rockets fired into Israel amounted to more than 8,600 between 2001 and 2009, then almost 6,000 of these rockets were fired after the Gaza disengagement.[28] According to UN figures, 1,194 Qassam rockets were fired at Israel in 2005 (an average of 100 rockets a month); in 2006 the rocket fire increased to 1,786 (an average of 149 a month); and in 2007, 1,331 rockets were fired (an average of 111 a month). According to figures provided by Israel's Security Agency, in 2008, 2,048 rockets and more than 1,672 mortar shells were fired from the Gaza Strip into Israel. From 2001 to the end of Israel's war on Gaza on January 17, 2009, eighteen people were killed in Israel by Palestinian rockets and mortar fire (between 2001 and Israel's withdrawal from Gaza, mortars and rockets fired on Israeli settlements in the Gaza Strip had killed another ten people).[29]

The aim of preventing the launching of these rockets, which increased in range and sophistication over the years, was the official reasoning behind Israel's decision to impose a blockade on Gaza after Hamas gained control over it in June 2007. Stopping the rocket attacks was also the main official motivation for the Israeli offensive in the Gaza Strip from December 27, 2008, to January 18, 2009, termed Operation Cast Lead. Israel's blockade of the Gaza Strip, imposed after the Hamas takeover, went unquestioned in Israeli politics. Likewise, Israel's continued control of Gaza's air space, its territorial waters, and, together with Egypt, its borders did not figure in Israel's political discourse or collective consciousness.

As with most of the history of the Israeli–Palestinian conflict, the justification and legitimacy of "Operation Cast Lead" remains highly controversial, together with the question of who violated the truce between Israel and Hamas that had been in place since June 19, 2008. Perhaps unsurprisingly, Israel and Hamas accused each other of violating the Egyptian-mediated cease-fire. As a matter of fact, rockets from Gaza never completely stopped during the truce, and Israel never allowed a major flow of goods and aid into Gaza. According to Hamas, it was Israel's raid into the Gaza Strip and the killing of six Hamas fighters on November 4, 2008, that broke the cease-fire. Israel claimed that its action was a legitimate step to destroy an immediate threat—namely, a tunnel on the Gaza–Israel border dug by militants to infiltrate into Israel and abduct soldiers.[30]

The extremely high number of Palestinian fatalities, the extent of the destruction in Gaza, and the fact that—courtesy of Israel *and* Egypt— Palestinians were jailed in the strip during Israeli air raids had a major impact on Israel's international reputation. Israel's conduct of the war on the Gaza Strip also further contributed to the ever-widening gap between Israeli collective consciousness and international public opinion. However, the perceived necessity of eliminating the Hamas regime went undisputed among Israel's political and military elites. The Israeli government under Ehud Olmert claimed the war was a legitimate defense against the terror of Hamas, and stressed that no country would accept repeated attacks on its civilian population by another entity (which incidentally happened to be a terrorist organization). Accusations by the international community that Israel had violated the laws of war were dismissed with dismay by Israeli politicians, public figures, and the media. The so-called Goldstone Report by the international fact-finding mission to investigate alleged violations of international law in the Gaza conflict, appointed by the UN Human Rights Council in April 2009 and headed by South African jurist Richard Goldstone, reached precisely these conclusions: it stipulated that Israel, along with the different Palestinian factions, had perpetrated war crimes by deliberately attacking civilians.[31] The report caused outrage on the Israeli side, along with harsh accusations of an anti-Israel bias.[32] Israel stressed that the high number of Palestinian civilian casualties resulted from Hamas deliberately hiding its fighters and weapons arsenal in densely populated areas.

The conviction that Israel had not only the right but also the duty to fight Hamas in Gaza in order to protect its citizens was widely shared by the Israeli Jewish public. Indeed, "Operation Cast Lead" enjoyed exceptionally vast support from day one, with the war being considered as just in a double sense: first, the reason for going to war was seen as justified and, second, there was full support for the way the war was conducted. Most Jewish Israelis considered the war as a war of "no choice." On the fifth day of the war, on December 31, 2008, 79 percent of respondents "strongly supported" the operation, and another 14 percent "largely supported" it.[33] A poll held on the third day of the ground offensive showed that a staggering 70 percent of the total Israeli population supported a continuation of the operation, while 20 percent called for a cease-fire. Because this poll had been taken among the total Israeli population, the pollsters assumed that some 80 percent of the Jewish population supported the continuation of the war.[34] According to another opinion poll among Jewish Israelis conducted about a week and a half after the war had started, 94 percent of respondents supported or strongly supported the operation, and 92 percent thought it benefited Israel's security. Despite the severe damage caused to infrastructure and notwithstanding the suffering of the civilian population in the strip, 92 percent of those polled justified the Israeli air force attacks in Gaza, and 70 percent considered the decision to send ground forces into Gaza a necessary move.[35] In February 2009, after the war had already ended, 66 percent of the Jewish Israeli public believed that Israel, instead of conceding to international pressure to stop the fighting, should have continued the operation until Hamas surrendered.[36]

Interestingly, the sample of Palestinian Israeli citizens maintained opposite positions to those of the Jewish public. Thus, 85 percent of Israel's Arab citizens opposed the 2008–9 Gaza war, and 93 percent thought Israel should end it, based on an agreement that included a cessation of Hamas's shelling in return for opening the crossings into the strip.[37]

The rockets and mortar shells launched into Israel during the military operations, which deliberately targeted civilians, killed three Israeli civilians and one soldier and wounded dozens. Nine Israeli soldiers were killed within the Gaza Strip, 4 by friendly fire, and more than 100 Israeli soldiers were wounded. However, the fact that the Israeli army caused the deaths of over 1,300 Palestinians (759 of whom did not take part in the hostilities), injured over 5,300 people, destroyed 3,500 houses, and left 20,000 Gaza Palestinians homeless apparently did not affect the Israeli consensus on the war's appropriateness and proportionality.[38]

Analyses of the coverage of the Gaza war in the Israeli media point to the usual pattern of adopting the government line in terms of justification. The Israeli media also praised the precision of the Israeli army as well as its "purity of arms" and dismissed any international criticism.[39]

The Israeli notion of being exposed to terrorism on all fronts also included the "terror from Lebanon," as Israel's Ministry of Foreign Affairs put it. More specifically, this refers to the repeated border incidents between the Lebanese Hizballah and the Israeli army, which did not cease after Israel withdrew from southern Lebanon in May 2000. These incidents include the kidnapping or attempted kidnapping of Israeli soldiers, the firing of mortar shells and antitank missiles at Israeli army positions in the Sheba'a Farms area (which Hizballah claims belongs to Lebanon[40]), sniper fire, roadside explosives, and antiaircraft fire at Israeli jets that violated Lebanese airspace. From 2002 Hizballah also sporadically resumed the firing of Katyusha rockets on Israeli territory.[41] Until 2006 Israel had reacted to these incidents "in proportion to Hezbollah's border provocations" while also seeking to hit Hizballah's Syrian patron, yet trying "not to rock the boat."[42] For instance, in reaction to Hizballah's abduction of Israeli soldiers in October 2000, Israel had sent warplanes against Hizballah targets, but it had also released Lebanese prisoners in exchange for its soldiers. In early 2004 Israel had released four hundred Lebanese prisoners to Hizballah in exchange for an Israeli reservist colonel and the bodies of three Israeli soldiers. Prior to 2006 Israel held at least five Lebanese prisoners, who were later swapped for the remains of two kidnapped Israeli soldiers (the number of Lebanese prisoners in Israeli jails is disputed).

In July 2006, however, the Israeli government decided to respond to the abduction of two Israeli soldiers on Israeli territory by starting a massive military campaign. This time Israel's political and military establishment presented the war as a necessary fight against the terror of Hizballah, with coalition partners Likud and Labor agreeing on the need to respond forcefully to the organization's act of aggression. The Jewish Israeli public was supportive of the war, at least initially, as well as of the declared objective to "turn Lebanon's clock back 20 years," if the two abducted Israeli soldiers were not returned, as former Chief of Staff Dan Halutz memorably stated. However, the support waned as the war proceeded. Hizballah, a semi–military organization of a few thousand men, resisted for weeks the strongest army in the Middle East and launched a barrage of rockets at Israel's civilian population throughout the war, with the Israeli army unable to stop it.

Israel's failures in the Second Lebanon War became apparent in the findings of the Winograd Commission, an Israeli commission of inquiry appointed to investigate Israel's conduct of the war. Presenting a purely Israeli perspective that ignored the war's impact on Lebanon, the commission found that there were serious failings in the strategic planning and decision-making process at both the political and the military level, as well as significant flaws in the army's preparedness and in the defense of the Israeli civilian population. The Winograd Commission also criticized Israel's decision to respond with an intensive military strike without having any comprehensive military plan or clearly defined goals.[43]

Terrorism and the Restructuring of Israel's Political Landscape

Terrorism continued to be a major concern throughout the decade, affecting the public mood in Israel. For example, according to a survey in 2009, 80 percent of the Jewish Israeli public believed that there was a real danger of terrorism on a large scale in the near future.[44] But the attacks of the Second Intifada and the general Israeli sense of being under siege also reshaped Israel's political landscape.

On the one hand, terrorism profoundly impacted the outcome of Israel's elections in the first post-Oslo decade, prompting a right-wing shift in Israel's voting behavior.[45] The dominance of the Likud party (and its offshoot, Kadima), with its uncompromising stance and focus on "national security," during most of the 2000s is a clear case in point. Second, terrorism destroyed the trust in the Palestinian side of those supporting peace negotiations. It persuaded the Israeli electorate that the PA under Arafat, who was perhaps not exactly a trust-inspiring statesman, was unwilling or unable to stop the violence. The frequent attacks also convinced Israelis that talking to "blood-thirsty Hamas" (or Hizballah, for that matter) was out of question. The continuous terror attacks and the consensus around their existentially threatening nature profoundly undermined the clout and credibility of the Israeli peace camp. Third, the intifada prompted part of the political Right to revisit its "Greater Israel" vision, as the country's withdrawal from Gaza and four minor West Bank settlements in the summer of 2005 demonstrates. The issue of terrorism also prompted Ariel Sharon's breakaway from the Likud party, of which he was a central figure, over the Gaza disengagement plan. He founded a new center-right party, Kadima.

More importantly, however, the consensus around the phenomenon of terrorism also provided the Israeli Right with the opportunity to reframe the Israeli–Palestinian conflict in terms of terrorism and to promote a hegemonic explanation for its persistence. Concurrently, it shifted Israel's preoccupation with the Palestinian problem during the Oslo years back to a broader concern with a hostile "Arab world," or "Muslim world," thus increasingly accentuating an ethnoreligious interpretation of the conflict.[46] Significantly, this (allegedly) hostile Arab/Muslim "world" also increasingly came to comprise Israel's Palestinian citizens, viewed as the "enemy within." The period after Oslo indeed witnessed a growing gap between the positions of Jewish and Palestinian Israelis, and a growing mutual suspicion. Israel's right-wing parties, particularly Avigdor Lieberman's Yisrael Beiteinu party, sought to capitalize on this development, portraying Israel's Arab citizens as a "fifth column" while supporting a number of discriminatory pieces of legislation.[47] Thus, as right-wing governments increasingly presented terrorism as a threat to Jewish national identity and associated the phenomenon with Israel's Arab citizens (as well as with Jewish left-wing groups), the issue of terrorism affected political tolerance and liberal values in Israel's political culture. As the authors of a study on the impact of terrorism on political tolerance in Israel noted, "there is every incentive for Israeli politicians, particularly those on the Right who clearly 'own' the issues of national security and terrorism, to use fear to manipulate the public for political gains and for justifying the repression of the Arab/Palestinian minority."[48]

Hence, as Israeli governments highlighted the terror exerted by Hamas and Hizballah in launching rockets on southern and northern Israel, respectively, and in attacking Israeli security personnel and civilians alike, the notion that terrorism was a an encircling and particularly menacing phenomenon came to underwrite Israel's political discourse. Israel's prevailing notion of regional order also stipulated that terrorism was endemic to the Arab/Muslim Middle East.

"There is no partner for peace"

The second pillar of Israel's foreign policy consensus post-Oslo relates to the question of why the Camp David negotiations of July 2000 between Israel and the PA failed. The explanation provided for the failure of these talks is pivotal to how Israelis came to see the regional environment post-Oslo. The account that became dominant in Israel (and to a large extent in the United States as well) is that Israeli prime minister Ehud Barak made the most generous offer to the Palestinians that any Israeli government had ever proposed. The Palestinians, however, turned every single Israeli proposal down, presumably because Arafat was not genuinely interested in peace and the concessions demanded from the Palestinian side.[49] According to this interpretation of events, while Israel went the extra mile to reach a deal, the Palestinians reacted with the violence of the Second Intifada, proving that there was no partner for peace on the Palestinian side. Thus, the negotiations at Camp David revealed the "true face" of Palestinian leader Yasser Arafat.

Background: Israel's Offer and Arafat's Rejection

From a purely Israeli perspective, Barak's offer at Camp David was far-reaching indeed. Regarding territory and borders, there are different accounts of what percentage of the Palestinian territory the Israeli side offered to their Palestinian counterparts at Camp David for a future Palestinian state. The map presented by the Israeli side in the informal discussions in Stockholm, prior to the Camp David talks, showed a Palestinian state covering 88 percent of the West Bank and Gaza Strip. This map served as a basis for discussion at Camp David, during which the Israeli position evolved. On the eighth day of the summit, Barak had offered to the Palestinians that Israel annex settlement blocks constituting 9 percent of the West Bank, with a 1 percent land swap in Gaza.[50] Arab Jerusalem would become the capital of the Palestinian state, with a division of the Old City into two equal parts and Palestinian functional rule over the Arab and Armenian quarter. A "more qualified Palestinian sovereignty" would apply to other parts of East Jerusalem.[51] As for the Haram al-Sharif / Temple Mount in Jerusalem's Old City, where the Al-Aqsa mosque (Islam's third-holiest site) is situated just above the remains of the Jewish First and Second Temples, the Palestinians would obtain a "sovereign custodianship." Thus, according to the dominant Israeli narrative, a state in almost all of the territories Israel had conquered in 1967, with East Jerusalem as its capital, was within reach for the Palestinians, but Arafat turned it down. The magnitude of Barak's offer resonates with the origin of the conflict, with the Arab side turning down the UN partition plan of 1947 and starting a war upon Israel's declaration of independence in May 1948. According to this perspective, the Palestinians could have had a state a long time ago, were it not for Arab rejectionism. Thus, the Camp David Summit ended without an agreement.

A central element of the narrative of not having a partner for peace (*ein partner le-shalom*) is the role Arafat allegedly played in the outbreak and continuation of the second Palestinian intifada that erupted shortly after the failed Camp David Summit. Barak insisted that the PA had responded with violence to his offer at Camp David in July by orchestrating the uprising, which erupted after opposition leader Ariel Sharon, accompanied by about one thousand riot police, visited the Temple Mount on September 28, 2000. Sharon's visit, which was approved by Prime Minister Barak, was mainly aimed at assessing Sharon's leadership within the Likud party. However, the Palestinians perceived Sharon's action as a blatant affront, particularly since the question of who controls the Temple Mount had been one of the key issues preventing an agreement at Camp David. Israel's official position leaves no doubt about Arafat's responsibilities. Stressing that Sharon's visit did not cause or spark the violence but rather served as "an excuse" for it, an Israeli government report asserts that the violence was "nurtured, planned, and prosecuted as an instrument of policy by the Palestinian leadership."[52] The Israeli government also succeeded in disseminating the message that it was acting with great restraint in its effort to curb Palestinian violence during the first months of the uprising.[53]

According to Israel's official explanation, the reason for the breakdown of the subsequent rounds of peace negotiations, which ended at Taba, Egypt, in January 2001, is once more to be found in Yasser Arafat's unwillingness to accept Israel's proposals. The talks at Taba on the Egyptian side of the Sinai Peninsula were based on the so-called Clinton Parameters, the bridging proposal that US president Bill Clinton had put forward in December 2000 in his last effort to save the Israeli–Palestinian peace negotiations from collapsing. These parameters stipulated the creation of a Palestinian state on 96 percent of the West Bank and the entire Gaza Strip, Israel's annexation of settlement blocks and land swaps in the range of 1 to 3 percent, plus free passage between Gaza and the West Bank. Jerusalem was to be divided according to the principle that "Arab areas are Palestinian and Jewish areas are Israeli," with the Palestinians obtaining full sovereignty over the Temple Mount. Israel would retain sovereignty over the underground space where the remains of the Jewish Temple might be buried, or, alternatively an international mechanism would be in charge of excavations under the Temple Mount. The Clinton Parameters also stipulated that Palestinian refugees had a right of return to the Palestinian state, with the solution of the refugee problem including return, rehabilitation, resettlement, and compensation. Israel would absorb a limited number of Palestinian refugees as a "humanitarian" gesture, subject to its discretion. On security, the Clinton Parameters stipulated a "nonmilitarized" Palestinian state, early-warning stations, and an international presence at the border with Jordan.

The official Israeli version of events is that the Israeli side accepted the parameters, but Arafat remained hesitant, presenting substantial reservations that in fact entailed their rejection.[54] The negotiations in Taba eventually ended on January 27, 2001, against the backdrop of continuous Palestinian violence that further undermined Barak's legitimacy. His government had already lost its majority in the Knesset, and elections were scheduled for February 6.

The official Israeli explanation of why the negotiations failed was circulated by the Israeli media time and again, significantly impacting Israeli public opinion. From the outset, Barak claimed that Camp David was a moment of crucial decision that would show whether the Palestinians were serious about peace. The Israeli media soon repeated the line that the negotiations would "reveal Arafat's true face."[55] From this vantage point, what eventually transpired was that, while talking peace, the Palestinian leadership (and population) were set on destroying the State of Israel, either by force or through the insistence on the right of return to Israel for Palestinian refugees.[56] Or, according to the more sophisticated explanation of Israel's former foreign minister Shlomo Ben-Ami (who was also a member of the Israeli negotiating team), "The Palestinian constituent ethos of the right of return and Islamic values, more than land and real estate, were the insurmountable obstacles that prevented an agreement at Camp David and later at Taba."[57]

A study of public opinion in Israel in 2000–2002 shows that the "there is no one to talk to" explanation became the widely accepted interpretation of events. In a poll of July 2000, 67 percent of Jewish Israelis believed the Palestinian side to be partly or entirely responsible for the failure of Camp David. In October 2000 a staggering 73 percent of respondents maintained that the PA had no vested interest in peace with Israel, and 71 percent believed that Arafat behaved like a terrorist. In November 2000 about 80 percent of the Jewish Israeli public held the Palestinians responsible for the eruption of the intifada. A poll in May 2001 showed that 70 percent of Jewish Israelis believed that Arafat was not willing or able to sign an agreement that would end the conflict with Israel. Moreover, in a poll of March 2001, 72 percent of Jewish Israelis supported more military force to deal with the Palestinian uprising.[58]

For the sake of comparison, in June 2000, before the Camp David Summit, Jewish Israelis were evenly divided between those who believed that the Palestinians wanted peace and those who maintained that they did not.[59] Compared to previous polls, the year 2001–2 thus marks an important shift in Israeli public opinion. A study investigating the reason for this shift points to the growing acceptance of the "there is no partner for peace" narrative as promoted by Ehud Barak and his government, particularly against the backdrop of the violence of the Second Intifada.[60]

With Ariel Sharon winning the Israeli elections of February 2001, the belief that there was no one to talk to on the Palestinian side was to remain with the Israeli collective psyche for years to come. The intifada would turn increasingly violent, and the resumption of Palestinian suicide attacks in February 2001 would further convince the Israeli public that this reasoning was correct. While increasingly depicting the intifada as an "existential threat," the Sharon government would adopt repressive policies toward the Palestinians while refusing to talk to the PA as long as the violence continued.

Challenges to the Dominant Explanation

The "no partner for peace" explanation of what happened at Camp David and Taba is, of course, too simplistic to reflect real world events. And, perhaps unsurprisingly, it has been challenged from the outset.[61] Some commentators pointed to the utter lack of preparation before the Camp David talks and the pressure exerted by the Israeli government (which had convinced the US administration) to schedule the summit in the summer of 2000. The Israeli pressure occurred for mainly domestic reasons: Barak's government coalition collapsed in early July 2000, with some parties leaving the coalition for internal reasons and others in opposition to concessions Barak was allegedly ready to make in the negotiations with the Palestinians. Hence, Barak reckoned that he needed an agreement. Moreover, these were the last months of Bill Clinton's presidency.[62] Yasser Arafat, for his part, remained convinced that the summit was premature and that it was a "trap" for the Palestinians.[63] Others have underlined Ehud Barak's flawed negotiation strategy and poor social communication skills, Clinton's inability to authoritatively lead the talks and his failure to present his parameters earlier, and the American bias in favor of Israel's negotiating positions.[64]

The (evolving) positions of Barak's negotiating team may well have been the most far-reaching proposals that any Israeli government had ever put forward. In particular, it was the first time an Israeli leader had proposed the division of "united" Jerusalem, thus breaking an Israeli taboo. Of course, in reality Jerusalem is hardly united. In spite of the legal unification of the city after 1967 (tantamount to Israel's annexation of the conquered eastern part of the city), Jerusalem has continued to be divided in practice: the residents of the two parts of the city—that is, Palestinian and Jewish Jerusalemites—rarely cross into the respective other side. In any event, while the notion of generosity already refutes any type of responsibility or obligation, some authors point out that the Israeli offer was not "generous" at all. According to this argument, it did not meet the pertinent requirements of international law, or at least the dominant interpretation thereof. Specifically, the Israeli proposals did not entail a full Israeli withdrawal from the territories it occupied in 1967 or the evacuation of all settlements it had built there.[65] It is worth recalling here that the majority opinion in international law views UN Security Council Resolution 242, which defines the acquisition of territory by force as unlawful, as stipulating an obligation for Israel to withdraw from *all* the territories it occupied in 1967. Israeli governments have tended to challenge this interpretation, insisting that the resolution calls on Israel to withdraw "from territories." Thus, according to the Israeli position, Israel has already fulfilled its obligations under international law, for instance, by withdrawing from the Sinai Peninsula in the context of the Egyptian–Israeli peace agreement. Similarly, Article 49 of the Fourth Geneva Convention forbids the transfer of population into occupied territory, thus rendering the Israeli settlements in the occupied territories illegal under international law. In contrast to the majority opinion in international law, as expressed, for instance, in UN Security Council Resolutions 446, 452, 465, 471, and 607, inter alia, Israel denies that the Fourth Geneva Convention applies to the West Bank and the Gaza Strip on the basis that these territories have never been part of an independent state.

By not insisting on a full Israeli withdrawal and the dismantling of all the Israeli settlements in the territories, the Palestinians had in fact made major concessions in the negotiations, as Hussein Agha and Robert Malley point out. According to these authors, the Palestinian negotiators had in principle agreed to Israel's annexation of settlements in exchange for land swaps while being "open to a division of East Jerusalem granting Israel sovereignty over its Jewish areas (the Jewish Quarter, the Wailing Wall, and the Jewish neighborhoods)."[66] The Palestinian side had also consented to alternative mechanisms to solving the refugee problem—as long as Israel would publicly acknowledge the right of return and its responsibility in creating the refugee problem in the first place. Altogether, the Palestinian side insisted on the principle of establishing a sovereign and contiguous state in the pre-1967 border with East Jerusalem as its capital, as a basis for negotiations, together with some sort of solution to the refugee problem. Yet Israel insisted on Israeli control over the Jordan

Valley (and hence the border with Jordan), which would undermine the notion of sovereignty. On this issue, Israel's position moved from an initial insistence on permanent control to a twenty-year (and later fifteen-year) lease of the Jordan Valley. However, Israel was initially also adamant on retaining two corridors running from Jerusalem, through the large settlement of Ma'ale Adumim, to the Jordan River, and in the north through the settlement of Ariel to the Jordan Valley.[67] The Israeli negotiators also refused to concede any "real" Palestinian sovereignty over the Haram al-Sharif / Temple Mount, and they declined to tackle the refugee problem in any meaningful way. Neither was there any Israeli recognition that the Palestinians had already made their historical compromise by agreeing to the June 4, 1967, borders, thus accepting a state in 22 percent of Mandatory Palestine and leaving the remaining 78 percent to Israel.[68] Thus, Israel's proposals not only fell short of the minimum Palestinian aspirations but also of anything any Palestinian leader concerned about his (or her) political survival could possibly have accepted.[69]

Notwithstanding the rather detailed accounts of the negotiations at Camp David by members of the three teams, different interpretations of what was offered and who is to blame for their failure persist. Even members of the *same* negotiations team, such as Dennis Ross and Robert Malley of the US delegation, defend highly divergent accounts and reached opposite conclusions as to why Camp David failed. This, in fact, adds an additional layer of complication to the quest for assessing social reality.[70]

Some disagreements also persist on the subsequent talks at Taba, where both sides conducted discussions on the basis of maps and so-called nonpapers.[71] Yet, while the positions of both sides on the thorny final-status issues apparently converged, Ehud Barak, who had sent the most "dovish" members of his government to Taba (including Yossi Beilin and Yossi Sarid), made it clear that those talks were merely "non-binding contacts between senior Israeli and senior Palestinians."[72] Ostensibly convinced that there was no chance of reaching an agreement, Barak stressed that at Taba "there would be no negotiations and there would be no delegation and there would be no official discussions and no documentation. Nor would Americans be present in the room."[73] Barak's noncommittal stance toward the Taba talks is an important detail that the "no partner for peace" narrative tends to ignore.

Perhaps more importantly, the widely circulated account that Israel accepted the Clinton Parameters at Taba while the Palestinians rejected them by way of asking for clarifications on substantial points has been challenged as well. The twenty-page list of reservations presented by the

Israeli side after it had officially agreed to the parameters concerned the status of the Temple Mount in Jerusalem and the right of return—not exactly minor issues. In fact, Barak stated that he had explained to Bill Clinton "over and over" that he would not sign any document that transferred sovereignty on the Temple Mount to the Palestinians and that no Israeli prime minister would accept even one refugee on the basis of the right of return.[74] According to Ahron Bregman, three days after Barak had officially accepted the parameters, he phoned President Clinton telling him that "I do not intend to sign any agreement before the elections."[75] Yet Barak's change of heart apparently did not make it into the headlines—or into the awareness of the Israeli public, for that matter.

The government's claim that Arafat had deliberately orchestrated the violence of the Second Intifada is also questionable, contrasting most notably with the findings of the so-called Mitchell Report—the report of the international fact-finding committee led by former US senator George Mitchell. Stressing that although Sharon's "provocative" and "poorly timed" visit to the Temple Mount did not *cause* the outbreak of the intifada, the Mitchell Report makes it clear that there was "no basis on which to conclude that there was a deliberate plan by the PA to initiate a campaign of violence at the first opportunity."[76] Strikingly enough, Israel's security establishment had initially provided a similar assessment, claiming that the outburst of violence was spontaneous, resulting from rising Palestinian frustrations. However, Chief of Staff Shaul Mofaz and his deputy, Moshe Ya'alon, soon adopted Barak's line.[77] In spite of the widespread agreement that Arafat did not make a consistent effort to control the violence once it began, in recent years, officials from Israel's different intelligence organizations have privately or publicly acknowledged that the intifada was not planned. For instance, Ephraim Lavie, who headed the Palestinian desk at the research department of Israel's military intelligence at that time, stressed that the Second Intifada "erupted as a grassroots uprising and was fought between an occupying state and a people aspiring for national liberation and self-determination."[78] Ami Ayalon, head of Israel's internal security service Shabak (or Shin Bet) from 1996 to May 2000, noted in an interview with *Le Monde* that Yasser Arafat neither prepared nor triggered the intifada.[79] However, the account that Arafat had orchestrated the intifada and was personally responsible for every single attack became—and remained—the dominant narrative.[80]

Finally, the high number of Palestinian victims during the first months of the intifada challenges the official claim that the Israeli army initially acted with great restraint. In the first two months of the Second Intifada, thirteen Israeli civilians and eleven military personnel were killed by Palestinian civilians in the occupied territories; another five Israeli security force personnel were killed by Palestinian security officials (suicide bombings would only resume in February 2001). However, with over two hundred Palestinian civilians and twenty-four security officials killed by the Israeli army and with more than ten thousand Palestinians wounded in the same time span, the government's notion of restraint was more of an illusion, as the Israeli human rights organization B'Tselem stated.[81] Conversely, Israel probably contributed to the spiraling of violence by using live ammunition against unarmed Palestinians during the demonstration the day after Sharon's visit to the Temple Mount, killing four people, and by continuing to use lethal weapons in the protests that subsequently started to spread all over the Palestinian territories.[82]

Altogether, it remains striking that the Barak government continued to propagate its claims about the "real" (i.e., murderous and dishonest) intentions of the Palestinians while continuing to negotiate in dozens of rounds with them. Indeed, over fifty rounds of negotiations took place between the Camp David Summit and the Taba meetings in January 2001, which marked the end of the negotiations. In fact, plainly contradicting Barak's "no partner for peace" mantra, the Palestinian and Israeli delegations jointly declared after the conclusion of the Taba talks that "they have never been closer to reaching an agreement and it is thus our shared belief that the remaining gaps could be bridged with the resumption of negotiations following the Israeli elections."[83]

Altogether, it is safe to assume that the Palestinian leadership made many mistakes at Camp David and after, but ostensibly so did the Israeli side. While the reasons for the outbreak of the Second Intifada are much more complex than the Israeli narrative would have it, the "no partner for peace" narrative constitutes a particularly one-sided interpretation of events, which assigns blame to one side only. So why did the "no partner for peace" explanation become so powerful in Israeli politics and society?

Constructing the Hegemonic Narrative

Considering the significant contradictions of the "no partner for peace" explanation, the question of how it became hegemonic is particularly intriguing. With regard to Israel's counterterrorism policies, there is evidence that the Israeli media played a major role in presenting a "one-sided, simplified, apocalyptic, and emotional representation of reality."[84] In this context, it has been noted that the Israeli media relied extensively on military, intelligence, and political sources in their reporting.[85] More importantly, a study of how three leading Israeli newspapers reported on the outbreak of the intifada suggests that alternative information to the government's version of events was marginalized as a result of a specific editorial policy in the three papers under investigation. This deliberate policy may have played a crucial role in the construction of a "new consensual narrative" that reflected the information provided by the Barak government.[86]

The role of the media in constructing Israel's reality must be seen particularly in the context of the acute sense of crisis and emergency, which tends to trigger a "rally around the flag" effect. As in other times and places—the United States after 9/11 being a good example—this entails that the differences between domestic parties and factions recede into the background, together with any criticism of government policies or the military. It has been noted that conflicts generally constrain any consideration of the other side and foster the consolidation of one's own point of view. The media is part and parcel of this social mechanism. Daniel Bar-Tal and Yona Teichman have argued that "in times of conflict the media is recruited to mobilize society members by presenting a one-sided account of the story."[87] While in many cases the media actually "recruit themselves," so to speak, it is important to note that the construction of a hegemonic discourse in conflict situations is not a one-sided process. On the contrary, important feedback processes between the media and the public take place insofar as the public sets limits on the ability of the press to criticize the establishment.

Specifically in the Israeli case, an additional number of constraints on the reporting of conflicts have been identified. These include the tendency of journalists and publishers in Israel to see themselves as actors of the Zionist consensus, which, in conflict, gains legitimacy. Second, criticism of the military—the institution that Israelis trust the most—is considered as being outside the Israeli consensus. Finally, it has been noted that most Israelis rely almost entirely on the information provided by Israeli sources (newspapers, radio, and television), particularly on issues related to conflict and security, in spite of their access to foreign media.[88] Considering the widespread consumption of Arab media such as Al-Jazeera, Al-Arabiyya, or the Lebanese LBC among Palestinian citizens of Israel, this observation is particularly relevant in explaining the widening gap of perceptions between Jewish and Arab citizens of Israel. All of these factors may explain why in times of acute crisis or war, the Israeli media is mobilized, glorifying Israeli political and military leadership and praising

Israel's moral and military might, thus creating conditions for support among Jewish Israelis. This mechanism may also explain the growing gap between Jewish Israelis and international public opinion—particularly in European countries, to say nothing of Arabic-speaking publics within or without—in how reality is framed and perceived in moments of crisis. Finally, it has been noted that the degree of trust in the Israeli mainstream media is traditionally much higher among Israel's political Left than among the opponents of a meaningful territorial compromise.[89] Hence, it can be assumed that in times of crisis a mobilized media is more likely to move the Israeli peace camp toward a shift of opinion, than it will the traditional opponents of peace negotiations.

In addition to the role of the media, it has been suggested that the source of the "no partner for peace" narrative was central in explaining its power of persuasion. Because most of the information of this narrative came from Ehud Barak himself, a look at his standing and personality is revealing. According to Eran Halperin and Daniel Bar-Tal, Barak was considered by the Jewish Israeli audience—and particularly by the Israeli peace camp—as an "epistemic authority," the source of information an individual relies on in his or her attempt to acquire knowledge about a specific issue.[90] Research has indicated that the reactions to a communication or a message are "significantly affected by cues as to the communicator's intention, expertness, and trustworthiness."[91] Hence, a message "tends to be judged more favorably when made by a communicator of high credibility," with the two main components of credibility being trustworthiness and expertness.[92] As the most-decorated soldier in Israel's history, Barak undoubtedly possessed the expertise and credibility of a truly authoritative source in the eyes of many Israelis—especially since a military background is often a crucial prerequisite for a political career in Israeli politics. The fact that Barak was deemed as both extremely sharp-minded and the political heir of the assassinated and highly respected Yitzhak Rabin only augmented his trustworthiness, particularly among supporters of peace negotiations. In fact, it is relevant that the Israeli peace camp considered Barak their leader. Lacking any comparative authority, a political leader from the right would probably not have succeeded in convincing the Israeli peace camp that there was no peace partner on the Palestinian side.[93]

It is similarly relevant that Barak's explanation for the eruption of the Second Intifada was soon supported by the highest military echelons, most notably the chief of staff, the deputy chief of staff, and the head of the Military Intelligence at that time.[94] Needless to say, in a country in which the army plays such a central role, military leaders enjoy a particularly high degree of trust, including among the Israeli Left. In fact, a study suggests that because of the characteristic of the Second Intifada as a low-intensity conflict and because of the inability of the political echelons to articulate a clear strategy, the Israeli military filled the gap by starting to generate the required knowledge needed for managing the violent confrontation. By creating an information dependency on the military, the army further transformed itself into an epistemic authority.[95]

According to a number of Israeli scholars and "insiders," the blame that was placed on the Palestinians for the breakdown of Camp David was part of a successful campaign that Barak had prepared well in advance, in the event of a failure.[96] Not exactly suffering from low self-esteem, Barak seemed to have genuinely believed that he had the ability to convince Arafat to accept Israel's proposal. In the first press conference after the summit, it was Barak himself who introduced the image of Arafat as "no partner," an image that struck particularly well with the Israeli public. Of course, in view of the upcoming Israeli elections, a significant and rather convenient side effect of this line was that it relieved Barak from any responsibility for the failure of the negotiations. President Clinton's public finger pointing at Arafat for the failure of Camp David—breaking his promise that he would not assign any blame should the summit fail—only provided further legitimacy to Israel's official version of events.[97] As the Palestinian side did not ostensibly succeed in communicating its position to the Israeli public (or the American one for that matter), including the significance of the concessions they had already made (or believed to have made), Ehud Barak had an easy game in laying the blame for Camp David's failure on the Palestinians. They were depicted as intransigent, passive, and uncompromising, thus once more seeming to confirm Abba Eban's famous dictum that the Palestinians "never miss an opportunity to miss an opportunity." Simultaneously, Israel's peace camp started to disintegrate, and Israeli politics witnessed a significant shift to the right.

Finally, the power of the "no partner for peace" theme also derived from the very nature of the message. The relevance of the communication, its repetition, the ability of the public to recognize the general idea, and the predisposition of the audience regarding the frame of reference are all factors believed to enhance persuasion.[98] Hence, the argument that Israel "did not leave any stone unturned" in its quest for peace but that it "had no one to talk to" provided a tremendously simple message that was repeated time and again. It received a high degree of recognition in a society for which conflict, and not peacemaking, was, and still is, the norm. At the same time, the uncertainty and violence of the Second Intifada provided the crucial environment that opened the door for a collective reinterpretation of reality. Hence, in such a situation, the need for an authoritative explanation favored Barak's "no partner for peace" narrative, persuading the Israeli peace camp, in particular.

Political Implications

What is the implication of the "no partner for peace" narrative? Clearly, if there is no one to talk to, then the logical consequence is that there is no point in even trying—at least as long as the Palestinians have not changed. The narrative thus justified the suspension of any peace negotiations that would demand far-reaching territorial concessions from Israel. Barak and, subsequently, Sharon may well have been truly convinced that there was no Palestinian partner for peace. But considering the intricacies of Israeli domestic politics and the international support for meaningful Israeli territorial concessions in the framework of a peace deal, the "no partner for peace" narrative was also instrumental for the Israeli government. And, arguably, it continues to be so. In particular, this explanation was convenient for Israel's political Right—whether religious or not— which opposes major territorial concessions for religious, ultranationalistic, or security considerations. Dov Weissglass, senior adviser to Prime Minister Sharon, highlighted the enormous benefit of the "no partner for peace" explanation, musing that "[we] received a no-one-to-talk-to certificate. That certificate says: (1) There is no one to talk to. (2) As long as there is no one to talk to, the geographic status quo remains intact. (3) The certificate will be revoked only when this-and-this happens— when Palestine becomes Finland. (4) See you then and shalom."[99]

The account of not having a partner also justified a series of unilateral policies, such as the reoccupation of Palestinian cities, the construction of the West Bank barrier, and the withdrawal from the Gaza Strip. It is important to note here that Israel's occupation of Gaza had increasingly turned into a strategic nightmare. Thus, parts of Israel's security and political establishment came to consider a withdrawal from the strip as a relatively good deal at the time. Unlike a negotiated peace agreement, withdrawing from the ideologically and religiously rather irrelevant Gaza Strip "only" involved the evacuation of around eight thousand Israeli settlers and the renunciation of a relatively small territory. By declaring that the "[Gaza] disengagement is actually formaldehyde," Sharon's senior adviser, Weissglass, described the logic behind the Israeli withdrawal from Gaza in a particularly graphic manner. According to Weissglass, who was one of the initiators of the Gaza withdrawal, the "significance of the disengagement plan is the freezing of the peace process."[100] As he stated: "And when you freeze that process, you prevent the establishment of a Palestinian state, and you prevent a discussion on the refugees, the borders and Jerusalem. Effectively, this whole package called the Palestinian state, with all that it entails, has been removed indefinitely from our agenda. And all this with authority and permission. All with a presidential blessing and the ratification of both houses of Congress."[101]

Ironically, the new Israeli foreign policy consensus around the "no partner for peace" narrative prompted large parts of Israel's political and military echelons to realize that keeping full Israeli control over all (or most) of the territories was not in Israel's strategic interest either. In fact, considering the continuing terrorist attacks and launching of rockets, the idea of a strict separation from the Palestinians, combined with an effective defense against terrorism, emerged as the most reasonable alternative to any type of negotiations. This alternative also entailed the withdrawal from strategically unfavorable areas and the investment in those areas that Israel wished to keep. Sharon's disengagement plan (*hitnatkut* in Hebrew, literally deriving from the verb "to cut yourself off," or "to separate yourself") can clearly be seen in this light. The specific route of the West Bank barrier further supports this perspective. Moreover, the idea of "convergence" (*hitkansut*) formulated in 2006 by Ehud Olmert, who took over the leadership of the Kadima party after Sharon's stroke, further translated this new strategy: Olmert's plan was that Israel would "converge" its settlers to those settlement blocs on this side of the West Bank barrier and withdraw unilaterally from the settlements on the other side of the barrier—while still retaining the right to intervene militarily beyond the new "border." The victory of Kadima under Olmert in the Israeli elections of March 2006 bears evidence to the relevance of this new thinking. The victory of Hamas in the Palestinian elections of January 2006 only seemed to further corroborate the adequacy of this strategy.[102]

In the face of continued rocket attacks from the Gaza Strip, the idea of *hitkansut* was soon abandoned. Ironically, however, a process of "convergence" characterized Israeli politics in these years. The Likud's ideology of holding on to *all* the occupied territories seemed discredited: it was the revolt of the Likud party against Sharon's Gaza disengagement plan that prompted Sharon to found the Kadima party in the first place. Simultaneously, the traditional belief of the Israeli Left in far-reaching territorial concessions in exchange for peace became the position of a small minority only.

Abu Mazen: Still No Partner

The Israeli government would continue to evoke the by now widely accepted "no partner for peace" narrative on every occasion, even though the main villain in the story, Yasser Arafat, died in November 2004. However, the line was easily transferred to Arafat's successor, Mahmoud Abbas (Abu Mazen), who, in fact, was (and still is) a moderate and a pragmatist, and who had been Israel's preferred successor to Arafat. Indeed, Abbas has constantly condemned the use of violence in the Palestinian struggle for statehood. Yet, interestingly enough, Israeli leaders—such as Ehud Barak himself and Foreign Minister Tzipi Livni—soon started to regret that there was no Palestinian partner for peace because Abbas was *too weak*. Particularly in light of the electoral victory of Hamas in 2006 and its takeover of the Gaza Strip in June 2007, Livni publicly reckoned that Abbas lacked the "public support needed to compromise over refugees and the right of return."[103]

This line would not change with the dying out of the Palestinian intifada and the resumption of peace talks in 2007. As a result of international pressure following the US-sponsored Middle East peace summit held on November 27, 2007, at the U.S. Naval Academy in Annapolis, Maryland, the revival of Israeli–Palestinian peace talks was certainly an exception to the ubiquitous "no partner for peace" theme.[104] In addition to US pressure, the resumption of negotiations also reflected the comparatively moderate positions of Olmert's Kadima-led government on peacemaking. This in turn raises the question of why challenges to the hegemonic vision, which certainly existed in the post-Oslo decade, did not succeed in taking hold. This question will be discussed further below. However, the Israeli government was quick in blaming the Palestinian leadership for the breakdown of the talks in late 2008, pointing to its unwillingness or inability to reach peace. Since the content of these negotiations was confidential, this was a relatively easy game. Olmert's successor, Netanyahu, who after the 2009 elections came to lead a government farther to the right than the one headed by Olmert, continued to stress that the "Palestinians are not ready for peace with Israel." Even in her new position as opposition leader after the 2009 elections, Livni occasionally concurred with the government's assessment.[105] Having participated in the peace negotiations with Abbas, Livni was regarded as a particularly authoritative source on the matter.

Public opinion polls continuously attested to the deep entrenchment of the "no one to talk to" theme in Israel's collective psyche: a 2007 poll found that 65 percent of Israeli respondents did not believe that the PA was a partner for peace.[106] According to another survey of 2007, 65 percent of Jewish Israelis did "somewhat not" or "absolutely not" believe that negotiations between Israel and the PA could lead to peace (61 percent of the general public, Arab citizens included, maintained this view).[107] A 2009 poll found that 62 percent of Jewish Israelis thought that the ultimate goal of PA chairman Mahmoud Abbas was to establish a Palestinian state that would *replace* Israel rather than establish a Palestinian next to it (only 27 percent of respondents believed that a Palestinian state next to Israel was Abbas's objective).[108] In a 2010 poll, 74 percent of Israeli Jewish respondents were convinced that the Palestinians were not interested in peace.[109] Another survey of 2011 found that a staggering 49 percent of Jewish Israelis believed that peace with the Palestinians would never happen, while 42 percent said it would happen but would take more than five years.[110] Expressing an even deeper disillusionment with the prospects of Middle East peace, in September 2011 two-thirds of Jewish Israelis said that there was no chance—*ever*—of achieving peace with the Palestinians, according to a *Yediot Ahronot* poll quoted in the *New York Times*.[111]

A closer look at Abbas's positions and policies, however, once more reveals that reality is far more nuanced than the prevailing Israeli narrative on the nonexistence of a Palestinian partner would have it. For one, there are very divergent accounts on what was offered during the negotiations with Olmert and on why the talks broke down. Interestingly, the first information on the talks that became available in 2009 portrayed Abbas as a serious negotiating partner. According to these reports, the main reason the negotiations led to nowhere was Abbas's refusal to sign a map, demanded in a take-it-or leave-it manner by Olmert, without prior consultations with his team. What is more, Olmert resigned only a few days later: the prime minster was under investigation on corruption charges. He had already announced in late July 2008 that he would resign once his party Kadima had elected a new leader.

Further details can be gleaned from the different accounts of these negotiations. Some insiders maintained that at the end of his term, Olmert had offered the establishment of a Palestinian state in 97 percent of the West Bank, while also acknowledging the "principle" of the right of return. He had allegedly also proposed an international regime (a consortium of Jordanians, Saudis, Israelis, Palestinians, and Americans) over Jerusalem's "Holy Basin" in the Old City—including the Haram al-Sharif (or Temple Mount), the Western Wall, and the Church of the Holy Sepulcher. This proposal was undoubtedly a novelty. According to Israeli accounts,

Abbas never replied to Olmert's offer and before too long, Olmert was out of office. Other reports claim that Olmert never accepted the right of return but was ready to acknowledge Palestinian suffering, offering an Israeli acceptance of a small number of returnees as a humanitarian gesture instead. According to these accounts, Olmert also suggested that some wording should be inserted to recognize the suffering of Jews from Arab countries who were forced to leave their homes after 1948. In addition, according to Palestinian chief negotiator Saeb Erekat, Olmert's "package deal" included Israel's annexation of the major settlement blocs in the West Bank as well as of all Israeli settlements in East Jerusalem. While East Jerusalem would be divided territorially along the lines of the Clinton Parameters, the issue of sovereignty over the "Holy Basin" would be delayed until a later stage. This issue would continue to be negotiated bilaterally between Israel and the Palestinians, with the nonbinding involvement of the United States, Saudi Arabia, Jordan, and Egypt. The "package" apparently made no mention of security; according to other accounts, this was because both sides had already agreed on the major security issues (a Palestinian nonmilitarized state; international patrolling of the Palestinian border with Jordan; Israeli access to Palestinian airspace, etc.). Still, according to the Palestinians, Olmert's team had showed a map of the proposed Palestinian state but refused to leave a copy of the plan, while the questions the Palestinian team had on specific issues (such as the calculation of percentages, Jerusalem, borders, and refugees) went unheeded. An additional reason for Abbas's refusal to conclude a deal with the outgoing Olmert government, according to Israeli and Palestinian officials involved in the talks, was that aides to Foreign Minister Livni, who had already been nominated to replace Olmert as head of the Kadima party before the upcoming Israeli elections, had signaled to Abbas not to sign: he would get a better deal with Livni, who was expected to win the elections.[112]

Although Abu Mazen was reportedly ready to continue the talks in Washington after Israel started the war on Hamas-ruled Gaza in "Operation Cast Lead" of December of the same year, the ongoing war eliminated the possibility of resuming the talks.[113] Netanyahu's Likud-led government that emerged after the elections of February 2009 had other priorities. The so-called Palestine Papers—the internal minutes of the negotiations that were leaked to Al-Jazeera in January 2011—in fact highlight the extent of concessions Abbas was ready to make for a peace deal. For instance, in the negotiations, Abbas consented to renouncing the right of return for Palestinian refugees if Israel acknowledged its responsibility in creating the problem. He also agreed to Israeli control over settlements built after

1967 in East Jerusalem (which Israel considers "neighborhoods"), such as Pisgat Ze'ev, French Hill (Ha-Giv'ah ha-Tsarfatit), Neve Ya'akov, and Gilo. Using the Hebrew name of Jerusalem, the Palestinians thus "offered the biggest Yerushalayim in history," as former Palestinian chief negotiator Saeb Erekat termed it.[114] Incidentally, it transpires from these internal minutes that a major stumbling block of these negotiations—albeit certainly not the only one—was Israel's insistence on retaining control over large settlement blocs. This includes most notably the settlement of Ariel, a town of around eighteen thousand inhabitants, located between Ramallah and Nablus, deep inside the West Bank.[115]

Sharply contrasting with the Israeli narrative, it is ironic that Al-Jazeera harshly criticized the PA precisely for its readiness to make important compromises, and depicted it as a sell-out of Palestinian rights and aspirations. It is also worth noting that Foreign Minister Livni does not emerge in the Palestine Papers as an especially forthcoming negotiator, particularly if compared to Mahmoud Abbas. While Israel certainly did not contribute to the strengthening of Abu Mazen's position, the Palestine Papers prove beyond doubt that Israel had a serious negotiating partner. In fact, the friendly and sometimes humorous atmosphere of the negotiations reported in the minutes is striking.

The US-sponsored security cooperation between the PA and Israel in the West Bank, which intensified toward the end of the 2000s, additionally challenges Israel's hegemonic conception of not having a partner in Abbas. In private, Israeli security experts and officials do not hesitate to recognize that Palestinian cooperation with Israel under Abbas contributed considerably to the significant decline in suicide attacks within Israel toward the end of the decade. In the Oscar-nominated documentary movie *The Gatekeepers*, Ami Ayalon, a former head of the Shabak, Israel's internal security service, is on record stating that the security cooperation with the Palestinians was the real reason why the terrorism in the West Bank diminished.[116] However, Israeli politicians seldom acknowledged the PA's cooperation in public, although they confirmed it behind closed doors. Thus, in 2009 Netanyahu, for instance, admitted to senior US officials that the PA was doing "a good job" on security.[117] In early 2012 President Shimon Peres and Ehud Olmert publicly declared that Abbas was a credible and "worthy" partner for peace. Yet, similar declarations by senior Israeli politicians were conspicuously absent during the first post-Oslo decade.[118]

Hence, while there are no specific grounds to the assertion that there is "no one to talk to," what is relevant is that the "no partner for peace" theme became hegemonic. As a central element in Israel's new foreign policy consensus after Oslo, the "no partner for peace" narrative links into the notion of being under constant terror attacks and under siege. The theme becomes even more compelling if combined with the notion of the new regional order that came to prevail in Israel. This is the focus of the next section.

Iran and the "Evil Alliance"

The third key element of Israel's foreign policy consensus post-Oslo was (and to a certain extent still is) the growing preoccupation with Iran's quest for regional hegemony in the Middle East. Iran's mounting regional involvement following the fall of Saddam Hussein in 2003 also entailed the consolidation or strengthening of its alliances with Hamas, Hizballah, and Syria—all of them hard-liners regarding Israel. Even more worrisome from an Israeli perspective were Iran's concerted efforts to develop a nuclear program. Contrary to Tehran's repeated claims that the program is meant for peaceful civilian use only, it is widely believed that the scope was the development of atomic weapons, or at least the ability to do so within a reasonable period of time. The following sections will explore the background, nature, and salience of the notion of the new regional order that became central to Israel's foreign policy consensus and public discourse after the demise of the Oslo process.

Hizballah, Hamas, and Tehran's Quest for Regional Hegemony

While, historically, fears and perceptions of foreign intervention have nurtured Iranian nationalism and foreign policy, after the 1979 revolution the new regime's sense of the importance of Iran became coupled to its determination to lead the "Islamic world."[119] Iran would particularly renew its ambitions of wanting to be recognized as a regional power in the Middle East after the end of the Iran–Iraq war in 1988, the end of the Cold War and the collapse of the Soviet Union shortly afterward, and the defeat of Iraq in the 1991 Persian Gulf War. Regarding the war between Iran and Iraq, it may be worth recalling that Saddam Hussein had invaded his neighbor Iran in September 1980 and subsequently fought the country in a bloody war for eight years, leaving an estimated half a million Iranians, soldiers and civilians, dead. Iraq, which at that time was widely supported by the West, also used chemical weapons extensively during the war. Significantly, in spite of the Iranian regime's repeated diatribes against Israel, the government in Jerusalem had supported Iran during the war against Iraq by secretly providing weapons to the Ayatollah's regime in Tehran.[120]

The impact of the terrorist attacks of 9/11 on the region and particularly the policies Washington subsequently adopted toward the Middle East cannot be underestimated. The US toppling of the Taliban in Afghanistan in late 2001 had eliminated an important foe of the Iranian regime, and, courtesy of the US invasion of Iraq in 2003, the elimination of Saddam Hussein's regime left Iran without its fiercest enemy. The sudden disappearance of Iraq's regional counterbalance in 2003 undoubtedly nurtured Tehran's ambitions for regional hegemony, at that point also in competition with traditional rival Saudi Arabia. Iranian foreign policy would turn increasingly assertive after Mahmoud Ahmadinejad became president in 2005. Iran's regional ambitions also witnessed the consolidation of its support for the Palestinian Hamas, which had started in the early 1990s, as well as of the Lebanese Hizballah, through the supply of money and weapons.[121] While developing closer ties with Turkey toward the end of the decade—hitherto Israel's most important Middle Eastern ally—Tehran also strengthened its relations with Syria under Bashar al-Assad. Syria, which officially was (and still is) at war with Israel, in turn assisted the Iranian weapons supply to Hizballah by permitting the transport of armaments through its territory. Damascus also hosted the political bureau of the Palestinian Hamas until early 2012.

Hence, in the 2000s Tehran had expanded its support for Israel's staunchest adversaries, which also happened to be situated in closest geographical vicinity, just across the borders (or would-be borders). Concurrently, Iranian president Ahmadinejad engaged in fierce anti-Israeli and anti-Semitic rhetoric. While sponsoring a conference on the Holocaust that featured some prominent Holocaust deniers in 2006, the Iranian president notoriously defined "the Zionist regime" as a "tumor" and a "stinking corpse," wishing for it to be "wiped off the map" (or, depending on the translation, to be "eliminated from the pages of history").[122] Regarding anti-Semitic statements, Hizballah's leader, Hassan Nasrallah, and the Hamas charter, for that matter, must be mentioned here as well.

But what exactly is the nature of the Iran-led alliance against Israel? And what is the background to Israel's prevailing notion of regional order post-Oslo? Starting with Hizballah, "the Party of God" developed ties to Tehran soon after it was created. As is well known, the Lebanese Shi'ite organization emerged against the backdrop of Israel's 1982 invasion of Lebanon, which killed thousands of Lebanese, many of them Shi'a.[123] Inspired by the 1979 Iranian Revolution and the teachings of Ayatollah

Khomeini, Hizballah forces were trained in Lebanon's Beqaa Valley by a contingent of the Revolutionary Guards, an elite branch of the Iranian army. Suicide attacks against Israeli and foreign targets soon became the signature of the organization. Indeed, the precursor of Hizballah, the Islamic Resistance, was responsible for the Beirut barracks bombings of October 1983. The attack involved two truck bombs striking the housing of the US Marines and French military forces who were members of the Multinational Force in Lebanon, killing 299 American and French security personal; most of the victims were US Marines. Hizballah is also held responsible for the 1992 bombing of the Israeli Embassy in Buenos Aires; the 1994 bomb attack on a Jewish community center, also in the Argentinian capital; and the 1996 truck bombing of a US military base in Saudi Arabia. For the regime in Tehran, which aims at spreading the Islamic revolution to the Arab Middle East, Hizballah provided an opportunity to gain a foothold in the region. On the other hand, Syria's secular regime under Hafez al-Assad, which controlled much of Lebanese politics at that time, supported Hizballah for strategic reasons. It served as a powerful bargaining card against Israel in Syria's quest to recover the Golan Heights that Israel had taken from Syria during the 1967 war.

Iran was to remain the major patron of Hizballah for the decades to come, with the Lebanese organization proving to be a formidable foe of Israel. It fought the Israeli army and its allies in southern Lebanon during the Israeli occupation. After Israel withdrew in 2000 from the self-defined "security strip" it had kept occupied, Hizballah repeatedly fired Katyusha rockets on Israel's northern region. In the summer of 2006, Iran launched rockets on Israel's northern border towns and attacked a patrol on the Israeli side of the fence, prompting the Second Lebanon War. Hizballah's firing of thousands of rockets on Israel during the war paralyzed the north of the country for several weeks. Ending the Israel–Hizballah war, UN Security Council Resolution 1701 of August 11, 2006 stipulated that there should be "no weapons without the consent of the Government of Lebanon" and that there should be "no sales or supply of arms and related materiel to Lebanon except as authorized by its Government."[124] Yet after the war Hizballah substantially increased its weapons arsenal, in blatant violation of resolution 1701. According to media reports, Hizballah succeeded in running arms, including surface-to-surface missiles that could hit the bigger population centers in Israel, from secret weapons depots in Syria to its bases in Lebanon. Some of these weapons originated in Iran.[125]

First fielding candidates for parliamentary elections in 1992, Hizballah developed over the years into a highly organized political force in

Lebanon with a strong social base.[126] Running a telecommunications network including a satellite TV station, various education and social development programs, and a well-armed and trained militia, Hizballah mutated into "a state within a state." While the organization and its leader, Hassan Nasrallah, are revered among large parts of the Arab population—Shi'a, Sunni, and Christians alike—for having fought Israel and forcing it to withdraw, Hizballah is considered a despicable terrorist organization by the United States, many European countries, Israel, and other governments. Defining itself as an Islamic resistance movement, Hizballah opposed the Oslo Accords and continued calling for the liberation of Jerusalem and the destruction of Israel. After Israel withdrew in 2000 to the so-called Blue Line—the UN-recognized Israeli-Lebanese border—Hizballah's rhetoric soon focused on "liberating" the disputed Sheba'a Farms (a fourteen-square-mile territory claimed by Lebanon and occupied by Israel but that argues it is Syrian). The image of continuous resistance undoubtedly foments the organization's political ambitions. Yet Hizballah has a pragmatic side as well, and a clear political strategy. However, its ideology and rhetoric have remained "a fiery mixture of revolutionary Khomeinism, Shiite nationalism, celebration of martyrdom, and militant anti-Zionism, occasionally accompanied by crude, neo-fascist anti-Semitism," as one observer has put it.[127]

Another ally of Iran, the Palestinian Hamas, has arguably been no less accommodating toward Israel. Rooted in the Egyptian Muslim Brotherhood, Hamas was a product of the first Palestinian intifada, which erupted at the end of 1987 in the territories and had weakened the PLO. Israel was not completely uninvolved in the emergence of Hamas: in the 1980s, Israel had turned a blind eye to the exponentially increasing number of foreign-funded mosques in the occupied territories. The government in Jerusalem had reckoned that a strengthening of Islamist forces in the territories would counterbalance the PLO—at that time considered a terrorist organization. Unsurprisingly perhaps, this brilliant logic backfired.

Hamas emerged as a basically social and religious movement. Following the usual recipe, by providing services to the poor and underprivileged through religious institutions, it succeeded in anchoring itself deeply into Palestinian society.[128] However, combining Palestinian nationalism and pan-Islamism, Hamas's ideology embraced the notion of armed struggle until the liberation of all of Palestine, which would occur through a holy war and the implementation of shari'a law. During the Second Intifada, Hamas became responsible for most terrorist attacks against Israel, with its charter and official discourse continuing to depict Israel—the "Zionist project"—as a Jewish conspiracy to control the world. The organization launched rockets on Israeli towns and continued to do so after Israel withdrew its settlers and soldiers from Gaza in 2005. It continued these methods of attack even after it won the Palestinian elections in January 2006.

A closer analysis of how Hamas operates indicates that the organization is far less dogmatic than it appears at first sight.[129] For instance, Ismail Haniyeh, prime minister of the Hamas government in Gaza after the 2006 elections, and other senior Hamas figures repeatedly called for the formation of a Palestinian state within the 1967 borders while offering Israel a *hudna*, or a truce.[130] In May 2006 senior Hamas members imprisoned in Israel joined their peers from Fatah and signed the "Prisoners' Document," initiated by incarcerated Fatah leader Marwan Barghouti. The document called for the establishment of a Palestinian state on "all territories occupied in 1967" while reserving the right to cling to "the option of resistance with the various means" in those territories only.[131] Similarly, Hamas committed itself to honoring any deal Mahmoud Abbas would negotiate with Israel, as long as it was submitted to a referendum (which Abbas promised to do). In late 2011 the external leadership of Hamas under Khaled Mesh'al declared—at least temporarily—a cessation of the principle of "armed struggle"—certainly not an irrelevant development. This declaration was probably motivated by the severing of ties with Iran (which entailed reduced funding), mainly because of a profound disagreement on the Syrian regime's bloody suppression of the popular upheavals that had started in early 2011. Unlike Iran, Hamas had sided with the Syrian people. The appeasing posture of Hamas toward Israel was probably also prompted by the renewed efforts to reach reconciliation with Fatah.[132] In August 2014 Mesh'al would reportedly reiterate his willingness to accept a Palestinian state within the 1967 borders.[133] While these developments in the positions of Hamas are undoubtedly significant, they do not seem to be unconditional or consistent, however.

As for the question of Hamas's allies and supporters, the organization was initially funded mainly through Palestinian sources, including Palestinian Islamic institutions financed from abroad as well as by wealthy donors in Saudi Arabia and Kuwait. According to some accounts, Iran's Revolutionary Guard armed and trained the organization as of late 1989, and in 1992 Hamas and Iran signed an agreement providing for political, military, and financial support.[134] According to Trita Parsi, however, Iran started supporting rejectionist Palestinian factions only in the aftermath of the 1991 Madrid peace process, to which it had not been invited. The snubbing of Iran had occurred in spite of Iranian president Ali Akbar Hashemi Rafsanjani's rather pragmatic attitude toward the Palestinian issue: departing from his hard-line predecessor, he had declared that if a peace deal with Israel was acceptable to the Palestinians, it would be acceptable to Iran. Tehran would increase its support to Hamas and other extremist Palestinian factions after the beginning of the Oslo peace process in 1993, which threatened to marginalize Iran and change the balance of power in the Middle East to its disadvantage.[135]

Hamas subsequently developed close ties to Syria, which also provided military training facilities, and to the Lebanese Hizballah. Ironically, Hamas's relationship to the Lebanese organization crystallized after the Israeli government under Rabin had deported 415 Palestinian Islamist activists to Lebanon in December 1992, following the murder of four Israeli soldiers and a border policemen by Palestinians. The presence of the Palestinian deportees in southern Lebanon for almost one year provided them with an unexpected opportunity to learn from the more seasoned Hizballah members about how to use suicide attacks and car bombs. And indeed, ready to apply these newly acquired skills, the first Hamas suicide attack was carried out shortly after the deportees had returned home to the occupied Palestinian territories.[136] With the outbreak of the Second Intifada, the American invasion of Iraq of 2003, and Yasser Arafat's death in 2004, the Palestinian Hamas was drawn closer to Iran. Hamas's rise to power made the organization very appealing for the regime in Tehran in its quest to expand its sphere of influence. Faute de mieux, the international boycott of Hamas after its 2006 electoral victory (as long as it refused to recognize Israel, renounce violence, and abide by previous agreements) only strengthened its reliance on Iran. However, the theological differences between the Shi'ite Iranian regime and Hamas, based on Sunni Islam, persist. In other words, the alliance is of a mainly strategic nature. In this vein, Prime Minister Ismail Haniyeh of the Hamas government in Gaza considered Iran a "strategic reserve" for the Palestinians.[137]

Altogether, it has been argued that Tehran's backing of hard-line organizations such as Hizballah and Hamas is at least partly a strategic response to the efforts of the international community (the United States in particular) to contain Iran and to deny it a significant regional role. As noted earlier, Iran's support for extremist groups became far more prominent after it had been excluded from the Madrid peace process, which started in 1991 and which was meant to define the new regional order after the end of the Cold War.[138] Its fierce opposition of Israel and of any type of peace process as long as Israel's occupation continues, together with its support for different "resistance groups," greatly contributes to Iran's popularity among Arab populations.

Finally, it is important to consider the background of Israel's obsession with Iran's nuclear program. Based on reports of Israel's military intelligence (whose accuracy is contested, however), evidence of Tehran's atomic ambitions began to surface in the early 1990s.[139] In 2002 a previously undeclared uranium-enrichment facility south of Tehran and a heavy-water reactor under construction were discovered. Iran's late notification of the two sites reached the UN's International Atomic Energy Agency (IAEA) only in September 2002, prompting the IAEA in 2003 to demand the Islamic Republic of Iran's full cooperation.[140] Following negotiations with France, Germany, and the United Kingdom, Iran, a signatory to the Non-Proliferation Treaty (NPT), agreed to correct past safeguard and disclosure violations. For two years it suspended all uranium enrichment and reprocessing activities according to the stipulations of the IAEA. However, the country resumed its activities because it claimed that the European negotiating parties had failed to respect their part of the bargain—namely, economic incentives and the recognition of Iran's "nuclear rights." In 2004 US documents—whose authenticity is disputed by Iran—alleged that Tehran had tested technologies that are necessary for delivering and exploding a nuclear device. This entailed the development of ballistic missiles that would be able to launch nuclear warheads against Iran's neighbors, Israel included. In the following years the IAEA recurrently criticized Iran's noncompliance with its obligations as NPT signatory and demanded that the country stop its enrichment program, with Tehran repeatedly obstructing IAEA investigations into the matter. Between December 2006 and June 2010 the UN Security Council passed six resolutions calling on Tehran to abide by its obligations under international law. In that time span, economic sanctions had been imposed in four different rounds, with Iran disclosing an additional covert underground enrichment facility in 2009.[141]

Although by November 2011 there was no evidence that Iran had succeeded in building an atomic bomb, a scathing IAEA report of that month deemed it "credible" that these were precisely Tehran's intentions.[142] However, Western intelligence services continued to differ in their assessment of how far Iran had proceeded. According to Robert Einhorn, special adviser for nonproliferation and arms control to the US Secretary of State at that time, in early 2012 US intelligence estimated that Iran would be able to build a bomb within a year and that it would be able to have missiles capable of launching nuclear weapons within three to four years—provided it decided to move quickly. But at that point US and Israeli intelligence believed that Tehran had not taken the decision to proceed swiftly. Concurrently, Israel insisted that sometime around summer 2012 Iran would enter into a "zone of immunity" in which it would be able to take such a decision with impunity. Israel would no longer be able to strike Iranian nuclear facilities, which by then would all have been moved underground.[143]

Existential Threat: Iran, Its Allies, and the Nukes

When and how did Israel start to depict Iran as a major—and even existential—threat? What was the nature of Israel's public discourse on this issue in the 2000s? By pointing to Iran's growing hegemonic allure and network of alliances, Israeli politicians and security experts began identifying the emergence of a new regional order in the Middle East after the end of the Cold War and the defeat of Iraq in the first Persian Gulf War.[144] At that point a new geopolitical competition between Israel and Iran started to emerge. Israel's portraying of Iran as a major threat to the region and to the world and as a major sponsor of international terrorism would become even more pronounced as the US invasion of Iraq was taking shape in late 2002.

Against the background of his declared "war on terror," US president George W. Bush had designated Iran as part of the "axis of evil" in his State of the Union address of 2002. Then–Israeli premier Ariel Sharon was quick to echo him, defining Iran "a center of world terror."[145] Similarly, in 2003 Shimon Peres, at that time leader of the Labor Party, called Iran a "double axis of evil" due to its role as the "largest terror nucleus in the Middle East."[146] Peres pointed out:

> In Israel, Iranian fingerprints can be found on the operations of a number of terror organizations. The Iranians fund, arm and train Hezbollah, a terror organization par excellence; around 100 officers of the Iranian Republican Guard are in Lebanon, helping Hezbollah prepare for, and put into effect, acts of terror. They train Hezbollah in the skills of launching the 10,000 rockets that they put at their disposal. They give Hamas and Islamic Jihad a hand in carrying out acts of terror inside Israel.[147]

Over the years the notion of an Iran-dominated regional order would increasingly take center stage in Israel's political discourse. For instance, in 2007 Defense Minister Shaul Mofaz, who would become leader of the Kadima party in 2012, publicly opposed an Israeli withdrawal from the

Golan Heights in exchange for peace with Syria, on the grounds that this would lead to an additional Iranian foothold on Israel's border.[148] Maj. Gen. Amir Eshel, then head of the Planning Directorate of the Israeli army, detected a well-thought-out design behind the Iran-lead alliance: "The radical axis in the region, headed by Iran ... has built up various capabilities for itself: It prepared a holding force in the north—Hezbollah; a logistical base—Syria and the weapons-smuggling networks; and a force tasked with wearing us down in the south—Hamas. There's method to the madness, there's a division of labor. Each one has its own role in the axis."[149]

Reflecting the same understanding of regional order, the 2009 platform of Kadima unequivocally stated that "the State of Israel is fighting against an extremist Islamist front, which is led by Iran and also includes both additional states and terrorist organizations, such as Hamas and Hizballah."[150] According to the platform, these "extremist forces work toward hurting the citizens of Israel and aim at destroying the State of Israel."[151] Similarly, in the run-up to the 2009 elections, Netanyahu, then the leader of the competing Likud, stressed emblematically that "we have had two wars with two Iranian proxies in two years and Persia has now two bases on the eastern Mediterranean."[152] Altogether, the electoral campaign leading up to Israel's general elections of February 2009 was an illustrative example of the salience of the new notion of regional order in Israeli politics. Indeed, the major political parties devoted the bulk of their attention to the threats emanating from Iran, Hizballah, and Hamas, with most candidates for the post of prime minister adopting a hard line. Although Kadima openly advocated a two-state solution, and both Kadima and the Labor Party supported a resumption of negotiations with the Palestinians, the major parties did not give this issue primary importance in the 2009 electoral campaign.[153]

Unsurprisingly, a pronounced anxiety over Tehran's nuclear program came to complement the notion of an Iranian-led march of evil forces set on Israel's destruction. In fact, Israeli leaders had been publicly calling for action to prevent Iran from acquiring nuclear weapons from the early 2000s. In November 2002 Prime Minister Sharon demanded that the international community deal with Iran as soon as the imminent war with Iraq ended.[154] For Shimon Peres, there was "no greater danger than the conjunction of an evil regime with nuclear capabilities," as he stated in June 2003.[155] And former head of the army's Planning Directorate, Eshel, warned that not just Iran but the whole "radical axis" was "trying to go nuclear."[156]

While Israeli governments did not believe in Tehran's assurances that the nuclear program was merely meant for the peaceful production of energy, Ahmadinejad's anti-Israeli rhetoric fomented Israel's concerns even further. Echoing the assessment of Yitzhak Rabin, who reportedly first received reports about Tehran's nuclear ambitions from Israel's military intelligence back in May 1992, many Israeli politicians and pundits defined a nuclear Iran as an existential threat to the State of Israel.[157] Significantly, while the regime in Tehran was regularly portrayed as an exceptionally sinister force, references to Jewish history and the Holocaust moved to the center of Israel's official rhetoric. As Yossi Klein Halevi and Michael Oren put it, "senior army commanders, who likely once regarded Holocaust analogies with the Middle East conflict as an affront to Zionist empowerment, now routinely speak of a 'second Holocaust.'"[158]

The public statements of Mofaz as well as of Netanyahu and other politicians are emblematic of this state of affairs. Claiming that (his native) Iran is "the root of all evil," Mofaz stressed that "Israel will not let a second Holocaust happen."[159] President Peres declared that "if Europe had dealt seriously with Hitler at that time, the terrible Holocaust and the loss of millions of people could have been avoided."[160] He also pointed out that "a nuclear weapon in Iranian hands has only one meaning—a flying death camp."[161] From the same vantage point, Netanyahu reminded that history had taught the Jewish people that threats against their collective existence should be taken seriously, and, if possible, preempted. Calling the Iranian leadership a "fanatic regime that might put its zealotry above its self-interest," Netanyahu also stated that no one wanted a "messianic apocalyptic cult controlling atomic bombs."[162] According to Netanyahu, "when the wide-eyed believer gets hold of the reins of power and the weapons of mass death, then the entire world should start worrying."[163] On the occasion of a 2009 state visit to Germany, during which German chancellor Angela Merkel called for an Israeli freeze of settlement construction in the territories in order to restart the peace process with the Palestinians, Netanyahu chose to focus on the Iranian issue: "we cannot allow those who wish to perpetrate mass deaths, those who call for the destruction of the Jewish people or the Jewish state to go unchallenged," he stressed.[164] Interestingly, Merkel was not convinced, responding to Netanyahu's statement via press conference by saying there was no comparison between the Holocaust and Iran's nuclear program.[165] In his speech to the UN General Assembly in September 2009 Netanyahu also focused exclusively on Iran's nuclear program, stressing that the "Iranian regime is fueled by an extreme fundamentalism that burst onto the world scene three decades ago after lying dormant for centuries."[166] It is also telling that Israel's Ministry of Foreign Affairs stressed that, for Iran, a war against Israel would serve a religious purpose: "President Ahmadinejad actively endorses chaos, so as to hasten the re-emergence of the Hidden Imam and spread true Islamic rule worldwide. He believes that the Hidden Imam will return only following an apocalyptic war against Israel and the West."[167]

In light of these assessments, it should come as no surprise that from the mid-2000s onward, different alternatives to countering the Iranian threat were discussed rather openly. In addition to, or sometimes instead of, international sanctions, Israel's preferred option was to have the United States take care of the problem—forcefully. Thus, the Israeli government sought to convince US president George W. Bush to force a regime change in Tehran as soon as the Iraq war ended.[168] Referring to Israel's bombing of the Iraqi atomic reactor in Osirak in 1981, which put an end to Saddam Hussein's nuclear aspirations, the government in Jerusalem also started publicly contemplating an Israeli strike on Iranian nuclear sites in "anticipatory self-defense."[169]

The subsequent US administration under Barack Obama expressed clear opposition to an Israeli surprise attack on Iran. This, however, did not prevent the Israeli government from regularly reminding Washington that the military option was still on the table.[170] Israel's government certainly welcomed Washington's attempts to impose sanctions on Iran after the discovery of a second uranium-enrichment facility near the Iranian city of Qom in September 2009, a clear indication of Tehran's cat-and-mouse game with the international community. However, it also repeatedly criticized the international community for not doing enough to counter the threat, yet another means of keeping up the pressure on Iran. Reportedly, an Israeli strike on Iran's nuclear facilities was imminent in 2010, had senior figures from Israel's security establishment not outright rejected this plan of attack by Netanyahu and Defense Minister Barak.[171] In late 2011 and early 2012, Israel would step up its rhetoric on the necessity to attack Iran, and to do it alone if necessary, exerting pressure on President Obama in an election year.

A significant side effect of Israel's growing obsession with Iran was the marginalization of the Palestinian question. In this vein, subsequent governments in Jerusalem defended the position that Iran was of far greater importance than the Israeli–Palestinian conflict. Netanyahu in particular, after becoming prime minister in early 2009, sought to convince President Obama that, since Tehran supported Hamas, reining in Iran was a precondition for solving the Israeli–Palestinian conflict. "I think we are

going to have to deal with neutralizing the power of the mother regime,"
Netanyahu told the 2009 World Economic Forum in Davos, in reply to
a question on his position on the Palestinian issue.[172] According to Netanyahu, the "Hamas stronghold would be about as important, if Iranian
power was neutralized, as Cuba was when the Soviet Union became irrelevant."[173]

Yet the US administration did not follow this logic, preferring diplomatic means to deal with Iran instead. The growing antagonism between
Netanyahu and Obama over the Iranian nuclear program would culminate
with Netanyahu addressing a joint meeting of the Republican-dominated
US Congress in March 2015, denouncing "the bad deal" that was being
negotiated with Tehran at that time. Signifying an unprecedented attempt
to undercut President Obama as well as a breaking of diplomatic protocol,
Netanyahu stressed that the deal would pave Iran's way to a nuclear bomb
and accused President Obama of putting Israel's very survival at risk.[174]
Netanyahu would lose the battle. In July 2015, after twenty months of
negotiations, Iran would sign a historic deal with the United States, the
European Union, and other major powers that would freeze or reverse
progress at all of Iran's major nuclear facilities for the next fifteen years in
exchange for the lifting of international economic sanctions.[175]

Considering how central this specific notion of regional order had become in Israel's political discourse from the early 2000s on, how did the
public react? In a nutshell, most Israeli citizens by and large internalized
the claims and fears propagated by their political leaders. Hence, for a
number of consecutive years, a majority of Israelis considered nuclear
weaponry in the hands of Iran as the most serious threat facing Israel. In
this vein, between 2004 and 2007, the Iranian nuclear issue scored between
5.8 and 6.2 on a 1–7 threat scale.[176] In February 2007, 82 percent of Jewish Israelis responded "yes" to the question of whether Iran possessing a
nuclear bomb would constitute an existential danger to Israel.[177] In a 2009
survey, 21 percent of Jewish Israelis believed that Iran would attack Israel
with nuclear weapons with the objective of destroying it. The same survey
showed that an astounding 59 percent of the Jewish public were in favor of
an Israeli military strike against Iran's nuclear installations, "should Israel
determine that Iran possesses nuclear weapons." The remaining 41 percent supported the use of all diplomatic means available to dismantle Iran's
nuclear capabilities.[178] Another 2009 poll, conducted on behalf of the
Center for Iranian Studies at Tel Aviv University, found that over 80 percent of Israeli respondents feared that Iran would obtain atomic weapons, and 74 percent believed that the attempts of the Obama administra-

tion to engage Tehran diplomatically would not persuade Iran to change its course. Concurrently, slightly more than half of the respondents—a staggering 51 percent—supported an *immediate* Israeli attack on Iran's nuclear installation, that is, without waiting to see whether the diplomatic track would lead to any results. The same poll found that 23 percent of Israelis would consider leaving the country if Tehran obtained an atomic bomb.[179]

At the beginning of the following decade, Israeli public opinion on Iran and the necessity to strike its nuclear facilities became more dissonant, as is discussed further below. However, during most of the first decade post-Oslo, Israeli Jewish public opinion was largely in sync with the official discourse on Iran, which, in the words of Ian Lustick, was dominated by the "specter of destruction" and the "psychological and mythic power of the Holocaust."[180]

Challenges to Israel's Notion of Regional Order

To be sure, no sovereign country would sit back and allow an organization to blow up bombs in its buses, restaurants, and shopping centers with impunity. And it is hard to think of any state that would accept the launching of rockets—however unsophisticated these may be—on its territory. Similarly, most governments would take saber-rattling leaders of well-armed militias and threatening statements by heads of states seriously. And the desire that Israel should disappear from the face of the earth is unfortunately not the opinion of only a few deranged individuals in the Middle East. Thus, particularly considering Ahmadinejad's ferocious rhetoric, Israelis had every reason to worry about the growing power of a soon-to-be nuclear Iran. The militancy of Hizballah and Hamas operating just across Israel's northern and southern border (or would-be border, in the case of Gaza) were valid reason for alarm as well. Throughout the 2000s, all of these players were sending signals about their intent that were far from reassuring to Israel.

The question is, however, whether the Holocaust-dominated discourse on Iran and its allies was the only valid description of regional realities. To begin with, the history of Israel's relations with Iran is significant, together with the geopolitical dimension of these relations. After Ayatollah Khomeini became Iran's supreme leader in 1979, relations between Israel and Iran were certainly not cordial. The new Iranian regime preferred to frame the Arab–Israeli conflict in terms of religion and political Islam, mainly in order to appeal to Arab populations, while undercutting Arab regimes that resisted Iran's ambitions for regional hegemony. However, until the early 1990s, the Ayatollah's fierce anti-Israeli and anti-Semitic tirades had not prevented Israeli secret arms dealings with Tehran. Considering Iraq a far greater menace to Israel than Iran, and seeing an advantage in both countries being preoccupied with fighting each other, the government in Jerusalem did not refer to Iran as a threat during much of the 1980s. According to David Menashri, one of Israel's leading experts on Iran, "[the] word was not even uttered."[181]

The growing antagonism between Israel and Iran would emerge after the end of the Cold War and the defeat of Iraq in the 1991 Gulf War, as the geopolitical conditions that had nurtured a consistent (albeit not officially acknowledged) alliance between the two countries during much of the latter part of the twentieth century had dissipated. Left without a common enemy, Israel and Iran soon found themselves in competition over the definition of the regional order, particularly after Iraq had been weakened in the second Persian Gulf War of 1991. Israel had, of course, no interest in seeing Iran emerge as the undisputed regional power in the Middle East. It is in this period that Israeli policymakers started depicting the regime in Tehran as fanatical and irrational. Trying to convince the incoming US administration under Bill Clinton that Iran, and not Iraq, had to be contained, the Israeli government also argued vis-à-vis Washington that Iran's renewed nuclear program would soon give the mullahs access to atomic weapons.[182] Iran's possession of the bomb would alter the strategic equation, depriving Israel of its "qualitative edge," one of the foundations of Israel's security doctrine.[183] This would leave the country particularly vulnerable to the Ayatollah's changing moods. Drawing attention to the Iranian menace also served Israel's objective of reinvigorating the strategic relationship with the US after the end of the Cold War, at a moment when Israel's strategic value to Washington was far from evident.[184]

The peacemaking efforts of the Israeli government under Yitzhak Rabin, which was formed after the Labor Party won a landslide victory in the June 1992 elections, were an equally important factor in explaining Israel's new approach to Iran after the end of the Cold War. Israel's accusations that Tehran was sponsoring not only the Lebanese Hizballah and rejectionist Palestinian factions but international terrorism in general grew louder after the 1994 attack on a Jewish community center in Buenos Aires. According to Israeli experts, this attack bore the fingerprints of Hizballah and Iran. Significantly, depicting Iran as a major threat entailed a reversal of the periphery doctrine that had underwritten Israel's security policy hitherto. Aimed at developing and maintaining relations with non-Arab and non-Muslim countries as well as with non-Arab minorities in "the periphery"—that is, beyond the hostile ring of Arab countries surrounding Israel—the periphery doctrine had been the basis of Israel's relations with Iran hitherto.[185] Initially many in Israel's political and security establishment remained unconvinced of the government's new approach toward Iran, but the new assessment soon started to take hold of the country's political and security establishment.[186] In this context, it has been argued that Rabin exaggerated the Iranian threat in order to "sell" the Israeli–Palestinian peace process, both domestically and internationally.[187]

Undoubtedly, the Iranian regime played its part in the ideological framing of the Israeli–Iranian competition for regional hegemony, and it openly supported Hizballah and, later on, rejectionist Palestinian groups. However, whether in the early 1990s the campaign against Iran championed by Yitzhak Rabin, Shimon Peres, and other Israeli strategists was based on clear-cut material facts remains disputed: in his efforts to moderate Iranian foreign policy post-Khomeini, Iranian president Rafsanjani had sought a rapprochement with Washington.[188] Iran had also massively reduced its military spending in 1992, and while it may have had some nuclear ambitions at that time, it was widely believed that Iran was not even close to any nuclear capability.[189]

Thus, while the government under Rabin started the discourse on the Iranian threat in the early 1990s, there is an important difference between the Labor government and subsequent Likud-led governments, particularly those headed by Binyamin Netanyahu: Rabin may have played up the Iranian threat partly in order to gain support for resolving the Palestinian issue. At the same time, the resolution of the Palestinian conflict would have enabled the Israeli government to build support for focusing on Iran, according to Rabin. For Netanyahu, however, the focus on the Iranian threat meant ignoring the Palestinian issue altogether.

The discourse on the evil and irrational regime in Tehran that became particularly salient in Israel from the mid-2000s onward was challenged from the outset. Israeli academics refuted, for instance, the assumption that the regime in Tehran was seeking to obtain nuclear weapons out of wicked insanity. According to this argument, insecurity and fear primarily motivated those ambitions, given that Iran was still surrounded by some powerful enemies. Indeed, even if Saddam Hussein was no longer a threat, Saudi Arabia, Egypt, and the Gulf monarchies loathed the Shi'a competitor in the quest for regional hegemony, with Saudi Arabia in particular being no less religiously fanatical. Moreover, the US invasion of two of Iran's neighbors, Afghanistan and Iraq, in the early 2000s, together with President Bush's designation of Iran as one of three members of "the axis of evil," was not exactly a reason to make Iran feel secure. Thus, according to this argument, a nuclear-armed Iran might not necessarily seek Israel's destruction.

Others stressed that Israel's (assumed, since undeclared) nuclear deterrence and second-strike capability would most likely prevent an Iranian attack with atomic weapons on Israel, unless the regime in Tehran was utterly suicidal.[190] Of course, the assumption that the regime in Tehran was rational did not automatically imply that it was not dangerous, as Emily Landau has pointed out. Considering that Iran had played the game of moving toward a nuclear bomb in the 2000s in a remarkably rational fashion, cost–benefit oriented rationality may still serve sinister goals, according to Landau.[191]

While still asserting the seriousness of a nuclear Iran, the prevailing discourse on the existential threat promoted by Israeli leaders was also challenged. For one, David Menashri, director of the Iranian Center at Tel Aviv University, described the pronounced Israeli anxieties as "worrying because they reflect an exaggerated and unnecessary fear."[192] Menashri identified the "public statements and talks of 'existential threat'" that Israeli politicians used in order to alert the world of its concern as the main culprit for this state of affairs.[193] More significantly, Defense Minister Ehud Barak himself—"Mr. Security" tout court—repeatedly dismissed out of hand the notion of Iran as an existential threat. Stressing that he would not "buy the relevance of comparing the situation with that of Europe in 1938," Barak rejected the recurrent comparison between Iran and Nazi Germany as well as between Ahmadinejad and Hitler.[194] "I don't think we are on the brink of a new Holocaust," he declared.[195] On another occasion he suggested that Ahmadinejad might be the "loudest and most colorful voice" but that he was not Iran's decision maker. Emphasizing that the "State of Israel is not European Jewry," Barak pointed to Israel's strength as a regional superpower, claiming that no one would dare to attack Israel.[196] Barak's refutation of Holocaust-loaded rhetoric and justifications did not, however, imply that he opposed a military option—on the contrary.

The notion of existential danger, together with the policy prescription of attacking Iran, was also refuted by a number of top Israeli security officials—once they retired. Former chief of staff Gabi Ashkenazi questioned whether Israel had the technological capabilities to bomb Iranian underground nuclear facilities, and he further pondered the extent of a possible retaliation in the event of an Israeli attack. Most notably, Meir Dagan, shortly after leaving his position as head of the Mossad, Israel's intelligence agency, declared in early 2011 that a military strike on Iran's nuclear capabilities would be "a stupid thing."[197] And, as noted previously, senior military figures rejected Netanyahu's and Barak's plan to attack Iran in 2010.[198] Criticism leveled at the Israeli government for its Iran-rhetoric and policy prescriptions would grow in 2012, with the former head of Israel's internal security service, Shabak, Yuval Diskin, leveling accusations at Netanyahu and Barak for misleading the Israeli public. According to Diskin, the claim that an attack on Iran's nuclear facilities would prevent the country from obtaining a nuclear bomb was baseless, stressing that an Israeli attack would actually accelerate the Iranian nuclear race instead. Former Mossad chief Dagan and former Prime Minister Olmert would soon back these positions, with some of these critics also pointing to Netanyahu's deliberate inactivity on the Palestinian track.[199] However, this type of outspoken criticism was almost absent within Israel during most of the 2000s. While some Israeli politicians expressed support for US-led diplomacy, a trigger-happy rhetoric and Holocaust-based analogies clearly prevailed.

The notion of the Iran-led radical axis posing an existential threat to Israel has also been challenged from without. According to one argument, it remained unclear whether Iran's objective was to become a full-fledged nuclear power or "merely" a nuclear threshold state, defined as a state that possesses the necessary capabilities to manufacture more than one atomic bomb within one year of the decision to do so. The warning that it remained impossible to gauge Tehran's real intentions accompanied this argument.[200] International experts also repeatedly stressed the point of the rationality of Iranian decision makers and speculated that fear or the need for recognition, or both, motivated Tehran's behavior. In this case, engaging Iran diplomatically would undoubtedly be the wiser strategy. Some argued that, while it would be preferable that Iran should not obtain atomic weapons, containment and deterrence could work in the case of a nuclear Iran, just as it worked with the Soviet Union during the Cold War.[201]

More generally, the notion of the new regional order according to the dominating political discourse in Israel can be challenged as well. While no one seriously doubted the Iranian support for Hizballah, Syria, and Hamas, the degree of influence that Tehran really had (and still has) over Hizballah has been questioned.[202] A similar argument has been made with regard to the Palestinian Hamas, which is believed to act rather independently of the regime in Tehran. If Hamas was simply a proxy of Iran, it would not have supported the Saudi peace plan of 2002 or backed the Sunni insurgents in Iraq, according to this argument.[203] And neither would it have taken a firm stance against Bashar al-Assad's violent response to the popular uprisings in 2011, thus alienating its most important allies, Syria and Iran. However, if the alliance between Iran and Hamas or other affiliates was primarily tactical and not an innate alliance between evil forces, then specific policies aimed at undermining that coalition are possible. In other words, the more the members of the alliance are autonomous, the more likely the success of diplomatic and nonconfrontational policies.

As much as the alliance between Iran, Hamas, Hizballah, and Syria is threatening to Israel, a number of other regional developments in the 2000s provide a far more nuanced picture of the regional order. Riyadh, for instance, emerged as an important regional player seeking to counterbalance the hegemonic ambitions of its traditional foe Iran. The Saudi peace initiative of 2002 can partly be explained in these terms. (Another important motivation was Riyadh's attempt to polish Saudi Arabia's international image, given the prominent role Saudi nationals played in the 9/11 terrorist attacks, with fifteen out of nineteen plane hijackers being Saudi nationals, in addition to Osama Bin Laden himself.[204]) The Saudi initiative, which was endorsed by the Arab League in 2002 and reproposed on different occasions, was undoubtedly a major development in the protracted history of the Arab–Israeli conflict.[205] Contrary to recurrent claims of Israeli critics and politicians, the peace plan did not seek to impose the Palestinian right of return on Israel. Rather, the Saudi peace plan refers to an "agreed upon" solution "in accordance" with UN General Assembly Resolution 194 of December 11, 1948, a resolution that is not very precise on the refugee issue to begin with.[206] Furthermore, there is no evidence that the Arab peace plan demands a full Israeli withdrawal *before* Arab states normalize their relations with Israel, as some Israeli critics asserted. Rather, the peace plan calls on Israel to "affirm" a "full Israeli withdrawal from all the territories occupied since 1967" without specifying any sequencing.[207]

An additional number of significant regional developments also took place in the 2000s. Qatar, for instance, had been showing a new interest in Middle Eastern diplomacy while assuming rather moderate positions toward Israel. As a result, Israeli political leaders visited Doha in 2007–8, and both sides started developing economic and political ties until Qatar suspended the latter, following Israel's war on Hamas at the end of 2008.

Concurrently, Egypt under Hosni Mubarak, which in spite of—or perhaps because of—its peace treaty with Israel had played a rather ambivalent role in the peacemaking arena, was de facto cooperating with Israel in seeking to fight Hamas in the Gaza Strip.[208] Cairo's decision to close, for most of the time, the Rafah crossing on the Egyptian–Gaza border after Hamas took control of the strip in 2007 bears evidence to a central (although not widely publicized) pattern of Egyptian–Israeli relations in the post-Oslo decade. It is worth noting that Egypt did not open the crossing even during Israel's war on Gaza of 2008–9, which left the people of Gaza with no place to escape to during the Israeli airstrikes.

Mubarak's regime also shared with Israel a deep aversion to Iran's nuclear ambitions. Thus, while Mubarak stated that a "nuclear armed Iran with hegemonic ambitions is the greatest threat to Arab nations today," the Egyptian regime was considering the development of an atomic program of its own in order to contain Iran.[209] Concurrently, government officials in Jordan and Bahrain publicly called for an intervention to halt Iran's atomic program—even militarily, if necessary—with the regimes of the United Arab Emirates, Saudi Arabia, and Egypt describing Iran as "evil." Behind closed doors several Arab governments were trying to convince Washington to strike Iran's nuclear facilities, as leaked secret cables from US embassies to the State Department demonstrate. The Saudi king was, for instance, reported as having frequently demanded that the US attack Iranian nuclear facilities, with the Saudi ambassador to Washington, Adel al-Jubeir, telling the Americans to "cut off the head of the snake."[210] These developments certainly point to the existence of shared interests between Israel and several Arab states in the region in that decade.

Similarly, from April 2007 onward Syria negotiated secretly on a peace deal with the Olmert government, with the help of Turkish mediation, but broke off negotiations when the Israeli government started "Operation Cast Lead" at the end of 2008.[211] In fact, several Israeli leaders explored the possibility of reaching a peace deal with Syria. These include Yitzhak Shamir following the Madrid peace process; Yitzhak Rabin; Binyamin Netanyahu during his first government from 1996 to 1999, and again in 2010; and Ehud Barak. Since the end of the Cold War, Israeli governments have clearly been considering peace with Syria as a strategic asset. The obstacles to the reaching of an agreement thus far include the extent of the Israeli withdrawal from the occupied Golan Heights, the sequencing of normalization and territorial withdrawal, water, security arrangements, and Syria's relations with its allies. Regarding the latter, the Olmert government insisted that in order to conduct negotiations, Syria must end its support of terrorism and break off its ties with Hamas, Hizballah, and Iran.[212] More problematic, however, is Syria's demand that Israel withdraw to the June 4, 1967, borders. This would include an Israeli withdrawal from a narrow strip along the Sea of Galilee (or Lake Tiberias), Israel's main water source. With the exception of Yitzhak Rabin, Israeli governments have thus far rejected this demand.[213] In any event, the sticking points in Israeli–Syrian peace talks plainly contradict the image of the Assad regime as "evil" and thus irrational.

The Palestinian scene is divided, but as uncompromising as Hamas may sound, it had offered Israel a long-term truce on several occasions, with numerous pundits observing some moderate undertones.[214] Palestinian president Mahmoud Abbas, whose US-trained security forces had been cooperating with Israel in fighting terrorism in the West Bank in the late 2000s, had undoubtedly been signaling his serious intention to reach a peace deal with Israel.[215] Moreover, it was an open secret that the PA profoundly disliked Iran's meddling in the Israeli–Palestinian conflict, although it was not until 2012 that Palestinian prime minister Salam Fayyad publicly voiced his concern over Iran's nuclear program.[216] Fatah also shared Israel's dislike for Hamas, of course.

Thus, in the decade 2000–2010, there were important peace overtures toward Israel, while some interesting patterns of converging interests between Israel and several Arab states emerged in the face of a strengthening Iran. However, the exclusive focus on the "axis" between Iran, Hizballah, and Hamas, together with the apocalyptic talk on the Iranian nuclear issue, meant that those developments were plainly disregarded. Hence, the hegemonic Israeli notion of regional order was but one understanding of regional developments; it was but one interpretation of reality.

The Consensus, Its Challengers, and What Is Left Out

The hegemonic vision of threats and regional order that prevailed in Israel post-Oslo is inherently coherent, simple, and powerful, as we have seen. It translates into a sense of besiegement and of not having any choice, together with a fear for survival. But considering the Gaza disengagement of 2005 and the peace talks with the Palestinians under the Olmert government in 2007–8, could it be argued that there were, in fact, some major challenges to Israel's new foreign policy consensus in that decade? To what extent did these initiatives challenge the new hegemony, or, alternatively, why did they not succeed in defying Israel's consensus on threats and regional order? Moreover, in order to understand the power of Israel's hegemonic vision and its political implications, it is also necessary to reflect on what was missing from it. These reflections will conclude this chapter.

Challenges to the Consensus

Israel's new hegemonic discourse during the first post-Oslo decade was certainly not monolithic. Dissenting voices and alternative policy pre-scriptions continued to exist, as exemplified by the Geneva Initiative of 2003. Initiated by two former key negotiators in Israeli–Palestinian peace talks, ex-Israeli minister and politician Yossi Beilin and minister of infor-mation and culture of the PA Yasser Abed Rabbo, the unofficial and non-binding document represents an extremely detailed and comprehensive draft agreement on permanent status to resolve the Israeli–Palestinian conflict. Supported by the Swiss government, the Geneva Initiative en-joyed broad international support. Its impact on Israeli politics and soci-ety remained limited, however. In addition, members of Israel's security establishment, such as former Mossad chief Efraim Halevy and former head of the Shabak Ami Ayalon, have publicly argued in favor of seeking to engage Hamas in a political process, thus departing from the official government position.[217] Perhaps more importantly, in at least four cases Israeli leaders did seem to move away from the consensus or perhaps even challenge it. This includes, most notably, Ariel Sharon's Gaza disen-gagement plan of 2005, Ehud Olmert's peace talks with the Palestinians in 2007–8, the indirect negotiations with Syria in the same period, and Ehud Barak's dissenting assessment of the "existential" nature of the Ira-nian threat.

But even while triggering some debates and disagreements in Israeli politics, did these initiatives really challenge the consensus? The Geneva Initiative represented perhaps the most important alternative to Israel's domestic consensus and neo-revisionist hegemony. Based on the idea of a two-state solution, the Geneva Initiative explicitly espoused the Oslo framework for negotiations with the Palestinians. However, initiated by Beilin, one of the most "dovish" political figures of the by then already dis-credited Zionist Left, and presented at the height of the second Palestin-ian intifada, the Geneva Initiative did not succeed in galvanizing sufficient political support in Israel. Although it had some backing among the Israeli population, the initiative was not endorsed or promoted by Israel's con-secutive right-wing governments, which the majority of Israelis continued to vote into power.[218] For Israeli governments, the far-reaching territorial concessions it proposed in unofficial negotiations with a counterpart that had already been branded as unworthy of being called a "partner" seemed out of touch with reality, as defined by the new foreign policy consensus. Prime Minister Ariel Sharon had an easy game in dismissing the initiative by labeling it an illegitimate and almost treasonous act, especially as it was funded by a foreign government.[219] Similar proposals promoted by Israeli public figures, often together with Palestinian counterparts, suffered a similar fate in that decade—and after.

As for Sharon's plan to withdraw Israeli settlers and soldiers from the Gaza Strip, it is true that the Likud party's fierce opposition to the initiative prompted Sharon to leave the Likud and form the Kadima party. Perhaps more importantly, it also set a precedent for territorial withdrawal in the context of Israel's conflict with the Palestinians. To a large extent, this explains the harsh opposition of the settler movement to Israel's withdrawal from the Gaza Strip. The disengagement plan, however, was not a radical departure from the consensus. Reflecting the priority Sharon had always given to security considerations over religious-ideological ones, the Gaza disengagement was a unilateral measure based on the belief that there was no one to talk to on the Palestinian side. Israel's Gaza withdrawal did not exemplify a return to the logic of Oslo, and neither did it signal Israel's readiness for significant territorial compromise. Rather, considering the mounting international pressure on Israel and the evolving Gaza security nightmare, Sharon's disengagement plan was a strategic move to increase Israel's security (erroneously, as it turned out) while avoiding the resurrection of Oslo. As noted earlier, Sharon's key adviser, Weissglass, had explained this logic eloquently.[220] The Gaza disengagement is thus an example of the variation that exists within the consensus, reflecting different lines of thought within Israel's political Right.

Importantly, however, for most Israelis, the rising number of rockets launched by Hamas on southern Israel after the Gaza withdrawal was to give the already unpopular idea of territorial withdrawal the coup de grace. This assessment conveniently ignores the fact that the problem was perhaps not the withdrawal per se but rather its unilateral nature— together with the fact that Israel still controls, indirectly, Gaza's territory.[221]

Ehud Barak's rejection of the existential nature of the Iranian menace is another indication of the variation that exists within Israel's new foreign policy consensus post-Oslo. Barak, the father of the "no partner for peace" narrative, refuted any comparison between Tehran's nuclear program and the Holocaust and refused to consider the Iranian nuclear threat as "existential." He still supported a strike on Iran's nuclear facilities, though.

Thus, while Barak did not subscribe to exaggerated politics of insecurity and fear, his position on Iran was still compatible with the dominant vision of threats and regional order in that decade.

The peace talks with the Palestinians conducted by the Olmert government after the 2007 Annapolis conference, on the other hand, marked a real departure from the "no partner for peace" narrative. The start of these negotiations may be explained by the mounting US pressure on the Israeli government, the decreasing number of terrorist attacks in that period, and the pragmatism and personal convictions of Ehud Olmert. However, the leaked minutes of these talks also show that until Olmert put forward his "package deal" in September 2008, Israel's inclination to offer any meaningful concessions to the Palestinians was extremely limited.[222] The prime minister also faced a consistent opposition to significant compromises on the major thorny issues—Jerusalem, settlements, territorial scope, borders, security, and the Palestinian right of return—from members of his own government coalition. Some may argue that Israel's engagement in these talks was merely a tactic to avoid further international pressure. It may be equally relevant that Olmert put a significant—albeit incomplete—peace proposal on the table in a take-it-or-leave-it fashion only after he was already under investigation for corruption, and after it was clear that new Israeli elections were imminent. Certainly, Olmert's intentions vis-à-vis the Palestinians may still have been serious, although one is left wondering why he gave the green light to "Operation Cast Lead" in December 2008, at exactly this point in time. As it was obvious that the PA would not have continued talking peace with Israel while its people in Gaza were being bombed by the Israeli army, it may be assumed that ending the conflict with the Palestinians may not have been Olmert's first priority. At any rate, as the Gaza war, Olmert's legal predicaments, and Abbas's hesitations were to put an end to the peace talks, at best it may be argued that the most relevant peace negotiations since the collapse of Oslo failed because of bad timing, poor leadership on both sides, and adverse circumstances. But had both sides reached a peace deal back then—and the gaps between them were reportedly not too large—could Olmert have succeeded in obtaining the support of the Israeli public in defiance of the new hegemonic discourse? While this remains open to speculation, it is interesting to note that, had a peace accord been reached, Olmert had reportedly planned to first secure the support of the UN Security Council, the UN General Assembly, the US Congress, the European Union, and other major powers *before* presenting it to the Israeli people.[223] Apparently Olmert was well aware of the power of Israel's new hegemony. More importantly, it was precisely the failure of these talks that seemed once more to confirm the Israeli perception of not having a partner for peace, with Israeli policymakers laying the blame solely on the Palestinians.

As for the indirect peace talks with Syria within the same time span, similar considerations apply. Israel's approach to Syria has always been marked by the precedence of purely strategic considerations—the Golan Heights, which Israel captured in the 1967 war, have no religious or historical significance for Israel whatsoever. Repeated Israeli attempts to negotiate a peace deal with Syria in the last few decades have generally followed the idea of seeking to drive a wedge in the "radical axis" of Iran, Hizballah, and the regime in Damascus. Yet, as in previous unsuccessful rounds of talks, a major problem has seemed to be the extent of the Israeli withdrawal from the Golan Heights, an issue on which the Syrian regime has never been willing to compromise one iota.[224] It is worth noting here that a return of the Golan Heights in the framework of a peace deal with Syria would face widespread opposition among the Israeli public. Indeed, various public opinion polls conducted over the last few decades show that between 62 and 65 percent of all Israelis, and between 71 and 76 percent of Jewish Israelis, oppose a full evacuation of the Golan Heights in return for a peace agreement with Syria.[225] Thus, while the talks with the Assad regime went somewhat against the prevailing preference for unilateral policies in post-Oslo Israel, they were not a novelty in post–Cold War Israeli policies toward the region. And whereas the peace talks in principle challenged the almost customary demonization of Syria, Olmert stressed that, in spite of the talks, he still considered the country to be "part of the axis of evil and a force that encourages terror in the entire Middle East."[226] Moreover, it remains baffling that Olmert should start the war on the Hamas-ruled Gaza Strip while peace talks with Syria (and the Palestinians) were under way. The Gaza war prompted Syria and the mediator, Turkey, to break off the talks—as was to be expected.

These examples show that Israel's hegemonic perceptions of threats and regional order post-Oslo were far from being monolithic. But they were extremely powerful nevertheless. Strategic considerations, external pressure, political calculations, and perhaps personal conviction prompted political leaders to depart, or try to depart, from the consensus, as exemplified by the 2005 Gaza withdrawal as well as by Olmert's peace talks with both the Palestinians and Syria. Yet these initiatives were unable to shake the new hegemony. On the contrary: some, such as the Gaza withdrawal, faced major opposition at the domestic level. Others, such as the peace talks with the PA and with Syria, would undoubtedly have faced resistance, had they been successful. The failure of these initiatives only reinforced the consensus further, providing additional proof for what Israelis considered they had known all along.

The power of the new consensus was also reflected in those critical facts and developments that were not, or were no longer, part of Israel's collective discourse and consciousness, as discussed in the following sections.

Regional Developments

A number of regional developments described earlier did not figure in Israel's political discourse, nor were they the subject of public debate. Thus, consecutive Israeli governments maintained an at-best ambivalent attitude toward the Saudi peace initiative. Admittedly, the timing was extremely unfortunate. The Arab League first endorsed the peace plan at its 2002 summit, precisely one day after Hamas had perpetrated the most atrocious terrorist attack of the Second Intifada: a suicide bombing in a Netanya hotel during a Passover Seder had left twenty-eight Israelis dead.

To a certain extent, the timing may explain why the Sharon government criticized the peace plan for demanding territorial concessions from Israel without addressing the issue of terrorism. However, while expressing reservations on the document's provisions regarding Jerusalem, refugees, and borders—the key issues of the conflict—the Israeli government also made it clear that a return to the 1967 borders was out of question. Ironically, Ariel Sharon, who had coined the phrase that there would be "no negotiations under fire," now denounced the Arab side for not talking to Israel. According to the former prime minister, "nobody among the Arabs thinks that the time has yet arrived to talk to Israel about this plan, which makes us a little suspicious."[227] Beyond these comments, the Israeli government by and large chose to ignore the peace initiative. The Arab League's renewed endorsement of the plan in March 2007 still did not prompt any official Israeli reaction, except for an extremely cautious welcome by Ehud Olmert. While categorically refusing any Israeli concessions over refugees, Olmert stressed that the initiative might be the starting point for future discussions.[228] However, there was no further follow-up. One and a half years later, Defense Minister Barak declared that the Israeli government was still "mulling" over the plan. Olmert, on his side, finally endorsed it *after* he had resigned from the position of prime minister on corruption charges at the end of 2008. Olmert's foreign minister, Livni, on the other hand, openly criticized the plan's provisions on Palestinian refugees and the 1967 borders. And Israel's subsequent prime minister, Netanyahu, flatly rejected it in public—but not in any official form vis-à-vis the Saudis or the Arab League.[229]

The government's eternal "mulling" of the plan was well reflected in Israeli public opinion. Although a group of former Israeli security officials had called on the government to engage with the peace plan, only 38 percent of Israelis supported the Arab League initiative, according to a poll of December 2008.[230] More interestingly, throughout 2009 the PA had placed advertisements in the main Israeli newspapers in support of the peace plan. These ads, however, went largely unnoticed. Only 25 percent of polled Israelis remembered seeing them at all, and only 14 percent actually read them.[231] This is a particularly intriguing indication of how preexisting convictions and ideas may act as filters on incoming information.

Israeli Policies in the Territories

Largely absent from Israel's public discourse—and from the collective consciousness—were the modalities and implications of Israel's continued control over the Palestinian territories. Except for the articles of a few journalists, most notably Amira Hass and Gideon Levy of the daily *Haaretz*, during most of the 2000s the impact of Israel's occupation on the daily lives of ordinary Palestinians was hardly a topic. This phenomenon was already observable during the Oslo process. Even in that period, public debates and the media mainly focused on the behavior and intentions of Arafat and the PA, with the recurrent terrorist attacks also featuring prominently. Once the Second Intifada broke out, the phenomenon of ignoring the fate and living condition of ordinary Palestinians became even more pronounced. Israeli politicians, pundits, and the media did of course discuss the operations of the Israeli army in the territories from 2000 onward, as well as the closures, the curfews, the arrests, the targeted killings, and, although less frequently, the destruction of infrastructure and the house demolitions. But these references generally occurred in the context of Israel's need to fight Palestinian terrorism. Hence, Israeli policies were presented as necessary measures, enjoying a broad public support.

Similarly, Israel's 2005 withdrawal from the Gaza Strip—entailing the end of Israel's occupation of that area, according to the narrative prevailing in Israel—was widely reported and discussed, and so was Israel's war on Hamas-ruled Gaza in the winter of 2008–9. Yet the question of whether Israel's control over the Gaza Strip really ended, let alone why Hamas continued to fire rockets on Israel, was not a topic of discussion. Certainly, the Israeli government withdrew the army and all settlers from the Gaza Strip in the summer of 2005. However, given that Israel still controls the airspace over the strip and—together with Egypt—all of its land or sea borders and thus the movement of goods and people from and into the Gaza Strip, it is more than questionable whether Israel's effective control over the Gaza Strip has really ended, or whether it has only changed in nature. While the appropriateness of Israel's economic blockade of the Gaza Strip following the Hamas takeover went unquestioned, any analysis of the conditions of a people living under occupation was missing. Similarly, the possibility that perhaps not all aspects of Israeli policies in the territories could be justified in terms of security was not, or was no longer, part of any public debate. Referring to Israel's counterterrorism policies during the Second Intifada, *Haaretz* journalists Amos Harel and Avi Issacharoff noted that Israel's security services, the army, and the West Bank barrier did not "just distance terror from Israelis in the center of the country; they pushed the territories out of Israeli awareness." According to these journalists, "for most Israelis, what happens there is taking place on the dark side of the moon, even if it's only a half hour's drive from their homes."[232]

Thus, we may assume that most Israelis did not know and no longer cared to know about the inherent arbitrariness and humiliations of military rule that—together with the killing and maiming of innocent civilians—accompanied Israel's counterterrorism policies. Likewise, the severe restrictions on the movement of people, the continuing expropriation of land for the construction of Israeli settlements or army bases, and Israel's constant exploitation of the West Bank's natural resources—including, most notably, water—were not a topic of public debate.[233] In fact, the occupation per se and the ways in which Israel's grip over people and territory had changed over a time span of more than four decades were simply pushed out of Israel's collective awareness. The growing settler violence against Palestinians and their property, which often went unpunished, did not take center stage in Israel's public discourse either. While any withdrawal from the territories faces great opposition in Israeli domestic politics, an additional explanation for this partly deliberate ignorance was that, after all, the Palestinians had only to blame themselves for their fate: Israel had offered them a state at Camp David, but they had nothing better to do than to resort to violence, according to the Israeli narrative.

◆

Israel's hegemonic vision of threats and regional order during the decade 2000–2010 describes a rather desolate reality: what most Jewish Israelis saw when looking at the regional environment was an encircling alliance of evil forces that were primed on the destruction of the Jewish state. One of the preferred means to achieve this objective—or at least to prevent Israeli citizens from living in peace—was terrorism. Thus, from Israel's vantage point, terrorism seemed to be endemic to the Arab/ Muslim worlds. Furthermore, the fanatic regime in Tehran, which was leading the anti-Israeli coalition, had deceived the international community in its quest to obtain nuclear weapons.

Concurrently, as Israelis became increasingly convinced that the refusal of "the Arabs," or perhaps of the whole "Muslim world," to accept Israel's existence was the core of the problem, no negotiated solution to the Israeli–Palestinian and the wider Arab–Israeli conflicts seemed possible. As Foreign Minister Lieberman expressed, the Israeli–Palestinian conflict was part of a broader "clash of values between civilizations."[234] According to the hegemonic narrative, the failed Camp David negotiations of 2000 proved beyond any doubt that the Palestinian side was not interested in peace. Ergo, Israel had no choice but to rely on its military doctrine of deterrence, preemption, and reprisal while continuing to "live by the sword," according to revisionism's Iron Wall doctrine. In this context, the option of giving up additional territory seemed suicidal, considering the rocket attacks Israel was exposed to from both Gaza and Lebanon after Israeli withdrawals. As the conflict became increasingly framed in ethnoreligious terms, no rational measure of peacemaking seemed appropriate to resolve it. The "no partner for peace" theme only fed into this conception.

However, while these notions of threats and regional order have undoubtedly a material basis, they can also be challenged on several accounts, as the discussion has shown. The fact that these convictions became hegemonic entails an absence of meaningful debate on these issues. Even though a few initiatives did seem to depart from the consensus in that decade, not all of them presented any meaningful challenge to the consensus. Their failure only reinforced the new hegemony. Concurrently, other significant developments at the regional level were not given the attention they may have deserved.

Focusing specifically on the legitimization of policies, the next chapter explores in more detail the implications of Israel's hegemonic vision in the post-Oslo decade. What was the impact of the new consensus on Israel's regional policies and international relations? And how did it affect domestic politics? In this context, the question is also raised as to whether Israeli policies have been counterproductive, perhaps contributing unintentionally to the cementing of the regional order that Israel's new hegemony prescribed.

Notes

1. For a good discussion, see Fletcher, "Indefinable Concept of Terrorism."

2. United Nations, *A More Secure World*, 52.

3. Maoz, *Defending the Holy Land*, 261.

4. Data based on "Fatal Terrorist Attacks in Israel since the DOP (Sept 1993)." Israel Ministry of Foreign Affairs, September 24, 2000, http://www.mfa.gov.il/mfa/ foreignpolicy/terrorism/palestinian/pages/fatal%20terrorist%20attacks%20in %20israel%20since%20the%20dop%20-s.aspx. The difficulty of defining terrorist attacks applies.

5. The Green Line is the demarcation line set out in the 1949 armistice agreements that also marks the border between the State of Israel and the territories it captured in the 1967 Six-Day War.

6. While these measures equal a form of collective punishment, which is illegal under international law, the effectiveness of closures and curfews in the fight against terrorism has been questioned. See, for example, Maoz, *Defending the Holy Land*, 262.

7. Data from "Fatal Terrorist Attacks in Israel (1993–1999)," Israel Ministry of Foreign Affairs, September 24, 2000, http://www.mfa.gov.il/mfa/ foreignpolicy/terrorism/palestinian/pages/fatal%20terrorist%20attacks%20in %20israel%20since%20the%20dop%20-s.aspx; and "Fatalities before Operation 'Cast Lead,'" B'Tselem, http://www.btselem.org/statistics/fatalities/before-cast -lead/by-date-of-event.

8. "Sharon: Past Peace Pacts Are Null," Associated Press, January 10, 2001; Deborah Sonntag, "Sharon Opens His Campaign; U.S. Diplomat Puts Off Trip," *New York Times*, January 11, 2001; and Sobelman, "PA Official: If Oslo Is Dead, Then We Might Withdraw Recognition," *Haaretz*, September 9, 2002.

9. Regarding another 445 Palestinians killed by the Israeli army or police between 2001 and 2006, it is not known whether they took part in hostilities. Data from "Fatalities before Operation 'Cast Lead.'"

10. Milstein, "A Decade since the Outbreak of the Al-Aqsa Intifada," 16–17.

11. Sharon, quoted in US Department of State, "President Bush Welcomes Prime Minister Sharon to White House: Question and Answer Session with the Press," The Oval Office, The White House, October 16, 2002, http://2001-2009 .state.gov/p/nea/rls/rm/14442.htm.

12. Doron Rosenblum, "The Philosophy and Thematics of Janana," *Haaretz Magazine*, January 24, 2002, p. 5.

13. The Roadmap stipulated that the "Palestinians must dismantle terrorist organizations, confiscate weapons, arrest the planners and perpetrators of terrorist acts, stop incitement and resume security cooperation with Israel. . . . These measures are imperative for renewing the peace process." See "Saving Lives: Israel's Security Fence," Israel Ministry of Foreign Affairs, November 26, 2003, http:// www.mfa.gov.il/mfa/foreignpolicy/terrorism/palestinian/pages/saving%20lives -%20israel-s%20security%20fence.aspx.

14. See Del Sarto, *Contested State Identities*, 126–27.

15. Ben-Ami, *Scars of War*, 177.

16. Sharon won the elections for prime minister (under Israel's old electoral law) of February 2001, with his term starting on March 7, 2001. He was reconfirmed after the elections of January 2003, in which the Likud won a resounding victory. Sharon left the Likud over the party's opposition to his Gaza disengagement plan and formed the Kadima party, which entered a coalition with the Labor Party in 2005, and thus remained prime minister until he suffered a stroke on January 4, 2006.

17. Palestinian citizens of Israel, who constitute about 20 percent of Israeli citizens, are usually excluded from Israeli opinion polls, reflecting the long-standing tendency of ignoring the political preferences of this relatively large minority.

18. Arian, "Israeli Public Opinion on National Security 2003," 29.

19. Ibid., 32.

20. Ibid., 32–34.

21. See Dor, *Suppression of Guilt*.

22. See Dor, *Intifada Hits the Headlines*.

23. Keshev, "'Liquidation Sale': Israeli Media Coverage of Events in Which Palestinians Were Killed by Israeli Security Forces," Keshev: The Center for the Protection of Democracy in Israel, March 2006.

24. "Saving Lives: Israel's Security Fence."

25. Shalom, "Disengagement Plan," 92.

26. Ariel Sharon, "Prime Minister Sharon's Speech at the Fourth Herzliya Conference," December 18, 2003, http://www.mfa.gov.il/mfa/pressroom/2003/pages/ address%20by%20pm%20ariel%20sharon%20at%20the%20fourth%20herzliya.aspx.

27. According to one poll, 56 percent of Jewish Israelis supported the withdrawal in 2004, and 50 percent of respondents supported it in 2005; Ben Meir

and Bagno-Moldavsky, "Vox Populi," 74. It can be assumed that the Palestinian Israeli public, which is often not considered, supported Israel's withdrawal from Gaza widely.

28. "Q&A: Gaza Conflict," BBC News, January 18, 2009, http://news.bbc.co.uk/2/hi/middle_east/7818022.stm.

29. Data based on a 2013 version of "Palestinian Terror: Victims of Palestinian Violence and Terrorism since September 2000," Israel Ministry of Foreign Affairs, http://www.mfa.gov.il/mfa/foreignpolicy/terrorism/palestinian/pages/victims %20of%20palestinian%20violence%20and%20terrorism%20sinc.aspx.

30. See for example Ethan Bronner, "Gaza Truce May Be Revived by Necessity," *New York Times*, December 19, 2008; and Rory McCarthy, "Gaza Truce Broken as Israeli Raid Kills Six Hamas Gunmen," *Guardian*, November 5, 2008.

31. United Nations General Assembly, Human Rights Council, "Human Rights in Palestine." A year and a half after the Goldstone Commission report was published, Justice Richard Goldstone "retracted" the findings of the committee that Israel had deliberately attacked civilians; see Richard Goldstone, "Reconsidering the Goldstone Report on Israel and War Crimes." *Washington Post*, April 1, 2011.

32. See, for example, "Initial Response to Report of the Fact-Finding Mission on Gaza Established Pursuant to Resolution S-9/1 of the Human Rights Council," Israel Ministry of Foreign Affairs, September 24, 2009, http://www.mfa.gov.il/MFA _Graphics/MFA%20Gallery/Documents/GoldstoneReportInitialResponse240909 .pdf. See also the response of the well-respected Hebrew University philosophy professor Moshe Halbertal, "The Goldstone Illusion: What the U.N. Report Gets Wrong about Gaza—and War," *New Republic*, November 9, 2009.

33. Ben Meir, "Operation Cast Lead," 31.

34. Ibid.

35. Ephraim Yaar and Tamar Hermann, "War and Peace Index—December 2008," Evens Program in Mediation and Conflict Resolution and the Tami Steinmetz Center for Peace Research, Tel Aviv University, 2008, http://www.peaceindex .org/files/peaceindex2008_12_3.pdf. This often-cited evaluation of public sentiments and attitudes was originally initiated by the Tami Steinmetz Center for Peace Research at Tel Aviv University in 1994 and became a project of the Israel Democracy Institute and the Evens Program in Mediation and Conflict Resolution at Tel Aviv University in January 2010. The project is headed by Professor Ephraim Yaar of Tel Aviv University and Tamar Hermann, a Senior Fellow at the Israel Democracy Institute.

36. Ephraim Yaar and Tamar Hermann, "War and Peace Index—February 2009," Evens Program in Mediation and Conflict Resolution and the Tami Steinmetz Center for Peace Research, Tel Aviv University, 2009, http://www.peaceindex .org/files/peaceindex2009_2_3.pdf.

37. Yaar and Hermann, "War and Peace Index—December 2008."

38. Data from "Statistics: Fatalities During Operation 'Cast Lead,'" B'Tselem, http://www.btselem.org/statistics/fatalities/during-cast-lead/by-date-of-event; and "Gaza Strip: Operation Cast Lead, 27 Dec. '08 to 18 Jan. '09," B'Tselem, January 1, 2011; updated September 18, 2014, http://www.btselem.org/gaza_strip/castlead_operation. For the argument that Israel's conduct of the Gaza war was morally—and, in most cases, legally—wrong and that the purpose of "Operation Cast Lead" cannot be justified as one of self-defense according to Just War philosophy, see Slater, "Just War Moral Philosophy and the 2008–09 Israeli Campaign."

39. Keshev, "Sikur Mivtsah 'Oferet Yetsukah' be-'Aza ba-Tikshoret ha-Israelit" [An analysis of "Operation Cast Lead" in the Israeli media], Keshev: The Center for the Protection of Democracy in Israel, 2009.

40. When the UN marked the border between Israel and Lebanon after Israel's withdrawal in 2000, the Sheba'a Farms were considered to be part of Syria. However, Damascus refused to commit to any binding demarcation until Israeli forces withdrew from the area, and Hizballah took advantage of the controversy to justify attacks on Israeli forces in the area. In 2007 the UN informally conveyed the message that the Sheba'a Farms were indeed Lebanese and that Israel should withdraw; however, the official UN position remained that the fate of the farms should be agreed between Syria and Lebanon. In the absence of an agreement with Syria, Israel refused to withdraw from the Sheba'a Farms because it could be seen as an additional victory for Hizballah. See for example Barak Ravid, "UN Tells Israel: Place Shaba Farms in Hands of UNIFIL," Haaretz, July 11, 2007. It is worth noting that the "Blue Line" is not identical to the demarcation line of the armistice agreement of 1949 between Lebanon and Israel.

41. Maoz, Defending the Holy Land, 256. See also "Main Events on the Israel-Lebanese Border since the IDF Withdrawal on 24 May 2000," Israel Ministry of Foreign Affairs, August 10, 2003, http://www.mfa.gov.il/mfa/foreignpolicy/terrorism/hizbullah/pages/main%20events%20on%20the%20israel-lebanese%20border%20since%20th.aspx.

42. Bregman, Israel's Wars, 274.

43. For a summary of the findings, see Winograd Committee, Press Release, April 30, 2007, http://www.imra.org.il/story.php3?id=34083. See also Lustick, "Abandoning the Iron Wall," 48; and Inbar, "How Israel Bungled the Second Lebanon War."

44. Ben Meir and Bagno-Moldavsky, "Vox Populi," 86.

45. Berrebi and Klor, "On Terrorism and Electoral Outcomes"; Berrebi and Klor, "Are Voters Sensitive to Terrorism?"; and Getmansky and Zeitzoff, "Terrorism and Voting."

46. See Klein, Shift.

47. For more on this issue, see chapter 2.

48. Peffley, Hutchison, and Shamir, "Impact of Persistent Terrorism," 830.

49. The literature on Camp David is far too extensive to mention, but see, for example, Sher, *The Israeli–Palestinian Peace Negotiations*; Benny Morris, "Camp David and After: An Exchange (An Interview with Ehud Barak)," *New York Review of Books*, June 13, 2002; Hussein Agha and Robert Malley, "Camp David: The Tragedy of Errors," *New York Review of Books*, August 9, 2001; Enderlin, *Shattered Dreams*; Ross, *Missing Peace*; Ben-Ami, *Scars of War*, 240–84; Pressman, "Visions in Collision"; Pressman, "Second Intifada"; Ari Shavit, "Eyes Wide Shut: Interview with Ehud Barak," *Haaretz Magazine*, September 6, 2002, 8–12; and Ari Shavit, "End of a Journey: Interview with Shlomo Ben-Ami," *Haaretz*, September 13, 2001.

50. Shavit, "End of a Journey"; Tessler, *History of the Israeli-Palestinian Conflict*, 802–3; and Bregman, *Elusive Peace*, 107.

51. Ben-Ami, *Scars of War*, 257.

52. "The Response of the Government of the State of Israel to the Report of the UN High Commissioner for Human Rights," Israel Ministry of Foreign Affairs, February 11, 2001, http://www.mfa.gov.il/MFA/MFA-Archive/2001/Pages/The%20Response%20of%20the%20Government%20of%20the%20State%20of%20Isr.aspx. See also Morris, "Camp David and After."

53. See, for example, Dor, *Intifada Hits the Headlines*, chap. 4.

54. Morris, "Camp David and After"; Ben-Ami, *Scars of War*, 273; Ross, *Missing Peace*, 756. President Clinton had publicly stated that both sides had accepted his parameters; see Enderlin, *Shattered Dreams*, 344.

55. Dor, *Intifada Hits the Headlines*, 148–54.

56. Morris, "Camp David and After"; Shavit, "Eyes Wide Shut"; Dor, *Intifada Hits the Headlines*; and Meital, *Peace in Tatters*, 111 ff.

57. Ben-Ami, *Lessons of the Israeli–Palestinian Peace Process*.

58. Halperin and Bar-Tal, "The Fall of the Peace Camp."

59. Ibid.

60. Ibid., 9. See also the various Peace Index polls for the period 2000–2002, at http://www.tau.ac.il/peace/.

61. See Agha and Malley, "Camp David"; Pressman, "Visions in Collision"; and Pressman, "Second Intifada."

62. Quandt, *Peace Process*, 365 ff.

63. Enderlin, *Shattered Dreams*, 171.

64. See, for example, Shamir and Maddy-Weitzman, *Camp David Summit*; Swisher, *Truth about Camp David*; and Miller, *Much Too Promised Land*.

65. See, for example, Falk, "Camp David II," 85–87.

66. Agha and Malley, "Camp David."

67. It is not clear whether Israel insisted on the two corridors as the negotiations proceeded. Tessler, *History of the Israeli–Palestinian Conflict*, 801–2.

68. Yatom, "Background, Process and Failure," 39; and Pressman, "Visions in Collision," 22–24.

69. See, for example, al-Abed, "Israeli Proposals," 74–81.

70. For the main narratives of what happened at Camp David, see Rabinovich, "Failure of Camp David," 14–17. See also Kacowicz, "Rashomon in the Middle East." For a rebuttal of the criticism, see Barak, "Myths Spread about Camp David."

71. For an account of the negotiations at Taba, see the so-called Moratinos Document, the document prepared by the special envoy of the European Union to the Middle East, Miguel Angel Moratinos, reproduced in Akiva Eldar, "The Peace That Nearly Was at Taba," *Haaretz*, February 14, 2002. Both the Israeli and the Palestinian negotiating teams accepted the document as a fair representation of the negotiations at Taba.

72. Barak, quoted in Shavit, "Eyes Wide Shut."

73. Barak, quoted in ibid.

74. Barak, quoted in ibid. See also Pressman, "Visions in Collision," 20.

75. Barak, quoted in Bregman, *Elusive Peace*, 145.

76. Sharm El-Sheikh Fact-Finding Committee, *Mitchell Report*, April 30, 2001, http://eeas.europa.eu/mepp/docs/mitchell_report_2001_en.pdf.

77. See, for example, the report of the IDF of November 2000, quoted in Enderlin, *Shattered Dreams*, 293–94. See also Akiva Eldar, "Popular Misconceptions," *Haaretz*, June 11, 2004.

78. Lavie, "Israel's Coping with the Al-Aqsa Intifada," 101. For further references to similar public pronouncements of intelligence community officials, see ibid., 117n1.

79. Ayalon, quoted in Sylvain Cypel, "L'urgence, c'est de se désengager inconditionnellement des territoires," Interview with Ami Ayalon, *Le Monde*, December 23–24, 2001.

80. See Dor, *Intifada Hits the Headlines*, chap. 2; Dor, *Suppression of Guilt*.

81. See "Illusions of Restraint: Human Rights Violations During the Events in the Occupied Territories, 29 September–2 December 2000," B'Tselem, December 6, 2000, http://www.btselem.org/Download/200012_Illusions_of_Restraint_Eng.doc.

82. Ibid. See also Sharm El-Sheikh Fact-Finding Committee, *Mitchell Report*.

83. Quoted in Tessler, *History of the Israeli–Palestinian Conflict*, 817.

84. Dor, *Intifada Hits the Headlines*, 157; and Wolfsfeld, *Media and the Path to Peace*, chap. 7.

85. See Meital, *Peace in Tatters*, 114–15.

86. Dor, *Intifada Hits the Headlines*, 3. See also Wolfsfeld, *Media and the Path to Peace*.

87. Bar-Tal and Teichman, *Stereotypes and Prejudice in Conflict*, 156.

88. See Liebes, *Reporting the Arab–Israeli Conflict*; Wolfsfeld, *Media and the Path to Peace*; Dor, *Intifada Hits the Headlines*; Dor, *Suppression of Guilt*; "War to the Last Moment: The Israeli Media in the Second Lebanon War," Keshev: The Center for the Protection of Democracy in Israel, July 2008; and Naveh, "Role of the Media."

89. Naveh, "Role of the Media," 32–35.

90. Halperin and Bar-Tal, "Fall of the Peace Camp."

91. Hovland, Janis, and Kelley, *Communication and Persuasion*, 35.

92. Ibid., 35 ff. See also Kruglanski et al., "Says Who?"; Kruglanski, *Lay Epistemics and Human Knowledge*.

93. Halperin and Bar-Tal, "Fall of the Peace Camp."

94. Ibid.

95. Michael, "The Israel Defense Forces as an Epistemic Authority."

96. Drucker, *Harakiri*, 284–86; Halperin and Bar-Tal, "Fall of the Peace Camp"; and Meital, *Peace in Tatters*, 84.

97. See Agha and Malley, "Camp David." Martin Indyk, member of the US delegation at the Camp David Summit and former US ambassador to Israel, considers Clinton's blaming of Arafat for the failure of Camp David as a mistake; see Indyk, "Sins of Ommission," 106.

98. Hovland, Janis, and Kelley, *Communication and Persuasion*, 246 ff.

99. Weissglass, quoted in Ari Shavit, "The Big Freeze: Interview with Dov Weisglass," *Haaretz Magazine*, October 8, 2004.

100. Weissglass, quoted in Ari Shavit, "Top PM Aide: Gaza Plan Aims to Freeze the Peace Process," *Haaretz*, October 6, 2004.

101. Ibid. See also Ari Shavit, "Yo'atso ha-Bekhir shel Sharon: Yiuzmanu et ha-Hitnatkut Kdei Lehakpi et Tahalikh ha-Medini le-Zman Bilti Mugbal" [Senior advisor of Sharon: We initiated the disengagement to freeze the peace process indefinitely], *Haaretz*, October 5, 2004.

102. Rubin, "Israel's New Strategy."

103. Barak Ravid, "Livni Menasah Leshakhneah et Artsot ha-Brit Lehanmikh Tsipiyot me-Pisgat November" [Livni tries to convince the US to reduce expectations regarding the November summit], *Haaretz*, September 2, 2007. See also Ehud Barak, "Nobody Can Push Me: Spiegel Interview with Israeli Defense Minister Ehud Barak," *Spiegel Online International*, August 4, 2008.

104. Organized and hosted by the United States, the Annapolis conference aimed to revive Israeli–Palestinian peace talks and implement the so-called Road Map for Peace. Israeli prime minister Ehud Olmert, Palestinian president Mahmoud Abbas, and US president George W. Bush attended the conference. The meeting ended with the issuing of joint statements; peace talks continued in the aftermath of the Annapolis conference.

105. Jonathan Lis, "Netanyahu: Palestinians Are Not Ready for Peace with Israel," *Haaretz*, March 22, 2011; and Galei Tsahal (Israel Army Radio), Interview with Tzipi Livni, 15:30 GTM + 2 (Israel time), May 29, 2011, in Hebrew.

106. "Public Opinion Survey for Peace Now, September 2007," Ma'agar Mohot, 2007, 28. This poll is no longer available on the Internet.

107. Ephraim Yaar and Tamar Hermann, "Madad ha-Shalom, September 2007" [Peace index, September 2007], Merkaz Tami Steinmetz le-Mehkarei Shalom, ha-Tokhnit le-Heker Sikhsukhim ve-Yishuvim 'al Shem Evens [The Tami Steinmetz Center for Peace Research, the Evens Program in Mediation and Conflict Resolution], Tel Aviv University, 2007, http://www.peaceindex.org/files/peaceindex2007_9_9.pdf.

108. "Israelis Would Accept Settlement Freeze on Both Israelis and Palestinians; Prefer Palestinian Autonomy to Sovereignty," Ma'agar Mohot, 2009, http://www.maagar-mochot.co.il, also reported in the *San Diego Jewish World*, July 26–27, 2009.

109. "Seker 'al ha-Yishuvim be-Yehuda ve-Shomron" [Poll on the settlements in Judea and Samaria], Ma'agar Mohot, 2011.

110. Telhami, *The 2011 Public Opinion Poll*.

111. Ethan Bronner, "Israelis Doubt Peace Prospects but Remain Happy, Polls Show," *New York Times*, September 28, 2011.

112. Jackson Diehl, "Abbas's Waiting Game," *Washington Post*, May 29, 2009; Kevin Peraino, "Olmert's Laments," *Newsweek*, June 13, 2009; Ethan Bronner, "Olmert Memoir Cites near Deal for Mideast Peace," *New York Times*, January 27, 2011; Ben Birnbaum, "The End of the Two-State Solution: Why the Window Is Closing on Middle-East Peace," *New Republic*, March 11, 2013; and Bernard Avishai, "A Plan for Peace that Still Could Be," *New York Times Magazine*, February 7, 2011. See also the document, marked "not for distribution," that outlines the Israeli proposal, according to information provided by Palestinian negotiator Saeb Erekat on September 9, 2008; reprinted in the *Guardian*, "The Palestine Papers: Olmert's Offer to the Palestinians," *Guardian*, January 23, 2011.

113. Avishai, "A Plan for Peace."

114. Erekat, quoted in Swisher, *Palestine Papers*, 186.

115. Ibid., particularly the documents on pp. 147–86, 187–93, 194–204, 205, 211, and 214–17.

116. Moreh, *Gatekeepers*.

117. "Codel Skelton's Meeting with Prime Minister Netanyahu," US Embassy in Tel Aviv, Cable, 09TELAVIV2777, December 23, 2009.

118. Yossi Verter, "Peres to Haaretz: Israel Could Reach a Peace Deal with Abbas," *Haaretz*, April 23, 2012; Yitzhak Benhorin, "Olmert: Abu Mazen Partner, me-Olam Lo Tamakh be-Terror" [Abu Mazen is a partner, he never supported

terrorism], *Ynet*, March 27, 2012; Attila Somalvi, "Peres: Rov ha-'Am Rotse Shteiy Medinot, Ledaber 'im 'Abas" [Peres: The majority of the people want two states, talking to Abbas (is necessary)], *Ynet*, March 11, 2012; and Natasha Mozgovaya, "Olmert be-J Street: Yiashavti 'Asrot Sh'aot 'im 'Abas, Iesh Lanu Partner" [Olmert to J Street: I sat dozens of hours with Abbas, we have a partner], *Haaretz*, March 27, 2012.

119. See, for example, Ehteshami, "Foreign Policy of Iran," 262–65.

120. Parsi, *Treacherous Alliance*, 97–135.

121. El-Husseini, "Hezbollah and the Axis of Refusal," 809–910.

122. "Ahmadinejad Brands Israel a 'Stinking Corpse,'" AFP, May 8, 2008; and Ethan Bronner, "Just How Far Did They Go, Those Words against Israel?" *New York Times*, June 11, 2006.

123. For a good account of Hizballah's history, see Norton, *Hezbollah: A Short History*.

124. UN Security Council, Resolution 1701, Adopted by the Security Council at Its 5511th Meeting, on 11 August 2006. S/RES/1701, http://daccess-dds-ny.un .org/doc/UNDOC/GEN/N06/465/03/PDF/N0646503.pdf?OpenElement.

125. See, for example, Richard Beeston, "Syria Accused of Arming Hezbollah from Secret Bases," *Times* (London), May 28, 2010.

126. Norton, "Hizballah and the Israeli Withdrawal"; Norton, "Hizballah: From Radicalism to Pragmatism?"; and El-Husseini, "Hezbollah and the Axis of Refusal."

127. Adam Shatz, "In Search for Hezbollah," *New York Review of Books*, April 29, 2004.

128. Mishal and Sela, *Palestinian Hamas*, 13–26.

129. Ibid. See also Gunning, *Hamas in Politics*.

130. See, for example, "Haniyeh Calls for Formation of Palestinian State on 1967 Lines," *Haaretz*, December 19, 2006; Waked, "Haniyeh: Anahnu be'ad Medinah be-Gvulot 67" [Haniyeh: We are in favor of a state within the '67 borders], *Ynet*, March 27, 2006; and Barak Ravid, "In 2006 Letter to Bush, Haniyeh Offered Compromise with Israel," *Haaretz*, November 14, 2008.

131. "Full Text of the National Conciliation Document of the Prisoners, May 11, 2006," Jerusalem Media and Communication Centre, 2006, https://web .archive.org/web/20060615183553/http://www.jmcc.org/documents/prisoners .htm; and Arnon Regular, "Joint Hamas-Fatah Plan Implies Acceptance of 1967 Borders," *Haaretz*, May 12, 2006.

132. Ari Issacharoff, "Is Israel Witnessing the Rise of a Kinder, Gentler Hamas?" *Haaretz*, December 30, 2011.

133. Jack Khoury, "Report: Hamas' Meshal Agrees for Palestinian State Based on 1967 Borders," *Haaretz*, September 5, 2014.

134. Mishal and Sela, *Palestinian Hamas*, 97.

135. Parsi, *Treacherous Alliance*, 172–89.

136. Ibid., 65–66.

137. Haniyeh, quoted in "Khamenei Pledges Iranian Support to Palestinian 'Resistance' Against Israel," *Haaretz*, February 12, 2012.

138. Parsi, *Treacherous Alliance*, 151–56; and Parsi, "Israel and the Origins," 283–84.

139. Yossi Klein Halevi and Michael B. Oren, "Israel's Worst Nightmare," *New Republic*, January 30, 2007. See also Mearsheimer and Walt, *Israel Lobby*, 283.

140. International Crisis Group, *In Heavy Waters*; and Ehteshami, "Foreign Policy of Iran," 279.

141. International Institute for Strategic Studies, *Iran's Strategic Weapons Programmes*; and International Crisis Group, *In Heavy Waters*.

142. IAEA Board of Governors, *Implementation of the NPT Safeguards Agreement*; and International Institute for Strategic Studies, *IAEA Report Puts Iran on Back Foot*.

143. Einhorn, *The Iran Nuclear Issue*. See also Ronen Bergman, "Will Israel Attack Iran?" *New York Times*, January 25, 2012.

144. Parsi, *Treacherous Alliance*, chap. 13.

145. Stephen Farrell, Robert Thomson, and Danielle Haas, "Attack Iran the Day Iraq War Ends, Demands Israel," *Times* (London), November 5, 2002.

146. Shimon Peres, "We Must Unite to Prevent an Ayatollah Nuke," *Wall Street Journal*, June 25, 2003.

147. Ibid.

148. "Mofaz: Land-for-Peace Will Put Iran in Golan," *Jerusalem Post*, April 29, 2008.

149. Eshel, quoted in Amos Harel, "Looking Ahead, with Guarded Optimism," *Haaretz, Week's End*, September 25, 2009.

150. The platform, once found at http://kadima.org, is no longer available on the internet.

151. Ibid.

152. "Netanyahu: Neutralizing Iran Would Reduce Danger of Hamas, Hezbollah," *Haaretz*, January 29, 2009.

153. Eran, "Ha-Behirot be-Israel"; Merav David, "Ha-Miflagot ha-Gdolot Matsigot: Matsa Bitkhoni" [Large parties present: Security platform], *NRG (Ma'ariv online)*, January 27, 2009; and Del Sarto, "Back to Square One?"

154. Farrell, Thomson, and Haas, "Attack Iran."

155. Peres, "We Must Unite."

156. Eshel, quoted in Harel, "Looking Ahead."

157. On Rabin's knowledge of Tehran's nuclear ambitions, see Klein Halevi and Oren, "Israel's Worst Nightmare."

158. Ibid.

159. Mofaz, quoted in Mazal Mualem, "Mofaz: Iran Is the Root of All Evil," *Haaretz*, August 6, 2008; and Mofaz, quoted in Haaretz Service and News Agencies, "Mofaz on Iran: We Won't Allow a Second Holocaust to Occur," *Haaretz*, August 1, 2008.

160. Peres, quoted in Natasha Mozgovaya, "Peres to Obama: No Choice but to Compare Iran to Nazis," *Haaretz*, May 6, 2009.

161. Peres, quoted in Roni Sofer, "Peres: Iranian Nuclear Bomb Akin to 'Flying Death Camp,'" *Ynet*, August 18, 2009.

162. Netanyahu, quoted in Jeffrey Goldberg, "Netanyahu to Obama: Stop Iran—or I Will." *Atlantic*, March 31, 2009.

163. Ibid.

164. Netanyahu, quoted in Barak Ravid, "Merkel: Settlement Freeze Crucial to Resumption of Mideast Peace Talks," *Haaretz*, August 27, 2009. See also Super, "Rosh ha-Memshalah Kibel et Tokhnit Auschwitz: 'La'atsor Resh'a ba-Zman'" [The prime minister accepted the Auschwitz plan: "Stop evil in time"], *Ynet*, 27 August 2009.

165. Super, "Merkel."

166. For a transcript of Netanyahu's speech, see "Prime Minister Benjamin Netanyahu's Speech to the UN General Assembly," *Haaretz*, September 24, 2009.

167. "Iranian Threat: Overview," Israel Ministry of Foreign Affairs, 2013, http://www.mfa.gov.il/MFA/The+Iranian+Threat/Overview/Iranian_Threat.htm.

168. Shimon Cohen, "Olmert le-Artsot ha-Brit: Shenu Mediniyut mul Iran" [Olmert to the US: Change policy towards Iran], *Aruts Shev'a* [Channel 7], November 13, 2006; Mearsheimer and Walt, *Israel Lobby*, 291–98; and Farrell, Thomson, and Haas, "Attack Iran."

169. Beres, "Israel, Iran, and Project Daniel," 1; Inbar, "Need to Block a Nuclear Iran"; and Ilano Marsiano, "Ba-Likud Hikhlitu: Lehaftsits et Iran" [They decided in the Likud: Bomb Iran], *Ynet*, January 1, 2006.

170. Goldberg, "Netanyahu to Obama"; and "Barak to Gates: Israel Not Ruling out Any Options on Iran," *Ynet*, September 21, 2009."

171. Jones, "Foreign Policy of Israel," 297.

172. Netanyahu, quoted in "Netanyahu: Neutralizing Iran."

173. Ibid.

174. Netanyahu's visit was organized by the Republican Speaker of the House without consulting the White House. In order to implement the deal, the president would eventually need US lawmakers to agree to permanently lift all of the sanctions on Iran, a prerequisite Tehran had insisted on. See Julie Hirschfeld Davis, "Administration Official Criticizes Israeli Ambassador over Netanyahu Visit," *New York Times*, January 28, 2015; and Peter Baker, "In Congress, Netanyahu Faults 'Bad Deal' on Iran Nuclear Program," *New York Times*, March 3, 2015.

175. Michael R. Gordon and David E. Sanger, "Deal Reached on Iran Nuclear Program; Limits on Fuel Would Lessen with Time," *New York Times*, July 14, 2015.

176. See Ben Meir and Shaked, "People Speak." The polls only consider Jewish Israelis.

177. Ephraim Yaar and Tamar Hermann, Peace Index, February 2007, Evens Program in Mediation and Conflict Resolution and the Tami Steinmetz Center for Peace Research, Tel Aviv University, 2007, http://www.peaceindex.org/indexMonthEng.aspx?num=5&monthname=February.

178. Ben Meir, *People's Voice*.

179. Center for Iranian Studies, "Public Opinion Poll: Main Findings" (Tel Aviv: Tel Aviv University, 2009). The sample included Arab Israelis. A summary of the poll is available at http://humanities1.tau.ac.il/iranian/images/CIS_Poll_English.pdf. See also Ofri Ilany, "1 in 4 Israelis Would Consider Leaving Country if Iran Gets Nukes," *Haaretz*, May 22, 2009.

180. Lustick, "Abandoning the Iron Wall," 49.

181. Menashri, quoted in in Parsi, *Treacherous Alliance*, 104.

182. Parsi, *Treacherous Alliance*, 157–65.

183. See, for example, Maoz, *Defending the Holy Land*, 12.

184. Parsi, *Treacherous Alliance*, 165–70.

185. Adopted shortly after the founding of Israel, the periphery doctrine was the basis of Israel's outreach to, or support of, Turkey, Iran, Ethiopia, Sudan, the Kurds, the Lebanese Maronites, and the Yemenite royalists, among others, during the first decades of Israeli statehood. On the periphery doctrine, see Alpher, *Periphery*.

186. For an excellent documentation of that period, see Parsi, *Treacherous Alliance*, 162–65.

187. Ibid., 165–70.

188. Ehteshami, "Foreign Policy of Iran," 269.

189. On Iran's military spending, see Parsi, *Treacherous Alliance*, 166.

190. See, for example, Sanders, "Israel and the Realities"; Yossi Yonah, "Lifnei she-Maftsitsim be-Iran" [Before we bomb Iran], *Ynet*, September 15, 2006; and Dror Zeevi, "Iran Motivated by Fear," *Ynet*, January 21, 2007.

191. Emily B. Landau, "Rational and Dangerous," *Haaretz*, June 3, 2011.

192. Menashri, quoted in Ofri Ilany, "1 in 4 Israelis Would Consider Leaving Country if Iran Gets Nukes," *Haaretz*, May 22, 2009.

193. Center for Iranian Studies, "Public Opinion Poll," 2.

194. "Barak: Palestinians Missing out on Huge Opportunity," *Ynet*, September 21, 2009.

195. Barak, quoted in Dan Williams, "Barak Says Nuke-Armed Iran Couldn't Destroy Israel," *Reuters*, September 17, 2009.

196. Gidi Weitz, "Barak: Netanyahu More Mature, Lieberman More Balanced Than He Seems, Interview with Ehud Barak," *Haaretz*, May 17, 2009.

197. Yossi Melman, "Ex-Mossad Chef Dagan: Military Strike against Iran Would Be Stupid," *Haaretz*, May 8, 2011.

198. Jones, "Foreign Policy of Israel," 297.

199. Barak Ravid, "Israel's Former Shin Bet Chief: I Have No Confidence in Netanyahu, Barak," *Haaretz*, April 18, 2012; "Former Mossad Chief Backs Shin Bet Counterpart over Criticism of Netanyahu, Barak," *Haaretz*, April 29, 2012; Anne Barnard, "Former Israeli Premier Assails Netanyahu on Iran," *New York Times*, April 30, 2012; and "Diskin neged Netanyahu ve-Barak: Lo Maamin be-Yekholtam" [Diskin against Netanyahu and Barak: I do not believe in their ability], *Walla News*, April 28, 2012.

200. Gareth Evans, "Inside Iran's Nuclear Reasoning," *Project Syndicate*, September 17, 2010, http://www.project-syndicate.org/commentary/evans2/English; and Goldschmidt, *Iranian Nuclear Issue.*

201. Barry R. Posen, "We Can Live with a Nuclear Iran," *New York Times*, February 27, 2006; and Mearsheimer and Walt, *Israel Lobby*, 284.

202. Shatz, "In Search for Hezbollah"; and El-Husseini, "Hezbollah and the Axis of Refusal."

203. McGeough, *Kill Khalid.*

204. Bahgat, "Arab Peace Initiative," 37–38.

205. "Arab League Summit: Beirut Declaration (March 28, 2002)," 583–84.

206. Ibid., 583. UNGA Resolution 194 resolves "that the refugees wishing to return to their homes and live at peace with their neighbors should be permitted to do so at the earliest practicable date, and that compensation should be paid for the property of those choosing not to return." Note that Resolution 194 refers to the refugee issue in item 11, after the fate of the Holy Places. For the text of the resolution, see "UN General Assembly: Resolution 194 (December 11, 1948)," 83–86.

207. "Arab League Summit: Beirut Declaration," 583.

208. Del Sarto, *Contested State Identities*, chap. 3; Sela, *Decline of the Arab-Israeli Conflict*; and Landau, *Arms Control in the Middle East.*

209. Mubarak, quoted in Amir Taheri, "Iran Has Started a Mideast Nuclear Arms Race," *Wall Street Journal*, March 23, 2009.

210. Ian Black and Simon Tisdall, "Saudi Arabia Urges US Attack on Iran to Stop Nuclear Programme," *Guardian*, November 28, 2010.

211. Allegra Stratton, "Assad Confirms Turkish Meditation with Israel," *Guardian*, April 24, 2008.

212. "Israel–Syria Negotiations," Israel Ministry of Foreign Affairs, May 21, 2008, http://www.mfa.gov.il/MFA/ForeignPolicy/Peace/Guide/Pages/Israel-Syria %20Negotiations.aspx.

213. On Rabin's agreement to withdraw to the 1967 borders, see, for example, Savir, *Process*, 268. Refuting Rabin's commitment, other Israeli leaders have insisted on the 1923 border drawn by Britain and France, which, according to Israel's position, is the only recognized border between the two sides. The difference between this border and the June 4, 1967, line is only twenty square kilometers, but the 1923 border would not grant the Syrians access to the Sea of Galilee and the upper Jordan valley. On the negotiations between Israel and Syria, see Rabinovich, *Brink of Peace*.

214. "Haniyeh Calls for Formation"; Ravid, "In 2006 Letter to Bush"; Gunning, *Hamas in Politics*; Mishal and Sela, *Palestinian Hamas*, 163–71; Issacharoff, "Is Israel Witnessing"; and Khoury, "Report: Hamas' Meshal Agrees."

215. See, for example, Ethan Bronner, "US Helps Palestinians Build Force for Security," *New York Times*, February 26, 2009.

216. Stephen Pollard, "PA Shares Israel's Nuclear Iran Fears," *Jewish Chronicle*, January 12, 2012.

217. Ari Shavit, "The Waiting Game: Interview with Efraim Halevy," *Haaretz*, September 4, 2004; Henry Siegman, "Hamas: The Last Chance for Peace?," *New York Review of Books*, April 27, 2006; and Thanassis Cambanis, "Political Newcomer Sees Hamas Dialogue as Crucial," *Boston Globe*, March 25, 2006.

218. See the various opinion polls conducted on behalf of the Geneva Initiative at http://www.geneva-accord.org/.

219. "A Welcome and Legitimate Initiative," *Haaretz*, October 12, 2003.

220. Shavit, "The Big Freeze"; Shavit, "Yo'atso ha-Bekhir shel Sharon"; and Shavit, "Top PM Aide."

221. Indeed, while incomplete, the Gaza withdrawal was not only decided unilaterally but also implemented unilaterally—that is, without coordinating it with the PA at all. Unsurprisingly, Hamas would capitalize most from it. For more on this issue, see chapter 2.

222. Swisher, *Palestine Papers*.

223. Avishai, "A Plan for Peace."

224. As noted earlier, for over thirty years, the objective of the Assad regime has been a full Israeli withdrawal to the June 4, 1967, lines; most Israeli governments regard the 1923 border as the basis of negotiations.

225. See, for example, the joint public opinion polls conducted by the Harry S. Truman Research Institute for the Advancement of Peace at the Hebrew University of Jerusalem and the Palestinian Center for Policy and Survey Research in Ramallah between March 2008 and December 2009, at truman.huji.ac.il/.upload/ Polls 2008 2009.pdf.

226. Olmert, quoted in "Israel–Syria Negotiations," Israel Ministry of Foreign Affairs, May 21, 2008, http://www.mfa.gov.il /MFA/ForeignPolicy/Peace/Guide/ Pages/Israel-Syria%20Negotiations.aspx.

227. Sharon, quoted in William Safire, "A Talk with Sharon," *New York Times*, April 1, 2002. See also "Response of FM Peres to the Decisions of the Arab Summit in Beirut." Israel Ministry of Foreign Affairs, March 28, 2002, http://www.mfa .gov.il/mfa/pressroom/2002/pages/response%20of%20fm%20peres%20to%20the %20decisions%20of%20the%20arab.aspx.

228. Rory McCarthy, "Olmert Says Peace Deal Possible within Five Years," *Guardian*, March 31, 2007.

229. "Barak: Israel Mulls Saudi Peace Plan," *USA Today*, October 19, 2008; and Bahgat, "Arab Peace Initiative."

230. Tobias Buck and Roula Khalaf, "Senior Israelis Back Arab Push for Peace," *Financial Times*, November 27, 2008.

231. Tovah Lazaroff, "Poll: Most Israelis Oppose Arab Peace Plan," *Jerusalem Post*, December 16, 2008; Palestinian Center for Policy and Survey Research, Joint Israeli–Palestinian Poll 31, March 5–7, 2009, http://www.pcpsr.org/en/node/414. The poll was carried out by the Palestinian Center for Policy and Survey Research in Ramallah and the Harry S. Truman Research Institute for the Advancement of Peace at the Hebrew University of Jerusalem.

232. Amos Harel and Avi Issacharoff, "Years of Rage," *Haaretz*, October 1, 2010.

233. See, for example, the documentation provided by B'Tselem, at www .btselem.org; also Gordon, *Israel's Occupation*.

234. Tim McGirk and Romesh Ratnesar, "Israel's Lieberman Raps US on Iran, Settlements," *Time*, June 25, 2009.

2

Israel's Foreign Policy Consensus

Impact and Implications

The previous chapter explored the building blocks of Israel's new consensus on regional foreign policy, together with its material basis. This chapter takes a closer look at its impact. What are the concrete political implications of Israel's new hegemonic notion of threats and regional order? On several occasions the discussion has referred to the power of the consensus in legitimizing specific policies toward the region, presented as the only alternatives. But did these policies actually achieve the desired outcome? Or did they, *nolens volens*, undermine Israel's security and contribute to the perpetuation of conflict? This chapter also assesses the impact of Israel's new hegemony on its relations with the international community, including some of Israel's key allies. As hegemony tends to sustain itself by silencing its critics, the domestic implications of Israel's new consensus is discussed subsequently, both regarding majority–minority relations in Israel and regarding the salience of tolerance and liberal values in Israeli society and politics in general.

Legitimizing Policies

One way of thinking about the legitimization of policies is to consider the issue of framing. Frames are underlying interpretative structures that are embedded in political discourse, and framing describes the process through which individuals develop a particular conceptualization of an issue or event and reorient their thinking about this issue.[1] Political science research on the process of framing confirms that the way in which political actors present their message may positively affect their ability to recruit adherents, gain favorable media coverage, and win elections. This is mainly so because the way in which ordinary citizens think about a specific issue shapes their political preference.[2] Likewise, the credible "packaging" of a political message is crucial for the legitimization of a specific line of policy.

The process of framing, however, usually presupposes intentionality as well as strategic action. A strong domestic consensus on threats and regional order, as in our case, points to the existence of a specific collective knowledge on those issues. Indeed, the majority of Israel's political elite and citizens have come to converge on a specific conception of the region. We may thus assume that a shared understanding of reality became a central feature of the Jewish Israeli collective experience after Oslo. In other words, for most Israelis, the organization of reality by and large followed the same taken-for-granted interpretative structures. This indicates that powerful frames may well have guided the collective assignment of meaning to regional developments in that period. Significantly, it is almost inherent in the construction of collective knowledge that specific lines of actions become intelligible and "normal." The persistence of a strong consensus during much of the decade also suggests that the process of making specific actions intelligible and legitimate became largely self-sustaining. In such a context, dissenting voices tend to have a slim chance of being heard.

Of course there is always the question of whether politicians make a specific argument out of conviction, or whether they follow crude strategic calculations. In many cases, we may never know. It must also be considered that uncertainty and educated guesses often underwrite the cases made by politicians and their advisers. This is particularly so if assessments of threats are involved, as these depend to a large extent on subjective perceptions. Governments also face the difficult decision of whether to classify a threat as serious enough to justify the use of exceptional means.[3] Furthermore, assessing the intentions of other states or actors is necessarily an approximate exercise, based on uncertainty.[4]

Yet there is ample evidence that actors also instrumentally frame situations so as to press their cases or in order to ensure support and money.[5] Thus, the possibility cannot be excluded that Israeli leaders may have exaggerated menacing notions of threats and regional order for a number of tactical and strategic reasons. Ehud Barak may have honestly believed there was no Palestinian partner for peace. However, his "no partner for peace" slogan may just as well have followed strategic considerations, most notably putting all the blame on Arafat for the failed Camp David Summit, while seeking to assure his own reelection.[6] Likewise, subsequent governments may have propagated the same line because they truly believed it, but nevertheless the "no partner for peace" argument was also instrumental in legitimizing specific counterterrorism policies. By the same token, Netanyahu's apocalyptic discourse on Iran may reflect the true conviction of its supporters, but it also served the aim of undermining Iran's regional ambitions, keeping up the pressure on Tehran, and diverting the attention from the Palestinian issue.

The previous chapter already touched upon the legitimizing power of Israel's foreign policy consensus post-Oslo, so a short summary should suffice here. First, the Israeli consensus on threats and regional order post-Oslo lent a strong legitimacy to policies of deterrence, the use of force, and unilateral action. Certainly, these principles also defined previous periods of Israeli politics. However, in the past these notions were usually also the subject of fierce domestic contestation. Post-Oslo, one result of the strong consensus on such policies across the political spectrum was that other options were no longer debated. Instead, alternatives were easily branded as naïve, suicidal, and occasionally even traitorous.

It was specifically the notion of not having a partner for peace on the Palestinian side that justified the use of force as well as the implementation of a series of unilateral actions, such as the construction of the West Bank Barrier and the withdrawal of Israeli settlers and soldiers from the Gaza Strip. The terrorism of the Second Intifada and the dominant explanation that Arafat had deliberately orchestrated it also legitimized Israel's reoccupation of the West Bank, together with forceful counterterrorism measures in the territories and the (at least temporary) attempt to wholly crush the Palestinian Authority. Altogether, Israel's hegemonic discourse on threats and regional order justified a complete disengagement from the idea of a negotiated peace deal with the Palestinians. The numerous suicide attacks of the Second Intifada only reinforced this conviction, thus providing an additional justification for these lines of policy.

Second, the Israeli consensus post-Oslo specifically delegitimized any further territorial compromise—in other words, Israel's withdrawal from territories it had occupied in 1967. Ironically, the deteriorating security situation after the Gaza disengagement, which may be seen as a variation of the prevailing consensus, reinforced this belief even further. Thus, the new consensus provided broad support—implicitly or explicitly—to the continuation of Israel's settlement project. According to the dominant Israeli version of events, the Oslo peace process, together with the unilateral withdrawal from southern Lebanon and Gaza, had given the wrong signals, presenting the country as yielding and "weak." Israelis thus came to believe that the withdrawal from the West Bank and the creation of the PA under Arafat had led to attacks with weapons that they themselves had provided; Israel's withdrawal from southern Lebanon in May 2000 prompted Hizballah to attack the country from there, and in exchange for the disengagement from the Gaza Strip, it was exposed to the firing of Qassam rockets onto its southern area. As one Israeli journalist noted in this context, "whether this reflects what really happened and why is not relevant. This is the way that the overwhelming majority of Israelis understand that reality."[7]

Perhaps even more importantly, further withdrawals from the territories came to be seen as potentially undermining Israel's security. This stands in clear contrast to the period of the Oslo process, when a majority of Israelis started to consider territorial compromise as enhancing Israel's security. From this vantage point, it is easy to see why any peace offer based on further Israeli withdrawals, including the Arab Peace Initiative of 2002, does not seem particularly appealing.

Third, regarding the broader regional context, Israel's hegemonic vision of threats and regional order entailed a reinterpretation of Middle East politics in general, and of the country's conflict with the Palestinians in particular. This process received a new impetus with the 9/11 terrorist attacks in New York and Washington, DC, which occurred almost one year after the outbreak of the Second Intifada. The attempts of the Sharon government to depict the Israeli–Palestinian conflict primarily as a fight between terrorists and the free world were also aimed at ensuring the support of the Bush administration in Washington. In fact, this specific way of portraying the conflict resonated perfectly with the world view of the neoconservative entourage of the American president.[8] And indeed, President George W. Bush gave Sharon a free hand to temporarily reoccupy most Palestinian cities and to seek to destroy the PA's infrastructure: this, according to some critics, was Sharon's prime objective all along.[9] As part of the same narrative, Israel increasingly portrayed itself as being at "the front line of the Western world in its civilizational battle with Muslim and Arab fundamentalists, obscurantist forces," as Ian Lustick describes this development.[10] Israeli foreign minister Avigdor Lieberman echoed this assessment by stressing that the Israeli–Palestinian conflict was part of a broader "clash of values between civilizations"; resolving it would therefore not be the key for bringing peace to the Middle East.[11] Indeed, if Israel was under siege by an evil alliance that engaged in terrorism and that, since it was fanatic, only understood the language of force, then a mix of deterrence and retaliation seemed the most appropriate response.

Finally, the exceptional legitimizing power of Israel's depiction of the Iranian regime as evil and irrational, together with the apocalyptic discourse tied to Jewish history, is almost self-evident.[12] An imminent and existential threat justifies the use of unconventional means—such as a strike on a country's nuclear facilities. Any collateral damage becomes, indeed, collateral.

These notions of threats and regional order went hand in hand with a growing sense of disillusionment once the Second Intifada started. An appropriate description of Israeli society in that period is that it "lost its faith in peace."[13] As one observer put it, Israelis stopped dreaming of driving their cars to Damascus to eat hummus for lunch; they were no longer interested in visiting Egypt or Jordan, and they were indifferent as to whether Jordanians or Egyptians came to visit their country.[14] The numerous terrorist attacks of the Second Intifada added anxiety and fear to the bitterness while destroying any empathy for Palestinian suffering. They also prompted the strengthening of illiberal, intolerant, and right-wing views in Israeli society.[15] Against this backdrop, the hegemonic construction of threats and regional order legitimized a deliberate show of military might at the expense of diplomacy. Israel's hegemonic vision also prescribed the idea of the absence of any alternative to the use force, especially as the country was confronting nonstate actors in an asymmetrical conflict. In this context, the consensus also postulated a profound sense of righteousness as to Israel's actions.

The country's 2006 war against Hizballah and the offensive in the Gaza Strip of 2008–9 provide two excellent examples of these legitimizing dynamics. Regarding Hizballah, in contrast to previous provocations, this time the Israeli government decided to react to the abduction of two Israeli soldiers "aggressively and harshly," as Israel's Foreign Ministry put it.[16] The strong domestic consensus on the right to self-defense against a "terrorist organization operating inside Lebanon" included broad support for the massive destruction of Lebanese civilian infrastructure beyond the southern area, presented by the Israeli government as an effective measure by which to pressure the Lebanese government to counter Hizballah.[17] Likewise, with the exception of Israel's Palestinian citizens, there was no notable domestic criticism of the high number of Lebanese casualties and the displacement of approximately one million Lebanese caused by Israel's military response.[18] A major legitimizing frame was the fact that Hizballah was seen to be operating from densely populated areas, tantamount to using civilians as human shields. Hence, according to the prevailing Israeli interpretation of events, Hizballah itself was ultimately the culprit for the killing of civilians and the damage to Lebanese infrastructure.[19]

Even as the international criticism of Israeli policies grew, the government in Jerusalem continued to present the war as a success. But with Hizballah's barrage of approximately four thousand rockets on civilian areas in northern Israel in the month-long war, the initial domestic consensus started to crumble. Significantly, however, the growing criticism did not take issue with the government's "logic of transformation through force" and the extensive collateral damage. Rather, it revolved exclusively around the lack of strategy and clearly defined objectives, and the surprisingly high level of unpreparedness of the Israeli army, which seriously undermined the country's deterrence. Israel's fact-finding Winograd Commission reached exactly these conclusions.[20]

In the eyes of most Israelis, the same notion of regional order provided legitimacy to Israel's war on Hamas in the winter of 2008–9. As in the case of Lebanon, "Operation Cast Lead" aimed at countering a terrorist organization that was viciously attacking Israel from across the border. The destruction of the "Hamas terrorist infrastructure in the Gaza Strip," as Israel's Foreign Ministry put it, to prevent the rocket fire that had deliberately targeted Israeli civilians in the preceding eight years was thus the campaign's main objective.[21] The definition of the problem in this specific way seemed to warrant massive retaliation and deterrence, not diplomacy. As former national security adviser Giora Eiland put it while addressing Hamas, "if our civilians are attacked by you, we are not going to respond in proportion but will . . . cause you such damage that you will think twice in the future."[22] Related to this was the hope that a suffering population would stop supporting Hamas—which it happened to have voted into power. Of course, as critical observers have pointed out, if Israel had wanted to protect its citizens from rockets, it could have observed or renewed the cease-fire with Hamas that was in place in the six months preceding the offensive.[23]

The question of whether terrorism can only be defeated with military means, as many counterterrorism experts maintain, is of course fiercely contested. Critics argue that the root causes of different types of terrorism must be addressed, with some of them warranting political solutions. While this is not the place to enter this debate, it should be stressed that the broad Israeli consensus around the Gaza war rested on the prevailing conviction that the country was defending itself against an evil force. As in the case of the conflict with Hizballah, this conviction explains the acceptance of the massive destruction of civilian infrastructure and the high number of civilian casualties on the other side. The belief in righteous self-defense against evil may also have nurtured the notion that

Israeli airstrikes against Hamas were carried out with "surgical precision," a claim heard repeatedly in the Israeli media during the first days of the war. And as in the case of the Lebanon war, the severe "collateral damage" was justified by the claim that the other side's fighters were cowardly hiding among civilians.[24] Hamas's firing of rockets into Israeli population centers—more than one hundred rockets were launched in the first two days of the war—only reinforced the view that Hamas was a ruthless terrorist organization that, in the final analysis, was to blame for *all* civilian casualties, including the Palestinian ones. Conversely, Israel presented its army as doing its utmost to protect Palestinian civilians from harm by such means as dropping leaflets and delivering phone messages warning of an imminent attack. As accounts of abuse of civilians committed by Israeli soldiers in the Gaza war started to emerge, Israel continued to cling to the concept of the "purity of arms" (*tohar ha-neshek*) of the Israeli Defense Forces, which, from an Israeli perspective, was and has remained a major guiding principle of the Israeli armed forces.[25] Investigations of the Israeli conduct during the Gaza war by the Israeli military advocate general resulted in military disciplinary actions against Israeli soldiers in some cases, although it concluded that there were no violations of the Law of Armed Conflict during that war.[26] The UN fact-finding mission led by Richard Goldstone came to a different conclusion in September 2009, stipulating that both Israel and Hamas were guilty of war crimes and crimes against humanity in their deliberate targeting of civilians during the operation. (In April 2011 Judge Goldstone would publicly retract this assertion regarding Israel; the three other panel members stood by the report's findings.[27])

To conclude, it is evident that the Israeli consensus on threats and regional order succeeded in justifying specific lines of policy among large parts of the population, policies that were in part morally questionable. But were these policies also effective?

Cementing the Regional Order

The question of how to confront a hostile theocratic regime with regional power ambitions does not lend itself to easy policy prescriptions. The same applies to the question of how to prevent suicide bombings and rocket attacks perpetrated by nonstate actors. While deterrence may be effective when dealing with terrorists, governments have the duty to protect their citizens, thus justifying the use of force to a certain extent. Governments, in fact, must necessarily choose between a range of bad options when confronting serious threats and hostile nonstate actors.

Keeping these complexities in mind, the following sections seek to assess whether the policies inscribed in Israel's new hegemony succeeded in addressing the threats it identified. Did Israel's response to suicide terrorism achieve its objectives? Was it successful in dealing with hostile non-state actors and the "Iranian threat?" Did Israeli policies strengthen moderate actors in the region while increasing the chances of peacemaking? The alternative is that Israeli policies were ineffective and did not change the status quo. A third option is that, *nolens volens*, the policies prescribed by Israel's hegemonic vision of threats and regional order may have empowered those very actors it aimed at weakening, cemented the existing regional order, and thus contributed to the perpetuation of conflict.

Fighting the Terrorism of the Second Intifada

The first aspect under investigation is Israel's reaction to the terror of the Second Intifada. Given that the number of suicide bombings and other attacks against Israeli civilians dropped dramatically from the mid-2000s onward, Israeli policies are generally considered as highly successful.[28] According to Israeli military analysts, several factors were crucial: first, the reoccupation of Palestinian cities in "Operation Defensive Shield" of March–April 2002 gave the Israeli army a greater space for maneuver in the territories while increasing its capacity for intelligence gathering. The reoccupation of the West Bank also established deterrence through the use of force; this included targeted killings, arrests, administrative detentions, curfews, house demolitions, and other measures. Second, the West Bank barrier is believed to have contributed to the reduction of terrorist attacks, as it constituted a physical obstacle to suicide bombers on their way to Israeli cities. Third, improved cooperation between different Israeli security services was identified as a significant factor in the dramatic reduction of suicide bombings from late 2004 and early 2005 onward.[29]

Whether the drop in the number of terrorist attacks was solely attributable to Israeli counterterrorism policies, however, has been questioned. Thus, critics raise doubts as to the efficacy of the West Bank barrier as a physical obstacle given that some parts were (and still are) under construction. Concurrently, it has been argued that the barrier's main objective was to mark the future border of Israel, as Justice Minister Tzipi Livni publicly affirmed.[30] Moreover, the prospects of Israel's disengagement from the Gaza Strip in 2005 may have acted as incentive for Hamas and other organizations to reduce the number of suicide attacks so as to not endanger the withdrawal. Finally, with Gaza sealed off, the resumption in 2006 of the US-sponsored security cooperation between the PA and Israel—denounced by Hamas as collaboration—is considered as having played a crucial role. Starting in the post-Sharon-Mofaz era (the former prime minister and his chief of staff were extremely reluctant to renew the cooperation with the PA), security experts affirm that the results of this cooperation have been impressive.[31]

Ironically, the greatly reduced level of Palestinian violence undermined the motivation of both the Israeli public and its leadership to engage in meaningful negotiations with the Palestinians, as Israeli government officials admitted off the record.[32] Moreover, according to Israeli security experts, Israel's extensive use of force during the first years of the intifada may have been plainly counterproductive in the long run. The decision of the Sharon government to define the Second Intifada as "limited armed conflict" planned and controlled by Arafat—counter to Israeli intelligence assessments—and to instruct the army to thwart it by force had two main consequences. First, it contributed to the spiraling of violence. The reaction of each side thus impacted on the reaction of the other, with the terrorist attacks triggering harsher policies by the Israeli army, which in turn led to an increase in the intensity of Palestinian violence. For instance, the targeted assassination of Abu Ali Mustafa, secretary-general of the Popular Front for the Liberation of Palestine in August 2001 led to an escalation of Palestinian violence, and Israel's killing of Fatah activist Ra'ed al-Karmi in January 2002 caused Fatah to join Hamas in employing the tactic of suicide terrorism. Conversely, the devastating Palestinian suicide attack during Passover at the Park Hotel in Netanya in March 2002 triggered Israel's partial reoccupation of Area A under "Operation Defensive Shield." In the absence of any political alternative—such as a return to the negotiating table—Israel's massive use of force in the territories thus triggered an escalation of violence and produced a prolonged conflict that both sides were unable to "win" decisively.[33]

Second, Sharon's handling of the intifada also impacted on how both sides came to see the confrontation. The Israeli government decided to define the conflict as an interstate war, which meant that the laws of war were (allegedly) applicable and that Israel's attempts to crush its enemy could be justified. Concurrently, Israel labeled the Palestinian suicide bombings, together with attacks on soldiers and armed settlers in the territories, as illegal and in fact inhuman. For the Palestinians, Israel's extensive use of force only reinforced the will to resist the onslaught of an occupying power by any possible means. Hence, Israel's growing consensus around the nature of the conflict and the appropriate policies also "shaped the security reality" on both sides, as Ephraim Lavie, former head of the Palestinian Desk in the Research Division of Israel's Military Intelligence, put it.[34] For Israelis, the Palestinian suicide bombings and the popular celebration of their "martyrs" only confirmed their perception of the other side as inherently evil. Conversely, Israel's hard-line response and the growing number of Palestinian casualties contributed to the prestige of those organizations that were able to "successfully" carry out suicide attacks, most notably Hamas and Islamic Jihad. They were subsequently joined by the al-Aqsa Martyrs' Brigades and the Tanzim under the leadership of Fatah's young guard. The numbers of Palestinian volunteers seeking to take part in such missions rose significantly in those years. The suicide attacks thus led to the "creation of new myths in which the suicide bombers—seen as sacrificing their personal good for the general welfare—became heroes. With it, terrorist organizations were seen as greatly powerful, with the proven ability to challenge Israel and cause it severe damage."[35]

Taken together with the Palestinian discontent with the corrupt and ineffective PA dominated by Fatah's old guard, in hindsight it is easy to see how Israeli policies unintentionally contributed to Hamas's growing strength and appeal. Indeed, the organization would win the Palestinian elections in January 2006. The growing popularity of Fatah's young guard under the leadership of Marwan Barghouti and the growing loss of legitimacy of the PA under Arafat in those years—with the Israeli army confining the Palestinian leader to his headquarters from 2002 onward—can also be explained in these terms.[36] These dynamics are in fact typical of asymmetrical wars, with the growing cycle of violence generally strengthening the domestic legitimacy of the nonstate actor that is perpetrating the attacks.

Confronting Nonstate Actors

A second aspect of the potentially counterproductive impact of Israel's hegemonic vision of regional foreign policy concerns Israel's attempt to confront Hamas and Hizballah, which it defined as "terrorist organizations acting as semi-states."[37] In asymmetrical wars, states usually face a real dilemma. On the one hand, they are often provoked to respond by the generally weaker party. But as asymmetrical wars are usually fought in population centers, responses tend to cause a high number of civilian casualties, thus damaging the state's international legitimacy. As Janice Gross Stein puts it, the "purpose of asymmetrical war is often to delegitimize

the other, to force it to behave in ways that are generally considered illegitimate and less than fully human."[38] While international law is not
sufficiently developed to deal with this type of conflict, nonaction, on the
other hand, undermines the domestic legitimacy of the government. In
addition, nonaction makes the stronger side look "weak." In its forceful
reaction to the Second Intifada, Israel clearly fell into this trap.

As for the other side, Hamas continued to consider itself as a legitimate
resistance movement against the ongoing Israeli occupation of Palestinian
territory. Boycotted by the United States, the European Union, Canada,
Japan, and (obviously) Israel after the 2006 elections because it refused to
recognize the latter, renounce violence, and abide by previous agreements
after its electoral victory, Hamas viewed itself as the legitimate and dem-
ocratically elected representative of the Palestinian people. According to
the organization, the suicide attacks were as much a legitimate form of
armed resistance against the persistent Israeli occupation of Palestinian
territory as the launching of rockets on southern Israel from the Gaza
Strip, both before and after Israel's disengagement of 2005. For Hamas
and the Palestinians at large—as for most international lawyers—Israel's
occupation of Gaza did not end with the withdrawal of its soldiers and
settlers, given that the country continued to control Gaza's airspace, wa-
terways, and, together with Egypt, its borders.

While defining the Hamas-ruled Gaza Strip as "enemy entity" and
affirming the end of Israel's occupation, a large majority of Israelis supported the official strategic objective to overturn, or at least to weaken,
Hamas's control over the Gaza Strip in order to prevent rocket fire. There
was an additional broad agreement that Israel should work to prevent the
international community from changing its conditions for dealing with
Hamas.[39] These objectives seemed to justify Israel's economic blockade
of Gaza, imposed shortly after Hamas took over the strip in the summer
of 2007. The same objectives also motivated Israel's attack on the Gaza
Strip in 2008–9, after a previous Egyptian-mediated cease-fire had collapsed. As mentioned earlier, the question of who infringed the accord is
disputed, with both sides accusing each other of violations and bad faith.[40]

However, both the blockade and the three-week-long battle in the
winter of 2008–9 may have unintentionally contributed to the strengthening of Hamas. In the Gaza war, Israel may well have demonstrated its
deterrence capability while ensuring a notable reduction in the rocket
fire after the war.[41] Thus, Israel clearly won a tactical victory. However, it
paid a heavy prize for it: on the one hand, at the international level Israel
fell into the "legitimacy trap which makes asymmetric warfare so treacher-

ous for the state," as Gross Stein put it.[42] Moreover, with 1.5 million people crammed into a tiny enclave of 360 square kilometers, and considering the high toll of Palestinian casualties and massive levels of destruction, Israel's operations in the Gaza Strip fueled anti-Israeli sentiments across the Middle East and beyond. Thus, Israel's war on Hamas contributed to the strengthening of radical regimes and states while undermining the moderate ones. More importantly, however, reflecting the dynamics described earlier, the appeal and legitimacy of Hamas among the Palestinian population only increased. Thus, polls conducted after the war show that almost half of the polled Palestinians (46.7 percent) claimed that Hamas had won the war, with the popularity of the latter soaring, especially in the West Bank.[43] While one poll found that Israel's war on Gaza contributed to a growing support for military action against Israel, immediately after the war Palestinians also expressed their satisfaction with radical actors, such as Iran and Hizballah, to the detriment of more moderate factions, such as Fatah.[44] For example, according to a poll conducted by the Jerusalem Media and Communication Center in January 2009, when asked about their preferences if Palestinian Legislative Council elections were to be held that day, the percentage of those who said they would vote for Hamas rose to 28.6 percent, compared with 19.3 percent according to a poll conducted by the same polling institute nearly a year earlier, in April 2008. The popularity of Fatah declined from 34 percent in April 2008 to 27.9 percent in the January 2009 poll. Similarly, the percentage of respondents who believed that locally made rockets helped achieve the Palestinian national goals rose from 39.3 percent in April 2008 to a whopping 50.8 percent in the poll of January 2009.[45]

Concurrently, according to most analysts, Israel had not succeeded in destroying Hamas's capacity for manufacturing mortars and rockets, nor its ability to secure supplies or ammunition.[46] Thus, in spite of tactical achievements, a stable security situation at Israel's southern border was not established without the necessity of negotiating with Hamas. While this is exactly what Israel wanted to avoid, the long-term sustainability of Israel's forceful approach thus remained more than questionable.[47]

Israel's economic blockade of Gaza presents an even more problematic picture. The economic siege, it is worth remembering, had a twofold objective: first, to weaken Hamas and prompt Gaza Palestinians to turn against the movement, and, second, to achieve the release of abducted Israeli soldier Gilad Shalit. However, the blockade did not achieve its objectives; it even had the opposite effect. The economic siege of Gaza led to the emergence of a thriving black market, with goods being smuggled through a network of tunnels connecting the Gaza Strip with Egypt. Trade through these over more than one thousand tunnels—some of them wide enough to let cars and cows go through—was controlled and taxed by Hamas. As John Ging, former director of the UN Relief and Works Agency for Palestine Refugees in the Near East (UNRWA) operations in Gaza, noted, the irony was that almost every commodity was available in Gaza after Israel imposed the blockade; however, most Gazans did not have the money to buy them. Those who could afford these goods were part of the new economic elite, those who controlled and profited from Gaza's tunnel economy—namely, Hamas and its supporters.[48] Thus, Israel's siege of Gaza, illegal under international law, made Hamas and its supporters only richer and more powerful.

As for the second objective, the blockade did not prompt Hamas to free abducted soldier Shalit. He was released in October 2011 after more than five years in captivity in exchange for Israel's release of 1,027 Palestinian prisoners. Once again, the prisoner swap had to be negotiated with Hamas. Needless to say, this measure further contributed to the popularity of the Palestinian organization, particularly since the Israeli government had not heeded Mahmoud Abbas's repeated requests to free a far lower number of Palestinians as a confidence-building measure.

At the same time, the Gaza blockade had devastating socioeconomic effects on ordinary Gaza Palestinians. While Israel made sure to let enough food aid into Gaza to prevent a full-fledged hunger crisis, poverty and malnutrition increased considerably among Gaza's 1.5 million inhabitants. According to Ging, eight hundred thousand people in Gaza depended on UN food aid in 2010, while the number of persons living in destitution—that is, absolute poverty—doubled from one hundred thousand to two hundred thousand after Israel imposed the economic siege on Gaza.[49] The blockade also affected UNRWA, which was unable to build schools and other infrastructure in the refugee camps because of the Israeli ban on importing cement to Gaza. The economic crisis also meant that the majority of factories were closed, with unemployment rising to over 70 percent of the workforce. Contacts between Gazans and Israelis (many Gaza Palestinians used to work in Israel or had business contacts) were completely cut off. Thus, Palestinian children in Gaza were (and still are) growing up without having ever met an Israeli—except for Israeli soldiers in war situations. These same children are also being constantly exposed to extremist propaganda by the Hamas leadership. This state of affairs provides a perfect breeding ground for more extremism in the future.

Israeli policies toward the Lebanese Hizballah may have been similarly counterproductive. However, as in the case of Hamas, the picture contains several shades of gray. While Hizballah emerged largely as a result of Israel's occupation of Lebanon in the 1980s and 1990s, the repeated rocket fire on northern Israel over the years undoubtedly exerted pressure on the government in Jerusalem to protect its citizens. It also highlighted Hizballah's claim as to rightfully resisting the Israeli occupation of Lebanese territory. Unsurprisingly, the firing of Katyusha rockets also boosted the organization's popularity, particularly among the relatively poor and underprivileged Shi'a population in Lebanon's south, Hizballah's main power base. However, Israel's self-declared security zone in southern Lebanon, the attempts to fight Hizballah there with the help of the South Lebanese Army (SLA) proxy, and the recurrent Israeli reprisals in the form of air campaigns did not achieve the declared objectives: the rocket fire continued and Hizballah remained highly popular. Conversely, the relatively high number of Israeli soldiers killed and injured in southern Lebanon started to foment a growing domestic opposition. Altogether, we may assume that Israel's presence in southern Lebanon "fed Lebanese radicalism," as Augustus Richard Norton has put it.[50]

Ehud Barak's decision to withdraw from the security zone in 2000 certainly responded to the popular will in Israel. But it had a number of adverse implications. First, following Barak's failed attempt to reach a peace agreement with Syria, and reflecting the emerging Israeli mind-set that there was no one to talk to, the withdrawal was unilateral. While it caught the SLA, until then Israel's major ally in southern Lebanon, completely by surprise, the Israeli withdrawal lacked any coordination or agreement with Hizballah's then-patron Syria, or Hizballah itself.[51] Thus, Hizballah was not compelled to affirm an end to all territorial claims (and of course it would not), and it would not be bound to any restraint in the future. And indeed, although Hizballah reacted with a surprising degree of discipline to Israel's withdrawal, the organization would soon start preparing for war by stockpiling weapons, building protected rocket launchers, erecting bunkers, training personnel, and collecting information on Israeli troop movements.[52] Second, the unilateral withdrawal constituted an enormous boost for Hizballah's popularity. In the Lebanese elections following the Israeli withdrawal, all the candidates fielded by Hizballah won, and the organization succeeded in increasing its representation in the Lebanese parliament by two seats, from nine to eleven. Significantly, the withdrawal transformed Hizballah leader Hassan Nasrallah into a hero not only in Lebanon but among the Palestinians too.[53] The message he promoted was clear: it was the organization's continued "armed resistance" that eventually prompted the Israelis to run away overnight; moderation and negotiations were useless.

In the following years Hizballah would continue to provoke Israel through repeated border incidents, rocket firing, and the occasional abduction of Israeli soldiers. Israel responded with air raids, hitting Hizballah targets, but also with the release of Lebanese prisoners. Israel's forceful response to the abduction of two Israeli soldiers in the summer of 2006, which led to the Israel–Hizballah war, was predominantly aimed at reestablishing Israeli deterrence. Together with his notorious statement that, if the two Israeli soldiers were not returned, Israel would "turn Lebanon's clock back 20 years," Chief of Staff Dan Halutz also advocated attacking infrastructure beyond southern Lebanon "to pressure the Lebanese government to counter Hezbollah."[54] While fully resonating with Israel's dominant conception of regional order post-Oslo, these policies nevertheless proved to be largely counterproductive. As mentioned previously, Hizballah remained in good shape until the last day of the war, as demonstrated by its continued launching of rockets on northern Israel. Moreover, Israel's conduct of the war seriously compromised the country's deterrence capacity.[55] And the abducted Israeli soldiers remained in captivity. Their bodies would only be released two years later in a prisoner swap, in exchange for four Hizballah prisoners and Samir Kuntar, a Palestinian sentenced to four life sentences by an Israeli court for his involvement in the kidnapping of an Israeli family in Nahariya that had resulted in the death of four Israelis, including a four year old girl.[56] As in the case of Israel's war on Hamas, the massive destruction of Lebanese infrastructure and the human costs on the Lebanese side prompted international criticism of Israeli actions and undermined moderate forces in the region. Of course, due to the internal fragmentation and strong polarization of Lebanese politics, the voices of Hizballah's opponents, blaming the organization for the war and for the destruction, also grew louder. Although it remains questionable whether an organization such as Hizballah can be deterred in the long term, it is clear that in Arab public opinion, Hizballah emerged as the clear victor of the 2006 war.

Israel's Strategy Toward Fatah and the PA

A final aspect to be assessed is the success of Israel's strategy toward the Fatah-dominated PA. Israel's course of action initially involved Ariel Sharon's attempts to crush it, particularly as long as Arafat was alive, followed by a period of seeking to plainly ignore it after Mahmoud Abbas (Abu Mazen) succeeded Arafat as PA chairman. Sharon's unilateral disengagement from Gaza and four West Bank settlements (*hitnatkut*) in 2005 and the so-called convergence plan (*hitkansut*) initially adopted by his successor, Ehud Olmert, must be put into this context.[57] Both the Gaza withdrawal and Olmert's plan to disengage from parts of the West Bank—while annexing the rest and incorporating most Israeli settlements into Israel— expressed the belief in unilateral action and defensible borders. They also kept a maximum of Israeli settlers in place. While the "convergence" plan was abandoned when Hamas won the Palestinian elections in 2006, Israel's strategy subsequently shifted to attempts at co-opting the PA in the fight against Hamas. In the context of the Annapolis process, which started in 2007, Israel started to insist that the Palestinians fulfill their security obligations and prevent the consolidation of Hamas in the West Bank.[58] In 2007–8 there would also be a renewal of negotiations, which was an exception of sorts to the dominant narrative, as discussed in the previous chapter. In light of the decrease in suicide bombings within the Green Line, Israel's co-opting strategy seemed successful.

However, considering Israel's refusal to resume negotiations during much of the decade and the lack of progress during the Olmert-Abbas talks in 2007–8, the PA's security cooperation with Israel undermined the public standing of the PA and Fatah. Indeed, prior to the withdrawal, the PA had sent Fatah spokesperson Hussam Zomlut to Gaza as main coordinator for the disengagement. As Zomlut put it, the PA was sure that the Israelis would call to coordinate the withdrawal. But the phone call never came.[59] Thus, mirrored by the simultaneous strengthening of Hamas, Israel's unilateral withdrawal from the Gaza Strip in 2005 further added to the dwindling legitimacy of Abu Mazen and his entourage. Repeated Israeli negotiations with Hamas over cease-fires and the release of Shalit in exchange for over one thousand Palestinian prisoners also contributed to the popularity of Hamas at the expense of Fatah and the PA.

In this context, it is important to mention Israel's continuous settlement expansion in the territories. During the Oslo years, the number of Israeli settlers had actually doubled. After Oslo's collapse, the settlement expansion continued, with Israel considerably tightening its grip over the territories and its people. To a large extent, the entrenchment of Israeli control and the growing limitation on the movement of ordinary Palestinians was a consequence of the Oslo Accords and of the failure to reach a final-status agreement. Indeed, the Oslo Accords had divided the territories into different areas of "sovereignty," with Israel erecting numerous roadblocks and other obstacles between these areas as part of its counterterrorism strategy. When Oslo collapsed, only 18 percent of the West Bank was under the exclusive administrative control of the PA (Area

A), mainly comprising Palestinian cities; 61 percent of the West Bank (Area C) remained under full Israeli civilian and security control; and the remaining 21 percent of the West Bank (Area B) was under Palestinian civil control and joint Israeli Palestinian security control. However, Israeli military rule remained the highest authority in all of the territories. Until today, this situation has remained unchanged while Israeli settlement construction has continued unabated in all these years. As of January 2016, there are over 125 Israeli settlements in the West Bank and approximately 100 "settlement outposts" located throughout the West Bank, in addition to 12 large settlement neighborhoods in Arab East Jerusalem. Over 540,000 Israeli settlers live in these settlements.[60]

Hence, for many Palestinians, the Fatah-dominated PA acted as Israel's "security contractor" while proving to be unable to significantly ameliorate their living conditions, let alone achieve an end to Israel's occupation. As Lavie notes, such a process was likely to enhance the relevance of Hamas as a political alternative while possibly also generating a shared interest between Fatah and Hamas to "pool their efforts and cooperate against Israel."[61]

However, with the Palestine Papers highlighting Mahmoud Abbas's readiness to compromise on a number of crucial issues, most notably Jerusalem and the question of refugees, in the long term Israel's strategy toward Fatah and the PA was clearly counterproductive.[62] The documents on the secret negotiations between Abu Mazen and Olmert in 2007–8 and the renewal of PA–Israeli security cooperation demonstrate that Israel had a partner in the PA chairman. Israeli policies, however, were constantly undermining Abbas—the same Abbas whom the Israeli government had wanted as successor after Arafat died in 2004. The more recent statements, mentioned above, of individual Israeli politicians, most notably Olmert himself, on Abbas's credibility as a partner for peace only add to this assessment.[63]

On the other hand, if the objective of Israeli governments was to refrain from meaningful territorial compromise in the context of a peace agreement, then Israel's strategy was highly successful. In fact, Israel succeeded in reducing the number of terrorist attacks within the Green Line, achieving a relative quiet in the West Bank, and setting the conditions for the continuation of the settlement project without being exposed to major international pressure. In any event, what is evident is that Israel's hegemonic vision of threats and regional order, together with the policies it prescribed, did not seek to honestly resolve the conflict with the Palestinians or to cultivate Abbas as a "partner for peace." Quite the contrary.

Confronting Iran's Nuclear Ambitions

How can we assess Israel's policy toward Iran? Again, it is extremely difficult to gauge the effectiveness of strategies to prevent states from going nuclear. Israel also faces a real dilemma in how to react to Tehran's extremely hostile posture.[64] However, a few points are worth noting. First, although the Israeli government did not succeed in persuading the US administrations under George W. Bush and Barack Obama to launch a strike against Iranian nuclear sites, Israel's constant lobbying efforts and apocalyptic rhetoric succeeded in drawing international attention to the Iranian nuclear issue. In spite of the repeated warnings by both US administrations to Netanyahu not to engage in any unilateral action, it is fair to assume that Israeli policies exerted influence on Washington and the broader international community to step up the pressure on Tehran and impose economic sanctions.

Second, Israel's bellicose stance toward Tehran, which included repeated threats to attack a sovereign country, echoed Ahmadinejad's despicable rhetoric in a surreal way, without, however, convincing the Iranian people of their regime's evil intentions. Quite the opposite: although Ahmadinejad was reportedly unpopular among the Iranian urban middle class and intelligentsia, a majority of Iranians defended the country's right to a nuclear program. These included the reformist candidate Mir Hossein Mousavi, who challenged Ahmadinejad in the 2009 Iranian presidential elections.[65] In light of the constant Israeli verbal confrontation, the rally-around-the-flag effect was thus, perhaps unsurprisingly, also observable in Iran.

Third, as we have seen, the Israeli strategy vis-à-vis Tehran under Netanyahu succeeded in diverting international and domestic attention away from the Palestinian issue. Indeed, at the end of the 2000s, the Iranian nuclear issue was the top priority in discussions between the government in Jerusalem and US administrations, with Israeli–Palestinian peacemaking ranking extremely low, if at all. The same list of priorities was reflected in Israel's foreign policy discourse at the domestic level, as explained earlier. Hence, particularly after the Gaza war, the attention paid to Iran and its allies was at the expense of any serious attempt to resolve Israel's conflict with the Palestinians. Concurrently, Netanyahu's outspoken hostility to US president Barack Obama's policy toward Iran contributed to a major dispute with Washington, the major guarantor of Israel's security. Altogether, the new foreign policy consensus on Iran may thus have had a negative impact on Israel's security in the medium and long term.

Looking beyond the domestic legitimization of Israel's policies toward the region, how did the new consensus impact on Israel's international standing more generally? To what extent did the international community follow the taken-for-granted justifications for specific lines of policies that prevailed in Israel?

Israel and the International Community

The new hegemony that increasingly took hold of the Israeli polity after Oslo is internally logical and coherent, as we have seen. However, over the last decade many actions of the Israeli government and of the army have been met with a rapidly shrinking degree of international sympathy and understanding. The heavy civilian death toll in Israel's war on Gaza in 2008–9, in particular, prompted a public outcry in Arab and Muslim majority states as well as in the wider international community. The more recent US–Israeli disagreement on the Iranian nuclear issue also suggests that Israel's new foreign policy consensus is not necessarily intelligible to the "outside world." In general, Israeli policies have increasingly clashed with the growing international consensus over the unlawfulness and illegitimacy of Israel's military rule over the Palestinian territories, as revealed in a recent report by Molad, an Israeli think tank cofounded by Avraham Burg, a former Labor member of Knesset (MK) and speaker of the Knesset.[66] Even more significantly, while pronounced criticism of Israeli policies had traditionally been voiced by Arab and some Western media as well as many academics and nongovernmental organizations (NGO), Western governments that had usually showed understanding for Israel's security concerns now adopted increasingly critical positions. Certainly, with its traditionally sympathetic view of Israel, the US may still be an exception. Even here, though, signs of divergence are discernible, as discussed in the following.

The US and the Israeli Consensus

During most of the 2000s, US administrations by and large shared Israel's hegemonic vision of threats and regional order post-Oslo, with President Clinton playing a significant role in the peacemaking efforts in the late 1990s. Indeed, when the intifada broke out at the end of 2000, Clinton initially sought to push all parties to end the violence through diplomacy and established a fact-finding commission led by former US senator George Mitchell. In December of the same year, he presented the so-called Clinton Parameters in a last-minute effort to resolve the Israeli–Palestinian conflict.

Significantly, President Clinton publicly blamed Arafat as the main culprit for the failure of Camp David, thus resonating with Ehud Barak's "no partner for peace" explanation. The memoirs of Dennis Ross, the American diplomat who held key positions on the Middle East in subsequent US administrations during and after Oslo, reveal that he also espoused Barak's interpretation of events.[67] Although Ross was criticized for his deference to Israeli government positions (even by some of his former colleagues[68]), his rather one-sided account of the peace talks and their failure contributed to the dissemination of one specific account of events in US circles and beyond.

Under the presidency of George W. Bush, Israeli policies by and large enjoyed full support. True, in his effort to gain support among Arab states for his war against al-Qaeda after 9/11, Bush was in 2001 the first American president to publicly call for the establishment of an independent Palestinian state. Yet, Israel's fight against Palestinian suicide attacks also resonated with Bush's declared "war on terror" after 9/11. Thus, the pro-Israel philosophy of some of the president's influential neoconservative advisers meant that the government in Jerusalem enjoyed a relatively free hand in its attempts to crush the intifada in the territories.[69] Bush clearly saw Arafat's support for terrorism as the main problem, a position that was well in line with Israel's dominant discourse. Israel's capture of the vessel *Karine A* in January 2002—with fifty tons of weapons, most probably destined for Arafat's PA—seemed to further confirm this position. Accordingly, influenced—by his own admission—by the book *The Case for Democracy* by former Soviet dissident Natan Sharansky, who had become an influential politician in the Israeli government, Bush developed his "freedom agenda."[70] He called for a new Palestinian leadership and pushed for democratic elections in the Palestinian territories. As is well known, however, after Hamas won these elections in 2006—the US had not objected to Hamas's participation in the elections as "List of Change and Reform"—the Bush administration once more aligned itself with Israel in boycotting Hamas until it recognized Israel, renounced violence, and recognized the Oslo Accords. It is interesting to note here that in a 2006 letter to President Bush, Hamas had proposed to accept a Palestinian state within the 1967 borders and offered Israel a truce for many years.[71] However, Hamas's offer did not impress the US administration: Washington did not oppose Israel's economic blockade of the strip after the Hamas takeover, and it acquiesced with Israel's war on the Palestinian organization in 2008–9.

The Bush administration also shared the Israeli vision of regional order. On the Lebanon war, the US initially opposed the implementation of a cease-fire as this would have comprised a return to the *status quo ante*. Most memorably, Secretary of State Condoleezza Rice defined the violence in Lebanon as the "birth pangs of a New Middle East."[72] Regarding Iran, the Bush government identified, at least rhetorically, with Israel's hegemonic vision as well, with a number of top-ranking members of the administration strongly voicing their support for an attack on Iran's nuclear facilities. Bush, however, refrained from giving in to the pressure.

The Obama administration initially showed far less understanding for Israel's dominant notion of threats and regional order. Obama's speech at Cairo University in June 2009, in which he promised to mend relations between the United States and the so-called Muslim world, is a case in point. Similarly, in 2009–10 the American president demanded a ten-month settlement freeze from the Israeli government while he sought to reignite Israeli–Palestinian peace negotiations. On the Iranian issue, President Obama has been even more unsympathetic to Israeli requests to strike Iran, causing quite some disharmony in US–Israeli relations. Although in the final analysis, the Obama administration by and large acquiesced with Israel's hegemonic worldview and the resulting policies, toward the end of the 2000s the official identification of the US government with Israeli positions started to show some cracks.[73] Thus, a number of high-ranking US officials publicly criticized both Israeli policies and Washington's blind support for the latter. These critics included David Petraeus, former chief of the US Central Command and former CIA chief; former US secretary of defense and CIA director Leon Panetta; and Sen. Chuck Hagel (R-NE), who replaced Panetta as secretary of defense in 2013.[74] Their criticism somewhat echoed the argument put forward in *The Israel Lobby*, the 2007 book written by US Ivy League scholars Stephen Walt and John Mearsheimer.[75] Perhaps unsurprisingly, the book was the object of many diatribes, mainly by representatives of that same (alleged) lobby. Concurrently, Netanyahu's increasing confrontation with the Obama administration prompted former Mossad director Meir Dagan to declare that Israel was gradually turning into a burden on the United States.[76]

The growing rift between the US and Israel would also become visible with Secretary of State John Kerry publicly blaming Israel for the collapse of Israeli–Palestinian peace talks in early 2014.[77] A few months later Washington would not condemn outright the emerging reconciliation between Fatah and Hamas, or the formation of a unity government, very much in contrast to Netanyahu's position—and expectation. Instead, while still expressing concern about Hamas's role in the new Palestinian government, the US administration said it would work with it while watching closely to see whether the new government would uphold the principles of renouncing violence, abide by existing agreements, and recognize Israel.[78] Bilateral relations would reach a low point with Netanyahu's visit to DC in March 2015, where he addressed Congress, warning against the nuclear talks that the Obama administration was conducting with Iran. Orchestrated by Republican Speaker of the House John Boehner without coordinating with the White House, the visit caused outrage among Obama's inner circle and angered a large number of legislators from the Democratic Party (and some Republicans as well).[79]

At the level of public opinion, American support for Israel remained strong. According to a 2007 Pew survey taken in a sample of over forty states worldwide, the public that sympathized most with Israel was, by far, that of the United States. According to the poll, about 60 percent of American respondents sympathized with Israel—as compared to 13 percent who expressed their sympathy for the Palestinians.[80]

However, there are clear indications that support for Israel among the US public has slowly been declining while it has also become less unconditional. First, over the last ten to fifteen years, US public support for Israel has increasingly taken a bipartisan dimension, with US citizens associated with the Democratic Party being increasingly critical of Israel.[81] Second, criticism of Israel's dominant vision of threats and regional order has also emerged from within the American Jewish community, as indicated by the founding of the left-of-center pro-Israel lobbying group J Street in 2008.[82] Challenging the far more powerful American Israel Public Affairs Committee (AIPAC), which supports Israel's right-wing policies and its justifications, J Street, Americans for Peace Now, and Meretz USA, among others, support the resumption of negotiations with the Palestinians in defiance of the "no partner for peace" narrative. These groups are also in favor of the establishment of a Palestinian state while specifically backing a proactive US role in bringing these objectives about. Finally, there is a clear trend among younger, secular, and liberal Jewish Americans to not identify with the persistent Israeli occupation of Palestinian territories, as Peter Beinart has pointed out.[83] Hence, they are also less likely to unconditionally accept Israel's new hegemony regarding the country's regional foreign policy.

Europe and the EU

A very different picture emerges on the European continent. It is worth noting here that economic relations between Israel and the European Union are well-developed; the EU and its member states are also the largest international donors to the Palestinians. After the collapse of the Oslo process, growing tensions characterized the official relations between Israel on the one hand and the EU and its member states on the other.[84] For instance, the Conclusions of the Council of the EU, for which the unanimity of the member states is required, regularly denounced Israel's harsh military response to the Palestinian intifada in the early 2000s. In particular, Brussels criticized the curfews, closures, extrajudicial killings, house demolitions, administrative detentions, destruction of infrastructure (which the EU had partly financed), and Israel's partial reoccupation of the West Bank from 2002 onward. It also consistently called for an end to the violence, for respect for human rights, and for the resumption of peace negotiations. Israel's 2003 decision to treat Yasser Arafat as "irrelevant" and to confine him to his Muqata headquarters also contrasted with the official position of the EU, which continued to maintain that Arafat was the elected leader of the Palestinian people. Accordingly, European officials continued to pay visits to the Palestinian *ra'is*, much to Israel's annoyance.[85] Furthermore, during much of the 2000–2010 decade Brussels continuously stressed the illegality of settlement expansion and the need for a two-state solution.[86] While this European criticism mainly drew on the heavy "collateral" damage of Israel's counterterrorism policies, for many Israelis, and certainly for Israeli governments, the EU's position at the height of the intifada only seemed to confirm that "the Europeans" lived on a different planet, at best, and that they were biased, at worst.

There was a moment of truce in EU–Israeli relations after Israel withdrew its soldiers and settlers from Gaza in 2005. As the withdrawal seemed to signify a resumption of Israeli–Palestinian peacemaking—erroneously, as it turned out—the EU offered financial aid and sent a border mission to the only crossing between Gaza and Egypt at Rafah. The border mission involved supervision by (unarmed) border guards from EU member states of the implementation of border procedures and practices to which Israel and the PA had previously agreed.[87] The victory of Hamas in the 2006 Palestinian elections also brought Israel and the EU closer, as Brussels joined the boycott of the Hamas-led government until it accepted the famous three conditions. However, the 2008–9 war on Hamas clearly signaled that the EU and its member states did not share Israel's hegemonic vision of threats and regional order, with Brussels demanding a lifting of the Israeli blockade on humanitarian aid.[88] The EU also stated that it would closely follow investigations into alleged violations of international humanitarian law during the war in light of Israel's reluctance to investigate the matter swiftly.[89] High-ranking Israeli soldiers and politicians were also facing the possibility of being indicted for war crimes upon entry into some EU member states, notably the United Kingdom. Altogether, the EU and its member states remained extremely critical of the delay in resuming peace talks as well as of the continuation of Israel's settlement project and the continuous human rights violations in the Palestinian territories. Growing criticism of the construction in the settlements has also been voiced by the one EU member state that has traditionally been most supportive of Israel—namely, Germany.[90]

The EU and single European governments also took a rather critical position toward Israel's conduct in the 2006 Lebanon war. On the one hand, the EU and its member states asserted Israel's right to defend itself and condemned Hizballah's abduction of Israeli soldiers. On the other hand, Finland, who held the rotating EU presidency at that time, expressed concern about the "disproportionate use of force by Israel in Lebanon in response to attacks by Hezbollah on Israel."[91] The Finnish government also defined Israel's air and sea blockade on Lebanon as unjustified. Concurrently, France condemned Israel's bombardment of Beirut airport as a "disproportionate act of war."[92] Although the official position of the EU refrained from such statements—calling for a cease-fire and offering humanitarian assistance instead[93]—the European reaction clearly points to a growing gap between the two sides in their perceptions of reality during much of the 2000s.

European publics were even more critical—and by far—than their governments. An EU poll carried out in October 2003 among 7,500 citizens of the EU's then fifteen member states, defined Israel as the top threat to world peace, ahead of North Korea, Afghanistan, and Iran.[94] The poll, which was accessible on the internet only for a very brief period, presented respondents with a list of fifteen countries with the request to indicate which of them represented a threat to world peace: a staggering 59 percent of respondents picked Israel. Causing an outcry on the Israeli side, the fact that the poll was taken at the height of the Second Intifada is relevant, seeming to indicate a widespread European disapproval of the policies the Sharon government put in place to crush the Palestinian uprising.

The results of surveys taken among European publics in the following years were less extreme (not least because that specific question was never asked again). However, they still illustrated a growing lack of apprehension of Israel's predominant vision of threats and regional order. At the same time, EU citizens tended to increasingly question Israel's willingness and genuine commitment to peacemaking. Thus, the 2007 Pew Global

Attitude Survey, mentioned earlier, evidenced an extremely low percentage of European citizens sympathetic to Israel. Asked about the side
with which they sympathized more, Israel or the Palestinians, favorable
attitudes toward Israel were relatively high in the Czech Republic, with
37 percent of Czech respondents favoring Israel.[95] Only 34 percent of
German respondents, 32 percent of French, and 31 percent of Slovaks
favored Israel. Interestingly, 21 percent of Germans favored the Palestinians, 3 percent of respondents expressed their sympathy for both sides,
and an astounding 34 percent of polled Germans responded that they
favored neither side. In the case of French respondents, 43 percent were in
favor of the Palestinians, 4 percent favored "both," and 16 percent "neither
side."[96] In the same poll, only 18 percent of Swedes and 16 percent of Britons expressed their sympathy for Israel.[97] In Spain, Italy, and Poland, the
percentage of respondents that favored Israel was even lower—11 percent
in Spain and only 9 percent in both Italy and Poland. These countries had
an exceptionally high percentage of respondents who said they sympathized with neither side, comprising 34 percent of Spanish respondents,
48 percent of Polish interviewees, and a staggering 50 percent of polled
Italians.[98] It should be noted that the survey was taken between May and
April 2007—that is, before the 2008–9 Gaza war, which would further
affect European public opinion, to Israel's disadvantage.

Similarly, the *Mavi Marmara* incident in May 2010, in which the Israeli
navy stormed the flagship of a flotilla of vessels crewed by pro-Palestinian
activists in defiance of the Israeli blockade of the Gaza Strip, had a decisively negative effect on European attitudes toward Israel. The Israeli
government had claimed that the organizers of the flotilla, a Turkish humanitarian group, were channeling funds and weapons to Hamas and had
links to al-Qaeda. Israeli naval commandos, who had boarded the ships in
an effort to force them to the Israeli port of Ashdod for inspection, also
claimed that they had fallen prey to a planned and vicious ambush on the
ships. Yet the Israeli show of force, which left nine Turkish activists dead
and more than fifty wounded, prompted outrage in Europe and beyond.[99]
For the Israeli public, on the other hand, the international outcry was incomprehensible in light of the (alleged) ambush of Israeli forces that had
happened on the ships.[100] Much to Israel's satisfaction, a UN report in the
fall of 2010 would find that Israel's naval blockade of Gaza was legal under
international law. The report, however, also defined the way Israeli forces
had boarded the vessels as excessive and unreasonable.[101]

The growing gap between Israel's new consensus and European public
opinion was further evidenced in repeated attempts by British higher ed-

ucation associations to adopt a motion to boycott Israeli academia during much of the 2000s, together with the growing hold of the Boycott, Divestment, and Sanctions (BDS) movement in European countries. Generally, there is no doubt that European academics and public intellectuals were far more outspoken in challenging Israel's hegemonic vision of threats and regional order than their counterparts in the United States.

A Growing International Isolation

While a majority of Israelis continued to stand united behind government policies and their justifications, Israel found itself increasingly isolated at the international level. Indeed, with the exception of the United States, Israel's foreign policy consensus and the resulting policies met with little international understanding. Thus, in that period, Israel's relations with former strategic Middle Eastern ally Turkey deteriorated to an unprecedented level. This development must be seen in the context of a reorientation of Turkish foreign policy under Recep Tayyip Erdoğan toward a predominantly Arab Middle East. But it can also be linked to the *Mavi Marmara* incident and Israel's initial refusal to apologize for the death of nine Turkish activists. Moreover, in spite of continuing economic and military relations, Israel's diplomatic ties with China, India, and South Korea did not improve, and its relations with Latin America and Africa did not fare much better.[102]

The UN General Assembly, although responsible for Israel's creation in the first place, may perhaps not be a particularly valid indicator of Israel's international status given that Israel is traditionally not very popular in this forum.[103] However, voting patterns in the UN Security Council and the support and the wording of resolutions critical of Israel point to Israel's growing international isolation. Between 2000 and 2009, nine UN Security Council Resolutions (UNSCR) sharply condemning different aspects of Israeli policies in the territories, or with regard to the 2006 Lebanon war, would have been adopted by the majority of its fifteen permanent and nonpermanent members had they not been vetoed by the United States. Another half dozen UNSCRs calling on Israel, as the occupying power in the territories under the Fourth Geneva Convention, to abide by its legal obligations did pass—generally following the abstention of the United States. One of these, UNSCR 1544, was adopted in 2004 and called on Israel to abide scrupulously by its legal obligations and to address its security needs within the boundaries of international law.[104] In comparison, in the 1990s the UN Security Council adopted eight resolutions that criticized Israel's behavior in the territories (including East Jerusalem) or regarding the deportation of Palestinians to Lebanon. In that period the US vetoed another four UNSRs critical of Israel's behavior in the territories. The increase in UNSCRs critical of Israel may only be gradual. However, it is significant that a draft resolution of February 2011, which would have condemned all Israeli settlements established in the occupied Palestinian territory since 1967 as illegal, was cosponsored by a large majority of over 120 states. The resolution was also supported by all the members of the Security Council except for the US, which vetoed it. The resolution would have demanded that Israel immediately and completely cease all settlement activities in the territories, including East Jerusalem.[105]

Israel's isolation at the United Nations would reach its peak with the recognition of Palestine as a nonmember observer state at the UN General Assembly in November 2012. Among the 193 UN members, only 7 countries sided with Israel in vetoing the resolution. These states included the US, Canada, the Czech Republic, Panama, Nauru, the Marshall Islands, and Palau—not all of them exactly major powers.

Israeli policymakers and observers identified with growing concern the increasing gap between what Israel deems as right and necessary, on the one hand, and what the international community thinks, on the other.[106] One analyst of the Israeli Institute of National Security Studies at Tel Aviv University stressed that

> a further negative aspect that arose over the decade is the increasing erosion of Israel's international legitimacy. Many Israeli actions in the past ten years were met with little understanding by the international community. These included Israeli military activity against the Palestinian Authority, erection of the separation fence, the policy of roadblocks in the West Bank, and Israel's military moves against Hamas in Gaza (especially Operation Cast Lead). Sharp and ever stronger criticism is instinctively leveled by political, public, academic, and media entities in the international arena that traditionally identify with the Palestinian struggle and tend to describe Israel as an illegitimate "colonial relic."[107]

While Israel's new hegemony thus seriously affected its international relations far beyond the Middle East, the country's growing international isolation also fed a vicious cycle sustaining its hegemonic vision: international critics could easily be accused of deliberately engaging in attacks on the legitimacy of Israel. In this vein, Israeli governments and affiliated think tanks have been using the delegitimization argument to dismiss and in fact delegitimize different lines of criticism, with the definition of what actually constitutes an attempt to delegitimize Israel being rather broad.[108] Similarly, pro-Palestinian activists have been accused of engaging in "lawfare"—the use of legal means and international law to counter Israel's (unlawful) policies. While Israeli governments have been focusing on *hasbarah* (explanation or propaganda), the sense of being under attack by the international community additionally feeds into the still predominant Israeli belief that "the whole world is against us" (*ha-'olam kulo negdeinu*).[109] For example, according to the Tel Aviv University Peace Index poll of August 2010, 56 percent of the Jewish Israeli public "totally" or "somewhat" agreed with this statement.[110]

In other words, the more Israel is criticized, the more it closes in on itself. This, in turn, has further strengthened Israel's dominant vision of threats and regional order. In this situation a consideration of alternative interpretations of Middle Eastern reality is highly unlikely.

Domestic Repercussions

Israel's hegemonic vision of threats and regional order post-Oslo also had important domestic implications. With the consensus in Israeli policy and society uniting Jewish Israelis of different political, religious, and cultural orientations, the gap between the Jewish majority and the Palestinian minority in Israel grew wider. As discussed in the following section, Israel's hegemonic conviction of being surrounded by enemies considerably affected majority–minority relations within Israel.[111]

Jewish–Palestinian Relations in Israel

Against the backdrop of the unresolved Arab–Israeli conflict, in conjuncture with Israel's self-definition as a "Jewish state," the standing of Israel's Palestinian citizens has always been precarious and difficult.[112] Indeed, from the outset, the state considered the approximately 160,000 Palestinian Arabs who remained in Israel after 1948, and who became an indigenous minority within the newly established State of Israel, as a potential security threat. Although they became Israeli citizens, they were subjected to military rule until 1966.

The so-called Orr Commission Report—the independent commission of inquiry led by Israeli justice Theodore Orr, which investigated the clashes between Israel's Arab citizens and the security forces in

October 2000—is perhaps the most authoritative Israeli official account of the decades of marginalization, discrimination, and neglect of the Palestinian minority by the Israeli state.[113] While approximately 1.6 million—around 18 percent—of Israeli citizens are Arab Palestinians, they have remained second-class citizens. Some collective rights are recognized in practice, such as the status of Arabic as an official language in Israel and the separate but state-controlled Arabic education system. However, the Arab citizens do not enjoy any officially recognized collective rights.[114] They face discrimination when it comes to the allocation of state budgets and resources, and they struggle with poor education, poverty, unequal opportunities in the job market, rising crime rates, and an insufficient integration and representation in government institutions. In addition, the Arab communities have constantly been put at a disadvantage in the distribution of land, rural and urban planning, and housing.[115]

Land and housing are perhaps the most sensitive issues, given that, after 1948, the State of Israel confiscated large amounts of lands belonging to either individual Arab citizens or the Islamic *waqf* (endowment). It subsequently allocated these lands for the development of mainly Jewish towns and neighborhoods, with different reasons and legal excuses.[116] For example, under the Absent Property Law of 1950 and subsequent regulations, land was confiscated from owners who by the date of the adoption of the UN partition plan on November 29, 1947, had property inside Israel but were living outside the newly defined borders of the newly created state. The Israeli authorities also expropriated land from Palestinians who had become Israeli citizens after Israel declared its independence in May 1948 but who left before September 1 of the same year—that is, during the second truce in the 1948 Arab–Israeli war—to areas beyond the state. Land was also confiscated from internally displaced persons, termed *nifkadim nokhahim* (literally, present absentees)—that is, Israeli Palestinian citizens who by September 1, 1948, found themselves in areas controlled by hostile forces. Under this law the inhabitants of sixty Palestinian villages were forbidden, partly by force, to return to their houses while their lands were expropriated. Palestinian-owned land was also confiscated for military purposes, infrastructure projects, "the public good," and the establishment of natural land reserves and parks.[117] While it is estimated that Palestinian Arabs who remained in Israel lost 40–60 percent of their land, confiscations have been continuing until today, although on a smaller scale.[118]

The constant deprivation and neglect of the Arab communities by the Israeli state saw a growing political awareness among Israel's Palestinian citizens over time, mainly due to rising levels of education, generational change, and access to alternative information. The Palestinian citizens' declining support for Zionist parties and the growing backing of Arab parties at the polls are a clear indication of this trend. Moreover, the Arab communities in Israel have witnessed the strengthening of Islamist movements from the 1990s onward and a growing—and publicly voiced—rejection of the mainstream Zionist paradigm in general.[119] The growing demands of the Arab Palestinian citizens of Israel for equal rights increasingly contrasted with the feeling of entitlement of the majority of the Jewish public. As Sammy Smooha put it over a decade ago, "Most Jews even fail to perceive . . . differential practices as discrimination against Arabs. Instead they consider them as preferences rightfully accorded to themselves as Jews in a Jewish state."[120]

With the beginning of the Oslo process, majority–minority relations in Israel temporarily improved. The country's then three Arab parties—one of them, Hadash, being actually a mixed party of Jewish and Palestinian Israelis that developed from the former Communist Party in Israel—strongly supported the peacemaking policies of the Rabin government.[121] They provided "external" backing in the Knesset (Arab parties have never been invited to join a government coalition in Israel). In fact, the Arab parties helped block the formation of a right-wing government after the 1992 elections, thus allowing the Labor Party to pursue the peace agreements with the PLO.[122] In return, the allocation of state resources to Arab communities noticeably increased, with the Rabin government also granting construction permits in Arab towns, establishing family health clinics in Arab localities, and increasing the recruitment of Arab university graduates into the civil service. These measures were temporary, however.[123]

While the peace process also meant that the Arab communities in Israel shifted the focus of their demands from the national Palestinian struggle to the civic dimension of their status in Israel, the outbreak of the Second Intifada in October 2000 reversed the temporary rapprochement abruptly, causing an unprecedented alienation of Israel's Palestinian citizens. The huge demonstrations by Arab citizens against the policies of Ariel Sharon, and especially the protests sparked by his visit to the Temple Mount, clearly showed that large parts of Israel's Arab citizens did not share the government's official line, according to which Arafat was to blame for the outbreak of the violence. The use of snipers by the Israeli police during these demonstrations led to the deaths of twelve Israeli Palestinian citizens and one Palestinian from the Gaza Strip. It caused outrage in the Arab communities. Their anger and frustration only increased as mainstream Jewish public opinion depicted them as "fifth column," thus recognizing the police's reaction as fully legitimate. As a result, most Israeli Arab citizens boycotted the February 2001 elections, marking a break with the traditional high voter turnout of the Arab communities and the customary high support for Israel's Labor Party. This trend of not participating in the Israeli elections continued throughout the first post-Oslo decade.[124]

As the intifada continued to unfold, relations between the Jewish majority and the Arab minority soured further, bringing a growing rejection of Israel's foreign policy consensus by the Arab communities to the fore. Israel's reoccupation of the West Bank in 2002 triggered further demonstrations against government policies among the Arab communities, giving Jewish Israelis yet another reason to identify their fellow Arab citizens as "the enemy within." During the 2006 war between Israel and Hizballah, the growing gap became once more visible. Although most Arab citizens of Israel living in the north of the country were directly exposed to Hizballah's barrage of rockets during the forty-three days of war, the main Arab-language media in Israel held the Israeli government responsible for the situation. And while Hizballah's Katyusha rockets caused eighteen Palestinian Israeli fatalities among the forty-two Israeli civilians killed by the rockets, the Arab Israeli media celebrated the courage of Hizballah leader Hassan Nasrallah in standing up against Israel.[125]

Israel's war against Hamas in Gaza in the winter of 2008–9 polarized Jewish and Palestinian Israelis even further. The widespread support of the war by Jewish Israelis contrasted with the large demonstration against Israel's military operations held by Palestinian citizens in the city of Sakhnin in January 2009. Whereas around 90 percent of Israel's Jewish citizens thought that both going to war and the way it was conducted were justified, around 85 percent of Israel's Arab citizens strongly opposed "Operation Cast Lead."[126] In other words, the positions of Arab and Jewish Israelis toward this war were diametrically opposed.

The participation of MK Haneen Zoabi of the Balad party in the *Mavi Marmara* flotilla in May 2010, which aimed at breaking Israel's blockade of Gaza, was a further indication of the divergent positions of the Arab communities' political leadership compared to their Jewish peers. Given the strong consensus among the Jewish public around the sinister intentions of the flotilla's organizers, together with the strong conviction that the actions of the Israeli navy were legal and legitimate, MK Zoabi's participation in the flotilla was perceived as an act of treason by parts of the Jewish public and of the political establishment. Thus, during a Knesset plenum in early June 2010, MK Miri Regev from the Likud party called on Zoabi to "go to Gaza, you traitor." One day later Interior Minister Eli Yishai sought to strip Zoabi of her Israeli citizenship on the basis that she had committed a "premeditated act of treason." Zoabi subsequently had some of her parliamentary privileges revoked, but an attempt to bring criminal charges against her failed. She was assigned special protection after receiving death threats.[127]

The position of Israel's Arab citizens on Iran also markedly differed from Israel's foreign policy consensus. According to a 2009 poll of six hundred Palestinian/Arab Israelis, 59 percent of respondents believed that Iran was indeed trying to develop nuclear weapons. However, 53 percent of those polled still believed that Tehran had the right to do so and that the international pressure should cease. In a 2010 poll, 61 percent of Arab Israeli respondents believed Iran aimed at obtaining nuclear weapons, with those maintaining it had a right to do so slightly decreasing to 50 percent. Interestingly, kinship to 1948 Palestinian refugees was a major factor influencing the position toward Iran's nuclear program, with respondents who had relatives among the refugees of the 1948 war being more inclined to defend Iran's right to an atomic weapons program. Similarly interesting is the fact that, notwithstanding the high support of Israel's Arab citizens for Iran's right to a nuclear program, 55 percent of respondents in the 2009 poll also believed that the outcome would be "more negative" if Iran acquired nuclear weapons.[128] While showing that the majority of the Arab public in Israel is far from being naïve, the poll proves that their positions still differ noticeably from Israel's hegemonic discourse on the existential threat of Iran's nuclear weapons program.

A number of other factors contributed to the deteriorating relations between the Jewish majority and the Arab minorities in the 2000s. First, Israel's Arab citizens were further alienated by the fact that no police officer was ever indicted for shooting and killing Arab demonstrators during the October 2000 events. The investigatory files were closed in 2008. Second, the recommendations of the Orr Commission Report remained unheeded. Third, the number of Palestinian citizens accused of involvement in terrorist attacks increased during the Second Intifada. While before the intifada these amounted to between two and four cases a year, in 2002, the peak year, seventy-four Arab Israelis were arrested on suspicion of helping prepare terrorist attacks committed by Hamas and other Palestinians factions or by Hizballah. These numbers then steadily declined, until the end of the decade, to pre-Intifada levels.[129] Concurrently, there has been an increase in religious preferences in Israel's Arab community over the last decades, a trend that can be observed all over the Middle East (Israel included). The growing appeal of religion entails that Islamist preferences, including radical ones that blame "the Jews" for every evil, are on the rise as well.[130] Fourth, Israel's general sense of being under siege was projected onto the Arab communities and their dissenting voices. In this vein, the Arab citizens were increasingly portrayed as a "security threat," and sometimes even as an existential one. For example, according to a poll published in the daily *Maariv* in the aftermath of the October 2000 events, 74 percent of the Jewish public defined the behavior of Arab citizens—that is, their protests—as "treason."[131] Nadim Rouhana and Nimer Sultany remarked on these findings that "Jewish Israelis felt deeply threatened by the 'discovery' that the people they had always called 'Israeli Arabs' or 'Israel's Arabs' are, in fact, Palestinians and part of the Palestinian people."[132] A series of polls conducted between 2001 and 2002 show that a majority of Jewish Israeli respondents consider Arab citizens as a security threat, increasing from 64 percent in 2001 to 72 percent in 2002.[133] A document of the Shabak of 2007 described Israel's Palestinian citizens as a "strategic danger."[134] Concurrently, the perception that Palestinian citizens represented a serious demographic problem that was putting the survival of the "Jewish state" at risk—not a new claim per se—grew considerably stronger. In late 2003 Binyamin Netanyahu, then finance minister in Sharon's government, bluntly described Israel's Palestinian citizens as "the real demographic threat."[135]

This placing of fellow Arab citizens into the category of "the enemy" within the new hegemonic vision of not having a partner for peace, of facing terrorism on all fronts while being surrounded by evil forces, also somewhat explains the preferred course of action of the Jewish public toward the minorities. According to a poll published in *Yediot Ahronot* in 2004, 64 percent of Jewish Israeli respondents expressed their support for the idea of "transferring" Arab Palestinian citizens out of the state.[136] A *Maariv* poll of 2008 found that 75 percent of Jewish Israeli respondents were in favor of such a measure.[137] Surveys taken during the 2000s consistently show that a large majority of Jewish Israelis rejected the granting of equal rights to their fellow Arab citizens—although they expressed their support for the idea of equality when asked about it in general terms. When asked about concrete measures, however, in a 2004 poll over 80 percent opposed granting Arab citizens the right to participate in "crucial national decisions," such as about the future borders of the state. About three-quarters of the sample opposed it in surveys taken in 2005, 2006, and 2007, and only 23 percent were in favor of this option in 2009. Similarly, according to a 2004 poll, 75 percent of Jewish Israeli respondents were opposed to the inclusion of Arab Israeli ministers in the government. In 2005 and 2006, 60 percent of respondents were against the participation of Arab ministers in the cabinet, and 63 percent opposed it in 2007. In 2009 only 30 percent of Jewish Israeli respondents were in favor of the participation of Arab Israeli ministers in the government.[138]

A growing number of Jewish Israelis were also in favor of encouraging voluntary emigration for Israel's Palestinian citizens. This number grew from around 50 percent in 2001 to 63 percent in 2006 and increased further from 66.3 percent of respondents in 2007 to an astounding 72.4 percent in 2009.[139] Similarly, a high percentage of Israel's Jewish citizens favored the "transfer" of Arab communities in Israel to a future Palestinian state, in the context of a land swap in final-status negotiations with the PA. In particular, this concerned the Arab towns in the so-called triangle in the northeast of Israel. In polls taken between 2006 and 2009, around one-third of Jewish Israeli respondents were in favor of transferring as many Arab communities as possible, and another approximately 15 percent were favorable to transferring a small number of communities. Only one-third of respondents were in favor of this measure being conditional on the Arab communities actually consenting to this swap.[140]

This set of polls also asked whether, vis-à-vis the Arab citizens, the state should emphasize "punitive measures for behavior that is not appropriate for Israeli citizens" or, alternatively, should seek to "equalize their conditions." Variation in the responses can be linked to concrete events such as the October demonstrations, the Lebanon war, or the Gaza war. The "punitive measure" option enjoyed a higher support (55 percent of respondents in 2009) whenever Israel's Arab citizens expressed dissent against Israel's hegemonic vision of threats and regional order.[141]

Representatives of Israel's political class clearly contributed to the growing suspicion of the Jewish majority toward the Arab minorities and their growing alienation. For example, there were repeated attempts to prevent Arab parties from participating at the Knesset elections. Israel's Central Election Committee, which is composed of Knesset members and headed by a Supreme Court justice, vetoed the participation of two well-established Arab parties prior to the elections in 2003 and again in 2009 on the grounds that they negated "the existence of the State of Israel as a Jewish and democratic state." Significantly, Israel's "Basic Law: the Knesset"—the procedures of the Israeli parliament in Israel's quasi-constitutional document—was amended in 2002 to allow the banning of political parties running for elections on the grounds that they reject the "Jewish and democratic" identity of Israel. In the case of the 2009 elections, which followed the Gaza war, the committee also claimed that these parties supported the "armed struggle by a hostile state or a terrorist organization" against the state. Israel's Supreme Court overturned the bans in both cases.[142]

Israel's right-wing parties and politicians clearly sought to capitalize on the deteriorating majority–minority relations for their own political gains. They increasingly voiced the proposition to transfer Palestinian citizens out of the state, with Avigdor Lieberman's idea of redrawing the borders so that Arab towns and villages in Israel would find themselves under PA rule gaining currency. It is worth noting that in the past the idea of "transfer" was considered as outside of the Israeli consensus. The decision of the Israeli government of 1988 to ban Meir Kahane's Kach party, which advocated this idea most vociferously, on the grounds that it was racist and undemocratic is a case in point. A few decades later, the slogan "no citizenship without loyalty" (*ein ne'emanut—ein ezrahut*) featured prominently in the 2009 electoral campaign of Lieberman's right-wing party Yisrael Beiteinu (Israel Is Our Home). Appealing in particular to Jewish immigrants from the former Soviet Union who arrived in Israel in the 1990s, the party has been eager to accuse Israel's Arab communities of being disloyal to the state by also pointing to the fact that most Arab citizens are not drafted to the Israeli army. While it is true that most Arab Israelis would not want to serve in the Israeli army against the backdrop of the persistent Israeli–Palestinian conflict, in his tirades Lieberman conveniently forgot to mention that the decision to draft only a small percentage of the Arab communities (such as the Druze) was obviously taken by the Israeli state. Moreover, in that period, Lieberman's campaign did not target ultra-Orthodox Jewish Israelis, who do not serve in the Israeli army either. Obtaining fifteen mandates, Yisrael Beiteinu became the third-largest party in the 2009 elections and entered the government coalition.

The rise of a populist and ultranationalist discourse targeting the Arab communities in Israel culminated at the end of 2010. In the northern city of Safed, a number of rabbis—state employees whose salaries are paid by (Jewish and Arab) taxes—ruled that it is forbidden for Jews to sell or rent property to Arabs and other gentiles. While none of the rabbis involved was fired, the rulings were followed by attacks by Jewish groups on Arab students.[143] Concurrently, Israel's mainstream public discourse and the media were regularly reporting the "radicalization" of the Arab Israeli public and their leaders, often in very alarmist tones, as Ilan Peleg and Dov Waxman note.[144] Depicting the Arab citizens of Israel as extremists, or even as terrorists, went hand in hand with verbal attacks on the political leadership of the Arab communities as well as on ordinary Palestinian citizens.[145] What the Israeli public and the media defined as radicalization referred, first, to the growing public opposition of Israel's Palestinian citizens to the notion of a "Jewish state," a concept they increasingly identified as being inherently discriminatory and racist. This trend became visible in a number of draft constitutions for Israel published by different Arab Israeli organizations and intellectuals in 2006–7, against the backdrop of the efforts by Israel's political elite to formulate a constitution for Israel at that time.[146] The most important documents put forward by Israel's Palestinian citizens gave a clear preference to "a state of all its citizens" with full equal rights for Jewish and Palestinian Israelis, as opposed to the concept of "a Jewish state." It provoked an outcry among Israel's Jewish majority. This outrage must be linked to the growing centrality of the notion of "the Jewish state" in Israel's collective self-definition in the 2000s and beyond. Certainly, the exact meaning of the concept remains deeply contested among Jewish Israelis, given that "Jewish state" can be defined in religious, ethnic, cultural, or even symbolic terms. In spite of this, the prevailing sense has been that the Jewish state, and thus the very existence of Israel, was under threat.[147] Second, for the official discourse and the media, the "radicalization" of the Arab minorities also entailed the contestation of any policies that departed from Israel's hegemonic vision of threats and regional order. In other words, the growing talk about the "radicalization" of the Arab communities didn't just disregard the fact that most Palestinians have been loyal citizens.[148] It also failed to distinguish between legitimate political opposition, which characterizes the overwhelming majority of the Arab community, and those rare cases in which Palestinian citizens were involved in terrorism.

The extent to which the perception of Israel's Arab citizens as a security or demographic threat (or both), thus allegedly justifying their unequal status, became a mainstream position was also visible in a series of bills and legislations that put the Arab communities at a disadvantage. This development also evidenced the growing emphasis on Israel as a Jewish state. For instance, Lieberman's "loyalty oath" campaign resulted in a bill aimed at amending Israel's Citizenship and Entry into Israel Law of 1952, which is the law that regulates Israeli citizenship for non-Jews. Whereas hitherto, candidates for naturalization had to pledge loyalty to the state without further specifications, the bill required non-Jews wanting to become Israeli citizens to pledge loyalty to Israel as a "Jewish and democratic state." The amendment would thus mainly affect Israeli-Arab

citizens' (Arab) spouses from abroad, who are likely to reject Israel's definition as a "Jewish state." It is worth noting that Jewish immigrants, including non-Zionist ultra-Orthodox Jews who would oppose pledging
alliance to a "Jewish state," would be exempted from taking the oath: they
are entitled to immigrate to Israel under a different law, the Law of Return of 1950, which does not contain these provisions. The bill aimed at
amending the citizenship law approved by the cabinet in October 2010,
but the Knesset has still to vote on it.

Lieberman's party sponsored an additional amendment to the 1952 citizenship law, which was adopted in March 2011. This amendment enables
a court sitting in criminal matters to revoke the citizenship of a person
who is convicted of serious terrorist offenses or serious offenses of treason
and espionage, in addition to any other penalty.[149] Revocation of citizenship
should not be ordered if it will result in the person becoming stateless.
However, should this happen, the state will grant a permit of residence in
Israel—which is of course not the same as citizenship. It should be noted
that in July 2008, courts sitting in administrative matters were already
granted the right to revoke citizenship on grounds of convictions for the
same types of offenses. These courts may also revoke Israeli citizenship
for having acquired citizenship or permanent residence in countries that
maintain a state of war with Israel—including, specifically, Afghanistan, the
Gaza Strip, Iran, Iraq, Lebanon, Libya, Pakistan, Sudan, Syria, and Yemen.[150]
Stressing that the already existing legislation was sufficient, critics of the
amendment—including Israel's internal security service, Shabak—pointed
out that "in Israel there is room to suspect that revocation of citizenship
would be carried out unequally and applied primarily to Arab citizens."[151]

In 2003, at the height of the Second Intifada, the citizenship law had
already been amended with a Law on Family Unification. This amendment explicitly denies citizenship and residency in Israel to Palestinian
spouses of Israeli citizens if they come from the West Bank and the Gaza
Strip.[152] Portrayed as a temporary measure based on a precarious security situation, the amendment has been renewed every year. The Israeli
Supreme Court upheld its constitutionality in January 2012 in response
to a number of petitions accusing the state of discriminating against its
Arab citizens.

A number of additional laws that specifically target Palestinian citizens were passed subsequently; others are pending.[153] Among the most
significant is the Community Acceptance Law of March 2011, which al-
lows vetting committees in Jewish Israeli communities to reject potential
(Arab) residents on the basis of "social incompatibility." Another example

is the Nakbah Law (Budget Foundations Law, Amendment 40), also passed in March 2011. It authorizes the finance minister to impose harsh fines on government-funded organizations that commemorate the *nakbah*—the catastrophe that befell the Palestinians in 1948—as a day of mourning.[154]

Other laws passed in the 2000s regard specifically land ownership. The Amendment to the Israel Land Administration Law of 2009 instituted, inter alia, a broad land privatization, which concerns about two hundred thousand acres of land confiscated by the state after 1948 from Palestinian refugees and internally displaced persons. Considering that the state owns 93 percent of the land in Israel, the rationale for the reform was to enable private ownership of land instead of leasing. However, the confiscation of this land was officially meant to be for public purposes and to be temporary; the privatization would make it impossible for the original owners to ever claim it back.[155] In a similar vein, the Amendment to the Land Acquisition Ordinance of February 2010 confirms state ownership of confiscated land if this land has not been used for the original purpose. According to the amendment, landowners cannot demand the return of confiscated land if the ownership has been transferred to a third party or if more than twenty-five years have passed since the confiscation.[156] This means in practice that Palestinian citizens of Israel have no chance of ever claiming back the land the Israeli government confiscated from them or from their families in 1948 or in its aftermath.

Thus, Israel's hegemonic vision of threats and regional order, of "us" and "them," together with the sense of besiegement, clearly puts the Jewish majority on a collision course with the Arab minorities. It also cements the unequal treatment of Arab-Palestinian citizens. In addition, it reverberates on Jewish critics and non-Jewish immigrants and refugees at large, as briefly discussed in the following.

Beyond Majority–Minority Relations

The new Israeli consensus on specific notions of threats and regional order witnessed a general tendency of seeking to silence its critics. Since the emergence of the new hegemony was intrinsically linked to a notable shift to the right and to the rise of ultranationalism in Israeli politics after the collapse of Oslo, the remaining left-wing and liberal Israeli intellectuals and organizations increasingly became the target of these attempts.

While organizations such as Im Tirtzu and Campus Watch started documenting and denouncing Israeli left-wing intellectuals and academics, at the end of the 2000s and in the beginning of the following decade opponents of the new hegemony were also increasingly the target of bills and laws. For instance, in early 2011, Israeli legislators sought to pass a law that, in its original form, would have revoked the status of tax exemption for Israeli NGOs that receive foreign public funding. While the existing law already obliges NGOs to make the sources of their funding public, the bill would have mainly concerned left-wing Israeli human rights organizations that are funded by foreign (often European) governments. Conversely, organizations that channel money to the territories in support of Israel's settlement project would have been excluded from the bill's provisions because they usually rely on private donations.

Similarly, in early 2011 the Knesset approved a motion, promoted by Yisrael Beiteinu, to investigate left-wing nongovernmental organizations and their funding sources because they had allegedly spread lies and incited criticism against Israel and the army. Presenting a detailed list of organizations that should be investigated—including Ittijah (an umbrella association of Israeli Arab NGOs), Yesh Din, Adalah, Physicians for Human Rights–Israel, the Public Committee against Torture, and others—Foreign Minister Avigdor Lieberman publicly claimed that these organizations "aid terrorism." In the same outburst he also denounced the renowned newspaper *Haaretz* for being anti-Israeli.[157]

The growing antagonism of Israel's right-wing politicians against domestic human rights organizations was also linked to their role in providing information to the UN fact-finding commission led by Richard Goldstone. The Israeli government had declined to cooperate with the fact-finding mission. As noted previously, in its investigation of the 2008–9 Gaza war, the so-called Goldstone Report accused Israel (as well as Hamas) of war crimes, prompting an outcry in Israel. In early 2010 a vicious campaign targeted Israel's liberal charity the New Israel Fund and its former chairwoman, scholar and former Knesset member Naomi Chazan. The campaign accused the New Israel Fund of supporting NGOs that gave evidence to the Goldstone commission of inquiry.

Lieberman's denunciation of Israeli human rights organizations and of *Haaretz* as collaborators of terrorism, however, occasionally crossed a red line, judging by the harsh reactions of other representatives of the Israeli government. Thus, Likud member Benny Begin commented that these developments were sending "a warning sign: here is darkness."[158] Experts on Israeli politics expressed their concern about an Israeli form of McCarthyism gaining currency.[159] In this vein, Mordechai Kremnitzer, law professor and vice president of the Israel Democracy Institute, identified an "ugly trend" toward a "McCarthyite campaign against civil society."[160]

In other instances, however, the growing restrictions on free speech were passed with the backing of Israel's mainstream politicians. This regards, for instance, the bill that exposes supporters of a boycott of Israel or the settlements to civil suits for compensation without the need to prove damages. The bill, which was sponsored by Likud MK Zeev Elkin, was passed in July 2011.[161] Similarly, the Nakbah Law mentioned earlier, which similarly infringes free speech, witnessed the loud opposition of the usual suspects only: that is, Israel's left-wing and liberal politicians and intellectuals, together with the Arab parties.

Finally, Israel's hegemonic sense of being under siege, together with the ethnoreligious definition of "us" and "them" it entails, was also reflected in Israel's dominant political discourse toward migrant workers in general, and the around sixty thousand refugees from sub-Saharan Africa who have entered Israel via the Egyptian Sinai Peninsula between 2006 and 2013 in particular. One indication of this is that it has become common in Israel's political discourse to call these refugees "infiltrators" (*mistanenim*). It is important to note that the term in Hebrew refers to those Palestinians and nationals of an enemy country who sought to enter Israel illegally after 1948—either to perpetrate terrorist attacks or, as in the case of most Palestinians in the early years after the war, to go back to their land and property and retrieve goods they had left behind.[162] The term clearly criminalizes the refugees and asylum seekers, equating them with potential terrorists while simultaneously constructing them as a major security threat.[163] Prime Minister Olmert even spoke about a "tsunami of infiltrators" in 2008, at a point at which the number of African refugees and undocumented migrants in Israel was actually substantially lower.[164]

Reflecting the growing securitization of the African immigrants and refugees, the government initially sought to apply the Prevention of Infiltration Law of 1954 to these persons, thus seeking to define them as hostile individuals from enemy countries, or as Palestinians who cross illegally into Israel with the intent to harm or kill Israelis. According to the 1954 law, these "infiltrators" are subject to criminal law and are tried by a military tribunal; they can be imprisoned for up to five years.[165] However, the government faced some judicial opposition to its intent of applying this law to the African immigrants, mainly because it was an emergency regulation. The government's subsequent attempt to amend the Prevention of Infiltration Law was overturned by the Israeli High Court of Justice in October of 2013. The amendment would have permitted the confinement of migrants and asylum seekers for up to three years before deporting them for illegally crossing the borders into Israel. After the court ruling, Netanyahu promptly announced he was preparing a new bill that would allow for the detention of the "infiltrators" for one and a half years.[166]

The construction of undocumented immigrants and refugees as security threat, which reproduces Israel's "frontier mentality," subsequently led to anti-African rallies in Tel Aviv in May and December 2012, at which Knesset members participated.[167] During the May rally, which also witnessed attacks on the African immigrant communities and their property in southern Tel Aviv, Deputy Defense Minister Danny Danon, who would be appointed Israeli ambassador to the United Nations in 2015, called for the immediate expulsion of the "infiltrators" in order to protect the Jewish character of the state. Likud MK Miri Regev, Minister of Culture and Sport at present, called the Sudanese migrants a "cancer in our body."[168] Thus, what had started as an identification by many Jewish Israelis with the first refugees from Darfur fleeing genocide progressively turned into the perception that the African migrants were another internal threat to the survival of the Jewish state. While the massive influx of poor and unskilled migrants and refugees creates problems in all Western societies, Israel's political elite seemed increasingly united in the preferred course of action of imprisoning and expelling the African migrants, often in contravention of international law on asylum.

◆

By way of summary, the Israeli consensus on threats, conflict, and regional order that characterized the first post-Oslo decade had a number of significant implications for the Israeli polity. Most notably, it legitimized and made feasible specific policies by presenting them as the only alternative. The predominant frames in Israel's foreign policy discourse in that decade explained events and developments in terms of Israel reacting in self-defense while presenting the other side—Hamas, Hizballah, Iran, and the Palestinians—as evil and even inhuman. Hence, Israel's new consensus on threats and regional order provided legitimacy to policies of deterrence, the use of force, unilateral action, and the deferral of territorial compromise with the Palestinians. The latter permitted the continuation of Israel's settlement project. Concurrently, the history of the Israeli–Palestinian conflict and Israel's role as an occupying power no longer figured in Israel's political consciousness post-Oslo. Israel came (again) to conceive of itself as being under siege, as having no choice, while fighting for its very survival. While similar ideas and policies had also been prominent in previous periods, including during the rule of the Israeli Labor Party, the new hegemony after Oslo entailed that other options, let alone a possible Israeli contribution to the de-escalation of conflict, were no longer debated. The post-Oslo period thus notably contrasted with previous decades, when contestation was part and parcel of Israel's political culture.

The regional policies prescribed by Israel's new consensus were only partly effective. Terrorist attacks dropped considerably from the mid-2000s onward, a certain degree of deterrence was, arguably, (re)established vis-à-vis Hamas and Hizballah, and Israel also contributed to the growing international pressure on Tehran to stop its nuclear program. While it remains contested as to whether these results were obtained through Israel's forceful policies, the country's foreign policy choices also ignored some converging interests across the region as well as a major Arab peace initiative.[169] Altogether, Israeli policies contributed to the growing legitimacy of Hamas and Hizballah and undermined pragmatist forces in the region, most notably PA chairman Mahmoud Abbas. Israeli actions thus reduced, rather than increased, the chances for Arab–Israeli peacemaking. Thus, Israel's new consensus on threats and regional order partly legitimized policies that, *nolens volens*, contributed to the cementing of precisely that regional order.

As for the international and domestic repercussions, Israel's new hegemony post-Oslo clearly gave rise to the country's growing isolation at the international level. With the exception of the United States—and even there some trends toward a growing gap in the medium term were discernible—Israel's hegemonic notions and the resulting actions were increasingly incomprehensible for foreign governments and international public opinion alike. In its relations with Europe and beyond, Israel perceived the growing international criticism of its policies as an attack on its legitimacy and its right to exist, thereby further reinforcing the hegemonic vision of threats and regional order. Part of the increasing failure of the international community to grasp Israeli logics probably results from the "legitimacy trap" posed by the confrontation of the state with terrorism and nonstate actors. However, given the growing international consensus that Israel's military control over the Palestinian territories is illegitimate, the role played by the country's continuing rule over the Palestinians cannot be underestimated. Yet this aspect of the problem has been completely removed from Israel's collective consciousness.

At the domestic level, Israel's sense of being under siege entailed a particular definition of "us" and "them" and specific policies of exclusion that also saw an ever growing emphasis on the concept of "the Jewish state." This focus on ethnoreligious conceptions of collective identity was reflected in Israeli policies toward its African immigrants and asylum seekers. As hegemony tends to sustain itself by delegitimizing any challenge to the notions it promotes, Israel's new consensus also called for attempts to silence its critics. In addition to left-wing and liberal Jewish Israelis and organizations that became the target of often vicious campaigns, the new policies of exclusion specifically target Israel's Palestinian citizens, with the consensus thus significantly impacting on majority–minority relations in Israel. Hence, the new hegemonic vision in Israel post-Oslo manifested itself in a decidedly illiberal, populist, and ultranationalist discourse. It also expressed itself in legislation that changed the meaning of citizenship for non-Jews in a state that increasingly defines itself in ethnic terms.[170]

Israel's new hegemony has thus significantly affected Israel's domestic policies, regional relations, and international standing alike. This raises the question of why Israel would maintain specific policies if they are partly counterproductive unless the explanation for this lies in the power of the new hegemony. The next chapter answers the question of how it emerged in the first place.

Notes

1. Chong and Druckman, "Framing Theory"; and Polletta and Ho, "Frames and Their Consequences."

2. Polletta and Ho, "Frames and Their Consequences," 188.

3. Buzan, *People, States and Fear*, chap. 3.

4. Edelstein, "Managing Uncertainty."

5. Polletta and Ho, "Frames and Their Consequences," 188.

6. Of course, successful strategic action also relies on previously diffused taken-for-granted convictions—in this case, that presenting Arafat as the main culprit was an intelligible and acceptable line of explanation.

7. Gershon Baskin, "In the Land of Miracles: Let's Get Real," *Haaretz*, September 29, 2009. Perhaps unsurprisingly, a total disillusionment with the prospects for peace, and with Israeli intentions, also characterizes Palestinian society after Oslo.

8. Zoughbie, *Indecision Points*.

9. Kimmerling, *Politicide*, 204.

10. Lustick, "Abandoning the Iron Wall," 38.

11. Tim McGirk and Romesh Ratnesar, "Israel's Lieberman Raps US on Iran, Settlements," *Time*, June 25, 2009.

12. See, for example, Natasha Mozgovaya, "Peres to Obama: No Choice but to Compare Iran to Nazis," *Haaretz*, May 6, 2009; Roni Super, "Rosh ha-Memshalah Kibel et Tokhnit Auschwitz: 'La'atsor Resh'a ba-Zman'" [The prime minister accepted the Auschwitz plan: "Stop evil in time"], *Ynet*, August 27, 2009; Roni Sofer,

"Peres: Iranian Nuclear Bomb Akin to 'Flying Death Camp,'" *Ynet*, August 18, 2009; and "The Iranian Threat: Overview," Israel Ministry of Foreign Affairs, 2013, http://www.mfa.gov.il/mfa/foreignpolicy/iran/pages/iranian_threat.aspx. For a culturalist explanation of Israel's obsession with Iran see Ram, "'To Banish the Levantine Dunghill'"; and Ram, *Iranophobia*.

13. Baskin, "In the Land of Miracles."

14. Ibid.

15. Peffley, Hutchison, and Shamir, "The Impact of Persistent Terrorism"; Getmansky and Zeitzoff, "Terrorism and Voting"; Berrebi and Klor, "On Terrorism and Electoral Outcomes"; Berrebi and Klor, "Are Voters Sensitive to Terrorism?"

16. "Special Cabinet Communiqué: Hizbullah Attack," Israel Ministry of Foreign Affairs, July 12, 2006, http://www.mfa.gov.il/mfa/pressroom/2006/pages/special%20cabinet%20communique%20-%20hizbullah%20attack%2012-jul-2006.aspx.

17. Ibid.

18. As noted in the previous chapter, Israel's military campaign in Lebanon left around 1,300 people, mostly Lebanese citizens, dead. According to Israel's Ministry of Foreign Affairs, on the Israeli side, the war caused 43 civilian casualties and the displacement of between 350,000 and 500,000 civilians.

19. Ali Waked and Hanan Greenberg, "Levanon: Asrot Harugim be-Haftsatsah be-Kfar Qana" [Lebanon: Dozens Killed in Strike on Qana], *Ynet*, July 30, 2006; "Incident in Kafr Qana," Israel Ministry of Foreign Affairs, July 30, 2006, http://www.mfa.gov.il/mfa/pressroom/2006/pages/incident%20in%20qana%20-%20idf%20spokesman%2030-jul-2006.aspx; and "Operation Cast Lead: Israel Strikes Back against Hamas Terror in Gaza," Israel Ministry of Foreign Affairs, January 21, 2009, http://www.mfa.gov.il/mfa/foreignpolicy/terrorism/pages/israel_strikes_back_against_hamas_terror_infrastructure_gaza_27-dec-2008.aspx#statements.

20. Winograd Committee, Press Release, April 30, 2007, http://www.imra.org.il/story.php3?id=34083; Inbar, "How Israel Bungled the Second Lebanon War"; Kober, "Israel Defense Forces in the Second Lebanon War"; and Cohen-Almagor and Haleva-Amir, "Israel-Hezbollah War."

21. "Operation Cast Lead."

22. Eiland, quoted in Ethan Bronner, "Parsing Gains of Gaza War," *New York Times*, January 18, 2009.

23. Shlaim, "Iron Wall Revisited"; and Slater, "Just War Moral Philosophy."

24. As noted in the previous chapter, according to B'Tselem, the Gaza war left over 1,300 Palestinian dead, more than half of whom did not take part in the hostilities; over 5,000 were injured and around 20,000 people were left without homes. Official Palestinian statistics put the numbers slightly higher; official Israel statistics put them lower. On the Israeli side, 9 soldiers were killed within

the Gaza Strip, 4 by friendly fire, and more than 100 soldiers were wounded. See "Statistics: Fatalities During Operation 'Cast Lead,'" B'Tselem, http://www.btselem .org/statistics/fatalities/during-cast-lead/by-date-of-event; and "Gaza Strip: Operation Cast Lead, 27 Dec. '08 to 18 Jan. '09," B'Tselem, January 1, 2011; updated September 18, 2014, http://www.btselem.org/gaza_strip/castlead_operation. On the claim of Hamas's use of civilian shields, see "Hamas Exploitation of Civilians," Israel Ministry of Foreign Affairs, January 6, 2009, http://www.mfa.gov.il/mfa/ foreignpolicy/terrorism/palestinian/pages/hamas_exploitation_civilians_jan _2009.aspx.

25. Ethan Bronner, "Israel Disputes Soldiers' Accounts of Gaza Abuses," *New York Times*, March 7, 2009; and "Soldier's Testimonies from Operation Cast Lead: Gaza 2009," Breaking the Silence, June 2009, http://www.breakingthesilence.org.il/ wp-content/uploads/2011/02/Operation_Cast_Lead_Gaza_2009_Eng.pdf.

26. "The Operation in Gaza: Factual and Legal Aspects," Israel Ministry of Foreign Affairs, July 29, 2009, www.mfa.gov.il/mfa/foreignpolicy/terrorism/pages/ operation_in_gaza-factual_and_legal_aspects.aspx; "Gaza Operation Investigations: An Update," Israel Ministry of Foreign Affairs, January 29, 2010, http://mfa .gov.il/mfa/foreignpolicy/terrorism/pages/gaza_operation_investigations_update _jan_2010.aspx; and "Gaza Operation Investigations: Second Update," Israel Ministry of Foreign Affairs, July 19, 2010, http://www.mfa.gov.il/mfa/foreignpolicy/ terrorism/pages/gaza_operation_investigations_second_update_july_2010.aspx.

27. Richard Goldstone, "Reconsidering the Goldstone Report on Israel and War Crimes," *Washington Post*, April 1, 2011; see also Ethan Bronner and Isabel Kershner, "Inquiry Chief Retracts Key Finding of Gaza Report," *International Herald Tribune*, April 4, 2011.

28. For the statistics of suicide bombings, see "Nituah Meafiyenei ha-Pigu'im ba-'Asor ha-Aharon" [An analysis of the features of terrorist attacks in the last decade], Israeli General Security Service (Shabak), September 14, 2010, http://www.shabak.gov.il/SiteCollectionImages/Hebrew/TerrorInfo/decade/ DecadeSummary_he.pdf, 5.

29. Schweitzer, "Rise and Fall of Suicide Bombings"; Schachter, "End of the Second Intifada?"; and Eiland, "IDF in the Second Intifada."

30. Yuval Yoaz, "Livni: Gader ha-Hafradah: Gvulah ha-'Atidi shel Israel" [Livni: The separation barrier, Israel's future border], *Haaretz*, November 30, 2005.

31. Interviews with members of Israel's security establishment, Tel Aviv, May 25 and 26, 2011, and June 29, 2012; Eiland, "IDF in the Second Intifada," 34; and Ayalon in Moreh, *Gatekeepers*.

32. Interview with Israeli Foreign Ministry official, Jerusalem, May 25, 2011.

33. Lavie, "Israel's Coping with the Al-Aqsa Intifada."

34. Ibid., 109.

35. Schweitzer, "The Rise and Fall of Suicide Bombings," 43. Members of Israel's security establishment confirmed this assessment (interviews, Tel Aviv, May 23, 2011).

36. After an unsuccessful assassination attempt, Marwan Barghouti was arrested in 2002 and subsequently convicted for murder to five consecutive life sentences. He is currently serving his sentence in an Israeli prison.

37. Etzion, "Ministry of Foreign Affairs Situation Assessment," 51.

38. Gross Stein, "Israel," 108.

39. Interview with senior Foreign Ministry official, Jerusalem, June 28, 2012; see also Etzion, "Ministry of Foreign Affairs Situation Assessment."

40. The rocket fire dropped considerably, though never stopped entirely during the cease-fire. The expectations that Israel would open the crossings to allow in goods that had been banned or restricted after June 2007 did not materialize. The cease-fire, for which there was no written text or verification mechanism, eventually collapsed following a raid by Israeli soldiers through a tunnel Hamas was digging into Gaza in early November 2008, killing six Hamas fighters. Ethan Bronner, "Gaza Truce May Be Revived by Necessity," *New York Times*, December 19, 2008; and Rory McCarthy, "Gaza Truce Broken as Israeli Raid Kills Six Hamas Gunmen," *Guardian*, November 5, 2008.

41. Etzion, "Ministry of Foreign Affairs Situation Assessment," 54.

42. Gross Stein, "Israel," 103.

43. "Poll No. 67, January 2009, Palestinian Opinions after the Gaza War," Jerusalem Media and Communication Center, http://www.jmcc.org/documentsandmaps.aspx?id=707; see also "Joint Israeli–Palestinian Poll 31, March 2009," Palestinian Center for Policy and Survey Research (PSR), 2009, http://www.pcpsr.org/en/node/414.

44. Poll No. 67.

45. Ibid.; and "Poll No. 64, April 2008: Palestinian's [sic] Opinions towards the Current Political Situation," Jerusalem Media and Communication Center, 2008, http://www.jmcc.org/documentsandmaps.aspx?id=435.

46. Cordesman, *Gaza War*; and Byman, "How to Handle Hamas."

47. Byman, "How to Handle Hamas."

48. Ging, "Siege on Gaza in 2010."

49. Ibid.

50. Norton, "Hizballah," 153.

51. Barak decided to withdraw unilaterally in spite of the opposition to this idea by the army's General Staff. Many senior SLA members requested, and obtained, political asylum in Israel, but this did not apply to regular SLA fighters.

52. Bregman, *Israel's Wars*, 273.

53. Norton, "Hizballah and the Israeli Withdrawal," 35.

54. Inbar, "How Israel Bungled."

55. Winograd Committee, Press Release; Cohen-Almagor and Haleva-Amir, "Israel-Hezbollah War"; Inbar, "How Israel Bungled"; and Kober, "Israel Defense Forces in the Second Lebanon War."

56. Kuntar would be killed by an explosion in the outskirts of Damascus on December 19, 2015.

57. On the "convergence plan," see, for example, Rubin, "Israel's New Strategy."

58. Etzion, "Ministry of Foreign Affairs Situation Assessment," 54.

59. Meeting with Hussam Zomlut during a SAIS Europe study trip to Israel and the West Bank, Ramallah, March 19, 2014.

60. See *Land Expropriation and Settlement Statistics*, B'Tselem, January 1, 2011, updated May 11, 2015, http://www.btselem.org/settlements/statistics. Settlement "outposts" are settlements that even Israeli law considers as illegal because they have been established without prior government authorization, often on private Palestinian land. On the government's policy of legalizing these outposts ex-facto, see, for example, Isabel Kershner, "Israel Quietly Legalizes Pirate Outposts in the West Bank," *New York Times*, August 30, 2016.

61. Lavie, "Israel's Coping with the Al-Aqsa Intifada," 66.

62. Swisher, *Palestine Papers*; and Ian Black and Seumas Milne, "Israel Spurned Palestinian Offer of 'Biggest Yerushalayim in History,'" *Guardian*, January 23, 2011.

63. Most notably, Natasha Mozgovaya, "Omert be-J Street: Yiashavti 'Asrot Sh'aot 'im 'Abas, Iesh Lanu Partner" [Olmert to J street: I sat dozens of hours with Abas, we have a partner], *Haaretz*, March 27, 2012.

64. Adler, "Damned If You Do."

65. Barzegar, "Paradox of Iran's Nuclear Consensus"; Gareth Evans, "Inside Iran's Nuclear Reasoning," *Project Syndicate*, September 17, 2010, http://www.project-syndicate.org/commentary/evans2/English; and Moshirzadeh, "Discursive Foundations."

66. *Brit be-Mashber: Ma'amad Israel be-'Olam ve-Sugiyat ha-Bidud* [Alliance in crisis: Israel's standing in the world and the question of isolation], Molad, The Center for the Renewal of Israeli Democracy, 2013, http://www.molad.org/images/upload/files/Brit-BeMashber.pdf.

67. Ross, *Missing Peace*.

68. Miller, *Much Too Promised Land*, 204–5; on Ross's one-sidedness, see also Mearsheimer and Walt, *Israel Lobby*, 114. For a different account of the Camp David talks by another member of the US negotiating team, see Hussein Agha and Robert Malley, "Camp David: The Tragedy of Errors," *New York Review of Books*, August 9, 2001.

69. Freedman, "George W. Bush, Barack Obama, and the Israeli–Palestinian Conflict," 36–78; Zoughbie, *Indecision Points*; and Gerges, *Obama and the Middle East*, chap. 2.

70. Shcharansky and Dermer, *Case for Democracy*. Sharansky published the book under his original name, using the traditional spelling.

71. Hamas had also offered the exchange of diplomatic personnel between Israel and the PA during the truce, and it had requested direct negotiations with Washington. Barak Ravid, "In 2006 Letter to Bush, Haniyeh Offered Compromise with Israel," *Haaretz*, November 14, 2008; and Ali Waked, "Haniyeh: Anahnu be'ad Medinah be-Gvulot 67 [Haniyeh: We are in favor of a State within with the '67 borders], *Ynet*, March 27, 2006.

72. "Transcript: Secretary Rice Holds a News Conference," *Washington Post*, July 21, 2006.

73. See Gerges, *Obama and the Middle East*; and Khalidi, *Brokers of Deceit*.

74. Hilary Leila Krieger, "'Arab–Israeli Conflict Hurts US': Petraeus Tells Congress Hostility Presents Challenges to US Interests in M-E," *Jerusalem Post*, March 18, 2010; Joby Warrick, "Panetta Chides Israel over Stalled Peace Process," *Washington Post*, December 2, 2011; and Glenn Kessler, "Chuck Hagel and Israel in Context: A Guide to His Controversial Statements," *Washington Post*, January 8, 2013. See also Marzano, "Loneliness of Israel."

75. See Mearsheimer and Walt, *Israel Lobby*.

76. Jonathan Lis, "Mossad Chief: Israel Gradually Becoming Burden on US," *Haaretz*, June 1, 2010.

77. Barak Ravid, "Kerry Places Blame on Israel for Crisis in Peace Talks," *Haaretz*, April 8, 2014.

78. Peter Beaumont, "Palestinian Unity Government of Fatah and Hamas Sworn In," *Guardian*, June 2, 2014.

79. Julie Hirschfeld Davis, "Administration Official Criticizes Israeli Ambassador over Netanyahu Visit," *New York Times*, January 28, 2015; and Peter Baker, "In Congress, Netanyahu Faults 'Bad Deal' on Iran Nuclear Program," *New York Times*, March 3, 2015.

80. Pew Research Center, *Global Unease with Major World Powers: 47-Nation Pew Global Attitudes Survey*, The Global Attitudes Project, June 27, 2007, http://pewglobal.org/files/pdf/256.pdf.

81. Cavari, "Six Decades of Public Affection."

82. See, for example, Waxman, "Pro-Israel Lobby."

83. Beinart, *Crisis of Zionism*, chap. 9.

84. These sections expand on Del Sarto, "Israel and the European Union." On the complex relations between the European Union, Israel, and the Palestinian territories, see Del Sarto, *Fragmented Borders*.

85. The *ra'is* is the Arab president or ruler.

86. Pardo and Peters, *Uneasy Neighbors*; and Pardo and Peters, *Israel and the European Union*.

87. Formally, the Palestinians were in charge of the border crossing, but Israeli officials observed the crossing via closed-circuit cameras and could request the Palestinians to detain or deny entry to suspected terrorists. The EU border mission (EUBAM Rafah) was suspended after Hamas took control of the strip in 2007.

88. Tocci, *Active but Acquiescent*.

89. Council of the European Union, *Council Conclusions on Middle East Peace Process*.

90. "Merkel: La'atsor Miyad et ha-Bniyah be-Hitnakhluyiot" [Merkel: Stop the construction in the settlements immediately], *NRG (Maariv)*, July 2, 2009; and Barak Ravid, "Merkel: Settlement Freeze Crucial to Resumption of Mideast Peace Talks," *Haaretz*, August 27, 2009.

91. "EU: Israeli Use of Force 'Disproportionate,'" *Haaretz*, July 14, 2006.

92. Ibid.

93. Council of the European Union, Press Release, "Extraordinary General Affairs and External Relations," 12023/06 (Presse 230), Brussels, August 1, 2006.

94. Peter Beaumont, "Israel Outraged as EU Poll Names It a Threat to Peace," *Guardian*, November 2, 2003.

95. Pew Research Center, *Global Unease with Major World Powers*, 55. Fourteen percent of Czech respondents sympathized with the Palestinians; 6 percent answered that they sympathized with "both," and 26 percent with neither side.

96. Ibid.

97. Ibid. Conversely, 29 percent of Swedish respondents expressed their sympathy for the Palestinians, 7 percent for both sides, and 28 percent for neither side. The numbers were similar in the case of British respondents: 29 percent of Britons favored the Palestinians, 9 percent expressed their sympathy for both sides, and 26 percent of British respondents said that they did not sympathize with either side.

98. Ibid. Twenty-seven percent of Spanish respondents favored the Palestinians and 14 percent both sides. In the case of Poland, 13 percent supported the Palestinians, and 9 percent sympathized with both sides. In Italy, the percentage in favor of the Palestinians was 16 percent, while 12 percent sympathized with both sides.

99. Isabel Kershner, "Deadly Israeli Raid Draws Condemnation," *New York Times*, May 31, 2010.

100. Ron Ben-Yishai, "Kakh Ze Karah: Mearav Metukhnan le-Shayietet 'al ha-Marmara" [This is how it happened: A planned ambush for the navy commandoes on the Marmara], *Ynet*, May 31, 2010; and Yaacov Katz, "Navy Commandos: 'They Came for War,'" *Jerusalem Post*, June 1, 2010.

101. Neil MacFarquhar and Ethan Bronner, "Report Finds Naval Blockade by Israel Legal but Faults Raid," *New York Times*, September 1, 2011.

102. Marzano, "The Loneliness of Israel"; and Shindler, *Israel and the Great Powers*.

103. It may be worth remembering that in 1975 the UN General Assembly passed a resolution equating Zionism with racism.

104. Data from the UN website, http://www.un.org/en/sc/documents/resolutions/.

105. "Palestinian Envoy: US Veto at UN 'Encourages Israeli Intransigence' on Settlements," *Haaretz*, February 19, 2011.

106. Interview with Israeli Foreign Ministry official, Jerusalem, May 25, 2011.

107. Milstein, "A Decade since the Outbreak of the Al-Aqsa Intifada," 18.

108. *Building a Political Firewall against Israel's Delegitimization: Conceptual Framework*, Reut Institute, March 2010, http://www.reut-institute.org/data/uploads/PDFVer/20100310%20Delegitimacy%20Eng.pdf.

109. Adler, "Israel's Unsettled Relations with the World," 9.

110. Ephraim Yaar and Tamar Hermann, Peace Index, August 2010. Israel Democracy Institute and the Evens Program in Mediation and Conflict Resolution, Tel Aviv University, August 19, 2010, http://www.peaceindex.org/indexMonthEng.aspx?num=56&monthname=August.

111. A brief note on terminology: the terms "Palestinian citizens of Israel," "Arab citizens of Israel," "Arab Palestinian citizens of Israel," and "Arab communities" are used interchangeably, reflecting the preferred (but also internally disputed) self-definition of the Arab citizens of Israel. The terms are used as synonyms in spite of the diversity within the Arab communities and even though some Arab citizens of Israel are not, or would not, define themselves as Palestinians or even as Arabs (such as the Druze). Mainly out of convenience, the terms "Palestinian Israelis," "Arab Israelis," "Israeli Palestinians," "Israeli Palestinian citizens" are also used as synonyms.

112. Smooha, "Minority Status in an Ethnic Democracy"; Rouhana, *Palestinian Citizens*; Rouhana and Ghanem, "Crisis of Minorities in Ethnic States"; Shafir and Peled, *Being Israeli*; Peleg and Waxman, *Israel's Palestinians*; and Rekhess, "Evolvement of an Arab-Palestinian National Minority."

113. Orr Commission, *Din ve-Heshbon* [Report], Jerusalem, Judicial Authority (of the State of Israel), August 2003, http://elyon1.court.gov.il/heb/veadot/or/inside1.htm.

114. Conversely, religious communities enjoy a large autonomy in religious affairs and personal status matters (note that there is no civil marriage in Israel).

115. Orr Commission, *Din ve-Heshbon*.

116. Ibid. Confiscated land was transferred to the Custodian of Absentee Property, the Israel Land Administration, and the Jewish National Fund. The latter two organizations, explicitly or implicitly, pursue the objective of developing and allocating the land exclusively or predominantly for the benefit of the Jewish people.

117. Ibid.

118. Yiftachel, *Ethnocracy*, 136–46; and *Land Expropriation and Settlement Statistics*.

119. See, for example, International Crisis Group, *Back to Basics*, 10–19.

120. Smooha, "Class, Ethnic, and National Cleavages," 329.

121. In the 2015 elections, the three parties ran on a joint list as the threshold to enter the Knesset was raised to 3.25 percent.

122. Arian, *Politics in Israel*, 162.

123. Peleg and Waxman, *Israel's Palestinians*, 89–91.

124. Ibid., 97–100; and Rekhess, "Evolvement of an Arab-Palestinian National Minority," 15–16.

125. Williams, "Israel's Independent Arabic Media in the 2006 War."

126. Ben Meir, "Operation Cast Lead."

127. Amon Miranda, "Havrei Knesset neged Zoabi: Mehumah, Klalot, ve-Kim'at Makot" [MKs against Zoabi: Chaos, curses, and almost beatings], *Ynet*, June 2, 2010; Barak Ravid, "Interior Minister Seeks to Strip Israeli Arab MK of Citizenship," *Haaretz*, June 3, 2010; and Jonathan Lis, "Israeli Arab MK Who Joined Gaza Flotilla: IDF Raid Was a 'Pirate' Operation," *Haaretz*, June 2, 2010. The Israeli Supreme Court overruled a decision by the central elections committee to disqualify her from seeking reelection as a member of the Israeli parliament in 2012; see Aviel Magnezi, "Supreme Court: MK Zoabi Can Run for Knesset," *Ynet*, December 30, 2012.

128. Telhami, *2010 Israeli Arab/Palestinian Public Opinion Survey*.

129. International Crisis Group, *Back to Basics*, 3n16.

130. See International Crisis Group, *Identity Crisis*, 23–25.

131. Cited in Rouhana and Sultany, "Redrawing the Boundaries of Citizenship," 9.

132. Ibid.

133. Ibid., 15.

134. Kobi Finkler, "'Arvei Israel: Sakanah Estrategit" [Israeli Arabs: A strategic danger], *Channel 7 News*, March 13, 2007.

135. Netanyahu, quoted in Gideon Alon and Aluf Benn, "Netanyahu: Israel's Arabs Are the Real Demographic Threat," *Haaretz*, December 18, 2003. See also Diana Behor-Nir, "Netanyahu: ha-Be'ayah ha-Demografit Ne'utsah be-'Arvei Israel" [Netanyahu: The demographic problem lies with the Israeli Arabs], *Ynet*, December 17, 2003.

136. Moran Zelikovitz, "Seker: 64% me-ha-Israelim be'ad Transfer shel 'Aravim" [Poll: 64% of Israelis are in favor of transferring Arabs], *Ynet*, June 21, 2004.

137. Arik Bender, "75% me-ha-Tsibur be'ad Transfer le-'Arvei Israel" [75% of the public are in favor of transferring Arab Israelis], *Maariv*, March 31, 2008.

138. Ben Meir and Shaked, "People Speak," 80; and Ben Meir and Bagno-Moldavsky, "Vox Populi," 93.

139. Rouhana and Sultany, "Redrawing the Boundaries of Citizenship," 15; Ben Meir and Shaked, "People Speak," 81; and Ben Meir and Bagno-Moldavsky, "Vox Populi," 93–94.

140. Ben Meir and Shaked, "People Speak," 81; and Ben Meir and Bagno-Moldavsky, "Vox Populi," 93–94.

141. Ben Meir and Shaked, "People Speak," 81–82.

142. See "Supreme Court Overturns Ban on Arab Parties from National Elections," *Haaretz*, January 26, 2009; and International Crisis Group, *Back to Basics*, 8.

143. Chaim Levinson, "Dozens of Top Israeli Rabbis Sign Ruling to Forbid Rental of Homes to Arabs," *Haaretz*, December 7, 2010.

144. Peleg and Waxman, *Israel's Palestinians*, 79; see also Sharon Roffe-Ofir, "Mashber Imun: Le'an Holkhim 'Arvei Israel?" [A crisis of trust: Where are Israeli Arabs headed?], *Ynet*, November 3, 2008.

145. For numerous examples, see Peleg and Waxman, *Israel's Palestinians*, chap. 3.

146. Israel does not have a constitution, but it has a series of basic laws. The most important documents put forward by Israel's Palestinian citizens are *The Future Vision Document of the Palestinian Arabs in Israel*, published by the National Committee for the Heads of the Arab Local Authorities in Israel, and *The Democratic Constitution*, published by Adalah; see The National Committee for the Heads of the Arab Local Authorities in Israel, *The Future Vision Document of the Palestinian Arabs in Israel*, Nazareth, 2006, published by Adalah, http://www.adalah.org/uploads/oldfiles/newsletter/eng/dec06/tasawor-mostaqbali.pdf; and *The Democratic Constitution*, Shafa'amr: Adalah, March 30, 2007, http://www.adalah.org/uploads/oldfiles/Public/files/democratic_constitution-english.pdf. On this issue see also Rekhess, "Evolvement of an Arab-Palestinian National Minority," 17–21; and Al-Haj, "Whither the Green Line."

147. On the domestic fault lines in Israel's identity contestation, see Del Sarto, *Contested State Identities*, chap. 3.

148. Peleg and Waxman, *Israel's Palestinians*, 215; International Crisis Group, *Identity Crisis*, 25; and International Crisis Group, *Back to Basics*.

149. The authorization to revoke the citizenship must follow the request of the minister of interior and with the written approval of the attorney general. See Levush, "Israel: Revocation of Citizenship."

150. Ha-Knesset [The Knesset], "Hok ha-Ezrahut (Tikun Mispar 9)."

151. Shai Lavi, "Revocation of Citizenship? Not in Israel," *Haaretz*, November 9, 2010; and Rebecca Anna Stoil, "Knesset Passes Law Revoking Citizenship for Treason," *Jerusalem Post*, March 28, 2011.

152. Ha-Knesset [The Knesset], "Hok ha-Ezrahut ve-ha-Knisah le-Israel."

153. See, for example, International Crisis Group, *Back to Basics*, 8–10.

154. See, for example, Roni Schocken, "Chilling Effect of the Nakba Law on Israel's Human Rights," *Haaretz*, May 17, 2011. The term "*nakbah*" is used to describe the suffering of Palestinians, including the around 750,000 who fled or were expelled from Israel in the war that led to the establishment of the State of Israel. Palestinians commemorate the *nakbah* on Israel's Independence Day. On the creation of the Palestinian refugee problem, see most authoritatively Morris, *Birth of the Palestinian Refugee Problem, 1947–1949*; and Morris, *Birth of the Palestinian Refugee Problem Revisited.*

155. Ha-Knesset [The Knesset], "Hok Minhal me-Karka'ei Yisrael, Tikun Mispar 7."

156. Ha-Knesset [The Knesset], "Hok le-Tikun Pkudat ha-Karka'ot."

157. Mazal Mualem, "Lieberman: Leftist Groups Are Terrorist Collaborators," *Haaretz*, January 11, 2011.

158. Begin, quoted in Jonathan Freedland, "McCarthyism—Israeli Style," *Jewish Chronicle*, January 24, 2011.

159. Ibid.

160. Kremnitzer, quoted in "Israel's Democracy: Under Siege Too," *Economist*, June 17, 2010.

161. Jonathan Lis, "Israel Passes Law Banning Calls for Boycott," *Haaretz*, July 11, 2011.

162. Morris, *Righteous Victims*, 269–72.

163. On the political discourse defining the African immigrants as a security threat, see Yacobi, "'Let Me Go to the City.'"

164. Roni Sofer, "Olmert: Yesh La'atsor Tsunami ha-Mistanenim me-Mitsrayyim" [Olmert: We must stop the tsunami of infiltrators from Egypt], *Ynet*, March 23, 2008.

165. Yaron, Hashimshony-Yaffe, and Campbell, "'Infiltrators' or Refugees?," 145.

166. Ilan Lior, "Netanyahu Backs Bill for Prolonged Detention of Illegal Migrants," *Haaretz*, October 19, 2013.

167. Yaron, Hashimshony-Yaffe and Campbell, "'Infiltrators' or Refugees?," 145.

168. Ilan Lior and Tomer Zarchin, "Demonstrators Attack African Migrants in South Tel Aviv," *Haaretz*, May 24, 2012.

169. For an analysis of Israel's notably improved regional environment in light of the Arab Peace initiative, see Kam, "Israel through Arab Strategic Lenses."

170. Rouhana and Sultany, "Redrawing the Boundaries of Citizenship."

3

A New Domestic Hegemony

Factors and Explanations

Why did one particular understanding of regional order become so powerful and so successful in taking hold of the Israeli collective? Which factors explain the emergence of a hegemonic vision of threats and regional order in post-Oslo Israel? Looking at a combination of factors and developments, this chapter offers an explanation for the remarkable lack of dissent in the Israeli body politic in the 2000s. The investigation starts by looking at the construction of Israeli identity and the dominant historical narratives that define the Israeli experience, showing that Israeli identity is deeply conducive to specific interpretations of the regional environment. The doctrinal foundations as well as the practices of Israeli foreign and security policy are an additional aspect that will be considered. Revealing a striking similarity with the collective understandings that prevail in Israel post-Oslo, long-established principles and practices of Israeli foreign policies partly explain why one interpretation of events is more likely to take hold of the Israeli foreign policy establishment than others. Next, the strengthening of neo-revisionist ideology since the 1970s and the constant shift to the right in Israeli policies are discussed. As we will see, the rise of neo-revisionism, with its embrace of territorial maximalism and ethnoreligious nationalism, deeply affected the Israeli collective perceptions of the region while increasingly intertwining the settlement project with security considerations. Psychological factors related to the end of the Oslo process and renewed violence and terrorism are similarly relevant. The argument here is that fear is a powerful instinct that tends to win over hope and cognition. Finally, the role of specific agents as well as politicians, the media, and the security establishment in promoting a specific vision of Israel and the world are revisited.

Israel's Collective Identity

Israel's collective identity is a relatively new phenomenon. It was molded by Zionism, the Jewish form of nationalism, before and after the establishment of the State of Israel in 1948.[1] As with other nationalisms, the impetus of Zionism was to provide a uniform history and a common sense of destiny to an emerging society, thus forging a bounded political community in the process of nation building.[2] There is reason to argue that the specific way in which Israel's collective identity has been constructed and reinforced throughout the decades is likely to forge specific interpretations of events and developments. This consideration is anchored in the extensive body of literature that highlights the impact of collective memory and identities on cognition. According to these findings, beliefs may act as a filter for understanding the present as well as for the formulation of expectations for the future.[3] As we will see, the hegemonic notion of threats and regional order in post-Oslo Israel mirrors the core themes of the Jewish Israeli collective consciousness. Israel's collective identity may thus act as a predisposition of sorts. It may explain why Israelis are more likely to focus on one set of factors in interpreting regional events than on others, particularly in the presence of a constellation of other enabling conditions.

Israel's collective identity was mainly shaped by secular Labor Zionism, the dominant stream of Zionism, in the prestate era and immediately after the establishment of the state. The construction of Israeli identity faced the challenge of a pronounced cultural heterogeneity characterizing the newly immigrated Jews to Palestine, and later Israel, who hailed from very different countries. In addition to the necessity of rescuing European Jews from destruction, Zionism had to provide legitimacy to Jewish statehood in Palestine. These objectives were achieved through the negation of two thousand years of Jewish life and culture in the Diaspora. Instead, Zionism emphasized a historical continuity of Jewish presence in Palestine, from antiquity to Israeli statehood, in order to underline Jewish historical rights to the land.[4] Concurrently, Palestinian history was expunged from the collective memory under construction. Dominated by the *Jewish* collective experience until today (Israel's Arab citizens are not part of the collective consciousness), Israel's identity thus came to espouse the Zionist narrative of return and liberation. It is important to note that, although Labor Zionism used the Old Testament as national history, at that time the dominant stream of Zionism was basically secular, relying on a mix of partly socialist-inspired and partly liberal-progressive beliefs.[5]

Another key element in Israeli identity is the history of oppression and persecution of the Jewish people that culminated in the Holocaust. The negative Diaspora experience, the Holocaust, and the consciousness of victimhood in Jewish Israeli collective memory undoubtedly nurtured the belief that the world was inherently hostile toward the Jewish people—"the whole world is against us" (*ha-ʿolam kulo negdeinu*).[6] It also provided the *raison d'état* to the State of Israel, with the "return to Zion" correcting "a cosmic injustice that had lasted for thousands of years," according to the Zionist narrative.[7]

The combination of Jewish history and the almost-constant experience of war, conflict, and threats regarding the Arab neighbors cultivated a basic "conflict formula" that specifically revolves around the notion of "the few against the many."[8] The commemoration of Jewish armed resistance in antiquity and in the prestate era, in Israel's official holiday and memorial cycle, bears evidence to this. Thus, as Yael Zerubavel puts it, Hanukkah commemorates the Maccabean revolt against the Greeks, Purim revolves around the threat to the Jews of Persia, Passover marks the liberation of the Jewish people from bondage in Egypt, Israel's Independence Day commemorates the war against Arab forces, Tisha B'Av remembers the destruction of the First and Second Jewish Temples, and Holocaust Day commemorates the Nazi atrocities.[9] The Israeli sociologist Baruch Kimmerling observed in this context the absorption of conflict into the institutions of society, with war and protracted conflict acquiring a central role in Israel's collective self-understanding.[10]

The Jewish reclaiming of power was no less significant, however. It reflected Labor Zionism's objective of creating the new "Hebrew man," who, in contrast to the Jews in exile, was strong, assertive, secular, and able to defend himself. The acquisition of Jewish power resulted in what Yaron Ezrahi has termed a "defensive ethos" in the first decades of statehood, with a growing military prowess coexisting with the constant sense of being a threatened minority fighting for its very survival.[11] According to Ezrahi, "The sense of siege continued for a long time to militate against the development of the kind of reserved and prudent stance toward the use of force which is the prerogative of the strong."[12] It should be noted that the centrality of security concerns and the conviction of facing an exceptional security situation explain Israel's investment in a technologically advanced army and the importance given to deterrence, preemptive strikes, and retaliatory military actions.[13] While the army acquired a central role and prestige in Israel, it was noted that the "Israelis' search for security is an obsession, a quest for an almost metaphysical security, even if they know that such protection is beyond their political and military capabilities."[14]

The concept of being a besieged and isolated island in a sea of hatred and rejection is thus disturbingly familiar to the Jewish Israeli collective memory. Post-Oslo, Israel's prevailing notions of existential threat and a menacing regional order thus reflect deeply entrenched cognitive patterns and collective beliefs. The idea of having no partner for peace also resonates surprisingly well with Israel's collective memory, which traditionally considers "the Arabs" as intransigent and evil.[15] It is worth noting that Ehud Barak's "no partner for peace" theme bears a striking resemblance to Israel's official narrative of "waiting for the Arab phone call" to trade territories for peace after the June 1967 war, a narrative that recent research has debunked as a myth.[16]

Likewise, the notion of an evil alliance set on Israel's destruction—figuring prominently in the post-Oslo consensus—resonates ominously with the long history of discrimination and persecution of the Jewish people. The centrality of the Holocaust in the Jewish Israeli collective memory also explains why former Iranian president Mahmoud Ahmadinejad's denial of the Holocaust—or Hamas's anti-Semitic charter, for that matter—touches a raw nerve in Israel.[17] It also explains the relative ease with which it is possible to generate consensus around the need to fight those enemies with exceptional means, if necessary. Anti-Jewish statements and attitudes also reinforce the conviction that anti-Semitism is endemic and will not disappear, a core belief of Zionism. The latter, it should be noted, has remained the matrix of Israel's political culture and collective identity.

Thus, the specific construction of the Jewish Israeli collective identity can be seen as a precondition for the emergence of Israel's hegemonic vision of threats and regional order in the 2000s. Seen in this light, the years of the Oslo peace process were an exception. In this specific period, political leaders were trying to change deeply entrenched thinking patterns in Israel's peacemaking efforts, as argued elsewhere.[18] Thus, Yitzhak Rabin called on Israelis to "revolutionize our thought and behavior patterns" so as to be part of the new reality that peacemaking required.[19] As Rabin stressed, "No longer are we necessarily 'a people that dwells alone,' and no longer is it true that 'the whole world is against us.' We must overcome the sense of isolation that has held us in its thrall for almost half a century."[20] Likewise, former Israeli president Ezer Weizman called Israel's sense of isolation a "ghetto mentality" that was an obstacle to the peace process, while Shimon Peres sought to convince Israelis that their country was, and should be, firmly anchored in a "New Middle East."[21]

The attempted manipulations of Jewish Israeli collective identity during the Oslo process were only partly successful. It is important to note in this context that persistent conflict and perceptions of external threat lend cohesion to societies. This is particularly significant in the case of traditionally heterogeneous and internally fragmented societies, such as the Israeli one. Conversely, the prospects of moving toward a radically different regional order in the context of peacemaking brought the deep fault lines of Israeli society to the fore. Implying a need to choose between very different conceptions of Israel and its society, the domestic divisions put a strain on foreign policymaking toward the region in that period.[22] The collapse of Oslo and the outbreak of the Second Intifada forged a renewed sense of unity among the Jewish Israeli collective while also prompting a "regression" to familiar patterns of collective thinking.

These dynamics are reflected, for instance, in Israeli schoolbooks. Pointing to the "need to construct a collective memory," Elie Podeh notes that for most decades of Israeli statehood, the historical narrative in Israeli textbooks was "replete with bias, prejudice, errors, misrepresentations and even deliberate omissions."[23] Concurrently, the Arabs (as a further unspecified group) were regularly portrayed "in stereotypical terms that in turn reinforced a distorted image in Israel society."[24] In the 1990s—that is, during the Oslo process—a shift in the official historical narrative and collective identity toward a less biased historiography has been observed; for some authors this has been a constant development since statehood.[25] However, Israeli school textbooks written in the 2000s—that is, after the end of Oslo—returned to extremely one-sided accounts of the conflict. These are coupled with narratives about Jewish persecution and victimhood, while significant geopolitical and social realities in Israel, the Palestinian territories, and the wider region are ignored.[26]

Significantly, the new consensus on threats and regional order post-Oslo also reinforces specific elements of Jewish Israeli collective identity. This partly explains the self-sustaining nature of the new hegemony. In other words, Israel's new consensus and the policies it prescribes are bound to strengthen the collective conviction of being under siege, which, in turn, lends itself to a specific interpretation of events. With regard to the link between collective beliefs and cognition, Ezrahi remarked almost two decades ago, when describing Israeli settlers in the Palestinian territories, that "Jews who built their homes in the midst of heavily populated Arab towns and villages, among Arabs enraged by the forced confiscation of their lands, were able to preserve, and even reinforce, a well-entrenched

ghetto mentality by reproducing the conditions and feelings of being surrounded by hostile enemies."[27]

It is reasonable to assume that the repeated narrative of the absence of
a Palestinian partner for peace and the eminently hostile regional environment produced a similar effect, strengthening the Jewish Israeli sense
of collective victimhood and the "siege mentality."[28] As intractable conflicts are conducive to the evolvement of a simplistic collective knowledge
in which the "enemy is presented . . . as violent, cruel, untrustworthy, and
primitive," the renewal of violence with the Second Intifada is likely to
have reinforced these one-dimensional collective beliefs.[29] At the same
time, Israel's forceful and unilateral policies of the first post-Oslo decade
invigorated the Zionist notion of righteous Jewish force and self-defense.

Of course, the rocket fire by Hamas and Hizballah, the frequent terrorist attacks, and the anti-Semitic statements of regional actors were not
particularly helpful to the dissipation of Israel's dominant perception of
threats and regional order. As mentioned previously, the suicide bombings and the rockets launched by Hamas had a profound impact on the
voting behavior of Israelis, contributing to Israel's shift to the right.[30] Yet
the Arab peace initiative and Israel's snubbing of it, together with the
country's own insistent continuation of the settlement project, obviously
fell through the cracks in this collective cognition.

Fear and insecurity are powerful tools in politics, justifying exceptional
means and frequently keeping politicians in power.[31] In the Israeli case, a
collective identity based on a sense of being under siege, combined with
a strong defensive ethos, lends itself particularly well to political manip-
ulation. Thus, with regard to the first decades of Israeli statehood, Zeev
Maoz noted that "the siege mentality that Ben-Gurion propagated may
have been a genuine perception. It was also a very useful social mobi-
lizer. And it may have also been an important aspect of the ruling party's
strategy for maintaining its political power. Finally, inflating the security
threat emerged as an extremely effective strategy for raising funds for
Jews all over the world."[32] Ezrahi too describes this evolving relationship
between Jewish power and perceived weakness, in that "while we were
gradually becoming wolves, we continued to feel and pose as lambs,"
while Peter Beinart speaks out against the perpetuation of a "narrative
of victimhood."[33] While threats to Israel persist, of course, the narrative
evades the "question of how to ethically wield Jewish power," exercised
over millions of Palestinians. Making Israel's occupation permanent, the
narrative of victimhood also puts a strain on peacemaking in the final
analysis, according to Beinart.[34]

Doctrines and Practices of Israel's Foreign Policy

The doctrinal foundations of Israel's foreign and security policy mirror the specific construction of Jewish Israeli collective identity surprisingly well. In the light of the experience of constant conflict with the neighbors that accompanied the Jewish settlement enterprise in Palestine, combined with the collective memory of the Holocaust in Europe, a central premise of Israel's national security is the notion that the country is engaged in a struggle for its survival in a hostile strategic environment. A second core assumption is that the conflict with its neighbors is "inherently and unalterably asymmetrical and that the Jewish state is and will always remain the weaker party."[35] David Ben-Gurion made this argument shortly after the establishment of the state, stressing that Israel was "a small island surrounded by a great Arab ocean extending over two continents."[36] This notion has been repeated by Israeli leaders ever since, and it is widely shared by the Jewish Israeli public, as various opinion polls taken over the decades show. Because of the pronounced numerical inequality, Israel perceived itself to be always on the defensive—even if it engaged in aggressive acts. This is because "the Arabs," usually conceived of as a unified front, could destroy Israel—but not the other way round. In fact, Israel's security doctrine is anchored in the conviction that the Arabs would annihilate Israel, given the chance, and that they would not recognize Israel's right to exist. Threatening Israel with annihilation was indeed rather common in the rhetoric of Arab leaders, particularly in the first decades of statehood, which witnessed a series of major wars. This is contrasted to Israel's longing for peace, a central element in the country's collective self-image.

Israel's security thinking thus put a strong emphasis on the country's own military might, together with an active deterrence, preemption, and the punitive and demonstrative use of force. The notion of the "Iron Wall," originally coined by revisionist leader Zeev (Vladimir) Jabotinsky but also implicitly adopted by Israeli Labor governments, assumed that only the use of force would ultimately guarantee Israel's very existence, with the Arab neighbors having ultimately no choice but to accept it. In fact, the military component of the Iron Wall doctrine became the basis of Israeli government strategies from 1948 onward.[37] Given the asymmetries, Israel's national security doctrine also emphasized the principle of "quality versus quantity." Accordingly, Israel invested massively in the army's technological advantage while establishing compulsory military service and a large reserve force, with Israel often being described as "a nation in

arms." Furthermore, Israel's small size and vulnerability in terms of territory gave rise to the concepts of strategic depth and defensible borders,
partly explaining the implicit consensus on keeping the territories Israeli
occupied in 1967 in the absence of peace.[38]

When the Islamic Republic of Iran became yet another part of the hostile strategic environment, seeking to prevent the acquisition of weapons
of mass destruction by hostile actors became a further major concern in
Israel's strategic thinking.[39] Finally, regarding the international community, a central assumption in the Israeli concept of national security is that
others cannot be trusted when it comes to defending the country. As history had proven, Jews could rely only on themselves; only they would risk
their lives in defending the country. This conviction reflects the theme of
a "people that shall dwell alone."[40]

Reflecting the construction of Israel's identity, which is based on historical experience, the country's security thinking clearly accentuates
the morality of Israeli motivation and behavior and the externally imposed need for protection and self-defense. It is no coincidence that the
Israeli army is called Israel *Defense* Forces (IDF; Tsva Haganah le-Israel,
or Tzahal, in its Hebrew acronym). Likewise, the belief in the "purity of
arms" (*tohar ha-neshek*) and the notion of the moral superiority of the
IDF (particularly in comparison to the armies of Arab states) are deeply
entrenched in Jewish Israeli society and politics.

However, Maoz notes that over the decades Israel's military superiority
and success on the battlefield also gave rise to a feeling of arrogance that
has been coexisting uneasily with the notions of victimhood and fight for
survival.[41] The basic understanding has been that the Arab side would
only negotiate with Israel from a weak position. This is tantamount to
the common belief in Israel that the "Arabs only understand force." While,
incidentally, the same assessment about Israel is frequently heard in Arab
societies, it is worth noting that when the other side is weak, Israel has
no reason to make concessions either, as members of Israel's security and
foreign policy community sometimes acknowledge.[42]

Significantly, the axioms of Israel's security doctrine have rarely been
questioned. However, as Maoz points out, reality did not exactly back up
the Israeli notion of an all-encompassing and coherent Arab coalition, and
the assumption of existential threat was widely exaggerated. According
to Maoz, the Arab states never invested in all that was necessary to annihilate Israel, and "most programs aimed at developing WMDs [weapons
of mass destruction] and delivery systems in the Arab world emerged
largely in response to Israel's nuclear policy."[43] Concurrently, the notion

of strategic depth legitimizing the continuous rule over the Palestinian territories may not have actually increased Israel's security in the medium and long term. Instead, this protracted rule over the territories is most likely to have nurtured resistance and extremism. Altogether, however, the notion that force may in fact exacerbate anti-Israeli violence is rarely considered in Israel's strategic thinking.

Also important are the blind spots of Israel's security thinking—the same blind spots that characterize the Jewish Israeli collective identity. What does not figure is even the slightest possibility that Israel may have inflicted some sort of injustice on the Palestinians in 1948 or that the Palestinians' rights to the land are at least as legitimate as the Jewish Israeli ones. Similarly, the key role played by the Israeli army in keeping the Palestinians under a protracted occupation—with military rule over another people inevitably entailing very ugly and immoral practices—is not part of Israel's strategic thinking. Altogether, a high sense of morality continues to characterize Israel's image of itself, the Zionist project, its strategic thinking and behavior. The notion of Israel's longing for peace is central, with unorthodox policies considered necessary, given the externally imposed struggle for survival. According to Israeli sociology professor Eva Illouz, while Israeli politicians, intellectuals, and different societal groups highlight Israel's quest for peace, thus reaffirming the country's moral identity, "Israel actually engaged in policies of neglect, obliviousness, and harsh domination. Israel built settlements; used the Israel Defense Forces to defend settlers against victimized Palestinians . . . ; seized land . . . ; created roadblocks breaking apart families and geographical movement . . . ; retaliated on Palestinians for wanting to be accepted by the UN or for forming a unity government."[44]

Israel's security doctrine is significant mainly because of the central role the military establishment plays in the Israeli body politic. First, at the societal level, the Israeli army has remained the most powerful tool of integration and socialization among mainly Jewish Israelis from different backgrounds and ethnicities, sabras and new immigrants alike.[45] Indeed, with the exception of the ultra-Orthodox community, whose military service was deferred, all Jewish Israelis are drafted into the army.[46] Conversely, while the Druze community is drafted to the army, most Muslim Palestinians citizens are exempted from military service (Christian Palestinian citizens and Bedouins may serve in the army on a voluntary basis). Thus, military service contributes considerably to the stratification of Israeli society as well as to the cohesion of the Jewish Israeli collective, while setting the boundaries of this collective. The centrality of the army in Israeli society must also be seen against the backdrop of the Holocaust and the image of the defenseless Jew in Israel's collective identity.[47] Thus, the army plays a key role in the nation-building process. Security and military service also act as cultural codes against this background. While Kimmerling defined security as a civil religion, he also noted that Israeli society "is oriented towards permanent war preparation in order to defend the collectivity's very existence."[48] The Israeli sociology professor remarked that such "preparation becomes part of social routine and is no longer considered a matter of public debate or political struggle."[49] While the military is also the institution that the Jewish Israeli public trusts and respects the most, army officials have an almost sacred authority in Israeli society and politics.[50]

Second, at the level of domestic politics, the political and military establishments are deeply intertwined in Israel, with the army being a formidable launch pad for political careers. Indeed, many Israeli prime ministers and key political figures have a significant military or security background; often they were former commanders or chiefs of staff. Examples include Yitzhak Rabin, Ehud Barak, Ariel Sharon, and Moshe Ya'alon, but also Moshe Dayan, Menachem Begin, and Yitzhak Shamir (with the latter two leading, respectively, the militias Etzel and Lehi in the prestate era). Powerful formal and informal networks connect the military and the political echelons in Israel, while Israel's security establishment is also linked to the lucrative and mainly state-owned Israeli defense industry.

Finally, and perhaps most importantly, the central role of Israel's security doctrine impacts significantly on Israel's regional and international relations, given the role of the defense establishment in Israeli policy. To put it bluntly, Israel does not have a foreign policy: it has a security policy. Maoz emphasizes the notion of a *"derivate foreign policy,"* showing that "Israel's foreign policy has always been a servant of Israel's security policy."[51] In other words, the security and defense establishment clearly trumps Israel's Foreign Ministry and the diplomatic corps in the foreign policy decision-making process, and the Foreign Ministry's department of policy planning is largely marginalized and kept outside the intelligence loop. As senior Foreign Ministry officials often complain—usually off the record—it is thus the Defense Ministry, together with the security establishment, that define Israel's foreign relations.[52]

The structures and practices of Israel's security policy clearly reflect the centrality of Israel's defensive ethos. Maoz's seminal study of Israel's foreign and security policy since the establishment of the state reveals that a "centralized, self-serving, and self-perpetuating security community" dominates the country's policymaking process.[53] Composed of the army and various security services, this community is strong, bureaucratically extremely efficient, and well-funded. Working largely in secrecy, it lacks civilian institutions and parliamentary oversight, with deferral generally characterizing the position and rulings of Israel's High Court of Justice toward the security establishment. Furthermore, the army has established itself as the main provider of the required knowledge for conceptualizing, planning, and managing violent confrontation. The political echelons thus rely on the military knowledge infrastructure, a "hegemonic knowledge that has almost no competitors."[54]

Michael Brecher noted that the structure of Israel's security establishment acts as a filter, influencing the perception of problems and the definition of possible solutions to address these problems.[55] The rigid axiomatic foundations of Israel's security policy, which are reflected in the operational environment, thus explain the prevalence of specific concepts of threat and regional order over others. They also account for the usually limited choice of alternative policies to address specific threats and developments.

Significantly, the prevailing axioms and structures of Israel's foreign policy also explain misconceptions, failed assessments, and outright policy failures. Providing numerous examples from the history of Israel's regional and foreign relations, Maoz argues that, independently of the government in power, Israel's security doctrine and the institutional framework of the country's foreign policy have produced a trigger-happy and risk-taking attitude. They have generated flawed and ineffective conflict management strategies, the inability to understand long-term political processes, the tendency to run covert and unsupervised operations and programs that often include interference in the domestic politics of other states, and the tendency of the security sector to cover up mistakes.[56] Stressing that the notions of defensive wars and "retaliatory" military actions rest "on shaky foundations," Maoz's scathing conclusion is that "most of Israel's wars were the result of deliberate aggressive designs or flawed conflict management strategies."[57]

In fact, since the establishment of the state, Israel has not been a particularly proactive partner for peace. Contrary to the prominent narrative of the country's longing for peace, Israel missed at least as many opportunities for peacemaking as its adversaries have missed. While rarely initiating peace initiatives, several diplomatic efforts failed because of usually badly timed (and sometimes also badly executed) Israeli military or intelligence operations. The talks with Egypt's Nasser in 1953–54 or the tacit understanding achieved with Jordan's King Hussein in the 1960s are cases in point.[58] Israel's military operations in the territories during the Oslo process are no exception here. In fact, the unfortunate timing of specific military operations while the Oslo process was still ongoing has often been explained in terms of a specific opportunity opening up (for instance, for assassinating a "wanted" Hamas operative), in plain disregard of political considerations. In discussions with members of Israel's security establishment, the explanation of "we did it because we could" is often heard. Moreover, because the military bureaucracy has traditionally been extremely suspicious of any peace overture from the Arab side, it usually prefers small and cautious steps to test the ground while being overly concerned with short-term security needs and procedures. In the case of Oslo, this strategy backfired.

In general terms, the juxtaposition of a siege mentality and what former chief of military intelligence and Hebrew University professor Yehoshafat Harkabi called a "policy of arrogance" in Israel's strategic thinking does not seem to be particularly conducive to peacemaking.[59] With a mixture of feelings of fear and superiority also characterizing the Israeli public at large, fear may nurture paranoia and mental closure, while arrogance is associated with scorn and contempt toward the other side.[60] Combined, they may cultivate a sense of self-righteousness and indifference to the needs and suffering of the other side.

Under these conditions, one may wonder, then, how the Oslo peace process could come about in the first place. In addition to a favorable constellation of international and regional conditions after the end of the Cold War, one answer is that the process started as secret track-II diplomacy talks in the Norwegian capital, from which the security establishment was initially excluded.[61] While Yitzhak Rabin had stressed that the issues discussed in Oslo were of a mainly political and ideological nature, the security establishment was soon brought in. Uri Savir, former director-general of Israel's Foreign Ministry and chief negotiator of the Oslo Accords between 1993 and 1996, explains that after the initial Declaration of Principles of 1993, Rabin appointed a new team of negotiators from the army. The result was that immediate security considerations became dominant. With the Foreign Ministry increasingly sidelined by the security establishment, the process was soon subjugated to the traditional patterns of Israeli foreign—or, rather, security—policy.[62] This may very well explain one aspect of Oslo's failure.

The discussion so far clearly shows that the prevailing axioms, structures, and practices in Israeli foreign and security policy are strongly favorable to one interpretation of threats and regional order over others. While supporting the view that there is no partner for peace in an inherently hostile and evil environment, they also legitimize sometimes ill-conceived military actions and the excessive use of force, unilateralism, the deflection of blame for escalating violence, and the general absence of a political matrix in which security policies operate. Hence, the prevalence of military considerations and bureaucracies over the policymaking process and of persistent strategic myths and psychological constraints are important factors in explaining the emergence of the consensus on regional foreign policy that took hold of Israeli politics after 2000.

Neo-Revisionism and Israel's Shift to the Right

The construction of Israel's collective identity, together with the foundations of Israel's foreign and security policy and its modus operandi, provides the matrix for a specific thinking on threat and regional order. However, a number of developments in Israeli politics and society are no less relevant here. Most significantly, these include the rise of neo-revisionism and Israel's constant shift to the right over recent decades.

While Labor Zionism aimed at providing a secure existence for the Jewish people through the "ingathering of the exiles" into a sovereign state, it was also secular, relatively progressive in its socialist-collectivist orientation, and open to universalist values and the world at large. Of course, different schools of thought existed within Labor Zionism from the outset, and the challenge of ensuring a Jewish majority in a state did not necessarily lead to particularly liberal or progressive prescriptions regarding the question of how to deal with the non-Jewish inhabitants in the British Mandate of Palestine, and later in Israel. The conquest of the territories in June 1967, however, provided the material basis to the rise of a rather different kind of Zionism—namely, revisionist Zionism, the belief system originally promoted by Zeev Jabotinsky. Israel's newly acquired control over important sites of the Jewish religion—most notably the Western Wall in Jerusalem's old city but also Hebron, Shechem (Nablus), and Beit El—exposed Jewish Israelis to Jewish history and tradition, raising strong religious (and often messianic) sentiments among a large part of the Jewish Israeli population. The conquest of the territories thus undoubtedly boosted the revisionist version of Zionism, with its focus on "Greater Israel." The establishment of the Movement for Greater Israel (Tnuah le-Erets Yisrael ha-Shlemah) in September 1967, which had the support of many politicians and intellectuals of the Labor movement,

lent additional legitimacy to the revisionists. Additionally capitalizing on
the widespread popular anger at the security establishment for failing to
predict the 1973 October Yom Kippur War as well as on the resentment
of Mizrahi Jews against the Ashkenazi Labor establishment, the Herut
and later Likud party of Menachem Begin would win the Israeli elections
in 1977.[63] Described as "upheaval" (*mahapah*), these elections ended the
dominance of the Labor Party that had marked the first decades of Israeli
statehood, bringing to power a movement that had hitherto been considered an extremist outsider.

Crystallizing in the 1920s and 1930s, Jabotinsky's original version of
revisionist Zionism took issue with the socioeconomic prescriptions of
Labor Zionism, but it also postulated a number of key principles regarding Israel's place in the region and in the world. These include the inevi-
tability of the struggle between Jews and Arabs, seen as a zero-sum game;
the belief in Jewish historical rights over the land on both sides of the river
Jordan; the principles of isolation and vulnerability of the Jewish people;
a deep distrust of the Gentiles; and the belief in the supremacy of the
use of force. As noted earlier, Jabotinsky's concept of the "Iron Wall" was
central in revisionist Zionism, thus the idea that the Zionist project was to
be carried out in defiance of the will of the Arab population—by force, if
necessary.[64] Classical revisionist thinking was nationalist and pessimistic,
often yielding to far-right pressure, but not necessarily religious. In fact,
Jabotinsky himself had been a secularist—although in 1935 he discovered
the "sacred treasures of Jewish tradition."[65]

The ascending revisionist thinking after 1967, termed neo-revisionism,
represented a radicalized version of classical Zionist revisionist thought.
Thus, under Prime Minister Begin, a strongly romanticized notion of the
nation was promoted, and the use of power was emphasized. The political
aspect of Jabotinsky's conception of the "Iron Wall," which considered it
as a means to an end, after which negotiations could bring about a political settlement, was ignored. Devoid of its political component, only
the doctrine's military aspect of endless war remained central. Concurrently, the idea of the relations between Jews and Gentiles were reinterpreted so that the world was now presented as being actively engaged in
attempts to destroy the Jewish people. Arab hostility to Israel was now
also associated with classical Christian anti-Semitism, although the two
phenomena are of course not identical. A tendency to dehumanize the
enemy—mainly "the Arabs" but also internal and external opponents—
has been observed as well. Moreover, as the notion of national redemption indicates, neo-revisionism incorporated messianic elements in its

attempts to revive Jewish tradition and religion as a national history.[66] Altogether, the strengthening of neo-revisionism entailed a stronger emphasis on ethnocentric primordial and religious elements in the definition of nationalism.[67] Equally important, Israel's control over the territories was placed above any other consideration. As Ofira Seliktar points out, "The Six-Day-War indicated to the new Zionists that Israel should assume the mission of securing a Jewish state within its proper Biblical border. Physical safety, normalization in international relations, and even the yearning for peace should be subordinated to this goal."[68]

Neo-revisionism is not necessarily a religiously motivated ideology. However, the absorption of messianic elements, the focus on Jewish ethnicity (which cannot entirely be separated from Jewish religion), and the notion of the unbreakable link between the biblical Land of Israel and the Jewish people made neo-revisionism highly compatible with religious Zionism, yet another thread of Zionism. Developed by Rabbi Abraham Isaac Kook and his son, this strand of Zionism views the establishment of the state not as an act of national liberation or as an attempt to rescue Jews from extermination. Rather, based on a reinterpretation of Jewish religious orthodoxy, religious Zionism considers the founding of Israel as the beginning of a divinely inspired process of redemption. Significantly, in this national-religious belief system, the idea of the integrity of the land is based on the religious conviction that God has given the land to the Jewish people. The 1967 Six-Day War is thus interpreted as divine intervention in the redemption of the land, in which the secular establishment is sometimes described as "the donkey": it plays an important role in the redemption process without being aware of the mission's divine nature. For religious Zionists, including the Gush Emunim movement, which emerged after 1967 and has remained the backbone of the religious settler movement, giving up any part of the Land of Israel is thus strictly forbidden on religious grounds.

Starting in the 1970s, the neo-revisionists tried to refashion the way Israelis thought about the state and its place in the region—and in the world. According to Ian Lustick, "Begin's objective was nothing less than the hegemonic establishment of a new Zionist paradigm, supported by a new history of the independence struggle, a new relationship between religion and politics, and a new emphasis on the people, Bible, and Land of Israel rather than on the boundaries, citizens and laws of the state of Israel."[69] Unsurprisingly, the fusion of a Hobbesian worldview with prophetic elements and territorial maximalism had a major impact on Israel's domestic and international policies. For one, the belief that Israel was forced to "live by the sword" increasingly informed the thinking of policy-makers. It strengthened the tendency to engage in unilateral and defiant policies, together with the determination to use force in Israel's continued conflict with its Arab neighbors. The Basic Law of 1980, declaring Jerusalem as complete and united capital of Israel, the bombing of Iraq's nuclear Osirak reactor in 1981, and—most prominently—the 1982 invasion of Lebanon are cases in point.[70]

Second, the neo-revisionist idea of "a nation that shall dwell alone" impacted on Israel's relations to the international community. The conviction that the world was inherently hostile to the Jewish people reinforced the tendency to view criticism as the result of anti-Semitism rather than as a rational response to specific Israeli policies.[71] In this context, and writing in the early 1980s, Seliktar notes that the growing "diplomatic isolation of Israel became to a certain extent self-sustained as isolation engendered a sentiment of insecurity and defiance among Israeli decision makers, who as a result engaged in unilateral actions that in turn reinforced international resentment."[72] With the exception of the period of the Oslo process, characterized by Israel's unprecedented honeymoon with the international community, including Arab states, this tendency has undoubtedly persisted.

Third, and perhaps most importantly, the attempts of the neo-revisionists to establish a new hegemony concerned the status of the territories, which were to remain an integral part of Israel. Accordingly, the construction of Israeli settlements in the occupied territories increased massively under Begin and subsequent right-wing governments, as is well known. If before the elections of May 1977 there were around fifty thousand settlers in the occupied territories, with forty thousand of them in Arab Jerusalem, within thirty years the number of settlers had increased tenfold.[73] Unlike previous Labor governments, which had started the settlement enterprise by building settlements in strategic positions, Likud governments now built settlements also in densely populated areas. While stressing Jewish rights to "Judea, Samaria, and Gaza," neo-revisionist thinking ruled out territorial compromise with the Palestinians in principle. As Likud prime minister Yitzhak Shamir pointedly put it in 1991, "I don't believe in territorial compromise."[74]

Territorial maximalism has remained central to the Israeli Right, acquiring an ever greater importance over the decades. As we will see further below, the constant rise of revisionist Zionism since the 1970s went hand in hand with a growing political influence of the settler movement, whose commitment to territorial maximalism is particularly ideological and fervent.

The continuously growing significance of the neo-revisionist belief system is evidenced by the fact that the Likud has been dominating Israeli politics since 1977. Indeed, the Likud has either ruled the country in coalitions with religious and ultranationalist parties to its right or it entered into grand coalitions with Labor, such as during the 1980s, and intermittently in the 2000s. Labor-led governments excluding the Likud, such as the coalitions led by Yitzhak Rabin and the not-so-leftish Ehud Barak in the 1990s, were an exception to the rule: a brief interlude, if a long-term perspective is taken. Following the collapse of Oslo and the outbreak of the Second Intifada, the electoral power of the Likud and its spin-offs, such as Kadima and Yisrael Beiteinu, increased even further. In general, there has also been a constant rise of the ultranationalist and extreme Right in Israeli politics since the 1980s.[75] Moreover, the most important religious party tied to the settler movement—the national-religious party and its current successor, the Jewish Home (Ha-Bayit ha-Yehudi)—have almost constantly been part of government coalitions. Almost-constant participation in government also characterizes the ultra-Orthodox parties, which, in spite of their traditionally anti-Zionist positions, are increasingly sympathetic to the settlement enterprise. The main reason for these new sympathies is the massive increase in subsidized housing for the ultra-Orthodox community in the West Bank since the mid-1990s, to the point that the fastest growing settlement in the West Bank, Beitar 'Illit, and the most populous one, Modi'in 'Illit, are predominantly ultra-Orthodox.[76]

Important demographic changes in Israeli society have supported Israel's constant shift to the right since the 1970s. The first change is the growing percentage of Mizrahi Jews in Israel's general population over the decades, whose vote against the Ashkenazi Labor establishment was a key factor in bringing the Likud to power in 1977. Although Israeli Jewish society has been marked by a diminishing salience of the Ashkenazi–Mizrahi divide as well as a constantly growing number of intermarriages between both groups, Mizrahi Jews, who continue to be overrepresented among the lower social classes, still constitute the backbone of the Likud party and the Israeli Right. While this support is partly anchored in the traditional Mizrahi resentment of the Ashkenazi elite, it is of course ironic that the leadership of the Likud party has traditionally been of Ashkenazi origin. Second, the immigration wave from the former Soviet Union in the early 1990s affected Israeli politics. By the end of the 2000s, these "Russian" immigrants represented around one million people and had an electoral strength of twenty to twenty-two seats in the Knesset.[77] As a broad generalization, this sector of Israeli society tends to be secular, right-wing, and partly ultranationalist. In the 2000s, the so-called Russian vote went predominantly to the Likud, Kadima under Sharon, and, more recently, the ultranationalist Yisrael Beiteinu (Israel Is Our Home) party of Avigdor Lieberman.[78] Third, the growing support for right-wing, ultranationalist, and religious parties in Israeli politics is also related to the higher birth rates among orthodox and national-religious Jews, with the ultra-Orthodox parties turning increasingly "hawkish" on territorial issues over the years. It is worth noting that the ultra-Orthodox community is the fastest growing sector in Israeli society: it has grown eightfold since 1948.[79]

While neo-revisionist thought established itself as the new hegemony in Israel, a key indicator of its ever-growing power has been the mounting political influence of the settler movement. Against the backdrop of the rising influence of religion in general and the growing fusion of revisionism with Jewish fundamentalism, the settlers and their supporters succeeded in penetrating all levels of the state, from politics to economics and the Israeli army.[80] As a general trend, supporters of the settlement project sitting in the Knesset and holding key positions in the government have grown considerably in number over the years, to the point that a *Haaretz* editorial termed the government formed under Netanyahu after the January 2013 elections a "settler government."[81] In that government, supporters of the settlement enterprise occupied the ministries of housing and construction, defense, interior, education, and foreign affairs, and controlled the Knesset's finance committee and the Israel Land Administration.[82] Interestingly, while the Likud and associates are supportive of the settlement enterprise by default, there has also been a strengthening of the faction of hard-line religious settlers *within* the Likud.[83]

It is important to note that through the building of alliances with key figures in the state bureaucracy, the settler movement succeeded in gaining influence in complete disproportion to their relative representation in the Israeli population. Of Israel's total population of around 8.3 million at the end of 2013, only roughly 4 percent—that is, approximately 350,000 people—lived in West Bank settlements; if the Jerusalem neighborhoods beyond the Green Line are included, the percentage of settlers amounts to not even 7 percent of Israelis, to a total of an estimated 547,000 people.[84] The majority of the settler population does not live in the settlements for ideological reasons, however, but because it is cheaper and often convenient.

The constant expansion of Israeli settlements became a well-funded government enterprise enjoying top priority. A government-commissioned survey by former state prosecutor Talya Sason published in March 2005 documents the official Israeli backing of the continuous settlement expansion and the diversion of millions of shekels for this purpose.[85] The increase of the Israeli settler population also occurred in the Oslo period in which Labor-led governments were in power. Indeed, according to the Israeli human rights organization B'Tselem, from the end of 1993—the year the Oslo Accords were signed—to the end of 2001, the Israeli population living beyond the Green Line rose from 247,000 to 375,000; focusing only on the West Bank, the number of West Bank settlers had doubled in that period.[86] In the 2000s the construction in the settlements continued unabated. Between November 2002 and February 2013, Israeli governments under Sharon, Olmert, and Netanyahu issued construction tenders for a total of 14,203 housing units in the larger settlements in the West Bank and East Jerusalem.[87] Between 2000 and 2010 the total number of Israelis living beyond the Green Line increased from approximately 388,000 to around 534,000.[88] True, in June 2009 Binyamin Netanyahu committed to the two-state-solution, and thus to territorial compromise, during a speech he delivered at Bar-Ilan University, much to the consternation of his supporters.[89] But Netanyahu's policy of massive settlement expansion clearly contradicts this verbal commitment. In fact, Netanyahu's premiership from April 2009 (until the time of writing) is characterized by a record number of tenders for new housing units in the settlements and significant planning and construction activities in Arab East Jerusalem.[90] While even outbidding Sharon's appetite for settlement construction in the early 2000s, the Netanyahu government also legalized "illegal outposts"—makeshift settlements established by radical settlers that even Israeli law considers as illegal.[91] And, reneging from his earlier announcement, during the 2015 electoral campaign Netanyahu would stress that, if elected, there would be no Palestinian state.[92]

While there are no official reports of Israel's investment in the settlement, there is ample evidence that the government, through six different ministries, subsidizes construction and the price of housing. The Israeli government provides mortgage aid and various tax benefits for individuals and companies, gives significant price reductions in the leasing of land, transfers a far higher percentage of government funding to settlement municipalities as compared to those within Israel proper, and subsidizes public services and commodities in the settlements. These expenses are in addition to the costs of maintaining army bases and a massive military presence in the territories. Regarding the levels of provision of education, housing, and welfare, Israeli governments clearly favor the settlements at the expense of cities and communities within Israel proper.[93]

The continuous settlement project has witnessed ongoing confiscation and expropriation of Palestinian lands through different Israeli laws and military orders, and sometimes also without these. A detailed database on the settlements compiled by the Defense Ministry in January 2008—obtained by *Haaretz* and placed online in February 2009 until it was removed—comprehensively documents all relevant government decisions and the mode of land confiscation in the establishment of each settlement.[94] In about three-quarters of the settlements, construction was carried out without appropriate permits. In more than thirty settlements, infrastructure and buildings were built on private Palestinian land, including entire settlement neighborhoods, roads, schools, synagogues, municipal offices, and police stations. The database thus plainly contradicts Israel's official position that it does not appropriate private Palestinian land for the establishment of settlements.

On the economic front, Israeli banks provide the financial infrastructure for all government and private economic activities in the territories, through mortgages and special loans for building projects in the settlements, while benefiting from access to the Palestinian monetary market, which is dependent on the Israeli one. Private Israeli (and foreign) companies benefit from various economic incentives and cheap Palestinian labor in the territories while others are contracted by the Israeli government to provide various types of security services. Checkpoints run by private Israeli firms are a case in point. By controlling the import and export of all Palestinian goods from and to the territories, for which Israel has remained the main market, and by exploiting the natural resources in the Palestinian territories, the Israeli economy reaps considerable benefits from the continuing rule over them.[95]

Perhaps most significantly, the settler movement and the security sector are increasingly intertwined. Menachem Klein observes in this context a new symbiosis between settlements and security in Israel.[96] Thus, representatives of the settler movement and its sympathizers succeeded in occupying key positions within the Ministry of Defense and the Ministry of Housing and Construction. These two ministries oversee Israel's settlement project in the territories, with the Defense Ministry having the final control over the territories. Indeed, the army's Civil Administration is in charge of administering state land, supervising infrastructure and construction, and granting different types of permits that affect almost every aspect of Palestinian life. There are 101 different permits to regulate Palestinian movement in the territories alone.[97] The Israeli army also grants permits for transporting caravans and construction vehicles; it supervises the connection of new settlements to water and electricity and deploys soldiers to protect the settlements. Hence, even the establishment and subsequent expansion of the so-called illegal outposts cannot take place without the support of the security establishment and, thus, the government.[98] In fact, Amana, the organization behind the construction of illegal outposts in the territories and headed by a militant settler, is extremely well connected to the government and the Defense Ministry.[99]

Moreover, through the establishment of so-called *hesder yeshivot*, combining military service with the study of the Torah, the percentage of national-religious soldiers serving in the army has considerably increased over the years. From 2000 to 2012, for instance, the percentage of national-religious soldiers in officer training courses rose from 15 to 43 percent.[100] By now they also represent a considerable percentage—estimated at around 30 percent—of soldiers serving in combat units and of those deployed in the West Bank.[101] Thus, a growing number of soldiers serving in the territories share with the settlers the same social, educational, and ideological background.[102] While the influence of army rabbis and their religious rhetoric on soldiers has increased, there have been numerous cases in which officers cooperated with militant settlers in the West Bank, for instance, by providing advance notice of the removal of outposts or by taking their side in confrontations with the Palestinians.[103] The institutional cooperation between the army and the settlers also extends to the regional settler militias in the West Bank. These are composed of reserve units and (armed) civilian security coordinators who have the power to stop and temporarily detain people. Set up to defend the settlements, these militias count approximately two thousand volunteers. While being trained by private security firms, they receive M16 machine guns from the IDF and privately purchase additional security equipment, such as armored cars, bullet-proof vests, and telescopic sights.[104] The widespread phenomenon of settlers attacking Palestinians and damaging or destroying their property, which usually goes unpunished, and the frequent cases of violence and harassment of Palestinian civilians by Israeli security forces in the territories are thus probably no coincidence.[105]

It is worth noting here that Israel's Supreme Court, the highest judicial authority in the country, has mostly refrained from condemning the policies of the Israeli government and the army in the territories. While it has so far avoided ruling on the status of the territories, over the decades the court has decided on numerous petitions against the actions of the army in the territories, filed by Palestinian individuals and Israeli or Palestinian human rights organizations. With a number of notable exceptions, the court has tended to side with the government and the army, usually espousing the security-based justifications of the latter.[106] The jurisprudence of Israel's Supreme Court on cases related to the Palestinian territories thus differs considerably from its ruling on cases relating to Israel proper, where it tends to uphold liberal values and the defense of civil liberties.

Thus, the settlement–security symbiosis observed by Klein thrives particularly well in a neo-revisionist ideological environment. Or, to put it differently, the constant rise of neo-revisionism in Israeli politics and in Jewish Israeli society has made the hijacking of Israel's security concerns by the settler movement possible. It has also added a crucial fundamentalist-religious element to this takeover.

The neo-revisionist belief system has been described as a "hermetically closed ideology, highly resistant to alteration, innovation, or even questioning," with an inherent tendency to radicalize even further.[107] But perhaps more importantly, it has promoted a bleak regional outlook and fostered the strengthening of basically tribal ethnonational values, whether in their religious or secular version. The rise of neo-revisionism has also fostered ultranationalism and intolerance in Israeli society and politics, together with a preference for territorial maximalism and forceful unilateral policies.

The growing hold of neo-revisionism on Israeli politics sustains the transformation of the Israeli–Palestinian conflict from a dispute over territory to a basically ethnic conflict, as Klein has observed, with all the regional and domestic implications this development entails. Significantly, and as we have seen, the rise of neo-revisionism since the late 1970s is not only an ideological development but also entails profound structural changes in Israeli politics and society, as the disproportionate power of the settler movement indicates.

Of course, it is true that under neo-revisionist rule, Israel did evacuate occupied territory on three occasions. Yet both the pullout from the Sinai in the context of the 1979 peace agreement with Egypt and the Gaza disengagement of 2005 involved territories that were of relatively limited importance to Jewish national history or religion. In both cases, strategic considerations won over ideology. Thus, the strategic importance of the separate peace with Egypt cannot be overstated; it also removed the pressure on Israel to reach a territorial compromise with the Palestinians. Similarly, the 2005 pullout from the Gaza Strip permitted Israel to exit a security quagmire while freezing the peace process.[108] The 1997 Hebron protocol, on the other hand, was an agreement implementing the Oslo

Accords, which were legally binding on the Israeli government. Stipulating a partial withdrawal from the city of Hebron, the protocol was signed
by the first Netanyahu government under massive US pressure.[109]

Thus, neo-revisionist leaders partly betrayed ideology in the face of formidable incentives and powerful international constraints. Yet the extent
to which this would be possible today is debatable. By gradually erasing
the Green Line both in practice and in Israel's collective consciousness, in
the 2000s the neo-revisionists succeeded in anchoring Israeli rule over the
West Bank both at the institutional level and in terms of hegemony—an
achievement they fell short of until the early 1990s.[110] This development
occurred in spite of the two short intervals of Labor-led governments in
the 1990s, during the Oslo years.

At this point it is worth raising the question of how the electoral victory of the Labor party in 1992 and again in 1999 can be explained. Indeed, if the strengthening of neo-revisionism has been a constant trend
since the 1970s, why did Labor win the elections twice in that decade?
A rather exceptional combination of international and domestic factors
may account for Labor's victory in 1992, which was rather narrow to begin with. These include the general feeling of vulnerability on the Israeli
side amid a fundamentally altered post–Cold War international order;
Washington's almost unprecedented pressure on Israel; and, crucially, the
personality and leadership skills of Yitzhak Rabin. Particularly considering the political implications of the first Palestinian intifada, Rabin came
to realize that neo-revisionist policies had not increased Israel's security
but rather led to a growing insecurity. Moreover, in reaction to the reluctance of Yitzhak Shamir's right-wing government to seriously engage
in the Madrid peace process that had started at the end of 1991, the US
administration under George H. W. Bush had decided to withhold loan
guarantees to Israel. At this point these loan guarantees were urgently
needed for the absorption of the massive wave of immigrants from the
former Soviet Union. Labor leader Rabin was thus able to present Israeli
voters with two alternatives: either engage in peacemaking, absorb immigrants, enhance Israel's security, and mend relations with the US, or
risk a serious confrontation with Washington, major economic hardships,
and an increasingly unfavorable strategic environment.[111] In this specific
situation and context, a majority of Israeli voters preferred the first option. Barak's victory in 1999, on the other hand, may be explained by the
trust most Israelis placed in his impressive military career, in conjunction with the despair over Netanyahu's regional and economic policies
at a time when, for most Israelis, peace with the Palestinians and the

resolution of a century-old conflict still seemed within reach. The collapse of Oslo was to put an end to the short intervals of Labor rule in the 1990s, enabling not only the return of neo-revisionism but also its growing power ever since.

Of Terrorism, Fears, and Hope

Insights from social psychology on group behavior in protracted conflicts provide additional elements in the understanding of the rise of the new hegemony in Israel after 2000. Considering the dynamics linked to collective perceptions of threat and enemies in protracted conflicts, it is interesting to reconsider the attempts of Labor-led governments to change Israel's collective thinking pattern during the Oslo process.

In light of the growing salience of neo-revisionism, these attempts faced an uphill battle from the very start, for a number of reasons. First, since Israel was born and continued to exist in a situation of conflict and war, trust and mental openness toward the possibility of making peace with former enemies were not the default options. Indeed, numerous studies in social psychology show that intractable conflicts—defined as protracted, violent, and costly and perceived as irreconcilable—nurture extremely biased perceptions of self and other.[112] One side is characterized by the justness of the cause, unity, coherence, patriotism, and a strong longing for peace while being victimized by the other side. With security becoming a central concern, intractable conflicts also prompt negative stereotyping and the enemy's delegitimization, the worst form of stereotyping. As a deviation from standard behavior, the delegitimization of an enemy means that the norm of justice and the equal treatment of all individuals are suspended. The other side is no longer seen as human, so harming it is considered as an appropriate, acceptable, and even just action. Feelings of hatred, fear, and anger take prevalence over rational thinking.[113] It has also been noted that the categorization of the enemy is stable and extremely resistant to change because the conflict ethos prevents any positive information about the enemy from being absorbed.[114] While these features obviously apply to both sides, changing collective perceptions of groups that are in protracted conflict with each other is extremely difficult. As Muzafer Sherif's famous social-psychological experiments involving teenagers in the 1960s demonstrated, it is much easier to generate hatred between groups of people that previously did not even know each other than it is to prompt antagonistic collectives to change their perceptions so they can overcome conflict.[115]

The case of the Arab–Israeli conflict displays all the characteristics of intractable conflicts.[116] Israeli Jewish society developed into a security-obsessed nation, with constant threat perceptions prompting a steady radicalization and delegitimization of "the Arabs," particularly of the Palestinians.[117] These dynamics explain the resilience of deeply entrenched perceptions of threats and regional order in Israel, even under favorable external conditions such as peacemaking attempts. While failing to end the conflict, the Oslo period was extremely short when compared to all the previous decades of threats, wars, and conflict.

Second, it has been argued that in societies involved in intractable conflicts, emotions of fear will override hope, even if this society embarks on the road to peace. This is because fear is an automatic response based on a memorized past. Fear also involves conservatism and the freezing of beliefs. Conversely, hope is based on thinking, thus involving a cognitive activity that requires an open mind, flexibility, and creativity.[118] In other words, fear trumps hope, so to speak, because instincts win over cognition.

Finally, during Oslo, there was no concerted domestic effort to change predominant perceptions on threats and regional order. On the contrary, the option of peace and territorial compromise brought the domestic fragmentation of Israeli society to the fore, with important segments of the political spectrum denouncing the Oslo Accords as plain stupidity at best and as betrayal at worst. The neo-revisionist Right, in particular, along with its national-religious and ultranationalist allies, mobilized massively in its opposition to territorial compromise during both Labor-led governments, particularly during Rabin's term. The demonstrations led by Israeli right-wing leaders (including Benyamin Netanyahu and Ariel Sharon) depicting Yitzhak Rabin in Nazi uniform and the religious ruling justifying the killing of Rabin that circulated in extremist settler circles are cases in point.[119] Seemingly confirming the neo-revisionist belief, repeated Palestinian suicide attacks additionally reinforced the old thinking patterns on threats and foes within Israeli society. In other words, staging a short comeback, Labor Zionism, in an unprecedented way, sought to promote new ideas about the regional environment and the former enemy during Oslo, fighting deeply entrenched beliefs that were embedded in neo-revisionism. It lost the battle.

As renewed violence and conflict tend to reinforce stereotypes of the enemy and closed-mindedness, the Israeli peace camp was given its coup de grace with the collapse of Oslo, the outbreak of the Second Intifada, and the rising number of suicide bombings.[120] If fear prevails over hope in fairly "normal" circumstances, situations of renewed violence and persistent terrorism nurture these dynamics even further—no matter the objective distribution of power and other rational considerations. Moreover, the collapse of Oslo and the Second Intifada prompted a complete disillusionment with a negotiated solution of the conflict on both sides. Within Jewish Israeli society, these developments reinforced the sense of regional isolation and the feeling of victimhood while eradicating any grain of trust in the other side that may have been cultivated in the previous decade. Feelings of anger accompanied the deep sense of disappointment. Jewish Israelis were no longer interested in peace—or in what was happening on the other side. Israel's counterterrorism policies, the territorial fragmentation, and the West Bank barrier additionally pushed the territories out of the Jewish Israeli collective conscience.[121]

The rise of a hegemonic vision of threats and regional order in Israel after 2000 must be put into the context of these psychological dynamics of conflict. It is worth noting here that a study in 2011 on sociopsychological barriers to peacemaking for Israeli Jewish society shows that people with rightist political orientation and authoritarian personalities tend to express a greater tendency to delegitimize the enemy and a higher level of collective victimhood. Both these tendencies decrease the openness to be exposed to new information that might contradict preexisting views. This lack of openness "ultimately supports the continuation of the conflict."[122] In addition, another study highlights the correlation between persistent terrorism and diminishing political tolerance in Israel.[123] The country's general shift to the right is therefore highly significant here.

While the discussion has so far concentrated on ideological and material structures, developments and dynamics in explaining Israel's post-Oslo consensus on foreign policy, the last part of the chapter focuses on agency. Significant actors who contributed to the shaping of specific notions in post-Oslo Israel have already been addressed in previous chapters within the specific context of the different building blocks of the hegemony. Hence, the next section is rather concise.

Politicians, the Media, and the Army

Politicians, the media, and the Israeli army played an important role in shaping and reinforcing the emerging consensus on conflicts, threats, and regional order after Oslo. More specifically, the line that there is no partner for peace after the failed Camp David Summit in 2000 must clearly be attributed to Prime Minister Ehud Barak, as discussed in chapter 1. Intrinsically linked to the blame assigned to Yasser Arafat for orchestrating the violence of the Second Intifada, the "no partner for peace" theme had a significant impact on Israeli public opinion in the early 2000s.[124] Echoing the long-held myth that Israel was "waiting for the Arab phone call" after it conquered the territories in 1967, the simplicity of the message was particularly attractive in a moment of renewed violence and, thus, uncertainty in Jewish Israeli society. Even more important was Barak's background, as the experienced and most-decorated soldier in Israeli history. Together with his (alleged) role as political heir of the assassinated Yitzhak Rabin and therefore the hereditary leader of the peace camp, his military experience turned Barak into what has been defined as an epistemic authority[125] His assessment had an enormous influence on the Jewish Israeli collective.

Barak's interpretation of events resounded well with the particular construction of Israeli identity, the salience of neo-revisionist beliefs, and the psychological dynamics described earlier. Indeed, his claim that the Camp David Summit of 2000 failed because of Arafat's unwillingness to make peace, his response to Israel's unprecedented offer by resorting to violence, became central to the notion that Israel was fighting for its survival against those who did not recognize its right to exist.[126] The subsequent repetition of this line ad nauseam by other key figures of Israel's political establishment—from Sharon to Livni, from Lieberman to Netanyahu—only reinforced this belief. The no-partner theme was easily transferred to PA chairman Mahmoud Abbas, who, incidentally, was the Israeli government's preferred successor to Yasser Arafat. Interestingly, it was not until 2014 that Barak bothered to mention that he had actually meant Arafat specifically, when stating that there was no Palestinian partner for peace.[127]

As we have seen, Israeli politicians also played a significant role in nurturing the sense of siege. They promoted the notion of a small and isolated nation surrounded by a powerful and hostile environment, time and again. Without regard for any historical, factual, or strategic consideration, in Israel's prevailing notion of threats and regional order post-Oslo, this environment was (and still is) populated by inherently evil and utterly irrational terrorists and an equally evil state actor, Iran. With analogies to Jewish history and the Holocaust emphasizing the Jewish collective sense of victimhood, there is ample evidence of how political figures promoted the conception that Israel, with one of the most powerful armies in the world, was facing existential threats and struggling for its very survival. While delegitimizing the enemy and justifying the use of exceptional means, these themes became the mainstream political discourse in Israel after the collapse of Oslo, as we have seen.[128]

In addition to leading politicians, unsurprisingly at this point, the army and the security establishment played a crucial role in the emergence of the new consensus on threats and regional order. The highest military echelons supported Barak's explanation for the eruption of the Second Intifada, together with the "no partner for peace" theme, in spite of contradictory initial assessments on Arafat's role in orchestrating the Palestinian uprising.[129] With the ongoing intifada and the inability of political leaders to articulate a clear strategy, the Israeli army in fact became the main source of knowledge on how to manage the conflict.[130] By and large, the security establishment also concurred with the notion that terrorism—from Hamas to Syria and Hizballah—was the main problem facing Israel, together with the maxim that there was no political solution for this phenomenon. While key exponents of the Israeli army also publicly stressed the notion of an evil alliance led by Iran, the security establishment was a bit less vociferous regarding the need to attack Iran.[131] Probably aware of the operational constraints of an Israeli go-it-alone operation, in the 2000s the army generally stayed out of the debate, leaving the warmongering to politicians and other self-declared experts while nevertheless opposing an Israeli strike on Iran behind the scenes. Considering the high standing the army enjoys in Israeli Jewish society and the key role that the security establishment plays in the formulation of Israeli foreign policy, it goes without saying that the security establishment is an important epistemic authority in Jewish Israeli society.[132]

Finally, the media played a crucial role in the emerging hegemony. In its coverage of the Second Intifada, for instance, Israel's mainstream media often adopted the positions of the political and military establishment. It happily repeated Barak's claim that Arafat had orchestrated the Second Intifada and that the Palestinians were not interested in peace. The media also echoed the official rhetoric and reasoning behind the country's forceful counterterrorism policies, including the justifications for the closures and curfews, the administrative detentions, the house demolitions, and the targeted killings. In the face of international criticism leveled at Israel's policies in the territories, the Israeli media also sided with the official government position, avoiding any critical discussion of Israeli policies or their rationale.[133] Analyses of the media coverage of the 2006 Lebanon and the 2008–9 Gaza wars evidence these same patterns, with the media glorifying Israel's political and military leadership, stressing the morality of the army, taking pride in Israel's social and military strength, and dismissing any criticism.[134] While in times of conflict the media tends to mobilize itself around the Zionist consensus, it presented a one-sided account of the story.[135] In this context, it is of course not irrelevant that during the Second Intifada, the media came to increasingly rely on military sources.[136] It is equally significant that most Israelis consume national news and far less foreign media. More than that, in times of conflict, the explanations and justifications promoted by a mobilized Israeli media is much more likely to influence the political Left, since their degree of trust in Israeli news sources is comparably higher.[137] Finally, the impact of the free daily newspaper, *Israel Ha-Yom*, in propagating the government line cannot be underestimated. First published in July 2007 and financed by the American casino billionaire Sheldon Adelson—a staunch supporter of the Israeli Likud—*Israel Ha-Yom* has served as a propaganda instrument for Netanyahu's government and the settler movement. Mainly because Adelson's paper is distributed freely, it has become the largest daily newspaper in Israel, prompting MKs (including some from the Likud) to propose legislation that would ban free newspapers in Israel. Thus, with its sometimes apocalyptic, emotional, and uncritical representation of events, the Israeli mainstream media contributed significantly to the construction of the image of Israel as a nation under siege in the decade following the collapse of the Oslo process.[138]

◆

To sum up, a combination of different factors can be said to explain the emergence and consolidation of a specific hegemonic vision of threat, conflict, and regional order in Israel after 2000. These factors include the particular construction of Jewish Israeli collective identity, which acts as a predisposition of sorts, and the axioms and practices of Israeli foreign policy, which institutionalize these collective beliefs and establish the predominance of the security establishment in the formulation of regional foreign policy. The constant rise of neo-revisionism after 1967, with its focus on territorial maximalism and ethnonationalism and with its fusion with religious fundamentalism, is a crucial development. It significantly affected Jewish Israeli collective perceptions of the regional environment and of Israel's role in the world. Coupled with the constantly growing influence of the settler movement in Israeli politics, the rise of religious preferences, demographic shifts, and a growing symbiosis between security and settlements, the rise of neo-revisionism is not only an ideological development. It also entails a significant structural change. The disproportionate influence of the settler movement on Israeli politics and society, with its domestic and regional implications, is a clear evidence of this development. The period of the Oslo process that started under Rabin's premiership in the early 1990s was in fact only a short interruption of the constant rise of neo-revisionism since the 1970s. Neo-revisionist thought succeeded in establishing itself as the new hegemony in Israel, providing the ideological matrix for the consensus on threats and regional order that would emerge in Israel post-Oslo. Finally, sociopsychological dynamics of conflict explain the resilience of threat perceptions and images of the enemy. The collapse of Oslo and the terrorist attacks of the Second Intifada fueled fear and anger, powerful instincts that override cognition and hope. Taken together, these factors condition the intake of information, making one interpretation of events more likely than others. They also legitimize forceful and defiant foreign policies toward the region, which, in situations of violence, are generally more convincing to a general public than policies of restraint or de-escalation.

Attempts to change predominant beliefs and practices in the initial period of the Oslo process thus faced formidable challenges from the outset. The renewal of conflict after the collapse of Oslo and the terror of the Second Intifada reunited Jewish Israelis in their beliefs about the regional order. The notion that Israel is a country under siege, fighting for its very survival in an eminently hostile environment, was reconfirmed and reinforced, together with the conviction that there was no one to talk to. Social structure, however, does not exist in a vacuum. Its emergence, consolidation, and change over time also depend on specific agents in a mutually constitutive process. Thus, significant actors who are in turn influenced by social structure and collective beliefs also contribute to the shaping of that same structure out of genuine conviction or for far less genuine political gains. While Ehud Barak can be singled out in his coining of the highly influential "no partner for peace" theme after the collapse of the Camp David Summit of 2000, political leaders, mainly from the political Right, time and again conveyed the notion of an eminently hostile regional environment, of the existential threat emanating from Iran, and of the irrelevance of a political solution in the face of terrorism in the 2000s. Influencing and defining the commonsense perception of social reality, which acts as background prior knowledge for the intake of new information, is a crucial aspect of politics: it serves as a vehicle for legitimizing specific policies and a precise political order. Thus, Israel's right-wing elites, including the settler movement, had a clear interest in promoting these specific conceptions because they benefited most from it. A highly mobilized and increasingly uncritical Israeli media, including the freely distributed newspaper *Israel Ha-Yom*, propagated the government line. The role of the security establishment, which not only is intertwined with the political echelons but also became the main source of information during the Second Intifada, is an additional key factor. While the conflict with the Palestinians became increasingly framed in ethnoreligious terms, the Green Line gradually disappeared from Israel's collective consciousness. Concurrently, alternative interpretations of regional developments, different solutions to the problem, and the realities in the territories were blocked out from Israel's dominant discourse and perspective.

Notes

1. On Israel's collective identity, see Zerubavel, *Recovered Roots*; Kimmerling, *Invention and Decline of Israeliness*; Kimmerling, *Israeli State and Society*; Ezrahi, *Rubber Bullets*; Sternhell, *Founding Myths of Israel*; Evron, *Jewish State or Israeli Nation?*; and Del Sarto, *Contested State Identities*, chap. 4.

2. Anderson, *Imagined Communities*.

3. A good overview of the relevant research findings and questions is still DiMaggio, "Culture and Cognition." See also Berger and Luckmann, *Social Construction of Reality*; and Bar-Tal and Kruglanski, *Social Psychology of Knowledge*.

4. Zerubavel, *Recovered Roots*, chap. 2; and Sternhell, *Founding Myths of Israel*, chap. 1.

5. On the history of Zionism, see, for example, Laqueur, *A History of Zionism*.

6. See, for example, Segev, *Seventh Million*; and Barnett, "Cosmopolitanism."

7. Kimmerling, *Invention and Decline of Israeliness*, 186.

8. Gertz, "Few against the Many."

9. Zerubavel, *Recovered Roots*, 216–21.

10. Kimmerling, *Invention and Decline of Israeliness*, 211.

11. Ezrahi, *Rubber Bullets*, 274.

12. Ibid.

13. Horowitz, "The Israeli Concept of National Security." For a critical assessment of Israel's security exceptionalism, see Merom, "Israel's National Security."

14. Perlmutter, "Israel's Dilemma."

15. Most notably, see Bar-Tal and Teichman, *Stereotypes and Prejudice in Conflict*.

16. Raz, *Bride and the Dowry*.

17. For the Hamas charter, see Mishal and Sela, *Palestinian Hamas*, app. 2.

18. Del Sarto, *Contested State Identities*, chap. 4. See also Barnett, "Culture, Strategy and Foreign Policy Change."

19. Rabin, "Address by PM Rabin at the National Defense College," 298–99.

20. Rabin, "Address to the Knesset," 2.

21. Weizman, "Interview with Ezer Weizman." For Peres's concept of the New Middle East, see Peres and Naor, *The New Middle East.*

22. Del Sarto, *Contested State Identities,* chap. 4.

23. Podeh, "History and Memory," 91.

24. Ibid.

25. Nets-Zehngut, "Origins of the Palestinian Refugee Problem"; and Nets-Zehngut, "Internal and External Collective Memories."

26. Peled-Elhanan, *Palestine in Israeli School Books.*

27. Ezrahi, *Rubber Bullets,* 274–75.

28. Bar-Tal and Teichman, *Stereotypes and Prejudice in Conflict,* 96.

29. Ibid., 378.

30. Berrebi and Klor, "Are Voters Sensitive to Terrorism?"; Berrebi and Klor, "On Terrorism and Electoral Outcomes"; Peffley, Hutchison, and Shamir, "Impact of Persistent Terrorism"; and Getmansky and Zeitzoff, "Terrorism and Voting".

31. Buzan, *People, States, and Fear;* and Buzan, Wæver, and de Wilde, *Security.*

32. Maoz, *Defending the Holy Land,* 584.

33. Ezrahi, *Rubber Bullets,* 274; and Beinart, *Crisis of Zionism,* 195.

34. Beinart, *Crisis of Zionism,* 195.

35. Yaniv, "A Question of Surivial," 87–88.

36. Ben-Gurion, quoted in ibid., 88.

37. As Avi Shlaim notes, the conceptions and policies of Labor Zionist leaders Ben-Gurion, Moshe Dayan, and others were an almost identical reflection of the Iron Wall concept. See Shlaim, *Iron Wall;* and Shlaim, "Iron Wall Revisited," 87 ff.

38. See, for example, Horowitz, "Israeli Concept of National Security."

39. Maoz, *Defending the Holy Land,* 12.

40. Yaniv, "A Question of Surivial"; Horowitz, "Israeli Concept of National Security"; and Maoz, *Defending the Holy Land,* 7–9.

41. Maoz, *Defending the Holy Land,* 558.

42. Interview, Israeli Foreign Ministry, Jerusalem, May 25, 2011; and interviews with members of Israel's security establishment and members of Israel's Council for Peace and Security, Tel Aviv, May 24 and 26, 2011.

43. Maoz, *Defending the Holy Land,* 546.

44. Eva Illouz, "How Peace Masks Israel's True Colors," *Haaretz,* July 2, 2014.

45. Kimmerling, *Invention and Decline of Israeliness,* chap. 7; and Levy, Lomsky-Feder, and Harel, "From 'Obligatory Militarism' to 'Contractual Militarism.'"

46. A law passed in 2014 is to phase out exemptions from the military service of the ultra-Orthodox community.

47. Arian, *Politics in Israel,* 328.

48. Kimmerling, *Invention and Decline of Israeliness,* 214.

49. Ibid.

50. Arian, "Israeli Public Opinion on National Security 2003."

51. Maoz, *Defending the Holy Land*, 7; italics in the original.

52. Interviews with Israeli Foreign Ministry official and former Foreign Ministry official, Jerusalem, May 25 and 26, 2011. See also Yaniv, "A Question of Surivial"; and Jones, "Foreign Policy of Israel."

53. Maoz, *Defending the Holy Land*, 499–500.

54. Michael, "Military Knowledge and Weak Civilian Control," 62.

55. Brecher, *Foreign Policy System of Israel*, 117–33.

56. Maoz, *Defending the Holy Land*, 502.

57. Ibid., 552.

58. Ibid., 479.

59. Harkabi, quoted in ibid., 482.

60. Arian, *Security Threatened*; and Arian, "Israeli Public Opinion on National Security 2003."

61. Interview with Israeli Foreign Ministry official, Jerusalem, May 23, 2011.

62. Savir, *Process*, 81–82.

63. The resentment is based on the discriminatory treatment Mizrahi Jews received from the country's Labor establishment after they immigrated to Israel in the 1950s and the 1960s.

64. Shlaim, *Iron Wall*; and Shlaim, "Iron Wall Revisited."

65. This, however, may have been a tactical move to ensure the support of religious circles. Laqueur, *A History of Zionism*, 365; see also Shindler, *Israel, Likud and the Zionist Dream.*

66. Peleg, *Begin's Foreign Policy*, 52 ff.; and Seliktar, "New Zionism."

67. Kimmerling, *Invention and Decline of Israeliness*; see also Smooha, "Ethnic Democracy: Israel as an Archetype"; and Smooha, "Minority Status in an Ethnic Democracy."

68. Seliktar, *New Zionism and the Foreign Policy System of Israel*, 94.

69. Lustick, *Unsettled States*, 356.

70. Peleg, *Begin's Foreign Policy*, 72 ff.; and Seliktar, *New Zionism and the Foreign Policy System of Israel*, 231–39.

71. Seliktar, "New Zionism," 131.

72. Ibid., 129.

73. Gorenberg, *Accidental Empire*, 358.

74. Shamir, quoted in Linda Gradstein, "Shamir Bars Losing Territory," *Washington Post*, July 25, 1991; see also Quandt, *Peace Process*, 309.

75. Mohanad and Ghanem, "Empowering of the Israeli Extreme Right"; Pedahzur, "Supporting Condition"; and Sprinzak, "Emergence of the Israeli Radical Right."

76. International Crisis Group, *Israel's Religious Right*, 13; "Settlements: Statistics on Settlements and Settler Population," B'Tselem, January 1, 2011, updated May 11,

2015, http://www.btselem.org/settlements/statistics; "Tenders for Residential Set-tlement Construction (Units), by Government and Settlement, November 2002 to February 2013," Foundation for Middle East Peace, January 13, 2013, http://fmep.org/resource/tenders-for-residential-settlement-construction-units-by-government-and-settlement-november-2002-february-2013/; and "West Bank Settlements Population, 1999–2012," Foundation for Middle East Peace, January 13, 2013, http://fmep.org/resource/west-bank-settlements/. Beitar 'Illit has a growth rate of over 600 percent, reaching a population of 44,000 people in 2015. Modi'in 'Illit, which was only established in 1996, reached over 60,000 inhabitants in 2012.

77. Khanin, "Russian-Jewish Political Experience," 57.

78. Ibid. The author makes an effort to stress the diversity of the "Russian" electoral vote, which is not fully convincing in light of the data he provides.

79. See International Crisis Group, *Israel's Religious Right*, 12.

80. See Haklai, "Religious-Nationalist Mobilization"; see also Newman, "From *Hitnachlut* to *Hitnatkut*."

81. "The Emergence of Israel's Settler Government," *Haaretz* (editorial), March 19, 2013.

82. Housing and Construction Minister Uri Ariel was from the national-religious Jewish Home party; in the past he was a top official in the Yesha Council, the umbrella organization of municipal councils of Israeli settlements in the West Bank (and formerly in the Gaza Strip). The chair of the Knesset Finance Com-mittee, Nissan Slomiansky, was also from the Jewish Home Party; he is a former secretary-general of Gush Emunim and a former member of the Yesha Coun-cil. Bentzi Lieberman, who headed the Israel Lands Administration, was also a member of the Yesha Council. The former education minister, who then became interior minister, Gideon Sa'ar, is known to be strongly supportive of the settlers, and Foreign Minister Avigdor Lieberman is a proud West Bank settler himself. As for the Defense Ministry, Minister Moshe Ya'alon was on the Likud's right wing and highly sympathetic to the settlement enterprise, and the same applies to his extremely right-wing deputy defense minister, Danny Danon (Netanyahu would fire Danon in July 2014 because of his blunt criticism of Netanyahu's hesitation to invade the Gaza Strip. This would not prevent Netanyahu from appointing Danon as Israeli ambassador to the UN in 2015).

83. See, for example, Yossi Verter, "Netanyahu Frets over Growing Strength of Right in Likud," *Haaretz*, January 31, 2012; and International Crisis Group, *Leap of Faith*, 23–27.

84. Of the estimated 547,000 settlers living in the West Bank at the end of 2013, 350,000 were living in West Bank settlements and another 196,000 people in the Israeli neighborhoods in East Jerusalem. Data from B'Tselem and Israel's Central Bureau of Statistics.

85. *Havat Da'at (beineyim) be-Nose Maahazim Bilti Morshim, Mugash le-Rosh ha-Memshalah Mar Ariel Sharon 'al-yiadei Talya Sason, 'Orekhet Din* [Opinion (interim) on the topic of unauthorized outposts, presented to the prime minister Ariel Sharon by Talya Sason, Adv.], Office of the Prime Minister (Israel), n.d. [2005], http://www.pmo.gov.il/SiteCollectionDocuments/PMO/Communication/Spokesman/sason2.pdf.

86. "Land Grab: Israel's Settlement Policy in the West Bank," B'Tselem, May 2002, http://www.btselem.org/publications/fulltext/200205_land_grab, 8. As there are no precise statistics, the size of the settler population is an estimate. According to the Foundation for Middle East Peace, the total settlement population in 1993 amounted to 281,000 people and increased to 388,000 in 2010. See "Comprehensive Settlement Population 1972–2011," Foundation for Middle East Peace, January 13, 2013, http://tmep.org/resource/comprehensive-settlement-population-1972-2010/.

87. "Tenders for Residential Settlement Construction." Because construction tenders are only issued for some of the larger settlements, the total number of new housing units in the settlements is likely to be much higher.

88. "Comprehensive Settlement Population 1972–2011."

89. For Netanyahu's speech, see "Address by PM Netanyahu at Bar-Ilan University," Israel Ministry of Foreign Affairs, June 14, 2009, http://www.mfa.gov.il/mfa/pressroom/2009/pages/address_pm_netanyahu_bar-ilan_university_14-jun-2009.aspx.

90. In 2013 alone the construction of new housing units in West Bank settlements doubled as compared to the previous year: 2,534 new units were built in 2013 as compared to the 1,133 new units constructed in 2012. See Chaim Levinson, "Settlement Construction More Than Doubled in 2013," *Haaretz*, March 3, 2014; Tova Lazaroff, "Gov't Spent 22.3% More in Settlements," *Jerusalem Post*, July 22, 2009; Tova Lazaroff, "Settler Housing Starts Up by 124% in 2013," *Haaretz*, March 3, 2014; "Settlements and the Netanyahu Government: A Deliberate Policy of Undermining the Two-State-Solution," Peace Now, January 16, 2013, http://peacenow.org.il/eng/sites/default/files/summary-of-4-years-of-netanyahu-government.pdf; "Tenders for Residential Settlement Construction"; and Isabel Kershner, "Israel Approves Additional Funding for Settlements in the West Bank," *New York Times*, June 19, 2016.

91. Israeli law considers the over one hundred outposts as illegal (or unauthorized) if they were not established by government decision, were not built with a proper construction plan, or are built on private Palestinian land.

92. Barak Ravid, "Netanyahu: If I'm Elected, There Will Be No Palestinian State," *Haaretz*, March 16, 2015."

93. See the various statistics on government spending on settlements at the Foundation for Middle East Peace, at www.fmep.org. See also Arieli et al.,

Historical, Political, and Economic Impact; Lazaroff, "Gov't Spent 22.3% More in Settlements"; "Study: Settlements Get More Funding Than Israeli Cities," *Haaretz*, July 21, 2009; Rowe, *Funding Illegal Settlements*; Klein, *Shift*, 47–54; and "The Price of Settlements, or: How Israel Favors Settlements and Settlers," Peace Now, August 2013, http://peacenow.org.il/eng/PriceOfSettlements.

94. The author is in possession of a copy of the document, downloaded while it was online. The database has no title and is in Hebrew. See also Uri Blau, "Secret Israeli Database Reveals Full Extent of Illegal Settlement," *Haaretz*, February 1, 2009. On the Israeli government's different ways of expropriating land, see Gordon, *Israel's Occupation*, 119–31; and "Land Grab: Israel's Settlement Policy."

95. Who Profits, *Financing the Israeli Occupation*; see also the various reports and documentation at www.whoprofits.org.

96. Klein, *Shift*, chap. 3.

97. Chaim Levinson, "Israel Has 101 Different Types of Permits Governing Palestinian Movement," *Haaretz*, December 23, 2011.

98. *Havat Da'at (beineyim) be-Nose Maahazim Bilti Morshim* [Opinion (interim) on the topic of unauthorized outposts]; see also the summary of the Sason Report, "Summary of the Opinion Concerning Unauthorized Outposts—Talya Sason, Adv.," Israel Ministry of Foreign Affairs, March 10, 2005, http://www.mfa.gov .il/mfa/aboutisrael/state/law/pages/summary%20of%20opinion%20concerning %20unauthorized%20outposts%20-%20talya%20sason%20adv.asp. The opinion established that the outposts were established in blatant violation of Israeli law.

99. Chaim Levinson, "The Organization Behind Illegal West Bank Outpost Construction," *Haaretz*, May 13, 2013; see also Haklai, "Religious-Nationalist Mobilization." The head of Amana, Ze'ev "Zambish" Hever, is a former member of the Jewish Underground, a terrorist organization that operated in the West Bank in the 1980s.

100. International Crisis Group, *Leap of Faith*, 22.

101. International Crisis Group, *Israel's Religious Right*, 21.

102. Klein, *Shift*, 83.

103. International Crisis Group, *Israel's Religious Right*, 22–23.

104. See ibid., 25–26; Klein, *Shift*, 84–86.

105. See, for example, "Human Rights in the Occupied Territories: 2011 Annual Report," B'Tselem, 2011, http://www.btselem.org/sites/default/files2/2011 _annual_report_eng.pdf; and International Crisis Group, *Israel's Religious Right*, 32 ff. Only in December 2011, B'Tselem documented ten cases in which Israeli settlers harmed Palestinians or Palestinian property in the West Bank; "Settler Violence against Palestinians and Palestinian Property," B'Tselem, December 29, 2011, http://www.btselem.org/settler_violence/20111229_settler_violence_in _dec_2012.

106. See Kretzmer, *Occupation of Justice.* On the numerous rulings of the Supreme Court on petitions filed by B'Tselem, see the website of the organization, http://www.btselem.org.

107. Peleg, *Begin's Foreign Policy*, 66.

108. See chapter 1; see also Ari Shavit, "The Big Freeze: Interview with Dov Weisglass," *Haaretz Magazine*, October 8, 2004.

109. Del Sarto, "Back to Square One?," 422.

110. Lustick, *Unsettled States*, chaps. 9 and 10.

111. See, for example, Del Sarto, *Contested State Identities*, chap. 4; and Barnett, "Culture, Strategy and Foreign Policy Change."

112. See, for example, Bar-Tal and Teichman, *Stereotypes and Prejudice*, 58–61.

113. Ibid., 67 ff.

114. Ibid., 71.

115. Sherif, *In Common Predicament.* See also Hogg and Abrams, *Group Motivations.*

116. See Halperin, "Group-Based Hatred"; and Halperin and Bar-Tal, "Socio-Psychological Barriers."

117. Halperin and Bar-Tal, "Socio-Psychological Barriers"; and Seliktar, *New Zionism and the Foreign Policy System of Israel*, 163–69.

118. Bar-Tal, "Why Does Fear"; and Jarymowicz and Bar-Tal, "The Dominance of Fear."

119. The murderer of Rabin, Yigal Amir, justified his action by the Jewish religious ruling of *din rodef,* stipulating that it is permitted to kill a person who endangers the life of Jews. This ruling circulated in extremist settler circles. Amir has never regretted his deed.

120. The disappointment of Israeli intellectuals of the (former) left-wing, pro-peace camp is probably best represented by the volte-face of renowned historian Benny Morris. See Benny Morris, "Peace? No Chance," *Guardian*, February 21, 2002.

121. Amos Harel and Avi Issacharoff, "Years of Rage," *Haaretz*, October 1, 2010; and Gershon Baskin, "In the Land of Miracles: Let's Get Real," *Haaretz*, September 29, 2009.

122. Halperin and Bar-Tal, "Socio-Psychological Barriers," 647.

123. Peffley, Hutchison, and Shamir, "The Impact of Persistent Terrorism."

124. Halperin and Bar-Tal, "Fall of the Peace Camp." See also the Peace Index polls of the Tami Steinmetz Center for Peace Research at Tel Aviv University for the period 2000–2002, http://www.tau.ac.il/peace/.

125. See Hovland, Janis, and Kelley, *Communication and Persuasion*, 35 ff.; Kruglanski et al., "Says Who?"; and Kruglanski, *Lay Epistemics and Human Knowledge.*

126. Hussein Agha and Robert Malley, "Camp David: The Tragedy of Errors," *New York Review of Books*, August 9, 2001.

127. Ehud Barak during the Haaretz Conference on Peace in July 2014; see "Ve'idat Israel le-Shalom" [Israel Conference on Peace], *Haaretz*, July 18, 2014, http://www.haaretz.co.il/israel-peace-convention/1.2370066.

128. See, for example, Ilan Marsiano, "Ba-Likud Hikhlitu: Lehaftsits et Iran" [They decided in the Likud: Bomb Iran], *Ynet*, January 1, 2006; Yossi Yonah, "Lifnei She-Maftsitsim be-Iran" [Before we bomb Iran], *Ynet*, September 15, 2006; Shimon Cohen, "Olmert le-Artsot ha-Brit: Shenu Mediniyut mul Iran" [Olmert to the US: Change policy towards Iran], *Aruts Shev'a* [Channel 7], November 13, 2006; Jeffrey Goldberg, "Netanyahu to Obama: Stop Iran—or I Will," *Atlantic*, March 31, 2009; Natasha Mozgovaya, "Peres to Obama: No Choice but to Compare Iran to Nazis," *Haaretz*, May 6, 2009; "Netanyahu: Neutralizing Iran Would Reduce Danger of Hamas, Hezbollah," *Haaretz*, January 29, 2009; and Stephen Farrell, Robert Thomson, and Danielle Haas, "Attack Iran the Day Iraq War Ends, Demands Israel," *Times* (London), November 5, 2002.

129. See, for example, the report of the IDF of November 2000, quoted in Enderlin, *Shattered Dreams*, 293–94; and Akiva Eldar, "Popular Misconceptions," *Haaretz*, June 11, 2004.

130. Michael, "Israel Defense Forces."

131. Former head of the army's planning directorate Amir Eshel, quoted in Harel, "Looking Ahead."

132. Michael, "Israel Defense Forces"; and Michael, "Military Knowledge and Weak Civilian Control."

133. Dor, *Suppression of Guilt*; Dor, *Intifada Hits the Headlines*; Wolfsfeld, *Media and the Path to Peace,* chap. 7; and Keshev, "'Liquidation Sale': Israeli Media Coverage of Events in Which Palestinians Were Killed by Israeli Security Forces," Keshev, March 2006.

134. Keshev, "War to the Last Moment: The Israeli Media in the Second Lebanon War," Keshev, July 2008; and Keshev, "Sikur Mivtsah 'Oferet Yetsukah' be-'Aza ba-Tikshoret ha-Israelit" [An analysis of "Operation Cast Lead" in the Israeli Media], Keshev, 2009.

135. Bar-Tal and Teichman, *Stereotypes and Prejudice*, 156; Wolfsfeld, *Media and the Path to Peace,* 205.

136. Michael, "Israel Defense Forces."

137. Naveh, "Role of the Media," 32–35.

138. See Dor, *Suppression of Guilt*; Liebes, *Reporting the Arab–Israeli Conflict*; and Wolfsfeld, *Media and the Path to Peace*.

4

The Return of Dissent?

2010 to the Present

The so-called Arab Spring, which started in December 2010 with the self-immolation of the Tunisian vegetable vendor Mohamed Bouazizi, in a way marks the end of the first post-Oslo decade—and probably of the old regional order in the Middle East altogether. In parallel to the waves of political contestation sweeping through Arab states, a protest movement demanding social justice emerged in Israel in the summer of 2011. At about the same time, former key figures of Israel's security establishment started publicly denouncing the government's flirtation with the idea of attacking Iran's nuclear facilities. The criticism triggered a heated public debate in Israel on the country's regional relations, a debate that had been absent during much of the previous decade. Thus, dissent seemed to be returning to Israeli politics and society, indicating that the neo-revisionist and hegemonic worldview post-Oslo may have started to crumble. However, the events around the Israel–Gaza war of July–August 2014 marked a clear reversal of this trend. The extremely strong consensus in Israeli politics and society on the righteousness of the war and the denunciation of domestic and international critics were the clearest indication of this.

Social Protests and Dissenting Ex-Generals

At the beginning of the 2010s, it seemed as if dissent and contestation had returned to the Israeli body politic. The summer of 2011 witnessed the emergence of a social protest movement in Israel, incidentally triggered by complaints about the high cost of cottage cheese—of all things. The demonstrations soon developed into a much broader protest movement against the continuously rising costs of living, the lack of affordable housing, and deteriorating public services, especially in the fields of health and education. What had started as a protest triggered by social media leading to the establishment of tents on Tel Aviv's fancy Rothschild Boulevard soon spread to other cities and involved hundreds of thousands of Israelis. Due to the constant preoccupation with security, social and economic policies had rarely been the topic of public debate in Israel. Even more surprisingly, the protest movement transcended left/right divisions. Israelis of different ages, backgrounds, and political opinions joined in with calls of "the people demand social justice," thus paraphrasing the demonstrators at the time in neighboring Arab countries.

The protests exerted pressure on the Netanyahu government. After implementing a series of measures to alleviate the housing shortage, Netanyahu set up a committee of experts and senior officials to examine how the movement's demands could be met.[1] With demonstrations continuing in the summer of 2012, the protests began to have a wider political impact. Claiming to represent the secular middle class and to heed the demands for social justice, the narcissistic TV show presenter Yair Lapid founded the party Yesh Atid (literally, There Is a Future) in 2012. Capitalizing to a considerable degree on the social protests, the party came in second place in the February 2013 elections, winning 19 seats in Israel's 120-seat parliament. Perhaps for the first time ever, or at least in decades, socioeconomic issues also played a central role in the electoral campaign leading up to the March 2015 elections.

In 2011 the conscious decision of the protest movement's organizers to avoid party politics in order to increase the movement's appeal meant that divisive issues were avoided, so the matter of Israel's settlement project became a taboo. The movement did not point out the state-subsidized housing in the territories or the unequal distribution of budgets to the benefit of the settlements beyond the Green Line. Likewise, Lapid's proclaimed aim of wanting to represent the center of Israeli society did not prevent him, after the 2013 elections, from entering an alliance with Naftali Bennett, the new leader of the national-religious Ha-Bayit Ha-Yehudi party (The Jewish Home). Representing the settler movement, this party is the successor of the veteran National Religious Party (Mafdal); the new incarnation, however, had moved considerably to the right. Besides rejecting any territorial compromise on Jerusalem, Lapid has also been conspicuously vague as to his vision of how to resolve the Israeli–Palestinian conflict. In the subsequent elections in 2015, the Likud and affiliated parties won a majority. This coalition was joined by former communications minister Moshe Kahlon's newly established Kulanu party, which sought to take over the socioeconomic agenda.

The social protests thus succeeded in drawing attention to the implications of the neoliberal economic policies in Israel that had transformed the country, from an originally egalitarian and socialist-oriented society—perhaps best symbolized by the kibbutz—to the second country among Western states in terms of socioeconomic inequality, after the US. Among member countries of the Organisation for Economic Co-Operation and Development (OECD), Israel has the fifth-highest income inequality, after Chile, Mexico, Turkey, and the US.[2] In spite of a relatively strong economic growth and low unemployment rates, among the thirty-four OECD members, Israel also has the highest rate of relative poverty—defined by the OECD as the share of people having less income than half the national median income. The income of about one in five Israeli households falls below the relative poverty line; among the Arab citizens of Israel and the ultra-Orthodox Jewish communities, poverty is over one in two.[3] Within the last couple of years, the country also witnessed a doubling of real estate prices and an increase of over one-third in the costs of renting a house, with salaries remaining static. Thus, to a certain extent, the social protests did mark the return of dissent in Israeli society and politics. However, they were a long way from challenging the hegemonic vision on threats and regional order that have been prevailing in post-Oslo Israel.

The issue that did start to trigger some dissent in the new decade was the question of Iran. In October 2011 Nahum Barnea, one of the most influential Israeli journalists, lambasted Prime Minister Netanyahu and Defense Minister Barak in an op-ed in the daily *Yediot Aharonot* for planning an attack on Iran's nuclear facilities. He based his analysis on the opposition to such a plan expressed by key figures of Israel's security establishment, represented by the heads of all four Israeli security and intelligence services and by several members of the government coalition. Indeed, according to Barnea, those opposed to an attack included the chief of staff of the Israeli army, Benny Gantz; the head of military intelligence, Aviv Kochavi; the director of Mossad, Tamir Pardo; and the head of Israel's internal security service, Shabak, Yoram Cohen, with none of them denying Barnea's claim.[4] Barnea's article gave rise to an unprecedented public debate on the possible consequences of an Israeli strike on Iran, with Labor leader Shelly Yachimovich calling the plan a "megalomaniacal adventure." Similarly, a much-quoted poll of March 2012 conducted by the Israeli daily *Haaretz* found that a majority of Israelis, 58 percent, opposed a strike on Iran's nuclear facilities without US backing.[5] Significantly, this poll, for which no methodological information is available, was taken after President Obama had made it clear to Netanyahu that, for now, the United States would not take any military action against Iran. Most of the public opinion surveys taken previously had not distinguished between military action taken by the US alone, by the US in cooperation with Israel, or by Israel alone.

Former Mossad chief Meir Dagan and former head of Shabak Yuval Diskin continued to express their opposition to an Israeli strike on Iran's nuclear facilities in a series of lectures, stressing instead the urgency of reaching an agreement with the Palestinians. This assessment was echoed in 2014 by Tamir Pardo, the acting head of the Mossad. During a meeting with thirty businesspeople in a private home, Pardo stated that it was the unresolved Palestinian issue that was the major threat to Israel's security, not Iran. He also dismissed the idea that Iran's nuclear program, while dangerous, was an "existential" threat to Israel.[6]

An image of the crumbling of Israel's post-Oslo hegemonic vision of threats and regional order also seemed to emerge from public opinion polls taken at the end of the 2000s. Seemingly at odds with Israel's constant shift to the right, the Israeli public had become more divided on the question of whether the solution to the conflict with the Palestinians needed to be predominantly political or military. Dropping from much higher percentages in the middle of the decade, in the polls taken in 2009 only a quarter of respondents agreed with the statement that there was no political solution to the conflict (however, half of the respondents agreed that the solution to the problem was *also* military).[7] Dissent around the rationale of, and justification for, Israel's conduct in the Palestinian territories also became visible in September 2014, when forty-three reservists from the army's elite intelligence unit, Unit 8200, wrote an open letter to Prime Minister Netanyahu, IDF Chief of Staff Gantz, and Kochavi, the head of the Military Intelligence Directorate. The signatories of the letter, which included a major and two captains, stated that they would refuse to do their reserve service because intelligence was an integral part of Israel's military occupation of the territories. According to the letter, the intelligence that was collected harmed innocent civilians and violated their civil rights; it was "used for political persecution and to create divisions within Palestinian society by recruiting collaborators and driving part of Palestinian society against itself."[8]

In spite of this substantial criticism coming from within the Israeli army and the country's security community, the shift to the right and the growing influence of the settler movement on Israeli politics persisted. The general elections in January 2013 and March 2015 clearly confirmed this trend, with the newspaper *Haaretz* dubbing the Israeli government that was formed in 2013 a "settler government."[9] In the March 2015 elections, a majority of votes went to the center-right and right-wing parties, enabling Netanyahu to form a right-wing government, thus consolidating the hegemony of the neo-revisionist Right in Israel.[10] True, the Likud primaries witnessed a defeat of the far-right faction within the party, led by Moshe Feiglin. However, during the electoral campaign, Netanyahu went on record as saying that there would be no Palestinian state under his watch.[11] And he continued to focus on the need to bomb Iran. As noted earlier, this caused an all-time low in US–Israeli relations after his visit to address the US Congress on this matter without informing the US president and against the background of Obama's attempts to seal a nuclear deal with Iran. And, in a last-minute attempt to attract voters on the right, in a thirty-second video posted on social media, Netanyahu warned of the danger of "the Arabs" (*ha-'aravim*)—that is, the Arab citizens of Israel—going to the polls in huge numbers (*be-kamuiot 'adirot*), driven there in buses by the "organizations of the Left" (*amutot ha-smol*), and threatening the "rule of the Right" (*shilton ha-yamin*).[12]

But even before the 2015 elections, the war between Israel and Hamas in the summer of 2014 was to confirm the resilience of Israel's new hegemony.

The Gaza War, Summer 2014

During Israel's war with Hamas of July–August 2014, the power of Israel's hegemonic vision of threats and regional order became visible in all its strength. The Israeli government presented the war, the third of its kind in the previous six years, as legitimate self-defense against the repeated launching of Hamas rockets on Israel's civilian population. As noted earlier, the deliberate targeting of civilians counts as a violation of the rules of war, and it is indeed difficult to imagine any state accepting such hostilities without reacting. However, the context and conduct of this war were very specific.

The goal of Israel's military operation, dubbed "Protective Edge," was, initially, to "deal a blow" to Hamas, or, as the Israeli government termed it, "to mow the lawn." The objective of the operation soon developed into the destruction of the "terrorist infrastructure," including the hundreds of tunnels in Gaza that connected the strip to Egypt's Sinai Peninsula and the around forty tunnels or so connecting Gaza to Israel. These tunnels not only allowed the smuggling of weapons and related material into the Gaza

Strip from Egypt but could also be used to stage terrorist attacks inside Israel. Aimed at destroying Hamas's rocket-launching capabilities, the military operation started on July 4, 2014, with repeated Israeli airstrikes on the Gaza Strip. It was soon followed by a ground invasion. The rockets launched from the Gaza Strip during the fifty-day war now also reached Tel Aviv and Jerusalem, prompting Israeli citizens to run to shelters several times a day. It is estimated that Hamas and other Gaza-based groups launched over 4,500 rockets and mortars into Israel during the war.[13]

According to UN figures of September 2014 and June 2015, Israel's military operation in the Gaza Strip led to the killing of over 2,200 Palestinians, almost 70 percent of whom were civilians (including over 550 children). It left over 11,000 Palestinians wounded, of whom 10 percent suffered permanent disability as a result. A total of 18,000 housing units in the Gaza Strip were destroyed or severely damaged, as was vital infrastructure such as hospitals, schools, and the only power plant in Gaza. The war left over 100,000 people homeless and almost half a million people without access to municipal water due to infrastructure damage. As of September 2014 approximately 110,000 internally displaced persons still remained in UNRWA emergency shelters or with host families.[14] On the Israeli side, the number of fatalities rose to 67 soldiers and 4 civilians, including 1 foreign national from Thailand. The war led to the injury of up to 1,600 Israelis.[15]

As if in a replay of Israel's 2008–9 war on Hamas-ruled Gaza, Israel faced growing international alarm over the soaring casualty figures in Gaza and the accusations that it was violating international law. The government in Jerusalem, on its side, continued to emphasize the terrorist and repressive nature of Hamas and the threat it posed to Israeli citizens, also pointing to the relations Hamas maintained with Ansar Beit al-Maqdis, the self-proclaimed branch of the Islamic State, or Daesh, in the Sinai.[16] The justification for Israel's military action, repeated time and again by government spokespersons in the Israeli and foreign media, was that no country would accept the deliberate firing of rockets on its civilians. According to the Israeli government, the renewed rocket fire by different "terrorist organizations" in the Gaza Strip on June 12, 2014, was unprovoked, with three hundred rockets hitting Israel in June alone. The Israeli government also continued to maintain the righteousness of its mission and the defensive nature of its actions.[17] For instance, on its website the Israeli Foreign Ministry placed information on the military operation under the headline "Operation Protective Edge: Israel under Fire."[18] Likewise, the Israeli ambassador to the UN, Ron Prosor, declared that "the international community should be very vocal in standing with Israel fighting terrorism today because if not, you will see it on your doorstep tomorrow."[19]

Regarding the high number of casualties on the Palestinian side and the massive destruction of Gaza's infrastructure, the government repeated that Hamas was hiding its weapons among civilians, including in schools and hospitals, and in a labyrinth of tunnels running beneath the densely populated Gaza Strip. In support of this claim, the Israeli army displayed a manual on "urban warfare" used by Hamas's al-Qassam Brigades.[20] With the UN discovering caches of weapons in at least three UNRWA-run schools in the Gaza Strip, according to the Israeli authorities, the culprit remained Hamas: it was brutal, cowardly, and used human shields.[21] The government in Jerusalem also took pride in stressing that it was doing its utmost to spare civilian lives, for instance, by warning of imminent attacks through phone calls, leaflets, and "knocking" on rooftops (that is, "warning strikes" before bombing the building). Moreover, the Israeli government pointed to the fact that Hamas prolonged the hostilities by repeatedly rejecting cease-fires or formally accepting them while violating them. For instance, it could have accepted a first Egyptian-brokered cease-fire on July 15, which did not differ from the one Hamas eventually accepted on August 26, 2014. Had Hamas accepted the first cease-fire, 90 percent of casualties could have been avoided, according to the government in Jerusalem.[22] Hence, the official discourse once more presented Israel as occupying the moral high ground, stressing for instance that "the IDF is a moral army unlike any other. We are fighting a very brutal enemy, and seek to avoid harming civilians as much as possible."[23]

As is so often the case, the timeline of events leading to the escalation along with the justification for the conduct of Israel's war on Hamas is highly contested. Or, to put it differently, while there is an evident material basis for the course of events as presented by the Israeli government, alternative interpretations challenging the neat black-and-white picture emerging from Israel's official description are plausible as well. What Israel considered as a response to an unprovoked attack actually marked the gradual erosion and eventual collapse of an Egyptian-brokered cease-fire between Israel and Hamas, reached in November 2012, in the aftermath of the previous round of fighting. In the period leading up to the start of the 2014 Israel–Gaza war, seven Israelis, five of whom were civilians, were injured due to rocket fire. A total of fifteen Palestinians, including one civilian, were killed, and another fifty-eight, mostly civilians, were injured as a result of Israeli airstrikes in the Gaza Strip.[24]

The question of who violated the cease-fire agreement, or perhaps of who is to take most of the blame for its collapse, is disputed. While in the first three months following the November 2012 cease-fire only a few rockets were launched from Gaza, the Israeli government repeatedly postponed indirect negotiations with Hamas on the cease-fire. The economic blockade of Gaza was thus left effectively in place, in spite of the Israeli commitment to lift the blockade under the cease-fire agreement.[25] As the rocket fire resumed, Israeli air raids on the strip intensified. Tensions further increased after the abduction and killing on June 12, 2014, of three Israeli teenagers studying at yeshiva schools in the southern West Bank, for which Israel immediately held Hamas responsible. Thus, according to Israel's official version of events, from late 2013 onward Hamas and other militant groups violated the cease-fire by firing rockets, then abducted and killed three Israeli youngsters in June, while also intensifying the rocket fire. Israel was forced to react.[26]

What remains somewhat disconnected from this version of events is the massive Israeli search operation across West Bank towns and cities, which followed the abduction and killing of the three teenage boys. Dubbed Operation Brother's Keepers by the IDF, the eighteen-day operation targeted Hamas members and institutions in the West Bank, leading to the arrest of over four hundred Palestinians—some sources indicate over six hundred, including over three hundred members of Hamas, at all levels of seniority. At least fifty of the arrested Hamas members had been released under the Gilad Shalit prisoner-exchange deal in 2011. The operation extended well beyond the Hebron area where the Israeli teenagers had been abducted and also included the entry of the Israeli army into PA-controlled Area A. Hamas-affiliated charity workers and journalists were arrested as well. In the course of the operation, the largest Israeli incursion into the West Bank since the Second Intifada, six Palestinians were killed by the Israeli army during clashes.[27] The PA initially cooperated with the Israeli efforts to find the abductors of the kidnapped Israeli teenagers, a position that, in the eyes of many West Bank residents, underscored its role as Israel's security contractor and docile collaborator.

The discovery of the bodies of the three kidnapped Israeli teenagers— Eyal Yifrach, nineteen, and Gilad Shaar and Naftali Fraenkel, both sixteen— in the backyard of a Hamas member in Hebron on July 1 prompted a revenge killing of a Palestinian Jerusalemite teenager, sixteen-year-old Mohammed Abu Khdeir, who was burned alive by Israeli extremists. Together with the Israeli crackdown on Hamas in the West Bank, this incident led to violent Palestinian protests in the West Bank and rocket attacks on Israel by Palestinian militants based in Gaza. While the Israeli government claimed from the outset that it had irrefutable evidence that Hamas was behind the operation, the Hamas leadership repeatedly denied that the organization had ordered or orchestrated the kidnapping.[28] This did not prevent Hamas leaders, however, from praising the abduction and killing of Israeli settlers, including that of the three teenagers, as legitimate actions of Palestinian resistance against Israel's occupation. With the Israeli promise of the lifting of the economic blockade on Gaza under the 2012 cease-fire agreement remaining unfulfilled, the Hamas leadership probably decided that a military confrontation with Israel was its best option at this point, preferable to a return to the status quo ante.[29]

In this context, it is significant that a few weeks before the kidnapping of the Israeli teenagers, Hamas and Fatah had agreed on a unity government, which was sworn in in early June. Headed by the incumbent prime minister, Rami Hamdallah, the government comprised seventeen independent ministers and no Hamas representative. The reconciliation agreement between Hamas and Fatah stipulated that thousands of the Fatah-dominated PA security forces would move back to the Gaza Strip and take control over Gaza's borders. Hamas was not granted any reciprocal concession in the West Bank. Perhaps more importantly, the new Palestinian government agreed to comply with the three conditions named by the international community: recognizing Israel, renouncing violence, and respecting past agreements.[30] Hamas agreed to Palestinian reconciliation out of weakness and a growing isolation following a combination of domestic and regional developments post-Arab uprisings. In particular, Hamas had lost its ally (and base) in Damascus after it refused to take the side of Assad in Syria's civil war; relations with Iran soured for the same reason. Mohamed Morsi and the Muslim Brotherhood were ousted and outlawed in Egypt, and Hamas lost financial revenues from the tunnel trade after the new Egyptian regime under Abdel Fattah al-Sisi closed most of the tunnels and severely restricted the crossing of the border. Turkey had its own domestic and regional problems. With the economic situation in the Gaza Strip deteriorating further—including the inability to pay the salaries of Gaza's civil servants—and with regular electricity blackouts, fuel shortages, and a growing contamination of the water aquifer, Hamas may have reckoned that it had not many alternatives left.

As for Israel, the government rejected the reconciliation deal out of hand. According to Netanyahu, the unity government was proof that Abbas had chosen terror over peace.[31] The Israeli government also immediately attempted to undercut the unity deal between Hamas and Fatah. As

Nathan Thrall put it in the *New York Times*, the government in Jerusalem decided to prevent "Hamas leaders and Gaza residents from obtaining the two most essential benefits of the deal: the payment of salaries to 43,000 civil servants who worked for the Hamas government and continue to administer Gaza under the new one, and the easing of the suffocating border closures imposed by Israel and Egypt that bar most Gazans' passage to the outside world."[32]

Much to the dismay of the Israeli government, the United States and the European Union cautiously agreed to work with the new government. From this perspective, it would seem that the abduction of the three Israeli teenagers in the West Bank less than two weeks after the new Palestinian government was sworn in may also have provided the Israeli government with an opportunity to disrupt Palestinian reconciliation. The fact that Israel immediately blamed Hamas for having orchestrated the kidnapping, together with the massive crackdown on the organization in the West Bank accompanying Israel's search-and-rescue operation, supports this perspective. In September 2014 documents related to the investigation and indictment of the man who is believed to have been the logistical commander of the kidnapping squad depict the action as a local initiative carried out by members of a clan in Hebron. There was no evidence that the Hamas leadership had ordered or had prior knowledge of the abduction.[33] The emerging picture thus confirms comments made previously by Israeli authorities that the kidnapping was carried out by a rogue cell—comments that were later denied as having been made.[34]

As for Hamas, the growing protests against Fatah's security cooperation with Israel in the West Bank and the firing of rockets by militants (probably Islamic Jihad) in the Gaza Strip in reaction to the Israeli operation prompted the organization to call for a "third intifada," and for an end to policing the militants launching those rockets. Hamas started officially taking responsibility for the rocket fire the day after an Israeli raid killed seven Hamas operatives on July 6. This in turn prompted Israel to launch "Operation Protective Edge."[35] Thus, while Hamas did not necessarily start the war, it deliberately chose an escalation that it knew would cost dearly in terms of human lives, for strategic reasons. Not only did Hamas aim at changing an unacceptable status quo, but it also used the situation to strengthen its position. Compared to the PA's collaboration with Israel, Hamas could claim to be the only remaining resistance movement. As for Israel, a consideration of the whole picture suggests that the Gaza war may indeed have also been the result of a decision to undermine the Palestinian reconciliation agreement of April 2014.[36]

With its interpretation of events, Israel found itself increasingly on a collision course with the international community. This occurred notwithstanding the fact that most governments accepted Israel's right to defend itself against the rocket fire. But particularly in light of the images of dead and maimed Palestinian civilians, including many children, and of bombed schools and hospitals, flattened neighborhoods, and the general extent of the destruction in Gaza, the explanations and justifications provided by the Israeli government seemed increasingly hollow in the eyes of the international community. Israel's interpretation of international law also diverged considerably from the majority opinion. By designating the Hamas government as an "enemy entity," the Israeli army's combat doctrine stipulated that facilities and objects were legitimate targets, including symbols of the Hamas government such as offices, buildings, and the police. Similarly, according to the IDF's legal experts, when fighting in urban areas, the entire area is a legitimate target as long as residents are warned in time. Yet the majority opinion in international law maintains the principle of differentiating between military targets, which are legitimate, and civilian targets, which are not, together with the principle of proportionality. Likewise, most international lawyers would dispute the effectiveness of Israel's advance warning given to Gaza's civilians, for most residents were, effectively, not able to leave the area: there were no safe passages and no help for the ill, the elderly, and children.[37]

With numerous anti-Israel demonstrations taking place in Europe, Australia, Latin America, and the United States, Israel came under mounting international pressure, especially after it shelled on July 28, 2014, an UNRWA school in Gaza that was being used as a shelter by some three thousand people, killing at least twenty people. A similar incident involving a UN school used as a shelter and leaving ten people dead occurred less than a week later.[38] Falling short of officially accusing Israel of deliberately targeting civilians, UN Secretary-General Ban Ki-moon blamed Israel for "pummeling" Gazans with "indiscriminate destruction."[39] While acknowledging that the UN had indeed uncovered cases in which Hamas weapons were stored "in a small number of abandoned buildings" and that there were "reports that Hamas rockets were fired from near UN premises," the secretary-general denounced Israel's repeated "shelling of UN facilities harboring civilians who had been explicitly told to seek a safe haven there" as "outrageous, unacceptable and unjustifiable."[40] Ban also questioned the proportionality of Israel's military operations, stressing that the 1.8 million people of Gaza "have nowhere to run."[41] According to the UN secretary-general, Gazans "are trapped, besieged on a speck of land. Every area is a civilian area. Every home, every school, every refuge has become a target."[42] Concurrently, the UN High Commissioner for Human Rights Navi Pillay accused both Israel and Hamas militants of violating the rules of war, with the UN Human Rights Council launching a commission of inquiry to investigate possible war crimes.[43] On the Israeli side, the accusation of possibly having committed war crimes prompted a reaction of disbelief and indignation. The "decision today by the HRC is a travesty and should be rejected by decent people everywhere,"[44] was the official reply of Netanyahu's office to the Human Rights Council's decision. Israel promised to investigate the shelling of UN schools and set up a team of legal experts to counter, or perhaps deflect, the anticipated UN investigation.[45] However, these measures would not convince Israel's most important human rights organization, B'Tselem, or human rights lawyers that the Israeli authorities were able to investigate effectively Israeli alleged violations of international law.[46] Shortly afterward, the Israeli government announced that it would not cooperate with the commission of inquiry given that William Schabas, who was initially appointed to head the commission, was known to be "anti-Israel," according to the government's official position.[47] Schabas would resign from the position in early 2015 following an Israeli complaint about a conflict of interest based on legal services Schabas had provided to the PLO in 2012. Issued in June 2015, the report of the UN Human Rights Council concluded that the commission of inquiry "was able to gather substantial information pointing to serious violations of international humanitarian law and international human rights law by Israel and by Palestinian armed groups," specifying that "in some cases, these violations may amount to war crimes."[48] Israel's own investigation of the military conduct in the Gaza war reached the opposite conclusions: the use of force against Hamas was necessary, proportional, and justified under international law.[49]

While tensions between Israel and the UN are of course no novelty, Israel's conduct in the Gaza war also fueled tensions between Washington and the government in Jerusalem. The White House called the deadly strikes at or near UN facilities in Gaza "totally unacceptable and totally indefensible."[50] Previously, US secretary of state John Kerry had expressed his frustration with the rising toll of civilians in the Gaza Strip, contrasting with Israel's official argument that its military strikes occurred with chirurgical precision. During a conversation caught on an open microphone before an interview on Fox News, he was caught saying sarcastically, "it's a hell of a pinpoint operation."[51] Indicating increasingly strained relations, particularly after the Israeli cabinet rebuffed a cease-fire agreement brokered by Kerry at the end of July 2014, the White House had repeatedly criticized Israel for not doing enough to spare civilians in Gaza.[52] While providing millions of dollars in additional funding for Israel's "Iron Dome" missile shield that intercepts incoming rockets, the White House decided one week into the war to temporarily suspend the shipment of Hellfire missiles—air-to-surface missiles fired from Apache helicopters—to Israel because they were considered offensive weapons.[53] This did not, however, prevent Washington from supplying additional grenades and mortars during the Israeli offensive.[54] In general, the popular support for Israel remained high in the US. But a poll taken during the war corroborates a key development noted earlier—namely, that this support is not as mono-lithic as is usually assumed and that younger people and minorities were far more critical of Israel. This demographic shift could be interpreted as a potential source of increased sympathy toward the Palestinians in US policy in the long term.[55]

European governments were altogether rather tepid in their criticism of Israel, condemning Hamas's indiscriminate firing of rockets and support-ing Israel's right to protect its population. Thus, at the European Coun-cil summit in July 2014, the heads of state of EU member states—more concerned with the unfolding events in the Ukraine at that moment—called on Israel to "act proportionally" when exercising its right to self-defense. Deploring "the loss of innocent lives and the high number of wounded civilians in the Gaza Strip," the EU foreign ministers called on both sides to "de-escalate the situation, to end the violence, to end the suffering of the civilian populations notably by allowing access to human-itarian assistance, and return to calm."[56] In the vote in the United Nations Human Rights Council on the establishment of a commission of inquiry over alleged war crimes, European governments abstained and the United States cast the only dissenting vote.[57]

Significantly, however, European publics were far more critical of Is-raeli actions, with anti-Israel demonstrations taking place all over Europe. Particularly in France, Germany, Britain, the Netherlands, and Italy, these were accompanied by a growing incidence of despicable anti-Semitic at-tacks. In France, for instance, extremist fringes of the pro-Palestinian demonstrators during the Gaza war attacked synagogues and Jewish shops and sought to storm two synagogues in Paris while chanting "Death to the Jews." In the course of a single week in July 2014, eight synagogues in France were attacked. Molotov cocktails were hurled at synagogues in Germany, where chants heard at pro-Palestinian protests have included "Hamas, Hamas, Jews to the gas." Jewish shop owners in Rome found swastikas sprayed on their walls. An Amsterdam rabbi had his front door stoned. And in Britain there was a spike in anti-Semitic incidents in that period.[58]

The European media generally took a firm position on the Gaza war, usually denouncing Israel's conduct. In the UK, the widely read *Economist* affirmed the legality of Israel's war aims but also stated that it is simply "wrong" to "hit buildings with no evident military purpose and houses packed with civilians, even if they harbor Hamas fighters or officials and the army gives warnings."[59] The TV news anchorman for the British Channel 4, Jon Snow, made no attempt to hide his dismay over the killing of children in Gaza.[60] Generally, the reporting on the war by the major news outlets in Britain, Germany, France, and Italy expressed a general disapproval of Israeli policies and of their justifications.

The trend of granting recognition to Palestine among European parliaments and governments is a further indication of the shift in European public opinion. In early October 2014 the Swedish prime minister announced that Sweden would recognize the State of Palestine, and the British parliament passed a nonbinding but highly symbolic motion on the same issue shortly afterward. On November 19, 2014, with a nearly unanimous vote, the Spanish parliament's lower house adopted a motion urging the Spanish government to recognize Palestine as a state. The French and Irish parliaments, together with the European parliament, would soon follow suit, voting in favor of recognizing a Palestinian state.

The growing international condemnation of Israeli actions contrasted more sharply than ever with the firm conviction in Israel that the country was the victim of Palestinian terror and that it acted in self-defense. The kidnapping of the three teenagers had caused shock and anger in Israeli society. It had persuaded Israelis that they faced an enemy full of hatred, which forged a strong sense of unity. When the bodies of the three boys were found, Jewish Israeli society remained convinced that Israel's retaliation against the terrorists was justified. According to the almost uncontested interpretation of events on the Israeli side, Hamas responded with indiscriminate rocket attacks on Israeli population centers, forcing the army to respond. As Hamas resorted to terror infiltration through tunnels, Israel had to expand its military operation. The high toll of Palestinian civilians was a direct result of Hamas launching its rockets from densely populated areas, for which ultimately Hamas was to blame, according to the dominant narrative. And because the population of Gaza had voted Hamas, a terrorist organization, into power, the population of Gaza was responsible for the situation. Or, to put it in the words of Giora

Eiland, former head of Israel's National Security Council, "[In] Gaza, there is no such thing as 'innocent civilians.'"[61] Most Jewish Israelis were convinced that Israel no longer bore any responsibility for the fate of Gaza's civilian population.

During the war, the consensus around these beliefs was extraordinarily strong, spanning from the government to the army and from journalists to the Jewish Israeli public at large. Significantly, an unprecedented militancy characterized the attempts to silence critics. Indeed, it was difficult to overlook the verbal and sometimes physical violence and the intimidation directed at those who dared question the hegemonic narrative.

On Israeli TV, footage from the Gaza Strip was rare, with the media generally supporting the Israeli government and the military. While the media's support for the government and the army during times of war is nothing unusual, some pundits and journalists did question what would or should happen after the end of the military operation. Among Israel's newspapers, the most critical one was undoubtedly *Haaretz*, in which questions were asked and attempts were made to give a voice to the people of Gaza. Likewise, Israel's human rights organizations questioned the appropriateness, legality, and proportionality of Israel's military operations. However, their voices were rarely heard in the news coverage and in the numerous programs in which (real or self-nominated) experts and pundits discussed the war. Thus, the objective of stopping the rocket fire and destroying the "terror tunnels" went largely unquestioned, with Israel's military operations and the casualties on both sides being presented as a necessary evil.

Israeli politics presented a similar picture. Certainly, there were divisions within the country's political and military leadership. Significantly, however, most of these voices came from coalition members further to the right of Netanyahu. Most notably, Foreign Minister Avigdor Lieberman, Economy Minister Naftali Bennett, and a number of senior army officers criticized Netanyahu for not acting forcefully enough, advocating the complete destruction of Hamas and the reoccupation of the Gaza Strip. As a minimum, they argued in favor of teaching Hamas a lesson it would never forget.[62] Moshe Feiglin, then the deputy speaker of the Knesset and a well-known supporter of the settlement movement, posted an open letter to Netanyahu on his Facebook page, calling for the conquest of Gaza and the "elimination" of all military forces "and their supporters." Feiglin's underlying argument was that Gaza is part of "our land" and that there are "not two states for two people, but only one state for one people."[63] Arguing in favor of a reoccupation of the Gaza Strip, Deputy

Defense Minister Danny Danon was fired by Netanyahu for his outspoken criticism of the government's strategy in Gaza; he had also commented that it was crucial to ensure that the government would not become a "construct of the left."[64] Danon had taken control of the Likud's central committee in 2013, so he is not exactly a marginal figure (in August 2014, Netanyahu would appoint Danon to be Israel's ambassador to the United Nations). Yet, although it was Netanyahu, Moshe Ya'alon, Lieberman, and Bennett who were beating the war drums, other coalition partners went along. Justice Minister Tzipi Livni, often considered a "dove," supported the idea of toppling Hamas while calling on Israelis "to unite around the understanding that terror must be fought." While Livni considered Israel's military operations in Gaza "a tough war, but a necessary one," Finance Minister Yair Lapid claimed that "we care about Gaza's children more than they do."[65] The mainstream Zionist Left in the opposition, represented by the Labor party, refrained from criticizing government policies. Occasionally it even engaged in explaining the necessity of the war to foreign diplomats. The head of the Labor Party, Isaac Herzog, invoked "an ethos of 'Quiet, we're shooting,'" as the *New York Times* put it.[66] Among the Zionist Left, Meretz leader Zehava Gal-On was perhaps the most outspoken critic of the war. However, most of the party members, and Meretz voters at large, supported the war, as indicated by several opinion polls conducted in that period.

Indeed, among the Jewish Israeli public, support for the war was astoundingly high. In three consecutive polls taken in July by the Israel Democracy Institute and the Evens Program in Mediation and Conflict Resolution of Tel Aviv University, between 92 and 97 percent believed that the Gaza operation was just. These numbers included a vast majority of the self-identified moderate Left and the Left.[67] Support among the Jewish Israeli public for the war remained remarkably strong even after the military operations came to an end, with 83 percent approving of the performance of Chief of Staff Benny Gantz, and with Netanyahu and Ya'alon receiving 77 percent approval ratings.[68] Interestingly, support for the war was independent of the question of whether Israel had achieved its war objectives, given that more than half of the respondents said that they believed only a small proportion of the war aims had been achieved.[69] These polls further confirmed the ever-widening gap between Israel's Jewish majority and the Arab Palestinian citizens of Israel, with 62 percent of Palestinian Israelis believing that the Gaza operation was not justified.[70]

Toward the end of the fifty-day-long war, dissent and protest against the war increased, with a demonstration in Tel Aviv on August 16 attracting around ten thousand people. Meretz and Peace Now, which until then had not participated in antiwar demonstrations, joined in, calling for negotiations instead of war, an end to the occupation, and the lifting of the blockade on Gaza. During the demonstration, author David Grossman expressed his dismay at Israeli society, which "in any other field is proactive and creative and innovative," for having become extremely passive. How is it possible, he asked, "that we accept to be collaborators of despair and failure on the most fateful issue of our existence?"[71] The demonstrators, however, represented only a tiny section of Israeli society.

In fact, political debate and dissent in Israel became major victims of the Gaza war. Militancy and violence against the Palestinians as well as against Israeli critics of the war became the norm. At the initially very small antiwar demonstrations in Tel Aviv, featuring a few dozen protesters, large groups of right-wing counterdemonstrators regularly showed up, yelling "leftists to the oven," along with the more common battle cry, "death to the Arabs." There were repeated incidents of antiwar protesters being chased through the streets and beaten up by right-wing groups, which also stormed and smashed bars and coffee shops identified with the Left.[72] Verbal attacks occurred almost as often as the throwing of eggs, stones, and bottles at antiwar protesters by the war's outspoken supporters. Similar clashes occurred in Haifa, Jaffa, and Jerusalem, with right-wingers organizing themselves into ad hoc militias to fight "the enemy at home" in the name of "national unity." While these events instilled a feeling of intimidation and fear among the antiwar protesters, there were repeated complaints about the failure of the Israeli police to protect the critics of the war.[73] In Jerusalem, there were also repeated incidents of right-wing gangs attacking Palestinians and Palestinian-owned businesses, leading to the hospitalization of two people in at least one case.[74]

Other attempts to silence the critics were no less forceful, these partly also involving the state's institutions. *Haaretz* journalist Gideon Levy was physically assaulted in Ashkelon after his column "dared" to criticize the conduct of Israeli pilots and their lack of conscientious objection to the bombing of Gaza. The physical assault followed a series of verbal attacks. While the *Haaretz* journalist resorted to body guards, Likud MK Yariv Levin declared that he wanted to charge Levy with treason because of his critical articles. Palestinian MK Haneen Zoabi, who after the flotilla incident became the preferred punching bag for the right, was barred from most parliamentary activity—with the approval of the Knesset's ethics committee—after she declared (rightly or wrongly) that the kidnapping of the three teenagers on June 12 could not be considered terrorism.[75] Another notable incident underscoring what Zeev Sternhell described as the "total conformism of the intellectuals" during the war took place at Bar-Ilan University, where a professor was rebuked and threatened with sanctions for having expressed empathy with the Gaza war victims of both sides in an e-mail to his students.[76] Students and parents had filed complaints over the e-mail.[77] Likewise, the Israel Broadcasting Authority took a paid radio advertisement of the human rights organization B'Tselem off the air. The advertisement read out the names and ages of Palestinian children killed in the Gaza war. Petitioned by B'Tselem, Israel's High Court of Justice upheld the Broadcasting Authority's decision in its ruling.

Unsurprisingly, the "war at home" also raged on social media. Israeli comedian and actress Orna Banai, director Shira Geffen, and singer Achinoam Nini (internationally known as Noa) were harshly attacked on Facebook after they expressed compassion for the victims of the war on both sides, called for a cease-fire, or identified with peace and the two-state solution. Responses ranged from calling these artists "a disgrace" to the country to "traitors" and much worse. A right-wing rapper, on the other hand, who also organized attacks on "lefties" and who liked to be photographed holding a rifle, openly called for action against the "left-wing hypocrisy" in social media. For him and his acolytes, the left is "the real enemy." Still, in early August 2014 *Haaretz* reported that the prime minister's office, in cooperation with the National Union for Israeli Students, had approved a project to set up units within Israel's universities to monitor social media and respond in support of the war. The students working in the project would become part of the "public diplomacy" (*hasbarah*) arm of the prime minister's office, with the heads of the units receiving scholarships. They would not, however, identify themselves as officially representing the government.[78] In some institutions of higher education, such units of volunteers had already been operating.[79]

Altogether, and as anyone talking to Israelis during the war would confirm, ordinary Israelis had become nationalistic, often revengeful and militant. Right-wing positions had become the mainstream and verbal violence and incitement the norm. To a large extent, Jewish Israeli society became involved in the government's *hasbarah* efforts, knowingly or unknowingly, as by default. The fragility of Israeli democracy and the gradual erosion of universal values became visible in this acute moment of crisis. According to historian Zeev Sternhell, an extreme nationalist and radical ideology that sees the nation as an organic unit took over.[80] Gideon Levy of *Haaretz* warned: "We will face a new Israel after this operation . . . nationalistic, religious in many ways, brainwashed, militaristic, with very little empathy for the sacrifice of the other side. Nobody in Israel cares at all."[81] In light of the repeated terrorist attacks in Jerusalem starting in the fall of 2014, and with a possible third intifada looming on the horizon, Israel's hegemonic notions of threat and regional order were unlikely to give room to criticism and dissent in the near future.

Hence, the Gaza war evidenced the power of Israel's hegemonic vision on threats and regional order and its neo-revisionist underpinning, with all its domestic and international implications. Particularly in times of re-newed violence, Israel turns into a country in which free speech, criticism, and dissent are no longer tolerated, let alone cherished. In addition, the new foreign policy consensus has placed the country on a collision course with the international community.

At this point it is worth asking whether the war achieved Israel's de-clared objectives. During the war, Netanyahu vowed that he would not rest until all the "terror tunnels" and the "terror infrastructure" were "neu-tralized" and the Gaza Strip was demilitarized.[82] Once the military opera-tions ended, Israel claimed to have destroyed 60–70 percent of the Hamas rocket arsenal and demolished thirty-two "terrorist tunnels." The Israeli government also claimed that it succeeded in "eliminating" over one thou-sand terrorists.[83] There are, of course, differing assessments of whether Israel "won" the latest round of fighting in Gaza. The army may well have destroyed large parts of the weapons infrastructure and the tunnels Hamas had built in the Gaza Strip. But while Hamas enjoyed an unprecedented boost of popularity after the war—in stark contrast to Mahmoud Abbas and the PA—there was no change in the balance of power. The Gaza Strip was not demilitarized, and neither did the military operation fully reestab-lish Israel's deterrence. Hence, in exchange for a largely unchanged situa-tion, Israelis were killed and the country was paralyzed for weeks because of the rocket fire, which now reached Tel Aviv. Israel suffered considerable economic losses, and the country's international standing was dealt a heavy blow. This is in addition to the casualties and destruction on the Palestinian side, which is also most likely to further foment hatred of Israel. And per-haps equally importantly, as after previous rounds of fighting, Israel even-tually had to negotiate with Hamas on a cease-fire, in contrast to its vows that the government would not talk to the organization. Yet, if the status quo remains unchanged and, for instance, the economic blockade is not lifted, it will only be a matter of time before Hamas will renew the rocket fire and Israel will respond. Thus, the next round of confrontation is to be expected. If everything remains unchanged, Hamas is likely to win in pop-ularity, and the PA of Abbas, if still in place, will be the loser. Democracy and political tolerance in Israel, along with the country's international standing, will once more be the victim of the next war.

Notes

1. See, for, example Isabel Kershner, "Protests Grow in Israel, with 250,000 Marching," *New York Times*, August 6, 2011; and Ilan Lior, "Israeli Demonstrators to Mark First Anniversary of Social Protest," *Haaretz*, July 13, 2012.

2. OECD, *In It Together*.

3. OECD, *OECD Economic Surveys*. See also Lior Dattel and Nadan Feldman, "Israel Has Highest Poverty Rate in the Developed World, OECD Report Shows," *Haaretz*, May 15, 2013.

4. Nahum Barnea, "Lahats Atomi" [Atomic pressure], *Yedioth Aharonot*, October 28, 2011. See also "Former Mossad Chief Backs Shin Bet Counterpart over Criticism of Netanyahu, Barak," *Haaretz*, April 29, 2012; and Yossi Melman, "Ex-Mossad Chef Dagan: Military Strike against Iran Would Be Stupid," *Haaretz*, May 8, 2011.

5. Yossi Verter, "Haaretz Poll: Most of the Public Opposes an Israeli Strike on Iran," *Haaretz*, March 8, 2012. The article states that the poll was a "Haaretz-Dialog poll, conducted under the supervision of Prof. Camil Fuchs of Tel Aviv University," but it does not give any information about the size of the sample, the survey method and on whether only Jewish or also Palestinian Israelis were polled. It appears that the poll was financed by Avi Dichter, a candidate in the upcoming *Kadima* primaries. See Gil Hoffman, "Livni Campaign Questions Pollster's Integrity," *Jerusalem Post*, March 9, 2012.

6. Barak Ravid, "Mossad Chief: Palestinian Conflict Top Threat to Israel's Security, Not Iran," *Haaretz*, July 5, 2014.

7. Ben Meir and Bagno-Moldavsky, "Vox Populi," 87–88.

8. Quoted in Gili Cohen, "Reservists from Elite IDF Intel Unit Refuse to Serve over Palestinian 'Persecution,'" *Haaretz*, September 12, 2014.

9. "The Emergence of Israel's Settler Government," *Haaretz* (editorial), March 19, 2013.

10. See, for example, Peters and Pinfold, "Consolidating Right-Wing Hegemony."

11. Barak Ravid, "Netanyahu: If I'm Elected, There Will Be No Palestinian State," *Haaretz*, March 16, 2015.

12. The video is available at Diaa Hadid, "Voters in Nazareth Cheer Gains by Arab Alliance," *New York Times*, March 17, 2015.

13. "Operation Protective Edge in Numbers," *Ynet*, August 27, 2014.

14. United Nations General Assembly, Human Rights Council, *Report of the Independent Commission of Inquiry*; and United Nations Coordination Office for Humanitarian Affairs (OCHA), "Occupied Palestinian Territory." See also Nich-

olas Casey and Joshua Mitnick, "Israel Bombards Hamas Symbols, Power Plant in Gaza," *Wall Street Journal*, July 29, 2014.

15. "The 2014 Gaza Conflict: Factual and Legal Aspects," Israel Ministry of Foreign Affairs, May 2015, http://mfa.gov.il/MFA/ForeignPolicy/IsraelGaza2014/Pages/2014-Gaza-Conflict-Factual-and-Legal-Aspects.aspx, xi; and UN General Assembly, HRC, *Report of the Independent Commission, Resolution S-21/1*.

16. "The 2014 Gaza Conflict," 12–14.

17. "Operation Protective Edge: Israel under Fire, IDF Responds," Israel Ministry of Foreign Affairs, August 26, 2014, http://mfa.gov.il/MFA/ForeignPolicy/Terrorism/Pages/Rise-in-rocket-fire-from-Gaza-3-Jul-2014.aspx.

18. Ibid.

19. Prosor, quoted in "Abbas Seeks Broad Support for War Crime Charges," *Washington Post*, July 31, 2014.

20. "Hamas Manual on 'Urban Warfare,'" Israel Ministry of Foreign Affairs, August 5, 2014, http://mfa.gov.il/MFA/ForeignPolicy/Terrorism/Pages/Hamas-manual-on-Urban-Warfare.aspx. See also Israel Ministry of Foreign Affairs, The 2014 Gaza War, xii–xiii.

21. "UN Says More Rockets Found at One of Its Gaza Schools," Reuters, July 29, 2014.

22. "The 2014 Gaza Conflict," xi.

23. Netanyahu, quoted in Barak Ravid, "Netanyahu: Israel Will Destroy Gaza Tunnels, with or without Cease-Fire," *Haaretz*, July 31, 2014.

24. OCHA, "Occupied Palestinian Territory: Gaza Emergency."

25. Thrall, "Hamas' Chances"; and Avi Issacharoff, "Hamas Fires Rockets for First Time since 2012, Israeli Officials Say," *Times of Israel*, June 30, 2014.

26. "Operation Protective Edge."

27. Jodi Rudoren and Said Ghazali, "A Trail of Clues Leading to Victims and Heartbreak," *New York Times*, July 1, 2014; Gili Cohen and Amos Harel, "IDF Scales Back West Bank Operation against Hamas, Shifts Focus to Intelligence," *Haaretz*, June 24, 2014; and "Israel: Hamas 'Will Pay Price' after Teenagers Found Dead," *BBC News Middle East*, July 1, 2014.

28. Isabel Kershner, "New Light on Hamas Role in Killings of Teenagers That Fueled Gaza War," *New York Times*, September 4, 2014.

29. Thrall, "Hamas' Chances."

30. Peter Beaumont, "Palestinian Unity Government of Fatah and Hamas Sworn In," *Guardian*, June 2, 2014; and Thrall, "Hamas' Chances."

31. Jodi Rudoren and Michael R. Gordon, "Palestinian Rivals Announce Unity Pact, Drawing U.S. And Israeli Rebuke," *New York Times*, April 23, 2014.

32. Nathan Thrall, "How the West Chose War in Gaza," *New York Times*, July 17, 2014.

33. Kershner, "New Light on Hamas Role."

34. Rudoren and Ghazali, "A Trail of Clues"; and Peter Walker and Tom McCarty, "Gaza Crisis: Kerry Says Ceasefire Deal Remains out of Reach," *Guardian*, July 25, 2014. Israeli Police Chief Micky Rosenfeld used the term "lone cell," but later denied having made this comment.

35. Issacharoff, "Hamas Fires Rockets." See also Thrall, "Hamas' Chances."

36. Thrall, "How the West Chose War."

37. See, for example, Michael Sfard, "A 'Targeted Assassination' of International Law," *Haaretz*, August 4, 2014.

38. Steven Erlanger and Fares Akram, "Airstrike near UN School Kills 10, Gaza Officials Say," *New York Times*, August 3, 2014.

39. Ban Ki-moon, quoted in Joe Lauria, "UN Secretary-General Escalates Criticism of Gaza Operations," *Wall Street Journal*, July 28, 2014. See also Sudarsan Raghavan, William Booth, and Ruth Eglash, "UN Says Israel Violated International Law, after Shells Hit School in Gaza," *Washington Post*, July 30, 2014.

40. UN Secretary-General, "Secretary-General's Remarks to the General Assembly on the Situation in Gaza," August 6, 2014, http://www.un.org/sg/statements/index.asp?nid=7913.

41. Ban Ki-moon, quoted in Lauria, "UN Secretary-General Escalates Criticism."

42. Ibid.

43. "Abbas Seeks Broad Support"; and Barak Ravid, "UN Rights Council to Form Commission of Inquiry over Israeli 'War Crimes' in Gaza," *Haaretz*, July 23, 2014.

44. Quoted in Barak Ravid, "Brazil Recalls Israel Envoy to Protest 'Disproportionate Force' in Gaza," *Haaretz*, July 24, 2014.

45. Gili Cohen, "IDF Puts Together Team to Deflect War-Crime Allegations," *Haaretz*, August 3, 2014.

46. "Israeli Authorities Have Proven They Cannot Investigate Suspected Violations of International Humanitarian Law by Israel in the Gaza Strip," B'Tselem, September 5, 2014, http://www.btselem.org/accountability/20140905_failure_to_investigate; and Sfard, "'Targeted Assassination' of International Law."

47. "Israel Will Not Cooperate with UNHCR Investigative Committee," Israel Ministry of Foreign Affairs, November 13, 2014, http://mfa.gov.il/MFA/PressRoom/2014/Pages/Israel-will-not-cooperate-with-UNHRC-investigative-committee-13-Nov-2014.aspx.

48. UN General Assembly, HRC, *Report of the Independent Commission of Inquiry*, 19.

49. "2014 Gaza Conflict," 28–31.

50. "White House Slams Israel, for 'Indefensible' Shelling of UN School," Reuters, July 30, 2014.

51. Jeff Mason, "Update 2: White House Pressures Israel over Civilian Deaths in Gaza," Reuters, July 21, 2014.

52. See, for example, Michael Gordon and Mark Landler, "Cease-Fire in Gaza Conflict Takes Effect as Talks Are Set," *New York Times*, July 31, 2014.

53. Barak Ravid, "US Halts Missile Transfer Requested by Israel," *Haaretz*, August 14, 2014.

54. "US Resupplies Israel with Munitions as Gaza Offensive Rages," Reuters, July 30, 2014.

55. Gram Slattery, "Americans Still Support Israel, but Views Vary by Age and Race, Poll Finds," *Christian Science Monitor*, July 29, 2014.

56. "European Council Conclusions on External Relations (Ukraine and Gaza)," European Council, Brussels, July 16, 2014, 3.

57. The European members of the UN Human Rights Council comprised Austria, France, Germany, Ireland, Italy, and the United Kingdom. The resolution passed with twenty-nine votes in the forty-six-member council, with support from Arab and Muslim majority countries, China, Russia, and Latin American and African states. See, for example, Ravid, "UN Rights Council to Form Commission."

58. Dan Bilefsky, "Israel's Gaza Incursion Sets off Protests in Europe," *New York Times*, July 21, 2014; "Heurts à Barbès et Sarcelles: Le gouvernement dénonce des 'actes antisémites,'" *Le Monde*, July 21, 2014; Christoph Sydow, "Gaza-Proteste in Berlin: Deutsche Behörden fürchten neue antijüdische Hetze," *Spiegel*, July 22, 2014; "Gaza Israele, svastiche e scritte contro gli ebrei sui muri di diverse vie di Roma," *Huffington Post* (Italian edition), July 28, 2014; and Jon Henley, "Antisemitism on Rise across Europe 'in Worst Times since the Nazis,'" *Guardian*, August 7, 2014.

59. "Stop the Rockets, but Lift the Siege," *Economist*, July 26, 2014.

60. "The Children of Gaza: Jon Snow's Experience in the Middle East," *Channel 4 News*, July 26, 2014.

61. Giora Eiland, "In Gaza, There Is No Such Thing as 'Innocent Civilians,'" *Ynet*, August 8, 2014.

62. Ari Shavit, "Reckless Kerry Risks Causing Escalation," *Haaretz*, July 28, 2014.

63. Moshe Feiglin, "Mikhtav Patuakh le-Rosh ha-Memshalah Netanyahu" [Open letter to PM Netanyahu], posted on Feiglin's Facebook page on August 1, 2014, https://www.facebook.com/MFeiglin/posts/695450140534104. This post has been removed from Facebook.

64. Danon, quoted in Gregg Carlstrom, "The End of Sympathy," *Foreign Policy*, August 5, 2014.

65. Livni and Lapid, quoted in Haviv Rettig Gur, "The War of the Doves," *Times of Israel*, July 30, 2014.

66. Jodi Rudoren, "Some Israelis Count Open Discourse and Dissent among Gaza War Casualties," *New York Times*, August 5, 2014.

67. Ephraim Yaar and Tamar Hermann, The Peace Index, August 2014, Israel Democracy Institute and Evens Program in Mediation and Conflict Resolution, Tel Aviv University, http://peaceindex.org/indexMonthEng.aspx?num=283.

68. Yossi Verter, "Haaretz Survey: Israelis Think Neither Side Won Conflict, but Approve of PM's Decisions," *Haaretz*, August 6, 2014.

69. Ibid. See also Yaar and Hermann, Peace Index, August 2014.

70. Ibid.

71. Speech by David Grossman (video), available at Gilead Moreg, "David Gross-man Be-Kikar Rabin: 'Meabdim et ha-Bayit'" [David Grossman at Rabin Square: "We are losing our home"], *Ynet*, August 17, 2014; author's translation.

72. Or Kashti, "At Right-Wing Protests, Freedom of Expression Is One Thing, Violence Another," *Haaretz*, 24 July 2014; Asher Schechter, "Punch a Lefty, Save the Homeland: Israel Rediscovers Political Violence," *Haaretz*, July 24, 2014; and Rudoren, "Some Israelis Count Open Discourse."

73. "Police Are Obliged to Protect Every Israeli Citizen," *Haaretz* (editorial), July 15, 2014.

74. Nir Hasson, "Two Palestinians Reportedly Assaulted by Jewish Mob in Jerusalem," *Haaretz*, July 26, 2014; and Kashti, "At Right-Wing Protests."

75. Carlstrom, "End of Sympathy."

76. Gidi Weitz, "Simanei ha-Fashism be-Yisrael Hig'iyu le-Si Mafhid be-Tsuk Eitan: Ra'iyon 'im Prof' Zeev Sternhell" [Signs of fascim in Israel reached a fright-ening apex during Protective Edge: Interview with Prof. Zeev Sternhell], *Haaretz*, Weekend Supplement, August 8, 2014.

77. Or Kashti, "Israeli University Rebukes Professor Who Expressed Sympathy for Both Israeli, Gazan Victims," *Haaretz*, July 20, 2014.

78. Barak Ravid, "Prime Minister's Office Recruiting Students to Wage Online Hasbara Battles," *Haaretz*, August 13, 2014.

79. Shachar Hai, "Be-Tachazit ha-Hasbarah: 400 Mitnadvim neged ha-Ta'amulah" [On the hasbarah front: 400 volunteers against propaganda], *Ynet*, July 13, 2014.

80. Sternhell, quoted in Weitz, "Simanei."

81. Levy, quoted in Carlstrom, "End of Sympathy."

82. Ravid, "Netanyahu: Israel Will Destroy Gaza Tunnels."

83. "Operation Protective Edge."

Conclusions

Insecurity and the Power of Neo-Revisionist Hegemony

Israeli politics and society have changed remarkably since the end of the Oslo peace process. A country in which disagreements about the means and ends of its relations with its Middle Eastern neighbors were the norm developed into a polity marked by a strong consensus and a lack of dissent on crucial foreign policy issues. The decade 2000–2010 in particular— that is, the time span between the collapse of the Oslo peace process and the beginning of the Arab uprisings—has been exemplary of this development. Marked by the disintegration of the Israeli Left and a conspicuous shift to the right, Israeli politics have witnessed the emergence of a new consensus on the threats Israel is facing, on the regional order in the Middle East, and on the prospects for peace with the Palestinians. Consisting of three main building blocks, the new consensus is inherently consistent: it combines the threat of terrorism from within Israel and from over the (partly undefined) borders of the state with the conviction that there is no Palestinian partner for peace. Moreover, it depicts Iran's regional ambitions, in conjunction with the Iranian nuclear threat, as a major menace to the very survival of the state. The essence of the new consensus is that Israel is under siege, encircled by an alliance of evil and irrational forces. Consecutive Israeli governments and opposition leaders have subscribed to this understanding of the regional environment. They have reiterated this assessment time and again, thus also disseminating a general sense of insecurity and fear. And as numerous public opinion polls taken during that decade have shown, a vast majority of the Israeli public came to share these notions.

The emergence of the new foreign policy consensus in Israel undoubtedly reflected regional developments and realities in that period. Threats to the security of Israel remained, and still remain, all too real. The second Palestinian intifada, with its numerous terrorist attacks, the barrage of rockets launched on Israeli towns from southern Lebanon and the Gaza Strip, and the increasingly defiant posture of Hamas, Hizballah, and their ally, Iran, provided the material basis of the new consensus. Tehran's nuclear ambitions also became a major focus of concern. Israel's prevailing notions of threats and regional order post-Oslo provide a fairly coherent and quite gloomy perspective on the region. The strong sense of besiegement these notions convey fueled the rise of identity politics whereby "us" and "them" are increasingly defined along ethnoreligious divides. Israelis also increasingly came to view the conflict with their neighbors in ethnic and religious terms rather than as a struggle over land and borders. The new hegemonic conceptions of threats and regional order in Israel also called for specific policies and lines of actions vis-à-vis the region. Most notably, these include deterrence, the use of force, and unilateral action. The consensus also prescribed the deferral of any negotiated solution of the conflict with the Palestinians that would entail a meaningful territorial compromise. The new foreign policy consensus espoused the beliefs of neo-revisionist Zionism, which emerged as the new hegemony in Israel.

Notions of threats and regional order, however, are social constructs built on material facts. Hence, different readings of reality typically compete in any fairly open and democratic polity, together with various lines of possible action. The discussion has shown that the convictions about the regional environment prevailing in Israel can be challenged on several accounts. For instance, it is debatable whether Yasser Arafat, who was certainly ambiguous and often deceitful in his dealings with the Israelis, really orchestrated the second Palestinian intifada. It is also far from certain whether the late Palestinian *ra'is*, and even more so his successor, Mahmoud Abbas, were really not interested in peace or whether they instead disagreed with Israel's terms for ending the conflict. Similarly, a convergence of interests between Israel and some regional actors can be observed in that same time span, with the launching of a major peace initiative in 2002 backed by the Arab League. The Arab peace plan plainly contradicts the notion of an inherently hostile environment. Moreover, Israel's prevailing sense of besiegement remains remarkably at odds with the country's military superiority and regional power status. In a similar vein, there could surely be different options as to how to counter the terrorism of Hizballah and Hamas and how to deal with the two organizations. As the nuclear deal reached between the major powers and Iran in 2015 shows, different strategies to respond to Iran's quest for regional hegemony and its ambitions to develop a nuclear program do exist. While some of these options may be more desirable or feasible than others, one would have expected serious domestic debates in Israel on all these issues. However, the emergence of a strong consensus on threats and regional order meant that significant developments at the regional level were ignored while meaningful debates on these crucial issues were largely absent in Israel during the first post-Oslo decade.

What have been the main implications of Israel's new foreign policy consensus? One major consequence was that the consensus legitimized specific policies, rendering other lines of action irrational and illegitimate. Being depicted as acting in legitimate self-defense while the other side— Hamas, Hizballah, Iran, and the Palestinians—were presented as callously motivated by a deep hatred of Israel and the Jewish people, Israel came to be perceived as having only one choice: deterrence and forceful policies. As the country's conflict with the Palestinians was reinterpreted along ethnoreligious lines, negotiations and territorial compromise seemed out of the question. The rockets from Hizballah in the north and from Hamas in the south, which intensified in both cases after Israeli territorial withdrawals, further undermined the idea of a meaningful territorial compromise with the Palestinians, thus also legitimizing the continuation of Israel's settlement project. In other words, with some exceptions, such as the negotiations between the Israeli government under Ehud Olmert and the Palestinian Authority in 2007–8, revisionism's Iron Wall doctrine came to dominate Israeli politics and society in the first post-Oslo decade. Infused with messianic beliefs about Jewish entitlement to settle and control the Palestinian territories, neo-revisionist thought became hegemonic. While embracing territorial maximalism and an ethnoreligious interpretation of politics, neo-revisionism acted as the ideological matrix for the new foreign policy consensus. The dominant perception was now that Israel had to fight, by forceful means, for its very survival in a menacing environment, with the other side only understanding force. Alternatives were no longer considered.

Presenting policies as the only possible option in the face of major constraints is of course a sure recipe to stifle political debates. In other countries, political leaders adopt this method as well; Israel is not unique here. Moreover, terrorism and political violence provide an exceptionally strong legitimacy to the claims of leaders that there is no alternative to the (usually forceful) policies they propose. Again, this phenomenon can be observed in other cases as well. However, Israel's new hegemony after 2000 has been particularly powerful and persistent, and it has far-reaching implications.

In view of the astounding lack of domestic dissent on crucial foreign policy, a significant question here is whether the policies prescribed by Israel's hegemonic vision of threats and regional order achieved their objectives. As has been pointed out, the answer to this question is not clear-cut. In the short term, Israeli policies recorded some results. Most notably, the number of terrorist attacks dropped considerably from the mid-2000s onward. However, it remains questionable whether this resulted solely, or mainly, from Israel's counterterrorism policies and the construction of the West Bank barrier. As many members of the Israeli security establishment maintained, often off the record, the Palestinian Authority's renewed cooperation with Israel on security played a major role in reducing the number of terrorist attacks. Arguably, Israel also (re)established a certain degree of deterrence vis-à-vis Hamas and Hizballah through its devastating wars on both movements. The government in Jerusalem also succeeded in drawing much international attention to Tehran's nuclear program, with the international sanctions regime subsequently prompting Iran to enter into negotiations with the international community. However, Israel's regional policy choices also entailed a complete disregard of any converging interests across the region, let alone the chances of resolving the Israeli–Palestinian and wider Arab–Israeli conflict. In fact, Israeli actions to a large extent contributed to an escalation of violence and the growing popularity of Hamas and Hizballah in their respective constituencies—and beyond. Similarly, Israel's fierce rhetoric vis-à-vis Tehran may also have been a factor in the rising popularity of President Mahmoud Ahmadinejad in Iran at that time. Concurrently, Israel's forceful and unilateral policies as well as the continuation of the settlement project in the territories undermined the pragmatists, most notably Palestinian president Mahmoud Abbas. Thus, to a certain extent, Israeli policies, *nolens volens*, have contributed to the consolidation of the very regional order that its new consensus conceived of. And so, a vicious cycle is established, with Israel's new foreign policy consensus reinforcing itself.

The strong consensus on crucial foreign policy issues in the first post-Oslo decade had a number of additional significant implications. By legitimizing specific policies, Israel's prevailing notions of threats and regional order negatively affected the country's international relations and standing, placing Israel on a collision course with the international community. Israeli actions and their justifications, which were supported by a large majority of Israeli citizens, became increasingly incomprehensible to foreign governments and public opinions alike. This concerns in particular European states, but growing tensions were also visible regarding the United States, where support for Israel has remained relatively strong. Israeli policies prompted an ever-growing international criticism, which contributed to an increasing isolation of Israel on the global stage. In part, this development seems to have been unavoidable. Indeed, in confronting violent nonstate actors, states almost inevitably step into what has been termed the "legitimacy trap"; in this type of conflict, the number of civilian casualties is usually much higher on the side of the nonstate actor. International criticism of the state actor (in this case, Israel) for violating international humanitarian law, together with the principle of proportionality, should thus not be surprising. In fact, in the fight against terrorism, a country inevitably has to choose between options ranging from bad to extremely bad, most of which entail substantial human rights violations. Israel is no exception here. However, the refusal to enter into negotiations with the Palestinians during much of the first post-Oslo decade, the ignoring of the Arab peace initiative, and the constant expansion of settlements in the Palestinian territories only added to the growing international disapproval of Israeli policies. As Israel portrayed the international condemnation of its policies as an attack on the country's legitimacy and right to exist, often in conjunction with a perceived anti-Israeli or even anti-Semitic bias, the international criticism prompted Israeli society to further close in and to close ranks, thus further reinforcing Israel's sense of besiegement. And of course, anti-Semitic incidents, such as in Europe, only reinforced these perceptions.

Israel's hegemonic notions of threats and regional order also deeply affected the country's domestic politics. This is particularly so as these notions go hand in hand with a growing emphasis on the concept of "the Jewish state" and an interpretation of "us" and "them" along ethnoreligious lines. Because large parts of Israel's Palestinian citizens did not share the new consensus, the new hegemony resulted in a growing divide between the Jewish majority and the Arab minorities. Consecutive right-wing governments adopted a populist and illiberal discourse depicting Israel's Palestinian citizens as the enemy within, and engaged in policies of exclusion vis-à-vis the Arab minorities. These discourses and policies only strengthened the divide further. The rise of ethnoreligious conceptions of collective identity also manifested itself in a discriminatory discourse toward Israel's African immigrants and asylum seekers, and in questionable policies toward this community under standards of international law—a phenomenon that has become sadly prominent in many Western countries as well. Beyond majority–minority relations, the emergence and consolidation of the new consensus in the first post-Oslo decade also saw a strong tendency of silencing critics *tout court*. Thus, left-wing and liberal Jewish Israeli critics and organizations, let alone their Palestinian Israeli counterparts, increasingly came under attack. They became the target of sometimes vicious campaigns, including verbal and physical violence. The events in Israel during the Gaza war in the summer of 2014 serve as a particularly strong example here. The domestic repercussions of Israel's new consensus thus are a further indication of how hegemony tends to sustain itself by silencing its critics and by delegitimizing any challenge to the notions it promotes.

Hence, it is evident that the implications of Israel's new foreign policy consensus post-Oslo, together with its anchorage in neo-revisionist thought, are far-reaching and significant. A crucial question, then, is how the new hegemonic notions of threats and regional order emerged and consolidated in the first place. If, in particular, Israel's political culture of contestation and dissent is taken into consideration, this question also becomes relevant in theoretical terms. As this book has shown, the rise of specific notions of threats and regional order is a complex process that cannot be reduced to monocausal explanations. Processes by which specific concepts and ideas emerge and become hegemonic involve both material structure and preexisting collective ideas as well as specific actors.

In terms of preexisting beliefs, the particular construction of Israeli identity is significant. Because it is based on a combination of the history of Jewish persecution, the Holocaust, and the experience of conflict and war before and after Israeli statehood, Jewish Israeli collective identity has acted as a predisposition of sorts. Put differently, the post-Oslo consensus, with its notion of struggling for survival in a particularly aggressive environment, the imperative of self-defense, and the ethnoreligious definition of "us" and "them," reproduces the basic tenets of how Jewish Israelis traditionally conceive of themselves and their relationship with the world. This explains to a large extent why the post-Oslo consensus became so powerful.

The study has also shown that the doctrines and practices of Israel's foreign policy nurtured the emergence of the new hegemony post-Oslo. These strategies and practices not only reflect and institutionalize Israel's historical narratives and identity but also established the dominance of the security establishment over the foreign ministry. Security considerations and military means have thus usually trumped political considerations and diplomacy in Israel's relations with its neighbors. The new hegemony clearly reflects these deeply ingrained priorities: Israel's regional foreign policy in the time span under consideration strongly relied on military means, and far less on diplomacy. Furthermore, the predominance of the notion of persecution and the unique experience of the Holocaust in Israel's collective psyche is relevant regarding any criticism of Israeli policies coming from the outside world. Such criticism tends to be viewed as deriving from the inability of others to understand the unique experience of the Jewish people, possibly combined with assumptions about persistent anti-Semitism.

Israel's intellectual and political history is similarly relevant when considering the question of why a specific understanding of threats and regional order became prevalent in the country after the collapse of the Oslo process. This regards in particular the constant rise of neo-revisionist Zionism and its alliance with religious Zionism after 1967. This alliance became even more pronounced after the Likud came to power in the 1977 elections. In this context it is crucial to recognize that the rise of neo-revisionism has been constant since the 1970s, interrupted only by the short interlude of two Labor-dominated governments during the Oslo peace process in the 1990s. In other words, if we take into account the development of Israeli politics and society over recent decades, it becomes clear that the years of the Oslo process were not the normalcy in Israel; they were an exception within a much broader trend.

The ever-growing relevance of neo-revisionist thought in Israel since the 1970s is a key factor in explaining the emergence of the new consensus on threats and regional order in post-Oslo Israel. With its bleak regional outlook and its embrace of a deep sense of besiegement, neo-revisionism provides the ideological foundation of Israel's new foreign policy consensus. The rise of neo-revisionist Zionism not only gave an ever-growing prominence to territorial maximalism and Jabotinsky's Iron Wall doctrine but also resulted in the strengthening of ethnoreligious nationalism, messianic beliefs, and illiberal values and worldviews. It explains the strengthening of the grip of the settler movement on Israeli politics and society over the decades, a grip that is disproportionate compared to the size of the settler population. Equally important, neo-revisionism forged a new symbiosis between the national-religious credo and security considerations, thus providing an even stronger justification for the continuation of Israel's settlement project.

If the specific makeup of Jewish Israeli identity, the doctrines and practices of Israel's foreign policy, and the constant rise of neo-revisionism since the 1970s provide the ideological and structural environment nurturing the emergence of the new consensus post-Oslo, a number of additional factors must be considered. For one, in recent decades Israel has witnessed significant demographic shifts that have further contributed to its constant move to the right. This concerns both the large-scale immigration from the former Soviet Union after the end of the Cold War and the constant growth of Israel's religious populations due to higher birthrates, whether ultra-Orthodox, Orthodox, or national-religious. While this is a strong generalization, it is safe to say that these constituencies in Israeli society, in their entirety, are generally not famous for championing liberal values or territorial compromise with the Palestinians. While Israelis in general have become more religious in recent decades, the shift toward more hawkish positions with regard to the Palestinian question in the rapidly growing ultra-Orthodox communities is worth noting here.

Against this backdrop, the collapse of Oslo's negotiation framework in the early 2000s, the renewed violence following the outbreak of the Second Intifada, and the continuous terrorism were crucial. Instilling sentiments of fear, anger, and disappointment in Israeli society, these events are critical for explaining the emergence and consolidation of Israel's new foreign policy consensus after 2000. They were conducive to the rise of beliefs about the inherently evil intentions of the Palestinians and of "the Arabs" or "the Muslims" in general. Undoubtedly, terrorism and political violence have a far-reaching impact on societies, boosting forceful and uncompromising policies advocated by the political Right while undermining tolerance and liberal conceptions of politics. Post-Oslo Israel is a textbook case for this state of affairs. Sociopolitical and psychological dynamics linked to terror and fear thus provide an additional explanation for the success of right-wing parties in consecutive Israeli elections throughout the 2000s, thereby establishing the hegemony of neo-revisionist thought.

Finally, agency matters. As this study has shown, specific actors and epistemic authorities played a crucial role in constructing the new foreign policy consensus by promoting its main elements time and again. Former prime minister Ehud Barak certainly deserves the credit for coining the "no Palestinian partner for peace" slogan. Presenting himself as the political heir of Yitzhak Rabin and enjoying a high credibility due to his outstanding military record, Barak had a tremendous influence on the Israeli Left and center-left, which came to accept his simplistic explanation for the failure of the Camp David Summit in 2000. In conjunction with the terror of the second Palestinian intifada, Barak thus played a key role in the collapse of the Israeli Zionist Left and the gradual adoption of a new consensus on threats and regional order. Along with other influential politicians such as Ariel Sharon, the security establishment in particular also played an important role. It is significant here that the security establishment traditionally enjoys a high standing and credibility among the Israeli public. Last but not least, in times of crisis, the contribution of a self-mobilized and increasingly uncritical Israeli media in disseminating the new consensus was crucial. The impact, in particular, of the freely distributed and thus widely read newspaper *Israel Ha-Yom*, in uncritically promoting the government line, must also be considered here.

Of course, the consensus in post-Oslo Israel is neither monolithic nor absolute. Critics and opponents of Israel's neo-revisionist hegemony have continued to exist. The nonbinding Geneva Initiative of 2003, initiated by former minister and politician Yossi Beilin and former PA minister Yasser Abed Rabbo, is a case in point. While enjoying some public support, the initiative was never endorsed by any of Israel's right-wing governments, which continued to win the elections in that decade. Other peace plans proposed by public figures and intellectuals in that decade suffered a similar fate. On a few occasions, however, Israeli governments and political leaders engaged in policies that departed, or seemed to depart, from the prevailing consensus. This includes, most notably, the peace negotiations between the government of Ehud Olmert and the Palestinian Authority in 2007–8, which collapsed with Olmert's indictment on corruption charges, Abbas's hesitations, and the decision of the Israeli government to launch "Operation Cast Lead" in Gaza in December 2008. At best, poor leadership on both sides and bad timing may explain the failure of the most significant challenge to the neo-revisionist consensus since the collapse of the Oslo process. Ariel Sharon's disengagement in 2005 from the Gaza Strip also seemed to somewhat defy the consensus by setting a precedent of territorial withdrawal in the context of Israel's conflict with the Palestinians. Yet Sharon's withdrawal from Gaza was not a radical departure from the consensus. While it promised to enhance Israel's security by escaping the growing security quagmire in Gaza, the unilateral disengagement plan was actually meant to prevent a return to the Oslo framework and, thus, to the idea of a negotiated two-state solution. The secret peace talks with Syria during the Olmert government, and again in 2010 during Netanyahu's tenure, may also somewhat qualify as a departure from the consensus. However, attempts to reach a peace deal with Syria—preferably without having to withdraw from the Golan Heights to the June 4, 1967, lines—have a history in Israeli foreign policy after the end of the Cold War. And the option of peace with Syria is disconnected from the Palestinian issue. Similarly, Barak's refusal to consider Iran as an "existential" threat may be seen as an interesting variation within the consensus. He still considered Iran as a threat, though, and he was still in favor of bombing the country's nuclear facilities. Thus, in spite of some challenges and variations, Israel's foreign policy consensus remained extremely resilient in the first post-Oslo decade.

With the beginning of the 2010s, some dissent returned to Israeli politics. Notably, however, the contestation primarily concerned socioeconomic issues against the background of an ever-growing gap between rich and poor in Israeli society. The social protest movement, which emerged in the summer of 2011 over the price of cottage cheese (of all things), refrained from linking the socioeconomic malaise of ordinary Israelis to the massive pouring of state funds into the settlements enterprise in the territories. And neither did politicians, new and old, who sought to capitalize on the protest movement articulate this linkage. The complete disregard in Israel's public discourse for the economic and political costs of maintaining and expanding Israeli settlements in the territories demonstrated yet again how powerful the new consensus had become. Some contestation also emerged with regard to Netanyahu's preferred option of bombing Iran's nuclear facilities, with retired key figures of Israel's security establishment taking the lead in publicly criticizing the prime minister and his defense minister. In fact, the fierce opposition from Israel's security services, which was not voiced in public, is probably the main reason the government did not proceed with its plan to attack Iran in that period. However, as demonstrated by the electoral results in 2013 and in 2015, the prevalence of right-wing politics in Israel persisted. And as evidenced by the exceptionally strong domestic consensus around the Gaza war of 2014, together with the repeated attempts to silence any critics of the war, the main notions of threats and regional order in Israel have largely remained unchallenged. Neo-revisionist hegemony prevailed.

What are the broader implications of the findings of this book? First, in conceptual terms, the concrete case of Israel post-Oslo highlights the key ingredients and underlying mechanisms of hegemony and its political consequences. The emergence and consolidation of the current foreign policy consensus in Israel is a striking example of how hegemonic notions of threats and regional order are to a large extent the product of social construction. This does not mean, of course, that these notions are entirely imaginary, that Israel is not facing a number of substantial security threats, or that bombs and rockets do not kill people. It does mean, however, that specific notions of threats and regional order are but one interpretation of reality, with alternative policies aimed at enhancing the security of the state and resolving conflicts also being possible. This perspective also opens the door for a consideration of the argument that notions of threats and regional order may be manipulated for political ends.

Processes by which hegemonic notions emerge and consolidate are extremely complex. A focus on a single factor alone will thus hardly provide a sufficient explanation. Rather, the interplay of various endogenous and exogenous factors must be considered, including the factual basis of threats and foreign policy preferences, historical developments, preexisting beliefs and ingrained political practices, the role of powerful actors, and political and socioeconomic contexts and developments. This study confirms that collective interpretations of material reality, which gradually become common sense and are no longer questioned, are the key mechanism underpinning the emergence and consolidation of hegemony. In these processes, structure and agency influence each other: in promoting their ideas and beliefs, influential actors respond to a preexisting normative environment—that is, the taken-for-granted understandings of social reality. But, in turn, influential actors also affect this environment by promoting specific notions and beliefs. A powerful example here is the role played by the Israeli media in situations of war and conflict. Respecting the parameters of what is "common sense" and socially accepted, it uncritically—and voluntarily—reproduced the explanations provided by the government and the security establishment. The media thus also contributed to the definition of what counts as a logical and legitimate explanation of events.

This study also suggests that several feedback processes are responsible for the consolidation of hegemonic notions. It confirms the assumptions that preexisting shared understandings act as a filter through which events and developments are interpreted at the collective level. In our case, the convictions that the environment is inherently hostile and that there is no interest in peaceful relations on the other side led to a complete disregard of any signals or events that could contradict these beliefs. The case of the advertisements in support of the Arab peace plan, placed by the Palestinian Authority in Israeli newspapers and largely ignored or overlooked by the Israeli public, is particularly revealing here. Similarly, Israeli politics post-Oslo are a clear example of how hegemonic beliefs tend to dismiss and delegitimize alternative interpretations of events, whether within or without the collective. The extremely harsh responses of the public and of single institutions to the few Israeli critics of the 2014 Gaza war, often branding those critics as traitors, are particularly illuminating here. The consensus thus sustains itself. An additional example of the various feedback processes underpinning the emergence of hegemony concerns the relationship between ideas on the one hand and material reality on the other. The case of Israel post-Oslo clearly shows that taken-for-granted collective understandings do not remain confined to the ideational level; they become institutionalized and thus part of material structure as well as of everyday political practices. The institutionalization of the specific nature of Israel's collective identity in the doctrines and conduct of the country's foreign policies is a case in point; the persistently central role of the security establishment in defining Israel's foreign policy is another example. Another telling illustration is the ever-growing political influence of the settler movement on Israel's state institutions, including the government, the army, and the Knesset. Supported by neo-revisionist hegemony, this development represents a significant structural change in Israeli politics.

Second, an investigation into the new consensus on threats and regional order in post-Oslo Israel draws the attention to the strong nexus between domestic politics and foreign policies. As this study has shown, the new hegemony at the domestic level lends legitimacy to unilateral and forceful foreign policies, and these in turn reinforce prevailing beliefs about threats and regional order. Concurrently, the stronger Israel's sense of besiegement, the more likely it is for these policies to be considered as legitimate, often out of a perceived lack of alternatives. These policies thus enjoy a broad public support, regardless of any potentially negative long-term implications. Fear is, of course, extremely powerful in legitimizing rule and in justifying exceptional policies. The book confirms that since the collapse of Oslo, Israel's right-wing governments have not only capitalized on fears and the general feeling of insecurity but have also profited considerably from this political climate. It ensured their reelections. Depicting the main threats as emanating from both the regional environment and the domestic scene, Israeli governments have stressed that the legitimacy and very survival of "the Jewish state" and of the Jewish collective at large are at stake, threatened by the Arabs or Muslims within or without the borders of the Israeli state. As a result, the new hegemony has not only sustained the promotion of security-dominated policies. It has also legitimized ethnoreligious and illiberal policies, thus creating an ever-deepening fault line between Jewish Israelis and "the other"—Arabs, Muslims, liberals, human rights activists, or anyone else who dares challenging the neo-revisionist hegemony. While an ambiguous overlap of domestic and foreign policies already characterizes Israel's relations with the Palestinians, the linkage between external relations and domestic issues in Israel has thus deepened even further. The boundaries between the two domains have become increasingly blurred. Altogether, domestic developments are highly relevant in explaining Israeli policies toward its neighbors. As this study has shown, these policies are not merely a response to the strengthening of Hamas and Hizballah, the alleged weakness of the PA, or other external factors. These policies, together with the meager prospects of peace with the Palestinians, also flow from Israel's new foreign policy consensus and the hegemony of neo-revisionist thought at the domestic level.

Third, in order to understand the wider political implications of the new foreign policy consensus in Israel after 2000, Antonio Gramsci's notion of hegemony is extremely useful. Indeed, with its focus on power relations, the concept of hegemony stresses the importance of a consensus culture—understood here as the ideas and discourses that define the everyday life of ordinary people—in maintaining the status quo. According to Gramsci, who was concerned with the empowerment of the working class from a Marxist perspective, hegemony describes a situation in which the worldview of the ruling elites becomes imposed and accepted as the norm. Therefore, the power of hegemony, "the common sense," lies in its indistinctiveness and invisibility. Hegemony thus justifies and legitimizes the political, social, and economic status quo as natural and inevitable while presenting it as beneficial for the whole collective.

Even without subscribing to a Marxist analysis, the concept of hegemony sheds light on power relations and the maintenance of the political and socioeconomic status quo in post-Oslo Israel. We have seen that, against the backdrop of a profound sense of besiegement by evil forces, a large majority of Jewish Israelis conceive of uncompromising and forceful policies toward the Palestinians and the wider region as necessary, justified, and legitimate. The inevitably ugly aspects of ruling over another people or the fact that many ideological settlers behave in the West Bank as if it was the nineteenth-century American Wild West do not figure in Israel's public discourse or in the collective consciousness. At the same time, the constant sense of danger is, of course, very powerful in uniting a population that is divided on many other issues. While lending legitimacy to a "strong" leadership with its promise of "security," it also distracts the attention from a number of other pressing political issues. The new consensus and the politics of insecurity thus justify the prevailing political and socioeconomic order in Israel, even though this order not only denies rights to the Palestinians in the territories but is also far from being beneficial to Israeli society as a whole. It is a consensus from which the settlement project draws perhaps the largest socioeconomic and political benefits. The defense industry, the army, and, of course, the political class that has been ruling the country for the last fifteen years at least benefit from the prevailing political and socioeconomic order as well. Conversely, the status quo prevails to the detriment of the Palestinian population in the territories, of course, but also at the expense of the poorest segments of Israel's population, such as ultra-Orthodox Jews, the Palestinian citizens of Israel, and the lower social classes living in the development towns as well as all across Israel. It also prevails at the expense of a constantly shrinking middle class, which is increasingly struggling to make ends meet. Considering the profound socioeconomic inequalities in Israel and the high rate of relative poverty, the prevailing neo-revisionist hegemony combined with long-standing inter-Jewish divides and grievances also explains why even those members of the collective who lose out from the predominant socioeconomic and political order still continue to sustain that same order. As evidenced in the electoral results over recent decades, constituencies suffering most from the prevailing socioeconomic order would still vote for right-wing and religious parties—that is, exactly those parties that either subscribe to the status quo or want to change it to the disadvantage of the weaker socioeconomic strata in Israeli society.

The final concluding remarks concern the question of whether the process described in this study is reversible, and if so, under which conditions. As we have seen, Israel's new hegemony has a strong tendency toward sustaining and reproducing itself, with critics being discredited. But it is also evident that counterhegemonic cultures, as Gramsci would call them, that would challenge the dominant power are present in Israeli society and politics. However, these critics constitute an increasingly embattled minority. As the absence of meaningful contestation and dissent on crucial issues—contestation that is perceived to be legitimate—seriously undermines the democratic quality of Israel's political system, the new consensus is remarkably resilient. Equally important, the new hegemony has witnessed the constant rise of right-wing politics, on the one hand, and a growing political influence of the settler movement, on the other. Resulting from ideological developments, these structural changes affect Israeli politics and society at large, acting against a possible disintegration of the consensus. However, on several occasions, as we have seen, Israeli politicians and influential public figures have articulated ideas and policies that challenged or at least seemed to depart from the prevailing consensus. The question then arises as to why these ideas did not succeed in shaking the foundations of neo-revisionist hegemony. Hegemonic beliefs, after all, may weaken and dissipate. The growing contestation of the hegemonic beliefs that marked the United States after 9/11 is a particularly good example here. The current disintegration of Kemalism in Turkey, which was hegemonic for decades, is another case in point. Under which circumstances, then, might Israel witness the weakening of neo-revisionist hegemony and the foreign policy consensus it sustains? Which conditions might facilitate a return to the politics of contestation that were so characteristic of Israeli politics in previous decades? Which factors might lead to the emergence of viable and legitimate foreign policy alternatives in Israeli politics?

For obvious reasons, there are no definite answers to these questions; only speculations are possible here. One possibility is that large numbers of Israeli citizens come to realize that Israel's current foreign policy course has significant political and economic costs, both at the international and the domestic level. Second, the emergence of a trusted and credible leadership that would be able to propose viable alternatives seems crucial. Third, it is conceivable that neo-revisionist hegemony loses its hold if Israel's security situation improved. Indeed, if Israel was not continuously threatened by bombs, rockets, and hate speech, a different vision of the region could perhaps emerge, according to this argument. Fourth, a weakening of the consensus could occur if the current course of action caused considerable and unsustainable economic and political costs.

At present, most of these conditions are absent. While fears and a profound sense of siege prevail, the majority of the Israeli public continues to believe that Israel has no choice. The politics of insecurity adopted by Israeli's right-wing governments continue to nurture these fears. There is no credible and courageous political leadership at present that could promote different notions of threats and regional order or highlight the costs of Israel's regional policies, including the continuous rule over the Palestinian territories. Indeed, the leaders of most mainstream opposition parties, Labor included, have by and large bought into the neo-revisionist consensus. Most opposition leaders in the last fifteen years have not truly challenged the consensus, and they have not proposed any real alternatives. And considering current political developments in the Middle East, it is unlikely that Israel will feel more secure—no matter that its policies may partly have contributed to an undermining of pragmatist Arab leaders as well as to the ever-diminishing chances of resolving the conflict with the Palestinians. But even if Israel felt more secure, the territorial maximalism enshrined in Israel's neo-revisionist hegemony may not automatically dissipate. In light of both the power of ideology and the structural changes that have marked Israeli politics and society in recent decades, any politician—left or right—would face an up-hill battle in gaining domestic support for any meaningful territorial (and ideological) compromise that a sustainable peace agreement with the Palestinians would require. In fact, it is possible that an improved security situation would reinforce neo-revisionist worldviews and policies. And regarding the political and economic costs of Israeli policies, these have not been as significant as to prompt a change of course: in spite of some disputes, Israel can still rely on powerful allies on the international stage, most notably the US and single European states. It remains a major regional power in a threatening environment; it is a "start-up nation" and a world leader in cutting-edge scientific research; and its macroeconomic indicators are sound.

For this reason, we may assume that without the occurrence of an internal or external shock to the system, Israel's new hegemony will be very difficult to reverse. This is even more so as post-Arab uprisings, violence, and ethnoreligious politics have been on the rise all over the Middle East. Particularly in the context of the disturbing political landscape in the region at present, developments in Israel and in its neighborhood region are likely to mutually influence and reinforce each other. The prospects of resolving the Israeli–Palestinian conflict within internationally accepted parameters will thus remain dim if left to the conflicting parties. Finally, Israel's neo-revisionist hegemony and the policies it prescribes are not only internally coherent and powerful but also largely immune to international criticism. As pointed out, international disapproval of Israeli policies only strengthens the country's sense of besiegement, thus lending further legitimacy to neo-revisionist hegemony. The recent rise of anti-Semitic incidents in the heart of Europe further feeds into this development. As a result, the gap between Israel and the unconditional supporters of its right-wing policies, on the one hand, and their critics, on the other, is likely to remain unchanged or to widen even further. Israel's international isolation, then, is not likely to recede.

APPENDIX A: KEY POLITICAL FIGURES

Abbas, Mahmoud (Abu Mazen)
President of the Palestinian Authority (PA) (2005–present); chairman of the Palestine Liberation Organization (PLO) (2004–present); head of the Fatah party (2004–present); prime minister of the PA (2003); awarded the Nobel Peace Prize for the signing of the Oslo Accords (1994); head of the Palestinian negotiating team at the Oslo talks; head of the PLO negotiations department (1994–2003); head of the PLO's national and international relations department (1984–2000); member of the PLO executive committee (1980–present); member of the Palestinian National Council (1968–present); founding member of Fatah; member of the Fatah Central Committee (1964–present).

Abdallah II, ibn al Hussein
King of the Hashemite Kingdom of Jordan (1999–present); commander of Jordan's Special Forces (1993–99); joined the Royal Jordanian Army in 1983 and became major-general in 1998.

Agha, Hussein
Representative of Mahmoud Abbas and deputy in the Oslo negotiations (1993–95).

Ahmadinejad, Mahmoud
President of the Islamic Republic of Iran (2005–13); mayor of Tehran (2003–5); governor general of Ardebil (1993–97); adviser to the ministry of culture and higher education (1993).

al-Assad, Bashar
President of Syria (2000–present); commander-in-chief of the Syrian Armed Forces (2000–present); secretary-general of the Syrian Baath party (2000–present); entered the military academy in Homs (1994)

and became a colonel (1999); postgraduate training in ophthalmology at Western Eye Hospital in London (1992–94); doctor at the military hospital Tishreen outside of Damascus (1988–92); graduated in medicine (1988).

al-Karmi, Ra'ed
Commander of the al-Aqsa Martyrs Brigade; assassinated in January 2002 (allegedly by Israel; officially the Israeli government did not claim responsibility).

al-Rantisi, Abdel Aziz
Cofounder of Hamas (the Islamic Resistance Movement); leader and spokesman of Hamas in the Gaza Strip (March–April 2004); killed by the Israeli air force in April 2004.

al-Sisi, Abdel Fattah
President of Egypt (2014–present); minister of defense (2012–14); head of the Egyptian Armed Forces (2012–14); director of military intelligence (2011–12); member of the Supreme Command of the Armed Forces (2011–present); obtained a master's degree at the US Army War College (2006). His military career includes the post of military attaché to Saudi Arabia, commander of the Northern Military Region–Alexandria, and commander of various infantry brigades; training at Joint Services Command and Staff College in the United Kingdom (1992); graduated from Egypt's Military Academy in 1977.

Arafat, Yasser
President of the Palestinian Authority (1996–2004); chairman of the PLO executive committee (1969–2004); head of the negotiations at Camp David (2000); awarded the Nobel Peace Prize for the signing of the Oslo Accords (1994); declared Palestinian independence at the Palestinian National Council meeting in Algiers (1988); spokesperson of Fatah (1968–2004); head of the Fatah party (1958–2004); cofounder of the Fatah movement in Kuwait (around 1958).

Ashkenazi, Gabi
Chief of staff of the Israel Defense Forces (IDF) (2007–11); director-general of the Israeli Ministry of Defense (2005–7); deputy chief of staff of the IDF (2002–5); head of northern command in the IDF (1998–2002).

Ayalon, Ami
Senior Fellow at the Israel Democracy Institute (2012–present); member of Knesset of the Labor Party (2006–9); director of the Shabak (or Shin Bet, Israel's internal security agency) (1996–2000); founder of the People's Voice peace initiative (2002); naval commander-in-chief (1992–96).

Barak, Ehud
Minister of defense of the State of Israel (2007–13); member of Knesset of the Labor/One Israel and later Ha-Atsma'ut (Independence) party (1996–2001; 2009–13); chairman of the Labor Party (1997–2001; 2007–11); prime minister (1999–2001); minister of foreign affairs (1995–96); chief of staff of the IDF (1991–95); deputy chief of staff of the IDF (1987–91); head of the IDF central command (1986–87); head of the IDF military intelligence directorate (Aman) (1983–85); holder of various commanding positions in IDF elite units; joined the IDF in 1959.

Barghouti, Marwan
Prominent Palestinian political figure (Fatah); is currently serving five consecutive life sentences in an Israeli prison for complicity in five murders carried out by the al-Aqsa Martyrs' Brigades (2002–present); elected to Fatah's central committee (2011); elected to the Palestinian National Council (2006) while imprisoned; drafted the Prisoners' Document, in which jailed leaders of all major Palestinian factions called for a Palestinian state to be established within the pre-1967 borders and the right of return for all Palestinian refugees (2006); master's degree in international relations from Birzeit University (1998); elected to the Palestinian Legislative Council (PLC) (1996); leader of the Fatah party in the West Bank (1994); joined Fatah and cofounded the Shabibah (Fatah Youth) in the West Bank in the mid-1970s.

Begin, Menachem
Prime minister of the State of Israel (1977–83); minister of agriculture (1983); minister of defense (1980–81; 1983); minister of foreign affairs (1979–80); recipient of the Nobel Peace Prize for the peace treaty with Egypt (1978); minister of justice, minister of labor and social welfare, minister of transportation, minister of communications (1977); cofounder of the Likud party (1973); minister without portfolio (1967–70); founder of the Herut party, the forerunner of today's Likud (1948); commander of the militia Irgun Tzvai Leumi (also known as "Etzel" or "Irgun") during the British

Mandate in Palestine (1943–48); head of the Polish branch of the Betar
Revisionist Zionist youth movement (1937–42).

Beilin, Yossi (Yosef)
Member of Knesset of the Meretz party (2006–8); chairman of the Meretz
party (2004–8); left the Labor Party and joined Meretz (2003); initiator
of the Geneva Initiative with Yasser Abed Rabbo (2003); member of the
Israeli negotiating team at the Taba Summit (2001); minister of religious
affairs (2000–2001); minister of justice (1999–2001); minister without
portfolio in the prime minister's office (1995–96); minister of economy
and planning (1995); deputy minister of foreign affairs (1992–95), one
of the main architects of the Oslo process; deputy minister of finance
(1988–90); member of Knesset (Labor) (1988 2003); director general
for political affairs of the Ministry of Foreign Affairs (1986–88); cabinet
secretary in the government of Shimon Peres (1984–86); spokesperson
of the Labor Party (1977–84).

Ben-Ami, Shlomo
Minister of foreign affairs of the State of Israel (2000–2001); member of
Knesset of the Labor/One Israel party (1996–2002); member of the Israeli
delegation at the Camp David Summit (2000) and the Taba negotiations
(2001); minister of public security (1999–2001); member of Israel's del-
egation to the Madrid peace conference (1992); Israel's ambassador to
Spain (1987–91); professor of Spanish and Latin American Studies at Tel
Aviv University (1986–91); head of the Graduate School of History at Tel
Aviv University (1982–86).

Ben-Gurion, David
First prime minister of the State of Israel and leader of Mapai (later to
become the Labor Party) (1948–54; 1955–63); defense minister (1948–
53; 1955–63); member of Knesset of Mapai and Rafi party (1949–70);
chairman of the Jewish Agency (1935–48); first secretary-general of the
Histadrut (Labor Union) (1921–35).

Bennett, Naftali
Minister of education and minister of diaspora affairs of the State of Israel (2015–present); minister of the economy, minister of Jerusalem and
diaspora affairs, and minister of religious services (2013–15); chairman
of Ha-Bayit Ha-Yehudi (Jewish Home) party (2012–present); member of
Knesset of Ha-Bayit Ha-Yehudi (2013–15).

Burg, Avraham

Speaker of the Knesset (1999–2003); chairman of the Jewish Agency for Israel (1995–99); adviser on diaspora affairs to Prime Minister Shimon Peres (1985–88); member of Knesset of the Labor Party (1988–2004).

Bush, George W.

President of the United States of America (2001–9); governor of Texas (1995–2000).

Clinton, Bill

President of the United States of America (1993–2001); governor of Arkansas (1978–92).

Dagan, Meir

Director of the Mossad (Israel's national intelligence agency) (2002–10); national security adviser to Prime Minister Ariel Sharon (2001); head of the counterterrorism staff at the office of the prime minister of Israel (1996); died in 2016.

Danon, Danny

Ambassador of the State of Israel to the United Nations (2015–present); minister of science, technology, and space (2015); deputy minister of defense (2013–14); member of Knesset of the Likud party (2009–15).

Dayan, Moshe

Minister of foreign affairs of the State of Israel (1977–79); minister of defense (1967–74); minister of agriculture (1959–64); Member of Knesset of Mapai, Rafi, and Labor Party (1959–81); chief of staff of the IDF (1953–58).

Diskin, Yuval

Head of the Shabak (or Shin Bet) (2005–11); deputy head of the Shabak (2000–2003); special adviser to Mossad director Meir Dagan (2003); commander of the Shabak's Jerusalem District (1997–2003); head of the intelligence and counterterrorism and counterintelligence division of the Shabak (1994–97); joined the Shabak in 1978.

Eban, Abba

Foreign minister of the State of Israel (1966–74); president of the Weizmann Institute of Science (1959–66); deputy prime minister (1964–65); minister of education and culture (1960–63); permanent representative of the State of Israel to the UN (1949–59); ambassador of Israel to the United States (1950–59); liaison officer with the UN Special Committee on Palestine (1947).

Elkin, Zeev
Minister of environmental protection of the State of Israel (2016–present); Minister of Jerusalem affairs and heritage of the State of Israel (2015–present); minister of immigration and absorption (2015–16); deputy minister of foreign affairs (2013–14); member of Knesset of the Likud party (2009–present); member of Knesset of the Kadima party (2006–9).

Erdoğan, Recep Tayyip
President of the Republic of Turkey (2014–present); prime minister of the Republic of Turkey (2003–14); established the Justice and Development Party (AKP) (2001); mayor of Metropolitan Istanbul (1994–98).

Erekat, Saeb
Secretary-general of the PLO (2015–present); head of the PLO negotiations affairs department (2003–15); member of the Palestinian National Council; member of the Palestinian Legislative Council (1996–2003); minister for local government of the PA (1994–2003); chairman of the Palestinian negotiation delegation (1994–2003; 2007–11); chief negotiator for the Declaration of Principles (Oslo I) (1993); deputy leader of the Palestinian delegation at the Madrid peace conference (1991).

Fayyad, Salam
Distinguished Statesman at the Brent Scowcroft Center on International Security of the Atlantic Council (2014-present); prime minister of the PA (2007–13); chairman of the finance committee of the PLC (2006–7); minister of finance of the PA (2002–5; 2007–12); IMF regional manager of the Arab Bank in Palestine (2001–2); IMF resident representative in the West Bank and Gaza Strip (1996–2001); joined the IMF in 1987.

Gal-On, Zehava
Chairwoman of the Meretz party (2012–present); member of Knesset of the Meretz party (1999–2009; 2011–present); cofounder of B'Tselem (the Israeli Information Center for Human Rights in the Occupied Territories) (1988).

Gantz, Benny
Chief of staff of the IDF (2011–15); deputy chief of staff of the IDF (2009–10); IDF military attaché to the United States (2007–9).

Halevy, Efraim

Head of Israel's National Security Council and adviser to Prime Minister Ariel Sharon (2002–3); director of the Mossad (1998–2002); appointed Israeli ambassador to the European Union (1996); deputy director of the Mossad and head of the headquarters branch (1990–95); played a major role in the conclusion of Israel's peace treaty with Jordan (1994); joined the Mossad in 1961.

Halutz, Dan

Chief of staff of the IDF (2005–7); commander of the Israeli air force (2000–2004); chief of staff of the Israeli air force (1995–98).

Hamdallah, Rami

Prime minister of the PA (2013–present); president of an-Najah University in Nablus (1998–2013).

Haniyeh, Ismail

Leader of Hamas and prime minister of the Hamas government in Gaza (2013–present); vice president of Hamas's political bureau (2013–present); prime minister of the PA (2006–7); head of the Hamas-affiliated political list in the Palestinian Legislative Council elections of 2006; member of the collective leadership of Hamas (2004–6); assistant to Hamas leader Sheikh Ahmed Yassin (1997–2004); appointed dean of the Islamic University in Gaza (1993).

Herzog, Isaac

Chairman of the Israeli Labor Party and leader of the opposition (2013–present); co-chair of the Zionist Union electoral list (including the Labor Party) (2015); minister of welfare and social service (2007–11); minister of the diaspora, society, and fight against anti-Semitism (2007–9); minister of tourism (2006–7); minister of construction and housing (2007); member of Knesset of the Labor Party / Zionist Union (2003–present); chairman of the Anti-Drugs Authority (2000–3); government secretary (1999–2001).

Jabotinsky, Zeev (Vladimir)

Revisionist Zionist leader during the British Mandate in Palestine and founder of the Revisionist Zionist movement; commander of the militia Irgun Tzvai Leumi (also known as "Etzel" or "Irgun") during the British Mandate in Palestine (1937–40); founder of the New Zionist Organization

(1935); founder of the Betar Revisionist Zionist youth movement (1923); served as a member of the Zionist Executive; one of the founders of Keren Hayesod (United Israel Appeal) (1921–25).

Kahlon, Moshe
Minister of finance of the State of Israel and chairperson of the Kulanu (All of Us) party (2015–present); minister of welfare and social services (2011–13); minister of communications (2009–13); member of Knesset of the Likud and later Kulanu party (2003–present).

Kerry, John
US secretary of state (2013–present); chairman of the Senate Foreign Relations Committee (2009–12); US senator (1985–2013); lieutenant governor of Massachusetts (1982–84).

Khatami, Mohammad
President of the Islamic Republic of Iran (1997–2005); adviser to President Ali Akbar Hashemi Rafsanjani (1992–97); minister of culture (1982–92).

Khomeini, Sayyid Ruhollah Musavi (Ayatollah Khomeini)
Supreme leader of the Islamic Republic of Iran (1979–89); led the 1979 revolution.

Kochavi, Aviv
Commanding officer of the IDF northern command (2014–present); chief of the IDF's directory of military intelligence (Aman) (2010–14).

Lapid, Yair
Chairman of the Yesh Atid (There Is a Future) party (2012–present); minister of finance (2013–14); member of Knesset of the Yesh Atid party (2013–present); previously TV presenter and news anchorman.

Lieberman, Avigdor
Minister of defense of the State of Israel (2016–present); minister of foreign affairs (2009–12; 2013–15); deputy prime minister (2006–8; 2009–12); minister of strategic affairs (2006–8); minister of transport (2003–4); minister of national infrastructure (2001–2); chairman of the Yisrael Beiteinu (Israel Is Our Home) party (1999–present); member of Knesset of the Yisrael Beiteinu party (1999–2003; 2005–present).

Livni, Tzipi

Co-chair of the Zionist Union electoral list (2015); founder and leader of Ha-Tnuah (The Movement) party (2013–15); minister of justice of the State of Israel (2006–7; 2013–14); leader of the opposition (2009–12); minister of foreign affairs and vice prime minister (2006–9); chairwoman of the Kadima (Forward) party (2008–12); minister of construction and housing (2004–5); minister of immigrant absorption (2003–6); minister of agriculture and rural development (2002–3); minister without portfolio (2001–2); minister of regional cooperation (2001); member of the Knesset of the Likud, Kadima, Ha-Tnuah, and Zionist Union party (1999–present).

Malley, Robert

Senior director at the National Security Council (NSC), special assistant to President Obama and White House coordinator for the Middle East, North Africa, and the Gulf Region, and senior adviser to President Obama for the counter–Islamic State campaign (2015–present); director of the Middle East Program at the International Crisis Group (2001–14); special assistant to President Clinton for Arab–Israeli affairs (1998–2001); member of the US team at the Camp David Summit (2000); executive assistant to National Security Adviser Sandy Berger (1996–98); director for democracy, human rights, and humanitarian affairs at the NSC (1994–96).

Mesh'al, Khaled

Leader of Hamas (2004–present); survived an Israeli attempt on his life in Jordan (1997); chairman of Hamas's political bureau (1996–present); member of Hamas's political bureau since the founding of Hamas in 1987; leader of the Kuwaiti branch of Hamas (1987–91); joined the Muslim Brotherhood in 1971.

Mofaz, Shaul

Chairman of the Kadima party (2013–15); leader of the opposition (2012–13); minister without portfolio (2012); vice prime minister of the State of Israel (2012); minister of transportation and road safety and deputy prime minister (2006–9); minister of defense (2002–6); member of Knesset of the Kadima party (2006–15); chief of staff (1998–2002).

Mousavi, Mir Hossein

Leader of the Green Movement in Iran (2009); senior adviser to President Mohammed Khatami (1997–2005); political adviser to President Rafsanjani

(1989–97); prime minister of the Islamic Republic of Iran (1981–89); foreign minister (1981).

Mubarak, Hosni
President of Egypt (1981–2011); vice president to President Anwar Sadat (1975–81); commander of the Egyptian Air Force (1972–75).

Mustafa, Abu Ali
Secretary-general of the Popular Front for the Liberation of Palestine (2000–2001); assassinated by Israeli forces in 2001.

Nasrallah, Hassan
Secretary-general of the Lebanese Hizballah (1992–present); member of Hizballah since the organization was created in 1982.

Netanyahu, Binyamin
Prime minister of the State of Israel (1996–99; 2009–present); minister of foreign affairs, internal affairs, regional cooperation, economy, and communications (2015–present); chairman of the Likud party (1996–99; 2005–present); minister of health (2009–13; 2015); minister of economic strategy and minister for senior citizens (2009–13); minister of foreign affairs (2002–3; 2012–13); minister of finance (1996–97; 1998–99; 2003–5); minister of religious affairs (1996–98); minister of science (1996–97); leader of the opposition in the Knesset (1993–96); ambassador of Israel to the UN (1984–88).

Obama, Barack
President of the United States (2009–17); US senator (2004–8).

Olmert, Ehud
Prime minister of the State of Israel (2006–9); minister of welfare and social services (2006–7); minister of finance (2005–6); acting prime minister (2003–6); minister of industry, trade and labor and minister of communications (2003–5); mayor of Jerusalem (1993–2003); minister of health (1990–92); minister without portfolio (1988–90); member of Knesset of the Likud and later Kadima party (1974–98).

Peres, Shimon
President of the State of Israel (2007–14); chairman of the Labor Party (1977–92; 1995–97; 2003–5); minister of foreign affairs (1986–88; 1992–95;

2001–2); minister of regional cooperation (1999–2001); prime minister (1984–86; 1995–96); minister of defense (1974–77; 1995–96); awarded the Nobel Peace Prize for the signing of the Oslo Accords (1994); founder of the Peres Center for Peace (1997); leader of the opposition (1990–92); minister of treasury (1988–90); deputy prime minister and minister of finance (1988–90); deputy prime minister and minister of foreign affairs (1986–88); minister of transportation and communications (1970–74); deputy minister of defense (1959–65); member of Knesset (1959–2007); died in 2016.

Qurei, Ahmed Ali Mohammed (Abu Ala')
Head of the PLO department for Jerusalem affairs and member of the PLO executive committee (2015); prime minister of the PA (2003–6); speaker of the PLC (1996–2003); minister of economy and trade and minister of industry of the PA (1994–96); chief negotiator of the Palestinian delegation during the Oslo Accords negotiations (1993–94); member of the Central Committee of Fatah (1989–present).

Rabbo, Yasser Abed
Secretary-general of the PLO's executive committee (2006–15); minister of cabinet affairs of the PA (2003); initiator of the Geneva Initiative with Yossi Beilin (2003); minister of information and culture of the PA (1994–2003); secretary-general of the Palestinian Democratic Union party (1993–2002); member of the Palestinian negotiating team at the Taba Summit (2001); head of the Palestinian negotiating team in final-status peace talks with Israel (1999–2000); member of the Madrid Peace Delegation (1991); head of the PLO's information department (1973–94); founder of the Palestinian Democratic Union party (1991); member of the politburo of the Democratic Front for the Liberation of Palestine (1968–91); member of the PLO executive committee (1971–present); founding member of the Democratic Front for the Liberation of Palestine (1968); leader of the Popular Front for the Liberation of Palestine (1967–68).

Rabin, Yitzhak
Prime minister of the State of Israel (1974–77; 1992–95); awarded the Nobel Peace Prize for the signing of the Oslo Accords (1994); chairman of the Labor Party (1992–95); minister of defense (1984–90); concluded the disengagement agreement with Egypt (1975); minister of communications (1974–75); minister of welfare (1975); minister of labor (1974); member of Knesset of the Labor Party (1974–95); ambassador of Israel

to the United States (1968–73); chief of staff of the IDF (1962–68); assassinated by an Israeli right-wing fanatic in November 1995.

Rafsanjani, Ali Akbar Hashemi
Chairman of the assembly of experts of Iran (2007–11); president of the Islamic Republic of Iran (1989–97); speaker of the Parliament (1980–89).

Regev, Miri
Minister of culture and sport of the State of Israel (2015–present); IDF spokesperson (2005–7); chief military censor for the press and media (2004–5); member of Knesset of the Likud party (2009–present); coordinator of public relations at the office of the prime minister of Israel (2003).

Rice, Condoleezza
US secretary of state (2005–9); US national security adviser (2001–5).

Ross, Dennis
William Davidson Distinguished Fellow and counselor at the Washington Institute for Near East Policy (2011–present); special assistant to President Obama and NSC senior director for the central region (2009–11); special adviser for the Persian Gulf and Southwest Asia to Secretary of State Hillary Clinton (2009); special Middle East coordinator (1993–2000); broker of the Hebron Accord (1997); facilitator of the Israel–Jordan peace treaty (1994); director of policy planning in the State Department under President George H.W. Bush; director of Near East and South Asian Affairs in the NSC and deputy director of the Pentagon's Office of Net Assessment (1982–84).

Sadat, Ahmed
Secretary-general of the Popular Front for the Liberation of Palestine (2001–present); imprisoned in Jericho jail (2002–present).

Shamir, Yitzhak
Prime minister (or acting prime minister) of the State of Israel (1983–84; 1986–92); chairman of the Likud party (1983–93); minister of Jerusalem affairs and minister of the environment (1990–92); minister of labor and social welfare (1988–92); minister of foreign affairs (1980–86); speaker of the Knesset (1977–80); member of Knesset of the Likud party (1974–96); served in the Mossad (1955–65); co-leader of the Lehi militia during the British Mandate in Palestine and during the 1948 war (1943–46; 1948–49).

Sharett, Moshe
Minister of foreign affairs of the State Israel (1949–56); chairman of the Mapai party (1953–56); prime minister (1954–55); member of Knesset of the Mapai party (1949–65); head of the political section of the Jewish Agency (1933–48).

Sharon, Ariel
Prime minister of the State of Israel (2001–6); founder and chairman of the Kadima party (2005–6); chairman of the Likud party (1999–2005); minister of transportation (2002–3); minister of immigration and absorption (2001–3); minister of industry and trade (1984–90; 2002–4); minister of foreign affairs (1998–99); minister of national infrastructure (1996–99); minister of construction and housing (1990–92); minister of industry and trade (1990–98); minister without portfolio (1983–84); minister of defense (1981–83); architect of Israel's invasion of Lebanon (1982); minister of agriculture (1977–81); security adviser to Prime Minister Yitzhak Rabin (1975); member of Knesset of the Likud party (and later Kadima party) (1974–2006); cofounder of the Likud party (1973); head of the IDF southern command (1969–73); head of the IDF northern command (1964–66); founder and commander of the IDF's special commando unit "Unit 101" and the paratrooper battalion into which it merged subsequently (1953–56); member of the Haganah militia (which would become the IDF after the founding of Israel) (1942–48).

Weissglass, Dov
Senior adviser to Prime Minister Ariel Sharon (2002–6).

Weizman, Ezer
President of the State of Israel (1993–2000); minister of science and technology (1988–90); minister of defense (1977–80); minister of transportation (1969–70); minister without portfolio (1984–88); member of Knesset of the Likud and later Labor Party (1981–92); head of IDF military operations and deputy chief of staff (1966–69); commander and chief of the Israel air force (1958–66); member of the militia Irgun Tzvai Leumi (also known as "Etzel" or "Irgun") during the British Mandate in Palestine (1946–48).

Ya'alon, Moshe
Minister of defense of the State of Israel (2013–present); vice prime minister and minister of strategic affairs (2009–13); member of Knesset of the

Likud (2009–15); chief of staff of the IDF (2002–5); head of IDF's military intelligence corps (1995–98).

Yachimovich, Shelly
Chairwoman of the Labor Party and leader of the opposition (2011–13); member of Knesset of the Labor Party (2006–present); radio and television columnist, Israel Channel 2 (2000–2005); journalist and anchorwoman of *Kol Israel* (1986–2000).

Yassin, Ahmed (Sheikh Ahmed Yassin)
Leader and cofounder of Hamas (1987–2004); released from Israeli prison following the Mossad's failed assassination attempt of Khaled Mesh'al in Amman (1997); arrested by Israel and sentenced to life in prison (1989); survived an Israeli attempt on his life (2003); killed by an Israeli missile in 2004.

Yishai, Eli
Chairman of the Yachad (Together) party (2014–present); minister of interior of the State of Israel (2009–13; 2001–3); chairman of the Shas party (1999–2013); deputy prime minister (2006–13; 2001–3); minister of industry, commerce, and labor (2006–9); minister of labor and welfare (1996–2000); secretary-general of the Shas party (1990–96); member of Knesset of the Shas party (and later Yachad party) (1996–2015).

Zoabi, Haneen
Member of Knesset (Joint List) (2015–present); member of Knesset (National Democratic Assembly, Balad) (2009–15); first Arab woman to be elected to Israel's parliament on an Arab political party list; cofounded the I'lam Media Center for Arab Palestinians in Israel (2003–9); senior member of the National Democratic Assembly (Balad) political party (1997–2015).

APPENDIX B: CHRONOLOGY

2000

January   Peace talks between Syria and Israel, launched at a summit meeting with US president Bill Clinton in Washington on December 15, 1999, end with no agreement.

May   Israel withdraws from the "security zone" in southern Lebanon.

June   Syrian president Hafez al-Assad dies.

July   Ehud Barak's government coalition collapses over the upcoming Camp David Summit: The ultra-Orthodox Shas party, the Russian immigrant party Yisrael Be-Aliyah, and the pro-settler National Religious Party all hand in their resignations.

Bashar al-Assad is elected president of Syria, succeeding his father.

Camp David Summit: US president Bill Clinton convenes a summit meeting between Israeli prime minister Ehud Barak and Palestinian Authority (PA) president Yasser Arafat to resolve the Israeli–Palestinian conflict. The summit ends without an agreement.

September   The leader of the opposition, Ariel Sharon, visits Jerusalem holy site—known to Jews as the Temple Mount and to Muslims as Haram al-Sharif. The visit triggers Palestinian protests and a forceful Israeli reaction, escalating to a new wave of violence.

The eruption of the Second Intifada (al-Aqsa Intifada) leads to violent clashes between Israel and the Palestinians marked by numerous Palestinian suicide bombings against Israeli civilians. Israeli policies in the territories consist of arbitrary detentions, curfews, house demolitions, and targeted killings. The Second Intifada formally ends at the Sharm el-Sheikh Summit in February 2005, but violence would continue. Between 2000 and 2005, it claimed the lives of over 3,200 Palestinians and over 1,000 Israelis.

During the Mohamed al-Durra "incident," the French television channel *France 2* broadcasts the footage of a father and his son caught in crossfire between Israeli soldiers and Palestinian security forces. It remains disputed whether they were actually targeted by Israeli fire and whether the boy died.

October   Three Israeli soldiers are abducted by Hizballah while patrolling the Israeli side of the border with Lebanon. Their bodies would be exchanged for Lebanese prisoners in 2004.

Demonstrations by Israel's Palestinian citizens against Israeli policies toward the Palestinians in the territories escalate into clashes with the Israeli police. Twelve Israeli Arab citizens and a Palestinian from the Gaza Strip are killed by the Israeli police.

December   Prime Minister Ehud Barak (Labor Party) formally resigns from his position.

Israeli–Palestinian peace negotiations resume at the Bolling Air Force Base in Washington, DC. President Bill Clinton presents the Clinton Parameters, his bridging proposal for a final-status agreement.

October   Two Israeli army reservists are lynched and their bodies dese crated by a Palestinian mob in Ramallah.

Sharm el-Sheikh Summit: Israeli and Palestinian leaders agree to a cease-fire after two days of talks in Sharm el-Sheikh, attended by US president Bill Clinton and hosted by Egyptian president Hosni Mubarak. The cease-fire does not hold.

2001

January   Republican George W. Bush is inaugurated president of the United States.

Taba Summit: A last round of Israeli–Palestinian peace talks are held at the Egyptian Red Sea resort of Taba. The talks end without an agreement.

Palestinian factions in the Gaza Strip for the first time fire mortar shells on Israeli settlements in the Gaza Strip.

February   Elections in Israel: Ariel Sharon (Likud) is elected prime minister under the old electoral law, defeating incumbent Ehud Barak (Labor). Sharon would form a "national unity" government coalition comprising Likud, Labor, Shas, the Center Party, the National Religious Party, United Torah Judaism, Yisrael Be-Aliyah, the National Union, and Yisrael Beiteinu.

Palestinian suicide attacks resume.

April   Publication of the Mitchell Report (Report of the Sharm el-Sheikh Fact Finding Committee): the report investigates the causes of the Second Intifada and provides recommendations for ending the violence. It refutes both the arguments that Sharon's visit to the Temple Mount was responsible for the eruption of the Second Intifada and that PA chairman Arafat deliberately orchestrated it.

June	Prime Minister Ariel Sharon suspends Israel's unilateral cease-fire following a major suicide attack in a Tel Aviv nightclub, the Dolphinarium.
	Presidential elections in Iran: Mohammad Khatami is elected for a second term.
August	Abu Ali Mustafa, secretary-general of the Popular Front for the Liberation of Palestine (PFLP) is killed by the Israeli army.
September	9/11: four planes are hijacked by al-Qaeda members and crash into the Twin Towers of the World Trade Center in New York City, the Pentagon outside Washington DC, and a field in Pennsylvania killing over three thousand.
October	Israeli minister of tourism Rechavam Ze'evi is killed by members of the PFLP.
	Hamas for the first time launches a rocket on the Israeli town of Sderot.
December	Palestinian president Yasser Arafat is placed under house arrest in his Muqata headquarters in Ramallah.

2002

January	*Karine A* incident: Israeli commandos seize the *Karine A*, a ship with fifty tons of concealed weapons on board, in the Red Sea. Israel claims that the weapons were destined for Arafat's PA.
	US president George Bush uses the term "axis of evil" in reference to Iran, Iraq, and North Korea.
	Fatah activist Ra'ed al-Karmi is killed by Israel (the Israeli government does not claim official responsibility). Fatah's al-Aqsa Martyrs' Brigades declare an end to the truce with Israel.
March	Arab Peace Initiative (also known as the Saudi Peace Plan): At the Arab League Summit in Beirut, the twenty-two members of the Arab League propose full peace with Israel in exchange for an Israeli withdrawal to the June 4, 1967, borders and a "just settlement" of the Palestinian refugee problem.
	Netanya bombing: In the deadliest attack during the Second Intifada, a suicide bombing in a hotel in Netanya during Passover celebrations kills 28 Israelis and leaves 140 injured.
	Start of "Operation Defensive Shield": The Israeli Defense Forces (IDF) reoccupies West Bank cities from which it had withdrawn under the Oslo Accords, resulting in approximately 500 Palestinian fatalities and over 1,400 injured.

April   Palestinian leader and member of the Palestinian Legislative
               Council Marwan Barghouti is arrested by Israeli forces. He
               later stands trial in an Israeli court where he is charged
               with five murders and sentenced to five consecutive life
               sentences.

June   Commencement of Israel's construction of the West Bank
               barrier.

               The Israeli army storms Arafat's headquarters, destroying build-
               ings in the compound.

               US president George H. Bush's Rose Garden Speech: Bush calls
               for a new Palestinian leadership, an end to the violence, and the
               establishment of an independent Palestinian state.

September   The Israeli Labor Party withdraws from the government coali-
               tion, mainly due to their opposition to the economic policy and
               the state budget.

December   First reports emerge on previously undeclared
               uranium-enrichment facilities in Iran.

2003

February   Elections in Israel: Prime Minister Ariel Sharon forms a govern-
               ment coalition composed of the parties Likud, Shinui, and the
               National Union (Yisrael Be-Aliyah had merged with the Likud).
               The National Religious Party would join the government in
               March.

March   Start of the US invasion of Iraq.

               Mahmoud Abbas is appointed prime minister of the PA.

June   Road Map for Middle East Peace: The Middle East Quartet,
               composed of the United States, the European Union, Russia,
               and the United Nations, proposes a plan to resolve the
               Israeli–Palestinian conflict. It calls for a cessation of violence,
               the reform of Palestinian institutions, an end to Israel's settle-
               ment construction, and the establishment of an independent
               Palestinian state.

September   Saeb Erekat is reappointed as chief negotiator of the PA.

               Palestinian prime minister Mahmoud Abbas resigns from his
               position. Ahmed Qurei (Abu Ala') is appointed as prime minister.

December   Geneva Initiative: The Draft Permanent Status Agreement to
               end the Israeli–Palestinian conflict, initiated by Yossi Beilin and
               Yasser Abed Rabbo, is published.

2004

January Israel releases 435 Palestinian and Lebanese prisoners in exchange for Hizballah's return of the remains of three Israeli soldiers and of a kidnapped Israeli businessman.

March Hamas leader Sheikh Ahmed Yassin is killed by an IDF missile attack.

April Sheikh Ahmed Yassin's successor, Abd al-Aziz al-Rantisi, is killed by an IDF attack.

June The Israeli government approves the Gaza disengagement plan; the National Union pulls out of the government in protest, leaving the government with a minority in the Knesset.

July Prime Minister Ahmed Qurei resigns but later retracts his resignation.

September UN Security Council Resolution 1559, calling for the disbanding of all Lebanese militia, is adopted.

October The Israeli Knesset approves Sharon's Gaza disengagement plan.

November President Yasser Arafat falls ill and dies in a hospital in France.

December The Labor Party joins Ariel Sharon's government.

2005

January Presidential elections in the PA: Mahmoud Abbas (Abu Mazen) is elected.

February Sharm el-Sheikh Summit: in the presence of Hosni Mubarak of Egypt and King Abdallah of Jordan, Ariel Sharon and Mahmoud Abbas declare the intention to end all violence against each other, marking a formal end to the Second Intifada (some violence would continue, however).

Lebanese prime minister Rafik Hariri is assassinated in a car bombing in Beirut.

April Syria withdraws its troops from Lebanon.

May–June Parliamentary elections in Lebanon: Fouad Siniora forms a government including the main political blocs; for the first time, Hizballah is represented in the cabinet.

June Presidential elections in Iran: Mahmoud Ahmadinejad is elected.

August–September Gaza disengagement: Israel withdraws the army from the Gaza Strip and evacuates all twenty-five Israeli settlements there. Israel also withdraws from four settlements in the northern West Bank.

November Prime Minister Ariel Sharon resigns as head of the Likud party, dissolves the parliament, and forms a new centrist party called Kadima (Forward).

2006

January Prime Minister Ariel Sharon suffers a severe stroke and falls into a coma; Ehud Olmert assumes the position of acting prime minister.

Palestinian Legislative Council elections: Hamas wins 76 out of 132 seats in the Palestinian parliament.

Israel declared that there would be no negotiations with Hamas until it disarms, recognizes Israel, and accepts existing Israel-PLO accords. Israel imposes an economic boycott on Gaza.

February Ismail Haniyeh (Hamas) is appointed prime minister of the PA. The US rejects the outcome of the Palestinian elections and boycotts the Hamas government; the Quartet follows suit.

March Elections in Israel: Ehud Olmert (Kadima) becomes prime minister and subsequently forms a government coalition composed of Kadima, Labor-Meimad, Shas, and Yisrael Beiteinu.

May The first version of the Prisoners' Document (officially the National Conciliation Document) is drafted by political figures from Fatah, Hamas, Islamic Jihad, PFLP, and the Democratic Front for the Liberation of Palestine, all incarcerated in Israeli prisons. Initiated by Marwan Barghouti, the document calls for the establishment of an independent Palestinian state within the 1967 borders.

Rockets fired from Lebanon into Israel; Israel bombs suspected rocket launch sites and exchanges fire across the Israeli–Lebanese border.

Ehud Olmert presents his "convergence plan" to the Knesset. The plan stipulates a partial Israeli withdrawal from the West Bank, the consolidation of Israeli control over large settlement blocs, and the unilateral delineation of Israel's borders with the Palestinians.

June Fatah, Hamas, and other Palestinian factions sign a slightly revised National Conciliation Document. The document does not contain essential changes when compared to the first version, the Prisoners' Document.

In a letter to US president George W. Bush, Palestinian prime minister Ismael Haniyeh of Hamas offers Israel a truce "for many years" in exchange for a Palestinian state within the 1967 borders and calls on Bush to open a dialogue with the Hamas government.

Iranian president Mahmoud Ahmadinejad calls for Israel to be "wiped off the map."

Israeli soldier Gilad Shalit is kidnapped from an IDF army post by the military wing of Hamas, the Izz al-Din al-Qassam Brigades.

Presidential elections in Israel: Shimon Peres is elected president of Israel.

July
Hizballah kills eight Israeli soldiers and kidnaps two more at the border with Lebanon.

Second Lebanon War: Israel launches air strikes on Lebanon, followed by a ground invasion; Hizballah launches a barrage of rockets on northern Israel. The war between Israel and Hizballah kills over 1,100 Lebanese and leaves 4,400 injured; on the Israeli side, 43 civilians and 119 soldiers are killed.

UN Security Council Resolution 1696 calls on Iran to suspend all uranium-enrichment-related and -reprocessing activities, threatening sanctions for noncompliance.

August
UN Security Council Resolution 1701, calling for a cessation of all hostilities and the disarmament of all armed groups in Lebanon, comes into effect.

December
UN Security Council Resolution 1737 makes it mandatory for Iran to suspend enrichment-related and reprocessing activities, demands full cooperation with the IAEA, and imposes sanctions banning the supply of nuclear-related materials and technology.

2007

January
Khaled Mesh'al declares that Hamas would consider recognizing Israel, once a Palestinian state is established.

February
Mecca Agreement between Fatah and Hamas: Both sides agree to stop the internal military confrontations in the Gaza Strip and to form a national unity government.

March
Fatah and Hamas form a national unity government, led by Ismail Haniyeh (Hamas).

UN Security Council Resolution 1747 imposes an arms embargo and expands the freeze on Iranian assets.

April
Indirect peace talks begin between Israel and Syria, mediated by Turkey.

June
Battle of Gaza between Hamas and Fatah: Hamas takes control of the Gaza Strip. Two rival governments are formed: Fatah in the West Bank and Hamas in Gaza.

President Mahmoud Abbas appoints Salam Fayyad as the new prime minister of the PA.

September   Israel's air force destroys a suspected nuclear reactor in Deir el-Zor, Syria ("Operation Orchard").

November   Annapolis Conference on Middle East Peace, sponsored by the US. Prime Minister Ehud Olmert and President Mahmoud Abbas commit to implementing the "Road Map" obligations and formulate the goal of reaching a peace treaty by the end of 2008.

Israeli–Palestinian peace negotiations resume.

2008

March   UN Security Council Resolution 1803 extends the freeze on Iranian assets linked to the nuclear program and calls on the international community to monitor Iranian banks and inspect Iranian ships and aircraft.

Arab League Summit in Damascus: The Arab League renews the Arab Peace Initiative of 2002.

April   Hamas leader Khaled Mesh'al offers a ten-year truce (*hudna*) and declares that Hamas would accept a Palestinian state in the West Bank and Gaza along Israel's pre-1967 border.

May   Iranian president Ahmadinejad calls Israel "a stinking corpse."

Syria and Israel officially announce that they have started indirect peace talks under the auspices of Turkey.

June   A six-month truce negotiated between Israel and Hamas goes into effect.

September   Israeli prime minister Olmert proposes his peace plan to Palestinian president Abbas.

November   IDF raids Gaza and kills six Hamas fighters; the Egyptian-mediated cease-fire between Israel and Hamas collapses.

Rocket barrages are fired from Gaza into southern Israel.

December   First Gaza War: Israel launches a military campaign on the Hamas-ruled Gaza Strip ("Operation Cast Lead"), which lasts until January 2009. The war claims over 1,300 Palestinian and 13 Israeli fatalities.

2009

January   Democrat Barack Obama is inaugurated president of the United States.

February	Elections in Israel: Binyamin Netanyahu (Likud) becomes prime minster and subsequently forms a government composed of the parties Likud, Kadima, Yisrael Beiteinu, Labor under Ehud Barak, Shas, Ha-Atsma'ut, and Ha-Bayit Ha-Yehudi.
June	Parliamentary elections in Lebanon: Saad Hariri eventually forms a national unity government after five months of negotiations; Hizballah obtains two cabinet posts.
	US President Obama's speech at Cairo University: Obama calls for Arab–Israeli peace based on the 2002 Arab peace plan and a halt to Israeli settlement building.
	Presidential elections in Iran: Ahmadinejad is elected for a second term.
September	Publication of the Goldstone Report (the report of the United Nations Fact Finding Mission on the Gaza Conflict): The report accuses both the Israeli army and Palestinian militants of war crimes and possible crimes against humanity.
	A second uranium enrichment facility is discovered near Qom in Iran.
October	In a speech delivered at Bar-Ilan University, Netanyahu agrees to the establishment of a demilitarized Palestinian state.
November	Prime Minister Netanyahu declares a ten-month partial freeze on settlement construction in the West Bank, under US pressure.

2010

May	The Israeli navy storms the Turkish-owned flagship *Mavi Marmara* of a flotilla of vessels crewed by pro-Palestinian activists whose aim is to break the Israeli–Egyptian blockade of the Gaza Strip. Nine Turkish citizens are killed.
June	UN Security Council Resolution 1929 bans Iran from participating in any activities related to ballistic missiles and tightens the arms embargo, the sanctions, the travel bans, and the freeze on assets of individuals, companies, and organizations linked to the nuclear program.
August	Clashes between the Israeli army and the Lebanese army along the border.
September	President Barack Obama initiates direct talks at a White House summit with President Abbas and Prime Minister Netanyahu.
	Netanyahu refuses to renew the settlement freeze; the talks collapse.

December   Start of the "Jasmine Revolution" in Tunisia, the beginning of the
              "Arab Spring."

2011

January   The Palestine Papers, a collection of confidential documents
              about Israeli–Palestinian talks between 1999 and 2010, is pub-
              lished by *Al Jazeera* and *Guardian*.

              Popular protests in Tahrir Square in Cairo, Egypt, mark the be-
              ginning of the 2011 Egyptian revolution.

              After the fall of the Hariri government, Najib Mikati is nominated
              to serve as prime minister of Lebanon.

February   Saeb Erekat (Fatah), the Palestinian chief negotiator, resigns from
              his position after it emerges that the source of the leaked Pales-
              tine Papers was in his own office.

              Egyptian president Hosni Mubarak resigns; power is turned over
              to the Supreme Council of the Armed Forces.

March   Popular protests in Syria, repressed by President Bashar al-Assad,
              lead to growing escalation resulting in what is to be a long lasting
              civil war.

April   PA president Mahmoud Abbas and Hamas leader Khaled Mesh'al
              sign the Cairo Agreement, stipulating the formation of a transi-
              tional government of technocrats to prepare for elections to the
              PA within one year. The talks on the formation of a unity govern-
              ment would be suspended in June.

June   Prime Minister Najib Mikati forms a new Lebanese government,
              a thirty-minister cabinet, following five months of negotiations;
              Hizballah obtains two cabinet posts.

August   Israeli soldiers and Lebanese soldiers exchange fire along the
              border.

October   Israel releases 1,027 Palestinian prisoners in exchange for kid-
              napped IDF soldier Gilad Shalit.

2012

January   Hamas closes its political bureau in Damascus after the organi-
              zation voiced support for the Syrian people against the regime
              of Bashar al-Assad. Hamas's political bureau relocates to Doha,
              Qatar.

February   PA president Mahmoud Abbas and Hamas leader Khaled Mesh'al
              sign a reconciliation agreement in Doha. No progress would be
              achieved, however.

May	Abbas and Mesh'al sign an additional agreement in Cairo to prepare for a unity government and the holding of elections in the West Bank and the Gaza Strip.
June	Presidential elections in Egypt: Muslim Brotherhood candidate Mohamed Morsi is elected president.
November	Barack Obama is elected for a second term as US president.

In an upsurge in cross-border violence in Gaza, different Palestinian militant groups, including Hamas's al-Qassam Brigades, fire rockets into southern Israel. The Israeli army shells and carries out air strikes on Gaza.

Second Gaza War ("Operation Pillar of Defense"): An Israeli airstrike kills the commander of Hamas's military wing, Ahmed Jabari; beginning of Israel's military campaign on the Hamas-ruled Gaza Strip lasting eight days; Hamas launches barrages of rockets on Israel. The war results in 174 Palestinian and 6 Israeli fatalities.

The UN General Assembly upgrades Palestinian representation status from "nonmember observer entity" to "nonmember observer state."

2013

January	Elections in Israel: Binyamin Netanyahu becomes prime minister for a second consecutive term, leading a government coalition composed of Likud Yisrael Beiteinu, Ha-Bayit Ha-Yehudi, Yesh Atid, and Ha-Tnuah chaired by Tzipi Livni.
April	Palestinian prime minister Salam Fayyad resigns.

Tammam Salam is designated as prime minister of Lebanon, and tasked with forming a new government after the resignation of Najib Mikati.

June	Rami Hamdallah is appointed Palestinian prime minister.

Presidential elections in Iran: Hassan Rouhani is elected, defeating incumbent Mahmoud Ahmadinejad.

July	Peace talks are initiated by US secretary of state John Kerry, with Israeli and Palestinian negotiators to meet in Washington DC. The talks are scheduled to last up to nine months and to reach a final-status agreement to the Palestinian–Israeli conflict by mid-2014. The PA commits to putting on hold its attempts to gain international recognition as a state by applying to international organizations; Israel commits to releasing four groups of Palestinian prisoners over the course of the talks.

Egyptian president Mohamed Morsi is deposed by Egyptian minister of defense and chief of the Egyptian armed forces, Gen. Abdel Fattah al-Sisi.

August   Israeli minister of justice Tzipi Livni and Palestinian chief negotiator Saeb Erekat conduct talks in Jerusalem.

2014

January   Netanyahu announces new tenders for 1,400 housing units in settlements in the West Bank and in East Jerusalem.

February   Lebanese prime minister Tammam Salam announces the formation of a new national unity government after ten months of negotiations.

March   Talks take place between Fatah and Hamas on possible reconciliation.

Israel delays the release of a fourth batch of Palestinian prisoners that it had committed to and issues new tenders for 1,500 housing units in Israeli West Bank settlements.

April   President Abbas pursues the joining of fifteen international agencies and organizations on behalf of the state of Palestine.

Reconciliation agreement between Hamas and Fatah: the two rival Palestinian factions agree to form a unity government.

Israel suspends peace talks.

May   Presidential elections in Egypt: Abdel Fattah al-Sisi is elected president.

June   Palestinian unity government, led by Rami Hamdallah, is sworn in. The government of "technocrats" does not include Hamas members.

Three Jewish Israeli teenagers are kidnapped and killed in the West Bank, followed by the murder of a Jerusalemite Palestinian teenager.

The Israeli army launches an eighteen-day search-and-rescue operation in the West Bank ("Operation Brother's Keeper"), resulting in the arrest of over four hundred Palestinians, including approximately three hundred members of Hamas.

A barrage of rockets is fired from the Gaza Strip into southern and central Israel.

July	Third Gaza War ("Operation Protective Edge"): Israel launches a military campaign on the Hamas-ruled Gaza Strip, which lasts through August; Hamas fires a barrage of rockets that reaches Tel Aviv. The war results in over 2,200 Palestinian fatalities; on the Israeli side, 67 Israeli soldiers and 4 civilians are killed.
August	Hamas leader Khaled Mesh'al reiterates his willingness to accept a Palestinian state within the 1967 borders.
December	Prime Minister Netanyahu fires Minister of Finance Yair Lapid and Minister of Justice Tzipi Livni and calls for dissolution of the Knesset and early elections.

2015

January	Airstrikes in the Quneitra District in Syria kill six Hizballah members and at least one Iranian Revolutionary Guard officer (Israel does not claim responsibility). Hizballah fires missiles at an Israeli convoy in the Sheba'a Farms and on the Israeli occupied Golan Heights, killing two Israeli soldiers; the IDF fires shells into southern Lebanon, killing one Spanish peacekeeper.
March	Netanyahu declares that his Bar-Ilan speech in support of the creation of a demilitarized Palestinian state is no longer valid.
	Elections in Israel: Binyamin Netanyahu is elected prime minister for a third consecutive term; he subsequently forms a government coalition composed of the parties Likud; Ha-Bayit Ha-Yehudi, chaired by Naftali Bennett; Kulanu, chaired by Moshe Kahlon; Shas; and United Torah Judaism.
April	Iran nuclear deal: The Joint Comprehensive Plan of Action is signed between P5+1 (the United States, the United Kingdom, France, China, Russia, and Germany, plus the European Union) and the Islamic Republic of Iran.
June	The Palestinian unity government, formed by Fatah and Hamas, resigns under protest from Hamas. Mahmoud Abbas reshuffles the government.
July	Prime Minister Netanyahu approves the construction of hundreds of settlement units in the West Bank and Arab East Jerusalem following a court ruling that two buildings in a West Bank settlement, built on private Palestinian land, had to be destroyed.

BIBLIOGRAPHY

Adler, Emanuel. "Damned If You Do, Damned If You Don't: Performative Power and the Strategy of Conventional and Nuclear Defusing." *Security Studies* 19, no. 2 (2010): 199–229.

———. "Israel's Unsettled Relations with the World: Causes and Consequences." In *Israel and the World: Legitimacy and Exceptionalism*, edited by Emanuel Adler, 1–23. New York: Routledge, 2013.

Adler, Emanuel, and Vincent Pouliot, eds. *International Practices*. Cambridge: Cambridge University Press, 2011.

Al-Abed, Samih. "The Israeli Proposals Were Not Serious." In *The Camp David Summit: What Went Wrong?*, edited by Shimon Shamir and Bruce Maddy-Weitzman, 74–81. Brighton, UK: Sussex Academic Press, 2005.

Al-Haj, Majid. "Whither the Green Line? Trends in the Orientation of the Palestinians in Israel and the Territories." In *Israeli Democracy at the Crossroads*, edited by Raphael Cohen-Almagor, 183–206. London: Routledge, 2005.

Alpher, Yossi. *Periphery: Israel's Search for Middle East Allies*. Lanham, Md.: Rowman & Littlefield, 2015.

Anderson, Benedict R. *Imagined Communities: Reflections on the Origin and Spread of Nationalism*. London: Verso, 1991.

"Arab League Summit: Beirut Declaration (March 28, 2002)." In *The Israel–Arab Reader: A Documentary History of the Middle East Conflict*, edited by Walter Laqueur and Barry Rubin, 583–84. New York: Penguin, 2008.

Arian, Asher. "Israeli Public Opinion on National Security 2003." Memorandum No. 67. Tel Aviv: Jaffee Center for Strategic Studies, October 2003.

———. *Politics in Israel: The Second Republic*. Washington, DC: CQ Press, 2005.

———. *Security Threatened: Surveying Israeli Opinion on Peace and War*. Cambridge: Cambridge University Press, 1995.

Arieli, Shaul, Roby Nathanson, Ziv Rubin, and Hagar Tzameret-Kertcher. *Historical, Political, and Economic Impact of Jewish Settlements in the Occupied Territories*. Israeli-European Policy Network (IEPN), June 2009. http://www.iepn.org/images/stories/papers/papershaularieli.pdf.

Bahgat, Gawdat. "The Arab Peace Initiative: An Assessment." *Middle East Policy* 15, no. 9 (2009): 37–38.

Barak, Ehud. "The Myths Spread about Camp David Are Baseless." In *The Camp David Summit: What Went Wrong?*, edited by Shimon Shamir and Bruce Maddy-Weitzman, 117–47. Brighton, UK: Sussex Academic Press, 2005.

Barnett, Michael. "Cosmopolitanism: Good for Israel? Or Bad for Israel?" In *Israel in the World: Legitimacy and Exceptionalism*, edited by Emanuel Adler, 32–50. London: Routledge, 2013.

———. "Culture, Strategy and Foreign Policy Change: Israel's Road to Oslo." *European Journal of International Relations* 5, no. 1 (1999): 5–36.

Bar-Tal, Daniel. "Why Does Fear Override Hope in Societies Engulfed by Intractable Conflict, as It Does in the Israeli Society?" *Political Psychology* 22 (2001): 601–62.

Bar-Tal, Daniel, and Arie W. Kruglanski. *The Social Psychology of Knowledge.* Cambridge: Cambridge University Press, 1988.

Bar-Tal, Daniel, and Yona Teichman. *Stereotypes and Prejudice in Conflict: Representation of Arabs in Israeli Jewish Society.* New York: Cambridge University Press, 2005.

Barzegar, Kayhan. "The Paradox of Iran's Nuclear Consensus." *World Policy Journal* 26, no. 3 (2009): 21–30.

Beinart, Peter. *The Crisis of Zionism.* New York: Times Books/Henry Holt, 2012.

Ben Meir, Yehuda. "Operation Cast Lead: Political Dimensions and Public Opinion." *Strategic Assessment* 11, no. 4 (February 2009): 29–34. Tel Aviv: Institute for National Security Studies.

———. *The People's Voice: Results of a Public Opinion Survey on National Security Issues.* Tel Aviv: Institute for National Security Studies, June 14, 2009. http://www.inss.org.il/index.aspx?id=4538&articleid=2041.

Ben Meir, Yehuda, and Olena Bagno-Moldavsky. "Vox Populi: Trends in Israeli Public Opinion on National Security 2004–2009." Memorandum No. 106. Tel Aviv: Institute for National Security Studies, November 2010.

Ben Meir, Yehuda, and Dafna Shaked. "The People Speak: Israeli Public Opinion on National Security 2005–2007." Memorandum No. 90. Tel Aviv: Institute for National Security Studies, May 2007.

Ben-Ami, Shlomo. *Lessons of the Israeli–Palestinian Peace Process.* Leonard Stein Lecture, Balliol College and St Antony's College, University of Oxford, May 15, 2008.

———. *Scars of War, Wounds of Peace: The Israeli–Arab Tragedy.* Oxford: Oxford University Press, 2006.

Beres, Louis René. "Israel, Iran, and Project Daniel: A Six Year Retrospective." Conference paper, Ninth Annual Herzliya Conference on the Balance of Israel's National Security and Resilience. Interdisciplinary Center, Herzliya, Israel. February 2–4, 2009.

Berger, Peter L., and Thomas Luckmann. *The Social Construction of Reality: A Treatise in the Sociology of Knowledge.* Garden City, NY: Doubleday, 1966.

Berrebi, Claude, and Esteban F. Klor. "Are Voters Sensitive to Terrorism? Direct Evidence from the Israeli Electorate." *American Political Science Review* 102, no. 3 (2008): 279–301.

———. "On Terrorism and Electoral Outcomes: Theory and Evidence from the Israeli–Palestinian Conflict." *Journal of Conflict Resolution* 50, no. 6 (2006): 899–925.

Bhaskar, Roy. *A Realist Theory of Science*. Leeds: Leeds Books, 1975.

Boulding, Kenneth E. *The Image: Knowledge in Life and Society*. Ann Arbor: University of Michigan Press, 1956.

Brecher, Michael. *The Foreign Policy System of Israel: Setting, Images, Process*. London: Oxford University Press, 1972.

Bregman, Ahron. *Elusive Peace: How the Holy Land Defeated America*. London: Penguin, 2005.

———. *Israel's Wars: A History since 1947*. London: Routledge, 2010.

Buzan, Barry. *People, States, and Fear: An Agenda for International Security Studies in the Post–Cold War Era*. New York: Harvester Wheatsheaf, 1991.

Buzan, Barry, Ole Wæver, and Jaap de Wilde. *Security: A New Framework for Analysis*. Boulder, CO: Lynne Rienner, 1998.

Byman, Daniel. "How to Handle Hamas: The Perils of Ignoring Gaza's Leadership." *Foreign Affairs* 89, no. 5 (2010): 45–62.

Caplan, Neil. *The Israel–Palestine Conflict: Contested Histories*. Chichester, UK: Wiley-Blackwell, 2010.

Cavari, Amnon. "Six Decades of Public Affection: Trends in American Public Attitudes Towards Israel." In *Israel and the United States: Six Decades of US–Israeli Relations*, edited by Robert O. Freedman, 100–123. Boulder, CO: Westview, 2012.

Chong, Dennis, and James N. Druckman. "Framing Theory." *Annual Review of Political Science* 10 (2007): 103–26.

Cohen-Almagor, Raphael, and Sharon Haleva-Amir. "The Israel–Hezbollah War and the Winograd Committee." *Journal of Parliamentary and Political Law* 2, no. 1 (2008): 113–30.

Cordesman, Anthony H. *The Gaza War: A Strategic Analysis*. Washington, DC: Center for Strategic and International Studies, February 2, 2009. http://csis .org/files/media/csis/pubs/090202_gaza_war.pdf.

Council of the European Union. *Council Conclusions on Middle East Peace Process*, 2921st External Relations Council Meeting. Brussels. January 26–27, 2009.

Cox, Robert W. "Gramsci, Hegemony and International Relations: An Essay in Method." *Millennium: Journal of International Studies* 12, no. 2 (1983): 162–75.

Del Sarto, Raffaella A. "Back to Square One? The Netanyahu Government and the Prospects for Middle East Peace." *Mediterranean Politics* 14, no. 3 (2009): 421–28.

————. *Contested State Identities and Regional Security in the Euro-Mediterranean Area*. New York: Palgrave Macmillan, 2006.

————, ed. *Fragmented Borders, Interdependence and External Relations: The Israel-Palestine-European Union Triangle*. Houndsmill, Basingstoke: Palgrave Macmillan, 2015.

————. "Israel and the European Union: Beween Rhetoric and Reality." In *Israel and the Great Powers*, edited by Colin Shindler, 155–86. London: I. B. Tauris, 2014.

Dessler, David. "What's at Stake in the Agent-Structure Debate?" *International Organization* 43, no. 3 (1989): 441–73.

DiMaggio, Paul. "Culture and Cognition." *Annual Review of Sociology* 23 (1997): 263–87.

Dor, Daniel. *Intifada Hits the Headlines: How the Israeli Press Misreported the Outbreak of the Second Palestinian Uprising*. Bloomington: Indiana University Press, 2004.

————. *The Suppression of Guilt: The Israeli Media and the Reoccupation of the West Bank*. London: Pluto Press, 2005.

Doty, Roxanne L. "Aporia: A Critical Exploration of the Agent-Structure Problematique in International Relations Theory." *European Journal of International Relations* 3, no. 3 (1997): 365–92.

Drucker, Raviv. *Harakiri: Ehud Barak be-mivhan ha-totsa'ah* [Harakiri: Ehud Barak facing the outcome]. Tel Aviv: Yedioth Ahronot, 2002.

Edelstein, David. "Managing Uncertainty: Beliefs About Intentions and the Rise of the Great Powers." *Security Studies* 12, no. 1 (2002): 1–40.

Ehteshami, Anoushiravan. "The Foreign Policy of Iran." In *The Foreign Policies of Middle East States*, 2nd ed., edited by Raymond Hinnebusch and Anoushiravan Ehteshami, 261–88. Boulder, CO: Lynne Rienner, 2014.

Eiland, Giora. "The IDF in the Second Intifada." *Strategic Assessment* 13, no. 3 (October 2010): 27–37. Tel Aviv: Institute for National Security Studies.

Einhorn, Robert J. *The Iran Nuclear Issue: Reaching a Critical Juncture*. Lecture, delivered at SAIS Europe at Bologna, Johns Hopkins University, March 7, 2012.

Eldridge, Albert F. *Images of Conflict*. New York: St. Martin's Press, 1979.

El-Husseini, Rola. "Hezbollah and the Axis of Refusal: Hamas, Iran and Syria." *Third World Quarterly* 31, no. 5 (2010): 803–15.

Enderlin, Charles. *Shattered Dreams: The Failure of the Peace Process in the Middle East, 1995–2002*. New York: Other Press, 2003.

Eran, Oded. "Ha-Behirot be-Israel: Ha-Hashlakhot ha-Diplomatiyot" [Elections in Israel: The diplomatic implications]. Tel Aviv: Institute for National Security Studies, February 17, 2009.

Etzion, Eran. "The Ministry of Foreign Affairs Situation Assessment for 2008–2009." *Strategic Assessment* 12, no. 1, June 2009: 47–58. Tel Aviv: Institute for National Security Studies.

Evron, Boas. *Jewish State or Israeli Nation?* Bloomington: Indiana University Press, 1995.

Ezrahi, Yaron. *Rubber Bullets: Power and Conscience in Modern Israel*. New York: Farrar, Strauss and Giroux, 1997.

Falk, Richard. "Camp David II: Looking Back, Looking Forward." *Journal of Palestine Studies* 36, no. 3 (2007): 78–88.

Finnemore, Marta, and Kathryn Sikkink. "International Norm Dynamics and Political Change." *International Organization* 52, no. 4 (1998): 887–917.

Fletcher, George P. "The Indefinable Concept of Terrorism." *Journal of International Criminal Justice* 4, no. 5 (2006): 894–911.

Freedman, Robert O. "George W. Bush, Barack Obama, and the Israeli–Palestinian Conflict from 2001 to 2011." In *Israel and the United States: Six Decades of US–Israeli Relations*, edited by Robert O. Freedman, 36–78. Boulder, CO: Westview, 2011.

Gerges, Fawaz A. *Obama and the Middle East: The End of America's Moment?* New York: Palgrave Macmillan, 2011.

Gertz, Nurith. "The Few against the Many." *Jerusalem Quarterly* 30 (1984): 94–104.

Getmansky, Anna, and Thomas Zeitzoff. "Terrorism and Voting: The Effect of Rocket Threat on Voting in Israeli Elections." *American Political Science Review* 108, no. 3 (2014): 588–604.

Ging, John. "The Siege on Gaza in 2010: A View from the Inside." Lecture delivered at the Middle East Centre, St. Antony's College, University of Oxford, June 1, 2010.

Goldschmidt, Pierre. *The Iranian Nuclear Issue: Achieving a Win–Win Diplomatic Solution*. Washington, DC: Carnegie Endowment for International Peace, 2012, http://carnegieendowment.org/2012/02/04/iranian-nuclear -issue-achieving-win-win-diplomatic-solution/9hb3.

Goodman, Russell B. *Pragmatism: A Contemporary Reader*. New York: Routledge, 1995.

Gordon, Neve. *Israel's Occupation*. Berkeley: University of California Press, 2008.

Gorenberg, Gershom. *The Accidental Empire: Israel and the Birth of Settlements, 1967–1977*. New York: Times Books, 2006.

Gramsci, Antonio. *Quaderni dal carcere*. Torino: Einaudi, 1977.

Gross Stein, Janice. "Israel: The Shard in a Fragmented Legal Order." In *Israel in the World: Legitimacy and Exceptionalism*, edited by Emanuel Adler, 97–109. London: Routledge, 2013.

Gunning, Jeroen. *Hamas in Politics: Democracy, Religion, Violence*. New York: Columbia University Press, 2008.

Haklai, Oded. "Religious-Nationalist Mobilization and State Penetration: Lessons from Jewish Settlers' Activism in Israel and the West Bank." *Comparative Political Studies* 40, no. 6 (2007): 713–39.

Ha-Knesset [The Knesset]. "Hok ha-ezrahut ve-ha-knisah le-Israel (Hora'at sh'aah)" [Nationality and entry into Israel law (temporary provision)]. *Sefer ha-Hukim* [Official gazette] 1901 (August 6, 2003): 544–45.

————. "Hok ha-ezrahut (Tikun mispar 9)" [Nationality law (amendment no. 9)].
   Sefer ha-Hukim [Official gazette] 2167 (August 6, 2008): 810–12.

————. "Hok le-tikun pkudat ha-karka'ot (Rekhishah le-tsorkhei tsibur, mispar 3)"
   [Amendment to the land acquisition ordinance for public purposes, no. 3].
   Sefer ha-Hukim [Official gazette] 2228 (February 15, 2010): 346–68.

————. "Hok minhal me-karka'ei Yisrael, tikun mispar 7" [Israel land administration law, amendment no. 7]. *Sefer ha-Hukim* [Official gazette] 2209 (August 10, 2009): 317–31.

Halperin, Eran. "Group-Based Hatred in Intractable Conflict in Israel." *Journal
   of Conflict Resolution* 52, no. 5 (2008): 713–36.

Halperin, Eran, and Daniel Bar-Tal. "The Fall of the Peace Camp in Israel: The
   Influence of Prime Minister Ehud Barak on Israeli Public Opinion, July
   2000–February 2001." *Conflict and Communication Online* 6, no. 2 (2007),
   http://www.cco.regener-online.de/2007_2/pdf/halperin.pdf.

————. "Socio-Psychological Barriers to Peace Making: An Empirical Examina-
   tion within the Israeli Jewish Society." *Journal of Peace Research* 48, no. 5
   (2011): 637–51.

Hermann, Tamar, and Ephraim Yuchtmann-Yaar. *Israeli Society and the Challenge of Transition to Co-Existence.* Tel Aviv: Tami Steinmetz Center for
   Peace Research, Tel Aviv University, 1997.

Hogg, Michael A., and Dominic Abrams, eds. *Group Motivations: Social Psychological Perspectives.* London: Harvester Wheatsheaf, 1993.

Holsti, K. J. *Change in the International System: Essays on the Theory and Practice of International Relations.* Aldershot, UK: E. Elgar, 1991.

Horowitz, Dan. "The Israeli Concept of National Security." In *National Security and Democracy in Israel,* edited by Avner Yaniv, 11–53. London: Lynne
   Rienner, 1993.

Hovland, Carl I., Irving L. Janis, and Harold H. Kelley. *Communication and
   Persuasion: Psychological Studies of Opinion Change.* New Haven, CT: Yale
   University Press, 1953.

Hunter, Shireen T. *Iran and the World: Continuity in a Revolutionary Decade.*
   Bloomington: Indiana University Press, 1990.

IAEA. *Implementation of the NPT Safeguards Agreement and Relevant
   Provisions of Security Council Resolutions in the Islamic Republic of Iran.*
   Gov/2011/65, November 8, 2011. Vienna: IAEA. https://www.iaea.org/sites/
   default/files/gov2011-65.pdf.

Inbar, Efraim. "How Israel Bungled the Second Lebanon War," *Middle East
   Quarterly* 4, no. 3 (2007): 57–65.

————. "The Need to Block a Nuclear Iran." *Middle East Review of International
   Affairs* 10, no. 1 (2006): 85–104.

Indyk, Martin. "Sins of Ommission, Sins of Commission." In *The Camp David
   Summit: What Went Wrong?,* edited by Shimon Shamir and Bruce Maddy-
   Weitzman, 100–107. Brighton, UK: Sussex Academic Press, 2005.

International Crisis Group. *Back to Basics: Israel's Arab Minority and the Israeli–Palestinian Conflict.* Middle East Report No. 119, March 14, 2012.

———. *Identity Crisis: Israel and Its Arab Citizens.* Middle East Report no. 25, March 4, 2004.

———. *In Heavy Waters: Iran's Nuclear Program, the Risk of War and Lessons from Turkey.* Middle East and Europe Report No. 116, February 23, 2012.

———. *Israel's Religious Right and the Question of Settlements.* Middle East Report No. 89, July 20, 2009.

———. *Leap of Faith: Israel's National Religious and the Israeli–Palestinian Conflict.* Middle East Report No. 147, November 21, 2013.

International Institute for Strategic Studies. *IAEA Report Puts Iran on Back Foot.* London, November 9, 2011, http://www.iiss.org.

———. *Iran's Strategic Weapons Programmes: A Net Assessment.* New York: Routledge, 2005.

Ish-Shalom, Piki. "Defining by Naming: Israeli Civic Warring over the Second Lebanon War." *European Journal of International Affairs* 17, no. 3 (2010): 475–93.

Jarymowicz, Maria, and Daniel Bar-Tal. "The Dominance of Fear over Hope in the Life of Individuals and Collectives." *European Journal of Social Psychology* 36, no. 3 (2006): 367–92.

Jervis, Robert. *Perception and Misperception in International Politics.* Princeton, NJ: Princeton University Press, 1976.

Jones, Clive. "The Foreign Policy of Israel." In *The Foreign Policies of Middle East States,* 2nd ed., edited by Raymond Hinnebusch and Anoushiravan Ehteshami, 261–313. Boulder, CO: Lynne Rienner, 2014.

Kacowicz, Arie M. "Rashomon in the Middle East: Clashing Narratives of the Israeli–Palestinian Conflict." *Cooperation and Conflict* 40, no. 3(2005): 343–60.

Kam, Efraim. "Israel through Arab Strategic Lenses: A Changed Reality." In *Strategic Survey for Israel 2009,* edited by Shlomo Brom and Anat Kuz, 41–52. Tel Aviv: Institute for National Security Studies, 2009.

Katzenstein, Peter J. *The Culture of National Security: Norms and Identity in World Politics.* New York: Columbia University Press, 1996.

Khalidi, Rashid. *Brokers of Deceit: How the US Has Undermined Peace in the Middle East.* Boston: Beacon Press, 2013.

Khanin, Vladimir (Zeev). "Russian-Jewish Political Experience in Israel: Patterns, Elites and Movements." *Israel Affairs* 17, no. 1 (2011): 55–71.

Kimmerling, Baruch. *The Invention and Decline of Israeliness: State, Society, and the Military.* Berkeley: University of California Press, 2001.

———. *The Israeli State and Society: Boundaries and Frontiers.* Albany: State University of New York Press, 1989.

———. *Politicide: Ariel Sharon's War against the Palestinians.* London: Verso, 2006.

Klein, Menachem. *The Shift: Israel–Palestine from Border Struggle to Ethnic Conflict.* New York: Columbia University Press, 2010.

Kober, Avi. "The Israel Defense Forces in the Second Lebanon War: Why the Poor Performance?" *Journal of Strategic Studies* 31, no. 1 (2008): 3–40.

Kretzmer, David. *The Occupation of Justice: The Supreme Court of Israel and the Occupied Territories.* Albany: State University of New York Press, 2002.

Kruglanski, Arie W. *Lay Epistemics and Human Knowledge: Cognitive and Motivational Bases.* New York: Plenum Press, 1989.

Kruglanski, Arie W., Amiram Raviv, Daniel Bar-Tal, Alona Raviv, Keren Sharvit, Shmuel Ellis, Ruth Bar, Antonio Pierro, and Lucia Mannetti. "Says Who? Epistemic Authority Effects in Social Judgment." *Advances in Experimental Social Psychology* 37 (2005): 345–92.

Landau, Emily B. *Arms Control in the Middle East: Cooperative Security Dialogue and Regional Constraints.* Brighton, UK: Sussex Academic Press, 2006

Laqueur, Walter. *A History of Zionism.* New York: Schocken Books, 2003.

Lavie, Ephraim. "Israel's Coping with the Al-Aqsa Intifada: A Critical Review." *Strategic Assessment* 13, no. 3 (October 2010): 101–22. Tel Aviv: Institute for National Security Studies.

Levush, Ruth. "Israel: Revocation of Citizenship Following Conviction for Serious Security Offenses." Law Library of Congress, April 1, 2011, http://www .loc.gov/lawweb/servlet/lloc_news?disp0_l205402600_text.

Levy, Yagil, Edna Lomsky-Feder, and Noa Harel. "From 'Obligatory Militarism' to 'Contractual Militarism': Competing Models of Citizenship." In *Militarism and Israeli Society*, edited by Gabriel Sheffer and Oren Barak, 145–67. Bloomington: Indiana University Press, 2010.

Liebes, Tamar. *Reporting the Arab–Israeli Conflict: How Hegemony Works.* London: Routledge, 1997.

Lustick, Ian. "Abandoning the Iron Wall: Israel and 'the Middle Eastern Muck.'" *Middle East Policy* 15, no. 3 (2008): 30–56.

———. *Unsettled States, Disputed Lands: Britain and Ireland, France and Algeria, Israel and the West Bank-Gaza.* Ithaca, NY: Cornell University Press, 1993.

Maoz, Zeev. *Defending the Holy Land: A Critical Analysis of Israel's Security and Foreign Policy.* Ann Arbor: University of Michigan Press, 2006.

Marzano, Arturo. "The Loneliness of Israel: The Jewish State's Status in International Relations." *International Spectator* 48, no. 2 (2013): 96–113.

McGeough, Paul. *Kill Khalid: The Failed Mossad Assassination of Khalid Mishal and the Rise of Hamas.* New York: New Press, 2009.

Mearsheimer, John J., and Stephen M. Walt. *The Israel Lobby and US Foreign Policy.* New York: Farrar, Straus and Giroux, 2007.

Meital, Yoram. *Peace in Tatters: Israel, Palestine, and the Middle East.* Boulder, CO: Lynne Rienner, 2006.

Merom, Gil. "Israel's National Security and the Myth of Exceptionalism." *Political Science Quarterly* 114, no. 3 (1999): 409–34.

Michael, Kobi. "The Israel Defense Forces as an Epistemic Authority: An Intellectual Challenge in the Reality of the Israeli–Palestinian Conflict." *Journal of Strategic Studies* 30, no. 3 (2007): 421–46.

———. "Military Knowledge and Weak Civilian Control: The Israeli Case." In *Militarism and Israeli Society*, edited by Gabriel Sheffer and Oren Barak, 42–66. Bloomington: Indiana University Press, 2010.

Miller, Aaron David. *The Much Too Promised Land: America's Elusive Search for Arab–Israeli Peace*. New York: Bantam, 2008.

Milstein, Michael. "A Decade since the Outbreak of the Al-Aqsa Intifada." *Strategic Assessment* 13, no. 3 (October 2010): 7–26. Tel Aviv: Institute for National Security Studies.

Mishal, Shaul, and Avraham Sela. *The Palestinian Hamas: Vision, Violence, and Coexistence*. New York: Columbia University Press, 2006.

Mohanad, Mustafa, and As'ad Ghanem. "The Empowering of the Israeli Extreme Right in the 18th Knesset Elections." *Mediterranean Politics* 15, no. 1 (2010): 25–44.

Moreh, Dror, dir. *The Gatekeepers*. Sony Pictures Classics, 2012 (Israel).

Morris, Benny. *The Birth of the Palestinian Refugee Problem, 1947–1949*. Cambridge: Cambridge University Press, 1987.

———. *The Birth of the Palestinian Refugee Problem Revisited*. Cambridge: Cambridge University Press, 2004.

———. *Righteous Victims: A History of the Zionist–Arab Conflict, 1881–1999*. New York: Knopf, 1999.

Moshirzadeh, Homeira. "Discursive Foundations of Iran's Nuclear Policy." *Security Dialogue* 38, no. 4 (2007): 521–43.

Naveh, Hanan. "The Role of the Media in Shaping Israeli Public Opinion, 1992–1996." Davis Occasional Papers No. 64. Jerusalem: Leonard Davis Institute for International Relations, Hebrew University of Jerusalem, 1998.

Nets-Zehngut, Rafi. "Internal and External Collective Memories of Conflicts: Israel and the 1948 Palestinian Exodus." *International Journal of Conflict and Violence* 6, no. 1 (2012): 127–40.

———. "Origins of the Palestinian Refugee Problem: Changes in the Historical Memory of Israelis/Jews 1949–2004." *Journal of Peace Research* 48, no. 2 (2011): 235–48.

Newman, David. "From Hitnachlut to Hitnatkut: The Impact of Gush Emunim and the Settlement Movement on Israeli Politics and Society." *Israel Studies* 10, no. 3 (2005): 192–224.

Norton, Augustus Richard. "Hizballah: From Radicalism to Pragmatism?" *Middle East Policy* 5, no. 4 (1998): 147–58.

———. "Hizballah and the Israeli Withdrawal from Southern Lebanon." *Journal of Palestine Studies* 30, no. 1 (2000): 22–35.

———. *Hezbollah: A Short History*. Princeton, NJ: Princeton University Press, 2007.

OECD. *In It Together: Why Less Inequality Benefits All.* Paris: OECD Publishing, 2015.

———. *OECD Economic Surveys: Israel.* Paris: OECD Publishing, 2013.

Onuf, Nicholas Greenwood. *World of Our Making: Rules and Rule in Social Theory and International Relations.* Columbia: University of South Carolina Press, 1989.

Pardo, Sharon, and Joel Peters. *Israel and the European Union: A Documentary History.* Lanham, MD: Lexington Books, 2011.

———. *Uneasy Neighbors: Israel and the European Union.* Lanham, Md.: Lexington Books, 2010.

Parsi, Trita. "Israel and the Originis of Iran's Arab Option: Dissection of a Strategy Misunderstood." *Middle East Journal* 60, no. 3 (2006): 493–512.

———. *Treacherous Alliance: The Secret Dealings of Israel, Iran, and the United States.* New Haven, CT: Yale University Press, 2007.

Pedahzur, Ami. "Supporting Condition for the Survival of the Extreme Right-Wing Parties in Israel." *Mediterranean Politics* 5, no. 3 (2000): 1–30.

Peffley, Mark, Marc L. Hutchison, and Michal Shamir. "The Impact of Persistent Terrorism on Political Tolerance: Israel, 1980 to 2011." *American Political Science Review* 109, no. 4 (2015): 817–32.

Peled-Elhanan, Nurit. *Palestine in Israeli School Books: Ideology and Propaganda in Education.* London: I. B. Tauris, 2012.

Peleg, Ilan. *Begin's Foreign Policy, 1977–1983: Israel's Move to the Right.* New York: Greenwood, 1987.

Peleg, Ilan, and Dov Waxman. *Israel's Palestinians: The Conflict Within.* Cambridge: Cambridge University Press, 2011.

Perlmutter, Amos. "Israel's Dilemma." *Foreign Affairs* 68, no. 5 (1990): 119–32.

Peres, Shimon, and Arye Naor. *The New Middle East.* New York: H. Holt, 1993.

Peters, Joel, and Rob Pinfold. "Consolidating Right-Wing Hegemony: The Israeli Elections 2015." *Mediterranean Politics* 20, no. 3 (2015): 405–12.

Podeh, Elie. "History and Memory in the Israeli Educational System." *History and Memory* 12, no. 1 (2000): 56–101.

Polletta, Francesca, and M. Kai Ho. "Frames and Their Consequences." In *The Oxford Handbook of Contextual Political Analysis,* edited by Robert E. Goodin and Charles Tilly, 189–92. Oxford: Oxford University Press, 2006.

Pressman, Jeremy. "The Second Intifada: Background and Causes of the Israeli–Palestinian Conflict." *Journal of Conflict Studies* 22, no. 2 (2003): 114–41.

———. "Visions in Collision: What Happened at Camp David and Taba?" *International Security* 28, no. 2 (2003): 5–43.

Quandt, William B. *Peace Process: American Diplomacy and the Arab–Israeli Conflict since 1967.* Washington, DC: Brookings Institution Press, 2005.

Rabin, Yitzhak. "Address by PM Rabin at the National Defense College, August 12, 1993." In *Israel's Foreign Relations: Selected Documents,* vol. 13: *1992–1994,* edited by Meron Medzini, 297–300. Jerusalem: Israel Ministry of Foreign Affairs, 1995.

———. "Address to the Knesset by Prime Minister Rabin Presenting His Government, 13 July 1992." In *Israel's Foreign Relations: Selected Documents*, vol. 13: *1992–1994*, edited by Meron Medzini, 1–9. Jerusalem: Israel Ministry of Foreign Affairs, 1995.

Rabinovich, Itamar. *The Brink of Peace: The Israeli–Syrian Negotiations*. Princeton, NJ: Princton University Press, 1999.

———. "The Failure of Camp David: Four Different Narratives." In *The Camp David Summit: What Went Wrong?*, edited by Shimon Shamir and Bruce Maddy-Weitzman, 14–17. Brighton, UK: Sussex Academic Press, 2005.

Ram, Haggai. "'To Banish the Levantine Dunghill' from Within: Toward a Cultural Understanding of Israeli Anti-Iran Phobias." *International Journal of Middle East Studies* 40 (2008): 249–68.

Ram, Haggay. *Iranophobia: The Logic of an Israeli Obsession*. Stanford, CA: Stanford University Press, 2009.

Raz, Avi. *The Bride and the Dowry: Israel, Jordan, and the Palestinians in the Aftermath of the June 1967 War*. New Haven, CT: Yale University Press, 2012.

Rekhess, Elie. "The Evolvement of an Arab-Palestinian National Minority in Israel." *Israel Studies* 12, no. 3 (2007): 1–28.

Ross, Dennis. *The Missing Peace: The Inside Story of the Fight for Middle East Peace*. New York: Farrar, Strauss, and Giroux, 2004.

Rouhana, Nadim. *Palestinian Citizens in an Ethnic Jewish State: Identities in Conflict*. New Haven, CT: Yale University Press, 1997.

Rouhana, Nadim, and Assad Ghanem. "The Crisis of Minorities in Ethnic States: The Case of Palestinian Citizens in Israel." *International Journal of Middle East Studies* 30, no. 3 (1998): 321–46.

Rouhana, Nadim N., and Nimer Sultany. "Redrawing the Boundaries of Citizenship: Israel's New Hegemony." *Journal of Palestine Studies* 33, no. 1 (2003): 5–22.

Rowe, Diana. *Funding Illegal Settlements in the Occupied Territories of Palestine*. Washington, DC: Jerusalem Fund for Education and Community Development, August 8, 2008.

Rubin, Barry. "Israel's New Strategy." *Foreign Affairs* 85, no. 4 (2006): 111–25.

Sanders, Ralph. "Israel and the Realities of Mutual Deterrence." *Israel Affairs* 15, no. 1 (2009): 81–97.

Savir, Uri. *The Process: 1,100 Days That Changed the Middle East*. New York: Vintage, 1998.

Schachter, Jonathan. "The End of the Second Intifada?" *Strategic Assessment* 13, no. 3 (October 2010): 63–70. Tel Aviv: Institute for National Security Studies.

Schweitzer, Yoram. "The Rise and Fall of Suicide Bombings in the Second Intifada." *Strategic Assessment* 13, no. 3 (October 2010): 39–48. Tel Aviv: Institute for National Security Studies.

Searle, John R. *The Construction of Social Reality*. New York: Free Press, 1995.

Segev, Tom. *The Seventh Million: The Israelis and the Holocaust.* New York: Henry Holt, 2000.

Sela, Avraham. *The Decline of the Arab–Israeli Conflict: Middle East Politics and the Quest for Regional Order.* Albany: State University of New York Press, 1998.

Seliktar, Ofira. "The New Zionism." *Foreign Policy* 51 (1983): 118–38.

———. *New Zionism and the Foreign Policy System of Israel.* Carbondale: Southern Illinois University Press, 1986.

Shafir, Gershon, and Yoav Peled. *Being Israeli: The Dynamics of Multiple Citizenship.* Cambridge: Cambridge University Press, 2002.

Shalom, Zaki. "The Disengagement Plan: Vision and Reality." *Strategic Assessment* 13, no. 3 (October 2010): 85–100.

Shamir, Shimon, and Bruce Maddy-Weitzman. *The Camp David Summit: What Went Wrong?* Brighton, UK: Sussex Academic Press, 2005.

Shcharansky, Anatoly, and Ron Dermer. *The Case for Democracy: The Power of Freedom to Overcome Tyranny and Terror.* New York: PublicAffairs, 2004.

Sher, Gilead. *The Israeli–Palestinian Peace Negotiations, 1999–2001: Within Reach.* London: Routledge, 2006.

Sherif, Muzafer. *In Common Predicament: Social Psychology of Intergroup Conflict and Cooperation.* Boston: Houghton Mifflin, 1966.

Shindler, Colin. *Israel and the Great Powers.* London: I. B. Tauris, 2014.

———. *Israel, Likud and the Zionist Dream: Power, Politics and Ideology from Begin to Netanyahu.* London: I. B. Tauris, 1995.

Shlaim, Avi. "Conflicting Approaches to Israel's Relations with the Arabs: Ben Gurion and Sharett." *Middle East Journal* 37, no. 2 (1983): 180–201.

———. *The Iron Wall: Israel and the Arab World.* London: Allen Lane, 2000.

———. "The Iron Wall Revisited." *Journal of Palestine Studies* 41, no. 2 (2012): 80–98.

Slater, Jerome. "Just War Moral Philosophy and the 2008–09 Israeli Campaign in Gaza." *International Security* 37, no. 2 (2012): 44–80.

Smooha, Sammy. "Class, Ethnic, and National Cleavages and Democracy in Israel." In *Israeli Democracy under Stress*, edited by Ehud Sprinzak and Larry Diamond, 309–42. Boulder, CO: Lynne Rienner, 1993.

———. "Ethnic Democracy: Israel as an Archetype." *Israel Studies* 2, no. 2 (1997): 198–241.

———. "Minority Status in an Ethnic Democracy: The Status of the Arab Minority in Israel." *Ethnic and Racial Studies* 13, no. 3 (1990): 389–413.

Sprinzak, Ehud. "The Emergence of the Israeli Radical Right." *Comparative Politics* 21, no. 2 (1989): 171–92.

Sternhell, Zeev. *The Founding Myths of Israel: Nationalism, Socialism, and the Making of the Jewish State.* Princeton, NJ: Princeton University Press, 1998.

Swisher, Clayton E. *The Palestine Papers: The End of the Road?* London: Hesperus, 2011.

———. *The Truth about Camp David: The Untold Story about the Collapse of the Middle East Peace Process.* New York: Nation, 2004.

Telhami, Shibley. *2010 Israeli Arab/Palestinian Public Opinion Survey.* Washington, DC: Brookings Institution, https://www.brookings.edu/wp-content/uploads/2016/06/israeli_arab_powerpoint.pdf.

———. *The 2011 Public Opinion Poll of Jewish and Arab Citizens of Israel.* Washington, DC: Brookings Institution, http://www.brookings.edu/research/reports/2011/12/01-israel-poll-telhami.

Tessler, Mark A. *A History of the Israeli–Palestinian Conflict.* Bloomington: Indiana University Press, 2009.

Thrall, Nathan. "Hamas' Chances." *London Review of Books* 36, no. 16 (August 21, 2014): 10–12.

Tocci, Nathalie. *Active but Acquiescent: The EU's Response to Israel's Military Offensive in the Gaza Strip.* Copenhagen: Euro-Mediterranean Human Rights Network, 2009.

"UN General Assembly: Resolution 194 (December 11, 1948)." In *The Israel–Arab Reader: A Documentary History of the Middle East Conflict*, edited by Walter Laqueur and Barry Rubin, 83–86. New York: Penguin, 2008.

United Nations. *A More Secure World: Our Shared Responsibility. Report of the Secretary-General's High-Level Panel on Threats, Challenges and Change.* New York: United Nations, 2004.

United Nations Coordination Office for Humanitarian Affairs (OCHA). "Occupied Palestinian Territory: Gaza Emergency, Situation Report (as of 14 September, 2014)." http://www.ochaopt.org/documents/ocha_opt_sitrep_04_09_2014.pdf.

United Nations General Assembly. *Report of the Commission of Inquiry on Lebanon Pursuant to Human Rights Council Resolution*, S-2/1. A/HRC/3/2, November 23, 2006. New York: United Nations, 2006. http://www2.ohchr.org/english/bodies/hrcouncil/docs/specialsession/A.HRC.3.2.pdf.

———. *Report of the Secretary-General on the United Nations Interim Force in Lebanon (UNIFIL) for the Period from 21 January 2006 to 18 July 2006.* New York: United Nations, 2006. http://www.un.org/en/peacekeeping/missions/unifil/reports.shtml.

United Nations General Assembly, Human Rights Council. "Human Rights in Palestine and Other Occupied Arab Territories: Report of the United Nations Fact-Finding Mission on the Gaza Conflict." A/HRC/12/48, September 25, 2009. New York: United Nations General Assembly, Human Rights Council, 2009. http://www2.ohchr.org/english/bodies/hrcouncil/specialsession/9/FactFindingMission.htm.

———. *Report of the Independent Commission of Inquiry Established Pursuant to Human Rights Council Resolution S-21/1.* A/HRC/29/52, June 24, 2015.

Vertzberger, Yaacov. *The World in Their Minds: Information Processing, Cognition, and Perception in Foreign Policy Decisionmaking.* Stanford, CA: Stanford University Press, 1990.

Waxman, Dov. "The Pro-Israel Lobby in the United States." In *Israel and the United States: Six Decades of US–Israeli Relations*, edited by Robert O. Freedman, 79–99. Boulder, CO: Westview, 2012.

Weber, Max. *Gesammelte Aufsätze zur Wissenschaftslehre*. Tübingen: J. C. B. Mohr, 1922.

Weissbrod, Lilly. "Israeli Identity in Transition." *Israel Affairs* 3, nos. 3–4 (1997): 47–65.

Weizman, Ezer. "Interview with Ezer Weizman." *Spectrum* 6 (1998): 10.

Wendt, Alexander. "Constructing International Politics." *International Security* 20, no. 1 (1995): 71–81.

———. *Social Theory of International Politics*. Cambridge: Cambridge University Press, 1999.

Williams, Simon. "Israel's Independent Arabic Media in the 2006 War with Hizbullah." MPhil thesis in Modern Middle Eastern Studies, University of Oxford, 2011.

Wolfsfeld, Gadi. *Media and the Path to Peace*. Cambridge: Cambridge University Press, 2004.

Yacobi, Haim. "'Let Me Go to the City': African Asylum Seekers, Racialization and the Politics of Space in Israel." *Journal of Refugee Studies* 24, no. 1 (2011): 47–68.

Yaniv, Avner. "A Question of Surival: The Military and Politics under Siege." In *National Security and Democracy in Israel*, edited by Avner Yaniv, 81–103. Boulder, CO: Lynne Rienner, 1993.

Yaron, Hadas, Nurit Hashimshony-Yaffe, and John Campbell. "'Infiltrators' or Refugees? An Analysis of Israel's Policy towards African Asylum-Seekers." *International Migration* 51, no. 4 (2013): 144–57.

Yatom, Danny. "Background, Process and Failure." In *The Camp David Summit: What Went Wrong?*, edited by Shimon Shamir and Bruce Maddy-Weitzman, 33–41. Brighton, UK: Sussex Academic Press, 2005.

Yiftachel, Oren. *Ethnocracy: Land and Identity Politics in Israel/Palestine*. Philadelphia: University of Pennsylvania Press, 2006.

Zerubavel, Yael. *Recovered Roots: Collective Memory and the Making of Israeli National Tradition*. Chicago: University of Chicago Press, 1995.

Zoughbie, Daniel E. *Indecision Points: George W. Bush and the Israeli–Palestinian Conflict*. Cambridge, MA: MIT Press, 2015.

INDEX

Arabic names beginning with the prefix 'al-' are alphabetized by the name itself.

ABOUT THE AUTHOR

Raffaella A. Del Sarto is associate professor of Middle East Studies at the Johns Hopkins University, School of Advanced International Studies (SAIS), SAIS Europe at Bologna, and a part-time professor at the Robert Schuman Centre for Advanced Studies, European University Institute in Florence, Italy. She is the author of *Contested State Identities and Regional Security in the Euro-Mediterranean Area* (Palgrave Macmillan, 2006), the coeditor (with Emanuel Adler, Beverly Crawford, and Federica Bicchi) of *The Convergence of Civilizations: Constructing a Mediterranean Region* (University of Toronto Press, 2006), and editor of *Fragmented Borders, Interdependence, and External Relations: The Israel–Palestine–European Union Triangle* (Palgrave Macmillan, 2015).

CPSIA information can be obtained
at www.ICGtesting.com
Printed in the USA
BVOW03s0719050417

480346BV00003B/3/P